Information Security Roles & Responsibilities Made Easy:

Job Descriptions, Mission Statements, And Reporting Relationships

CHARLES CRESSON WOOD
CISA, CISSP, CISM

VERSION 2.0

Information Security Roles & Responsibilities Made Easy

by Charles Cresson Wood, CISA, CISSP, CISM
Independent Information Security Consultant
ccwood@ix.netcom.com

© Copyright 2000-2005, Information Shield, Inc. All rights reserved.
Printed in the United States of America.

Published by Information Shield, Inc., 2660 Bering Dr. Houston, TX 77057.

Editor: David J. Lineman

Cover Design: Kristi Sadler

Printing History: June 2001:   First Edition.
                    April 2005:   Second Edition.

ISBN: 1-881585-12-3

Dedication

To Deborah

CONTENTS

Chapter 1 WHAT THIS BOOK AND CD-ROM CAN DO FOR YOU

The total cost of ownership (TCO) models developed by a variety of industry analysts such as the Gartner Group indicate that labor represents anywhere from two-thirds to three-quarters of the on-going cost associated with information technology. In this context, on-going costs include system configuration, administration, maintenance, training, and the like. Information security is just one of many niche areas within the information technology field, but its costs are also dominated by labor. In spite of what information security vendor sales representatives may tell you (the reader), the information security field is still in an embryonic state, and many essential activities have not yet been automated, or have not yet been automated to any significant extent. This means that all organizations, no matter how sophisticated they happen to be, will be critically dependent on the work of people to achieve a truly secure information technology environment.

Management in many organizations doesn't fully appreciate the labor required to achieve information security goals. This book is intended to provide the specific words needed to define roles and responsibilities so that management will truly understand and acknowledge the importance of labor in the information security area, and so that management will pay more attention to the increasingly important information security function. This in turn is intended to cause management to start allocating more realistic budgets for information security staffing. With this book, the author seeks to generate greater respect for, and understanding about, the information security function by pointing out the many, and often behind-the-scenes ways that the information security team adds value to an organization. The author also hopes that you will be surprised to see that the information security staff does so much, or at least could do so much, in so many ways working to make sure that things turn out right.

In the real world, the typical organization's information security efforts are characterized by a surprising amount of chaos and unnecessary internal politics. At a large number of organizations, lack of clearly articulated roles and responsibilities has become one of the most serious impediments to information security progress. Confusion and ongoing arguments about roles and responsibilities distract and deter workers from attending to the time-consuming work that needs to be done. Such confusion and ongoing arguments prevent both departments and individuals from creating the strong cooperative relationships that are needed for a successful information security effort. With this book, you can change all of that for the better by creating a formalized information security team, a team where each member has acknowledged and agreed-upon roles and responsibilities.

Who Needs Motivation?

According to a Gallup Poll reported in USA Today (10 May 2001):

- 55% of employees are not engaged in their jobs,
- 19% of employees are actively disengaged from their jobs, and
- 26% of employees are engaged in their jobs.

What realistic hope can management have of motivating employees to pay attention to information security if fully 74% of the workers don't really care about their jobs? To clearly show how important information security is, this book urges management to specifically state and document how information security is a part of every worker's job. Only by engaging workers in a discussion about the need for their cooperation, in conjunction with explicit written statements describing the support that is required from every worker, can management start to have confidence that information security activities are in fact being attended to as they should be.

If your organization has not yet clarified information security roles and responsibilities, then the organization is much less likely to be successful with other tasks related to information security. For instance, if the responsibility for information security training and awareness has not yet been assigned, the probability is high that are this job is not being done, or it's not being done adequately. For example, workers at your organization may wonder whether this work should be done by the Human Resources Department, the Training Department, or the Information Security Department. Thus, it is not an exaggeration to say that clear roles and responsibilities are an essential prerequisite for all information security activities. To genuinely be effective in the information security arena, every organization needs to consciously specify and coordinate the activities of a team of people, each with different information security roles and responsibilities (the reasons why a team is needed are covered in Chapter 3.)

As another example, consider the development of a hypothetical and innovative new Internet business application system. The programmers involved may be concerned about security, and may even know a thing or two about how best to implement security. Yet, the performance evaluations of most programmers today do not directly deal with how well the programmers build secure systems. Other factors, such as how fast they write code that works, receive much greater emphasis. In the absence of clear roles and responsibilities for building security into this application, and feeling deadline pressure, the programmers most likely will decide that serious security will be incorporated into a future version of the code. Thus important security decisions will be made by default, but they may not be what's best for the organization. To have security-related decisions that are truly in the best interests of an organization, management must clearly have assigned definitive roles and responsibilities.

On a related note, management at many organizations has assumed that the information security function, because it is still relatively new, is in great flux and is inherently unspecified. Thus management has believed that the information security function is much like the research and development function, where there is a great diversity of tasks as well as great unpredictability about which of these tasks will be performed. To the contrary, the author believes that the information security field has now developed to a point where the tasks to be performed are in fact part of a generally accepted standard of due care. The author thus advances the notion that the information security function can now be viewed and dealt with in a more mechanistic and deterministic fashion. To adopt this new perspective, and to therefore specify roles and responsibilities as defined in this book, brings many benefits including significantly greater management control, the ability of information security staff to competently handle a much larger group of complex tasks, and the ability of management to more rapidly evolve the function to respond to the rapidly changing risks in both the business and technical domains. These topics are addressed in greater detail in Chapter 2.

This book is intended to provide you with all the content you need to immediately develop or update mission statements, job descriptions, organizational reporting relationship diagrams, and other documentation dealing with information security roles and responsibilities. The book assumes that you must quickly compile roles and responsibilities documentation-that you do not have the time or budget to hire consultants, go to classes, or perform extensive research. To this end, this book provides the most comprehensive collection of practical ideas and ready-to-use documentation about information security roles and responsibilities available anywhere.

The author's intent is to give you the reader a compendium of the best standard practices found in successful organizations operating in industrialized nations. You are expected to pick and choose only those practices which best match the needs of your organization (certainly no organization would want to adopt all of the material found in this book). The author's information security document development consulting practice has proven that it's a lot faster to choose items from an already-developed list than it is to develop a new list from scratch. You will, of course, also need to tailor the material found in this book so that it fits in with your organization's documentation standards (format, length, graphics, topics, etc.).

There is no need for you to worry whether you have the requisite technical expertise to understand and use the material in this book. The book is written for a newly-appointed information security manager who has only a cursory knowledge of information systems concepts, and no particular technical information security expertise. Because the material is written with a management perspective, the book can also be used by technical writers, user department managers, project managers, consultants, auditors, and others who find themselves in a position where they need to quickly prepare information security roles and responsibilities documentation. Although the language will be oriented towards managers, seasoned information security specialists will nonetheless discover that this book provides many useful tips and templates.

The entire process of developing and/or revising information security roles and responsibilities documentation has been scripted for you. The chapters in this book are deliberately sequenced so as to step you through all the important tasks on the road to developing professional, relevant, and effective information security roles and responsibilities documentation. The book provides you with all the detailed information you will need to prepare credible and meaningful memos to management to advance an information security roles and responsibilities project. Accordingly, you are urged to at least skim the material found in each of the chapters to identify material that could be used within your organization. After this skimming process has been completed, you should prepare a document development plan using the ideas found in Chapter 2 through 10. After this plan has been approved by management, and after you have conducted initial interviews with the stakeholders, then you can start modifying the files provided on the accompanying CD-ROM. This modification process typically involves changing organization names, department names, and job titles to be consistent with existing organizational structures and naming conventions. The process could also include the addition of references to relevant laws, industry specific regulations, and other external require-ments that are unique to your organization. The process should additionally involve the provision of references to other relevant documents at your organization, such as a Human Resources Manual. Also advisable during the modification process is the addition of introductions or prefaces that will help to integrate the material found in this book into the documentation now found within your organization.

One of the easiest ways to proceed is for you to go through the hardcopy book using a highlighter, pen, or pencil. As you read or skim, you should mark the material that seems relevant for your organization. Later, after your plan has been developed and approved, you should open the relevant chapter's file on the CD-ROM. You can then cut-and-paste information from this file into another word processing document so that it may be uniquely tailored to the needs of your organization. In the course of this editing process, you will need to make some changes, add some additional words, change some of the terminology, and in other ways make it truly responsive to your organization's current situation. Besides following the specific directions found in each chapter, getting management approval, and interviewing the primary stakeholders in advance, the process is very straightforward.

Under great pressure to produce roles and responsibili-ties documentation, you may use the materials found in this book without anything more than changing organi-zation names and department names. Although this approach may sound attractive at first glance, the author strongly discourages it. You are instead advised to prepare a project justification memo, a project schedule, a list of interviewees, and related planning documents. These topics are discussed in Chapter 2 through Chapter 10. By spending some time to plan the project, you can

help ensure that the material that you develop dovetails nicely with the organization's current business activities, the so called "corporate culture," and other prevailing conditions at your organization.

Before submitting roles and responsibilities documents to management for approval, you should also have the material reviewed by a human resources specialist, an intellectual property lawyer, and a seasoned information security specialist. Chapter 7 discusses the best ways to get management approval and support for your roles and responsibilities documents, so this will not be explored further here. Suffice it to say that a considerable amount of your time on a roles and responsibilities project will be devoted to justifying and explaining the reasons why certain words were included in memos that you issue. This book is intended to provide all the necessary ammunition not only to fight these battles successfully, but also to staunchly and resolutely defend the importance of the information security function.

Since all of the material in this book is provided on the accompanying CD-ROM, you do not need to retype anything. Topics of interest can be quickly located using the Table Of Contents, the Index, and the Web Help Search tabs. The author, working in conjuction with the publisher, has done everything that he could think of to speed your development of professional and credible information security role and responsibility documenta-tion. Nonetheless, there is always room for improvement. If you have suggestions for the next version of this book, please contact the author at the electronic mail address shown in Appendix I, "About the Author."

The scope of the material licensed with this product should also be mentioned. The legal words can be found on the inside title page to the hardcopy book. This material is licensed on an organization-specific basis (based strictly on legal organizational name). A perpetual and worldwide license to edit, copy, and internally republish the derivative material at your organization is extended to all registered and licensed individuals. This license is for a single organization only; if more than one legal organizational name is involved, then a multi-organization license is required. If you take a job at a different organization, then a new organiza-tion-wide license is required to use this material. Consultants and other third parties must likewise obtain a separate license for each organization using this material.

꙰ ꙮ ꙰

Chapter 2   REASONS TO ESTABLISH CLEAR ROLES & RESPONSIBILITIES

This chapter discusses the major reasons why you should establish clear role and responsibility statements for all of the workers performing information security tasks. Each of the following paragraphs discusses a separate reason, and each of these reasons are summarized on a single line in a box at the end of the chapter. If management support for a role and responsi-bility clarification project is still missing at your organization, you are strongly urged to write a project justification memo using the material found in this chapter. If you seek a quick-and-dirty justification memo, you can simply copy the bullets found in the "Summary List of Reasons" found later in this chapter.

DISCUSSION OF REASONS

Having specific documented role and responsibility statements is advisable for every organizational unit, not just the information security group. Those organiza-tional units with fully developed role and responsibility statements will enjoy greater respect and greater resources. At many organizations, information security is a new or still-undeveloped organizational function. This means that these same organizations are often missing documents that cover information security job descriptions, mission statements, and reporting relationships. When these roles and responsibilities are documented and approved, the information security function will be increasingly recognized as a legitimate and on-going organizational function, worthy of respect and its own share of organizational resources.

One of the most important reasons to document role and responsibility assignments is to demonstrate top management support. Information security specialists often feel as though many people oppose what they are trying to do. Occasionally information security special-ists must take an unpopular position, for example, postponing the cut-over to a new software application until appropriate controls can be included. If the information security specialists aren't going to be outvoted, outmaneuvered, and otherwise overruled, clearly documented top management support for the information security function must have been documented. Thus, with documented and approved roles and responsibilities, information security special-ists can prevent or expediently resolve many arguments, and then get on with their work.

At many organizations, the information security function has been repeatedly moved from department to department. Many of these departments may not have known what to do with the information security function. These departments often treat the information security function like an unwanted foster child that really never had a home. As a result, departmental management may not have seriously considered the recommendations offered by information security specialists. Consequently, management may have postponed or failed to fund a number of important information security projects. But when roles and responsibilities for the information security function are specified and approved by top management, all this can quickly change. Then the information security function will have a real home, in other words, it will know where it fits into the organizational structure. In the course of defining a formalized and permanent home for the information security function, the ways that this function works with other internal groups will be defined. Then the information security function will have formal communication channels with top manage-ment that can be used to help get important projects underway.

For a newly-appointed or a relatively-isolated profes-sional working in the information security field, one very important reason to document roles and responsi-bilities involves negotiating good personal relationships with co-workers throughout the organization. The process of documenting roles and responsibilities will bring you into contact with all the other people who in one way or another have something to do with informa-tion security, or people who should have something to do with information security. It is this last group that can most importantly be reached through a roles and responsibilities interviewing process, which is discussed at length in Chapter 7. This interviewing process will allow you to establish many open and trusting personal relationships with co-workers, and these relationships will often be an important part of subsequent information security efforts.

Every effective democratic government must gain the confidence and support of the people it represents before it is given the power to govern. Something similar should happen with information security professionals. They must convince people throughout the organization that there is a problem, that their involvement will significantly help alleviate this problem, and that the proposed approach is an effective way to proceed. Thus, in the course of conducting information security roles and responsibilities interviews with co-workers, you will be indirectly gaining the right to govern and manage the information security activities of workers throughout the organization. This perceived authority will be absolutely essential to the success of all of your information security efforts.

Information itself knows no individual or organizational boundaries. It travels around at the speed of sound, light, or electricity, and ends up distributed to those who are interested in it, those who request it, and those who don't know how to stop it from coming. Intangible and by its very nature difficult to corral, information can only be secured adequately when all the people who have access to it consistently observe certain policies, standards, procedures, and other requirements. In other words, information security is a team effort that requires extensive interpersonal coordination. The coordination required has gone far beyond a team within the Information Technology Department. Now this coordination must include end-users, contractors, consultants, temporaries, outsourcing firm personnel, customers, suppliers, and business partners. This coordination should of course include clearly documented information security roles and responsibilities. This critically important topic is addressed at length in Chapter 3, and so will not be expanded upon here. Only through roles and responsibilities documentation can all of the individuals and organizations on this team work in both unison and harmony.

One additional important reason to document information security roles and responsibilities involves overcoming an erroneous viewpoint that information security is something that can be handled by specialists in the Information Security Department working alone. The job is way too big and way too important to be left to the Information Security Department. When roles and responsibilities are documented, specific people inside and outside the Information Security Department will be held accountable, and this in turn will cause them to become proactive. Without this accountability, in

many cases they will wait until there is a problem, and then do their best to handle whatever has taken place. Today, organizations, can no longer approach information security with a "fix on failure" mentality. Research studies show that information security is ten times less expensive when it is built into application systems before these same systems go into production use, as opposed to when security is added-on after these systems have already been placed into production operation. Said a bit differently, when it comes to information security, proactive planning and management is considerably less expensive than reactive repair and correction efforts.

On a related note, if management wishes to outsource some or all of the information security function, or if management wishes to retain contractors, consultants, or temporaries to assist with information security, then roles and responsibilities must first be specified. Unless roles and responsibilities have been clearly defined, management will find it difficult or even impossible to adequately draw up requests for proposals, legal contracts, outsourcing agreements, service level agreements (SLAs), and other documents with these third parties. Thus clear roles and responsibilities can be a significant enabler which allows management to better allocate organizational resources. Additional considerations about the engagement of third parties can be found in Chapter 16 and Chapter 17.

A related business management reason to establish clear roles and responsibilities is that, in so doing, management will reduce costs to adequately handle information security. Through the specification of job descriptions, management can select and retain people who are adequately qualified, but not over-qualified. This will in turn help to keep salary costs down. Likewise, a number of organizations are increasingly taking the security tasks performed by Systems Administrators and assigning these tasks to new information-security-specific positions like Access Control System Administrator. Not only does this change provide better separation of duties, it also allows the organization to lower costs because the security-specific jobs often pay less than the Systems Administrator jobs. On a related note, when clear roles and responsibilities documentation exists, management will know exactly what types of training programs it should send internal staff to, and this will help avoid wasting resources on training that is not directly relevant to the jobs that the involved individuals perform.

Many Internet Service Providers (ISPs), Application Service Providers (ASPs), hosting firms, facilities management firms, outsourcing firms, and other third parties have not paid adequate attention to information security. Organizations that rely on these third parties may be lowering their short-term costs, but unless information security roles and responsibilities are crystal clear, the organizations retaining these third parties are also significantly increasing their reputation risk. Reputation risk in this sense refers to the adverse publicity, loss of customer confidence, and even loss of customers that can be caused by a major information security problem. If information security roles and responsibilities are included in negotiations with third parties, then the initial cost will typically go up, but the issue is really summarized by the well-known phrase "pay me now, or pay me later-either way you're going to pay." When negotiations with third parties include a detailed examination of information security roles and responsibilities, management will be indirectly notified that there is a significant reputation risk associated with a decision not to specifically assign critical information security tasks to certain persons, groups, or organizations. In other words, by not assigning these tasks, management knows it is taking a risk, and that risk may adversely affect the organization's reputation. These specific tasks are discussed in Chapter 17.

Information security is inherently inter-disciplinary and inter-departmental, and at many organizations, it is fast becoming inter-organizational. For example, an effective communications encryption system requires a mix of human resources ideas (such as training), computer science ideas (such as mathematics to determine key length), and management ideas (such as procedures for key recovery when a key is lost). To implement an encryption system, a variety of people are needed including: Systems Administrators, technical information security staff, physical security staff, Information Systems Auditors, and networking technologists. In addition, to have an encryption system such as a virtual private network (VPN) work with business partners, these same people must work with their counterparts at other organizations. All this complexity requires a great deal of coordination if it's going to be effective. The roles and responsibilities of these individuals and organizational units must be clearly delineated if significant confusion and serious security lapses are going to be avoided.

Rather than eliminating the need for human involvement, the new information systems that organizations are using today (such as Internet commerce systems) are increasing the reliance on certain types of people with specialized skills. For example, if a critical technical person were to abruptly leave his or her employer, the organization might be hard pressed to continue certain technical computer operations without this person. This increased reliance on people with highly specialized skills and training can be reduced by backup personnel, cross-training, sharing job responsibilities, documenting the work, and other tasks associated with the development of clear information security roles and responsibilities (these topics are discussed in Chapter 18, "Adjustments For Smaller Organizations.") This book assists you in an effort to reengineer the information security function so that the people working within information security do not themselves become a single point of failure.

The information security field is still embryonic when compared to the marketing or accounting fields. While some interesting new technological solutions to information security problems are now on the market, in most organizations the achievement of effective information security critically depends on people. At this point in the evolution of the technology, there are many information security problems that can only be handled by people. For example, there is no commercially-available technological solution to the social engineering (masquerading) threats that all organizations face. All too often, the people within organizations don't understand what management expects them to do, and this in turn will prevent the achievement of information security goals. Only after roles and responsibilities have been clarified and documented, and after selected people are then appropriately trained, can these same people participate as essential members of the team that handles information security.

Management at many organizations has never clearly stated its intentions about the work it wanted an information security function to perform. For example, does it expect the Information Security Department or the Information Systems Auditing Department to do compliance checks to make sure that user departments were operating in a manner consistent with information security policies and standards? Likewise, does it expect the Information Security Department or the Business Contingency Planning Department to do information systems contingency planning work? These and other turf battles can consume an excessive amount of time and money, which would be better spent addressing prevailing information security vulnerabilities. When clear role and responsibility documentation is in place, staff can refocus their efforts on those things that truly advance the organization's goals. When this documentation is in place, departments will not "step on each other's toes" (anger one another because they are doing something that the other is expected to do). Similarly, when this documentation is in place, people will be much less likely to duplicate information security work already done in another internal department.

It's hard to do a "good job" if you don't know what your job is supposed to be. As perverse as this situation may sound, many information security specialists have been asked to do just that. When things go wrong, they often get blamed even though they didn't know these same things were important. This situation obviously demoralizes and discourages staff. But when roles and responsibilities are clarified, when management clarifies its expectations for the individuals working in the Information Security Department, workers will be much more likely to be focused, motivated, and working in accordance with management's intentions.

Some people deny that there is an information security problem, while others deny its importance. No doubt you have come across individuals who claim that doing something "is not my job." These individuals are often unwilling to find out whose job it is when they notice an information security problem. They deny that reporting a problem or finding out who to report it to is their job. With all this denial, it's very hard to get people to view information security as their own personal responsibility. But when roles and responsibilities are documented and approved by management, these people can't avoid it any longer. When this type of documentation exists, workers are a lot more serious about incorporating information security into their regular work activities. When this type of documentation has been prepared, workers can also readily determine who is responsible for specific tasks related to information security.

Management theorist Peter F. Drucker claims that people are inherently deeply resistant to being managed. This trend is especially pronounced with technical staff, or so-called knowledge workers, who often know far more about their jobs than their managers do. Knowing this resistance, good managers will help people to manage themselves. To achieve this, these good managers clearly articulate departmental mission statements, job descriptions, and the like, so that these knowledge workers can realistically evaluate and correct their own performance. To the extent that managers avoid dealing with matters such as performance expectations and what workers are actually supposed to be doing, they are missing a great opportunity to teach their staff what is valued by the organization, what gets rewarded, and where they need to improve. Only by clarifying these matters, and putting them in writing, is

there any hope of successfully managing knowledge workers in the still-evolving area of information security.

A voluntary approach to information security is not generally effective. If an organizational structure defining required information security activities is not specified, the work simply will not get done. This is because information security is in competition with other business objectives such as low cost, high performance, ease-of-use, and compressed time-to-market for a new product or service. Because worker performance is generally evaluated with these other factors and not with information security, there is a tendency for information security to be compromised in favor of other objectives. Stated differently, workers must be explicitly instructed how to act in ways that maintain information security. Some of the most effective ways to accomplish this are through specific words appearing in job descriptions and organizational unit mission statements. Even in those rare and progressive organizations where worker performance evaluations include consideration of information security, there is still a need to be clear about just what workers should be doing. When management is clear about roles and responsibilities, the proper balance between security and competing objectives will also be much easier to strike.

One of the most basic problems, but still one of the most difficult problems of the information security field, involves determining who should get what system privileges within a specific organization. In many organizations, managers don't really understand which users require which system privileges and powers, and in an effort not to interfere with the efficient flow of work, they define system access control privileges way too broadly. These relaxed access control privileges in turn prevent the organization in question from defining separation of duties in a strong and logical way. Likewise, relaxed privileges invite users to try things that they ordinarily should not be able to do, and this may lead to problems such as privacy violation, fraud, sabotage, errors, and system downtime. When an organization clearly defines roles and responsibilities related to information security, management will then be able to more clearly specify who should have what system privileges. This will in turn tighten-up access controls and allow the effective use of separation of duties, dual control, and other management techniques. This topic is explored in greater depth in Chapter 20.

Roles and responsibilities documentation will also help a great deal with disciplinary actions up to and including termination. These intermediate disciplinary actions include denial of pay raises, denial of bonuses, denial of promotions, denial of transfers to other organizational units, denial of special training, and forced time off without pay. Besides providing a reference point for the worker performance review process, clearly documented roles and responsibilities show what people should be doing, how they should be doing it, and when they should be doing it. This documentation may be essential when there is a so-called wrongful termination lawsuit (where an employee alleges that he or she was fired for inappropriate reasons). For example, if a worker is fired for not performing a certain job described in his or her job description, then sufficient basis for the termination has not only been previously communicated to the employee but some documentation supporting the termination has been established. In a broader sense, role and responsibility documentation supports fair and efficient management decisions that in all well-managed firms include a disciplinary process.

Experienced information security specialists are currently in great demand. According to recent market research studies, the demand for information security specialists is growing at an annual rate much higher than the rate for other information technology specialists. In other words, organizations will need to offer an attractive pay and benefits package if they are going to be successful with efforts to hire experienced information security specialists. These much-sought-after specialists will want to know what the prospective job entails. Nothing quite communicates the answer to that question as well as a job description and an Information Security Department mission statement. Having clear role and responsibility documentation will additionally let you accurately match an organization's needs with the skills and knowledge of people who have applied for a job. If your organization is using temporaries, consultants, or contractors rather than employees, having documented roles and responsibilities will also speed the selection of appropriate people.

If your organization has operations in the United States, be sure to discuss the implications of documenting roles and responsibilities with your accounting manager. The Internal Revenue Service (IRS) has a twenty question test that it uses to determine whether consultants and contractors are really employees (and whether the employer owes additional taxes). These questions include the lack of instructions how to accomplish a job and the lack of a continuing relationship. If contractors or consultants are used, there is still significant merit to documenting clear roles and responsibilities; this documentation should, however, be prepared so as to be consistent with IRS requirements.

Many organizations are now turning to outsourcing firms to handle their information security needs. While some management responsibilities such as making final decisions about information security policies should ultimately rest on the shoulders of internal management, a considerable amount of the security work can be outsourced. If roles and responsibilities are not clearly established at the time that a contract is negotiated, the organization that contracted the outsourcing firm may find itself in a difficult spot. The outsourcing firm may claim that the requested service (such as forensic investigation of a system break-in) is not in the contract, and that the customer must pay an additional fee. All this of course assumes that the outsourcing firm has technically-competent people available at the time they are needed. Of course, other consulting firms can also be called in, but with any of these options, precious time will be wasted negotiating fees, defining the work to be done, etc. While all of these ad-hoc business arrangements are being made, a hacker could be on the loose inside the internal network at your organization. To keep losses to a minimum, it is absolutely essential that roles and responsibilities for all important information security activities be defined in advance in outsourcing contracts (this topic is explored at length in Chapter 17.)

While many of the people working at your organization are likely to be concerned about information security issues, such as viruses, they often don't know who to contact. Imagine an ordinary end-user who has just inadvertently infected his personal computer with a virus thanks to downloaded software from the Internet. If he doesn't know who to contact, he may try to eradicate the virus himself. In the process, he may destroy data or spread the virus to other computers. On the other hand, if he knows who to contact for immediate expert assistance, these negative consequences can be minimized. Thus clear statements of roles and responsibilities facilitate communications that are needed to promptly resolve information security problems.

Another good reason to document roles and responsibilities is to demonstrate compliance with internal policies as well as external laws and regulations. Auditors and government examiners are impressed with documentation. It gives them the feeling that things are under control. A surprising number of modern laws include the requirement that information security roles and responsibilities must be specified. For example, within the United States, the Health Insurance Portability and Accountability Act (HIPAA) requires that firms in the health care industry document information security related roles and responsibilities. (See Appendix E,

"Responsibility and Liability," for a list of regulations that require proper documentation of information security roles and responsibilities.)

On a related note, with clear documentation defining information security roles and responsibilities, an organization can show that it is operating in a fashion which is consistent with the standard of due care. Being able to demonstrate this consistency may be very important in terms of reducing or eliminating management liability for losses and other problems. Such documentation may help with a variety of liability concerns including computer professional malpractice and breach of management's fiduciary duty to protect information assets. One example of an authoritative statement of the standard of due care, which includes the requirement that information security roles and responsibilities be clearly specified, is entitled "Generally Accepted Information Security Principles" (GASSP), published by the Information Systems Security Association (ISSA). Further discussion about the standard of due care is found in Appendix E.

One of the most important reasons to document roles and responsibilities is to clearly show business partners that your organization can adequately protect information which has been entrusted to it. Assume, for a moment, that your organization was approached by another organization which wished to establish a joint venture. In order to enter into this new business, the other organization would need to disclose proprietary information to your organization. Until the other organization's management can be convinced that your organization has its information security act together, it may legitimately be reluctant to disclose this proprietary information. Being able to quickly produce clear and up-to-date information security roles and responsibilities documentation would greatly encourage the other organization to proceed with the deal. Not being able to promptly provide professional looking information security documentation may cause the deal to be abandoned.

Another important reason to document information security roles and responsibilities involves the provision of assurance to management that people are doing their jobs. This is one of the primary tasks of an Internal Audit Department, but this task cannot be adequately performed unless auditors have a reference point against which to compare current worker activities. Without clearly documented roles and responsibilities, auditors will not be in a position to provide an opinion indicating whether individuals or departments are doing the work that management intends them to do. If management

doesn't know whether these people are doing their jobs, then they will be prevented from making personnel adjustments in order to improve information security.

A critical question that every top manager in charge of information security should be prepared to answer is "Does the organization have adequate expertise to deal with increasingly complex information security issues and problems?" This expertise might be provided by full-time permanent employees, or it might be provided by contractors, consultants, outsourcing firms, or other third parties. If outsiders are used for this purpose, the specific individuals with this expertise must be identified, their expertise must be evaluated, and their services must be explicitly retained. It is not enough for management to say: "Oh, not to worry, we will call on such-and-such consulting firm if we have any problems." However this necessary expertise is provided, it is management's responsibility to determine what expertise (training, skills, knowledge, etc.) is needed in order to adequately perform essential information security tasks. A definition of the required expertise is a natural next step after essential tasks have been clarified, and of course the essential tasks get clarified in the course of specifying roles and responsibilities.

Management often doesn't appreciate it, but if you do a good job when it comes to documenting information security roles and responsibilities, you will enable management to better perform IT staff succession planning, career planning, and career development. This in turn will assist with efforts to hire and retain quality staff members. This will also help management do forecasting about the number of, and nature of staff necessary to perform essential functions. Succession planning, career planning, and career development will additionally help to ensure that the right people, with the right skills and knowledge, are currently employed by, or otherwise working at your organization. To the extent that this effort is connected to both the business strategy and IT strategy, it will additionally allow you to ensure that the right people, with the right skills and knowledge, will in the future be employed by, or working at your organization.

Yet another reason to document information security roles and responsibilities involves the capture of organizational knowledge to prevent mistakes from happening again. If roles and responsibilities are documented, an organization can codify what it knows. If this information is not captured, new staff members are more likely to repeat the mistakes of their predecessors. Consider the common mistake where an Information Security Manager reports directly to the Chief Information

Officer (CIO). This hierarchy involves an inherent conflict of interest. The CIO is likely to give the information security function inadequate resources and attention because he or she is measured primarily with competing objectives (low response time, low cost, rapid new application development time, etc.). The CIO and Information Security Manager may have had several discussions about this problem, but may not have written anything down. If both the CIO and the Information Security Manager were then to leave the organization, this problem may not be appreciated by those who remain, and the dysfunctional reporting relationship may thus be perpetuated. Reporting relationships are discussed at length in Chapter 13.

In management circles, it is fashionable to talk about the Japanese concept of *kaizen* (continuous improvement). While the quality assurance and quality control disciplines have been around for a long time, the move towards ISO 9000 certification is relatively new and clearly an effective way to achieve competitive advantage. If information security roles and responsibilities are clearly documented, then one additional starting point for a process of continuous improvement has been created. Over time, staff can upgrade and refine the roles and responsibilities to better suit the organization's needs. The very act of writing these things down often illuminates important distinctions that were never previously considered. This in turn engenders both a new thinking process and a new revision process that would not otherwise occur.

Recent research on the criteria for organizational success and growth indicates that both tension and disequilibrium are vital. This tension and disequilibrium helps to encourage rapid evolutionary changes in response to changes in both the business and the technological environments. As the research of Margaret Wheatley in the book entitled Leadership And The New Science indicates, the tension and disequilibrium that leads to change and growth is dependent on a certain organizational order. The author of the book you are reading strongly argues that the necessary order is supported by clarifying information security roles and responsibilities in a manner that meets organizational objectives. The tension and disequilibrium in turn can be created via separation of duties, dual control, supervisory checking of the work of others, and other tactics that are further explained in Chapter 18 and Chapter 20.

Some managers will want to start an information security training and awareness effort as a way to get the ball rolling in the information security area. While their motivation may be laudable, this approach often produces less than stellar results. A training and awareness effort that is not built on an underlying statement of roles and responsibilities, as well as a current set of policies, is bound to have little impact. This is because the recipients of the training and awareness effort will naturally ask: (1) "Who's our contact point?", (2) "What should I do?", and (3) "How should we be using information systems in a more secure fashion?" Any training that lacks answers to these roles and responsibilities questions is likely to be ineffective, and is likely to tarnish the image of the sponsoring information security function for years to come. To ensure that a training effort illuminates the activities that an Information Security Department performs, and to ensure that it illuminates the participants' own information security responsibilities, written roles and responsibilities must first be prepared.

Perhaps the most significant reason to establish and document clear roles and responsibilities involves increasing worker productivity. Statistical studies of business economics indicate that about half of productivity growth over time comes from more efficient equipment, and about half comes from better trained, better educated, and better managed labor. Thus the clarification and publication of information security roles and responsibilities can have a substantial positive impact on productivity, and thereby markedly improve profits. The information security field is a new area, and there is still great confusion about who should be doing what. For example, when a worker has his or her laptop computer stolen, who should this event be reported to? Should a notice be sent to the Information Security Department, the Physical Security Department, or the Insurance Department? Maybe the notice should go only to the worker's manager? Without clear roles and responsibilities, users will unnecessarily spend time figuring out the answers to questions such as these. Likewise, if roles and responsibilities are clarified and documented, employees will not waste their time trying to figure out who to invite to certain meetings, who needs to sign-off on certain proposals, etc.

SUMMARY LIST OF REASONS

- Garner greater respect and greater resources for the information security function

- Foster acceptance of information security as a legitimate business function

- Establish demonstrable top management support for information security

- Establish formal communication channels with top management

- Negotiate good personal working relationships with co-workers throughout the organization

- Gain the right to govern and manage the information security activities of workers throughout the organization

- Foster coordinated team effort to safeguard information as it travels around

- Establish accountability for information security and thereby encourage proactive efforts to improve

- Enable management to better allocate organizational resources to outsourcing firms, consultants, etc.

- Minimize the costs associated with the provision of adequate information security services

- Lower the risks to the organization's reputation due to information security problems

- Manage the complexity of modern information systems and networks

- Reduce chance that information security staff will be single point of failure

- Clarify exactly what information security activities management expects

- Motivate and focus the work of specialists and rank-and-file staff

- Force staff to view information security as their personal responsibility

- Allow knowledge workers to manage their own performance and make corrections themselves

- Eliminate or reduce turf battles and related problems with internal politics

- Strike an appropriate balance between information security and competing objectives

- Restrict system access control privileges because management understands who does what tasks

- Leverage performance reviews to get people to take information security seriously

- Support a variety of disciplinary actions up to and including termination

- Speed selection and hiring of appropriate workers including contractors and consultants

- Allow outsourcing firms to quickly handle incidents without contract renegotiation

- Facilitate communications that are needed to resolve information security problems

- Demonstrate compliance with internal policies, as well as laws and regulations

- Demonstrate compliance with the standard of due care, and thereby shield management from negligence and related liability claims

- Encourage third party organizations to confidently disclose confidential or proprietary information

- Assist internal auditors in determining whether people are doing the necessary work

- Determine whether the organization has adequate expertise to deal with information security problems and issues

- Enable the organization to better do IT staff succession planning, career planning, and career development

- Capture organizational knowledge to prevent mistakes from being repeated

- Provide starting point for a process of continuous improvement (ISO 9000)

- Establish the required tension and disequilibrium needed to rapidly evolve the organization

- Lay a foundation for an information security training and awareness effort

- Increase worker efficiency and productivity by eliminating confusion

Information Security Roles & Responsibilities Made Easy

Chapter 3 PERSUADING MANAGEMENT TO DOCUMENT ROLES AND RESPONSIBILITIES

If you or others involved with information security at your organization have not yet had a serious discussion about roles and responsibilities with top management, one perspective probably prevails. Specifically, top management probably believes that the scope of information security roles and responsibilities is confined to the Information Security Department. If that old-fashioned view is used to determine roles and responsibilities, then the organization will be prevented from creating a truly effective information security organizational structure. If this happens, the resulting roles and responsibilities will leave major areas without sufficient attention and resources, and this will most likely lead to serious information security related losses.

Information Security Is A Team Effort

With the intention to change top management's perceptions, this chapter discusses the reasons why information security has become a team effort rather than simply an activity performed by a relatively isolated department. To acquaint top management with the true nature of modern information security, you should at least write a memo such as the one provided. This memo is intended to open management's eyes to the need for not just a team approach, but a multi-organizational team approach.

The memo provided below seeks management's approval to discuss roles and responsibilities with interested parties within your organization. While this may at first appear unduly conservative to you, there is merit to going through the proper management channels and in advance making sure that all involved managers are aligned with the project's objectives. If you don't observe the proper management communication channels, you run the risk of being accused of trying to build an empire, trying to undercut the managers in your own management chain, or trying to stur up trouble.

As this memo implies, the development of new roles and responsibilities should be done in accordance with, and in a manner that is respectful of existing organizational structures. The roles and responsibilities discussed in this book seek only to augment existing organizational structures so that information security objectives can be appropriately met. Unlike a reengineering project, the roles and responsibilities provided in this book are not intended to achieve any other organizational design objective besides the establishment of a strong and effective information security function. This approach is used because management requests which are simple and straightforward are more likely to meet with approval. With the intention to quickly obtain management approval, you should refrain from merging an information security roles and responsibilities project with any other project.

Beyond a memo, a brief meeting to discuss the project scope and the involvement of other groups is also recommended. At such a meeting, you can solicit management's ideas about all the different job titles and departments that in one way or another have something to do with information security. A good agenda for such a meeting would be:

1. Impediments to information security progress (see Chapter 4, "Before You Document Roles & Responsibilities," for further details.)

2. Benefits that come from clarifying information security roles & responsibilities (see Chapter 2, "Reasons To Establish Clear Roles & Responsibilities.")

3. Potential participants in an information security team (see Chapter 12, "Job Descriptions For Specific Team Players," well as the subsection which deals with "Memo To Management" in this chapter.)

Throughout this book the words "Company X" are intended to be replaced with your organizational name (whether that be a partnership, a corporation, a government agency, a non-profit agency, or some other entity). This designation is just a place-holder and in no way is meant to imply that anything in this book is designed exclusively for, or is limited in its applicability to, for-profit entities.

MEMO TO MANAGEMENT

Regarding: Information Security Has Become A Team Effort

To: [*insert your manager's name*]

From: [*insert your name*]

Date: [*insert today's date*]

Classification: Internal Use Only

Thank-you for authorizing me to develop new roles and responsibilities for the information security function at Company X. This memo describes the reasons why job descriptions (and perhaps mission statements and reporting relationships) outside the information security department need to be modified to achieve effective information security. This memo ends by seeking your permission for me to work with individuals in other functional groups besides information security, to concretely and responsively define appropriate information security roles and responsibilities.

Two or three decades ago, the only people who worked with computers were in what was then called a Data Processing Department. As local area networks, minicomputers, departmental servers, and personal computers became widespread, information was dispersed away from a central data processing organizational function and away from an isolated "computer machine room." This distribution of information continues with the spread of the Internet, telecommuting, and wireless remote access. Over the last few decades, the number and diversity of people who have access to Company X sensitive, critical, and valuable information has grown tremendously. This information is now in the hands of temporaries, contractors, consultants, strategic business partners, and other third parties. The information handling activities of these people must be coordinated if security is going to be achieved.

As the technology evolved, the ability to locally capture and manipulate information has grown exponentially. The computer terminals with no local storage capabilities and local connections to a mainframe that were common several decades ago, for the most part, have been replaced by small portable computers (such as the personal digital assistants) with local storage capabilities and international networking connections. This local storage and manipulation of information has placed much greater reliance on users as the key to achieving information security goals. For example, now a user can steal Company X trade secrets simply by copying that information to a floppy disk and removing it from Company X offices. This type of easy removal of sensitive information would have been much more difficult in the mainframe world of days gone past. Because users are now in a significant position of power when it comes to information security, they need to be enlisted as motivated participants on an information security team.

In some respects, technology itself is now dictating organizational structure. This is especially true to the degree that technology is dictating increased communication, for example, through the use of groupware (like Lotus Notes) and teleconferencing. An organization's use of these new tools implies the assignment of certain roles such as Security Administrator. Because there is so much more interaction between people than in years gone past, there is now an expectation that resources in other departments will be used to achieve certain organizational goals and objectives. For example, e-mail is now used to notify workers about new viruses distributed over the Internet, and each user is expected to play some role in the prevention of damage from viruses. To coordinate this type of increased communication with a larger number of people, there needs to be an associated clarification of information security roles and responsibilities.

While the original focus of attention in the information security field was on the technology, that has also changed, and now the focus is on information and information systems. For example, the information security field used to be called "computer security" but now that anachronistic term is rarely encountered. While an isolated organizational function in days gone past could handle the technical aspects of computer security, Company X now needs an organizational unit which deals with the technical, the business, and the human relations sides of secure information management. The latter of these three aspect of information security will of necessity involve clarification of roles and responsibilities.

The increasing focus on information has shown up in the recent emphasis on knowledge management systems. These systems capture, store, and appropriately disseminate critical information to those insiders who need certain information in order to do their jobs. In an age where global competition is heating up, when just about every other aspect of an organization (people, technology, buildings, etc.) can be replaced, it is the critical working knowledge, the reputation, and the relationships that have been built up over the many years of business that sets one business apart from another. This working knowledge is in many cases expressed as patents, copyrights, and trade secrets. A fine reputation is often attached to a trademark or service mark. The relationships are often captured in customer databases and supplier agreements. These examples show how competitive advantage is now dependent on the secure handling of information by people throughout Company X, and by implication they also show why assigned responsibility for information security should also be pervasive throughout the organization.

What's more, information itself frequently changes form as it is used for various purposes. To make a decision, a manager may read a computer-generated hardcopy report and then discuss the numbers appearing in the report via telephone with a specialist at a remote site. In this process, information will have morphed from paper form to verbal form. These and other dynamic transformations of information require that people outside the Information Systems Department be involved with information security. For example, the Telecommunications Department needs to assist with voicemail security, and the Corporate Records Manager needs to assist with paper records storage and retrieval. Thus, in order to properly protect sensitive, valuable, and critical information, no matter what form it takes, it is necessary for Company X to clarify the roles and responsibilities of all people who come into contact with this information.

Over the last several decades, the workplace has changed and there are now many fewer full-time permanent employees. These days, many organizations use contractors, consultants, temporaries and outsourcing firms. To do their jobs, these non-employee workers must also understand their information security roles and responsibilities. Unlike employees, many of these non-employee workers cannot simply be instructed to do things in the moment. For example, an information systems facilities management outsourcing firm must be very explicitly told what to do in a contract. Likewise, consultants generally cannot have their activities changed without a contractual revision. Other regulations, such as the US Internal Revenue Service stipulations on the relationship between a consultant or a contractor on one hand, and a client on the other, may further erode an organization's ability to define roles and responsibilities with little advance notice. For example, IRS regulations indicate that consultants and contractors should have the ability to determine where, when, and how to perform certain duties. Unless the specific roles and responsibilities are clear in advance, these laws and regulations can interfere with the successful accomplishment of information security objectives by non-employee workers.

The discipline of information security has also changed dramatically over the last few decades. While it used to be primarily focused on computer access control and contingency planning, it now includes a wide variety of issues such as web site privacy, credit card fraud prevention, and identity theft detection. This expansion of the information security field has meant that specialists in areas like criminal investigations, employee training, and internal auditing must assist to achieve effective information security. Information security has become, now more than ever, multi-disciplinary. The complexity of the information security field, combined with its multi-disciplinary aspects, have in turn meant that individuals must specialize to effectively and efficiently achieve information security goals. These new specialists in turn need clear roles and responsibilities documentation to properly work together.

Information security has also become multi-departmental and multi-organizational in nature. Extranets and electronic data interchange (EDI) systems provide good examples of how modern information systems must incorporate a clear understanding of the roles and responsibilities of people in several organizations. Just to handle problems within a single company, it is now clear that cooperation between multiple departments is required. For example, to investigate a systems intrusion, organizations often need cooperation from the Information Security Department, the Legal Department, and the Physical Security Department. To investigate security incidents such as Internet fraud, the participation of multiple organizations such as an Internet Service Provider (ISP) and the government agency in charge of criminal investigations may also be required.

Just as specialists are needed in the information security area, so too they are needed in other functional domains such as insurance and risk management. The increased division of labor, and the division of organizations into specialized subunits, unfortunately brings with it a tendency for specialists to see only their own activities, and fail to see how what they do fits in with other activities throughout the organization. This in turn erodes the ability of specialists to make decisions that include an organization-wide perspective. Often called "suboptimization," this process often occurs in the information security area, for example, where user departments make local decisions without considering the impact on others who share the same computer-network-connected resources. A project to clearly define information security roles and responsibilities across the organization will reduce suboptimization problems and will encourage a broader understanding of the ways that various specialists work together to achieve common information security goals.

Information security is furthermore dynamic in that every change in an information system, or even a change in the way an existing information system is used, can have significant information security implications. It is no longer sufficient for information security to be handled as a project, where vulnerabilities get examined from time to time. In most organizations of medium to large scale, a permanent full-time staff composed of knowledgeable, trained, and motivated people needs to be established and supported by clear roles and responsibilities.

If one examines the statistics of information system related crime and abuse, it is clear that the majority of the losses are caused by errors and omissions, and not by high profile hacker intrusions that often get reported by the news media. Frequently those responsible for these losses failed to pay attention to the mundane details associated with information systems management. Often those responsible failed to understand that they must perform certain tasks, such as backup a database daily. Clearly specified roles and responsibilities are an essential tool to help ensure that necessary information systems management activities are taking place, and that they are being performed by those who should be doing them.

If management believes that information security can be adequately dealt with by a single department working largely alone, the scope of an information security roles and responsibilities project will be unduly restricted. This in turn will mean that the Information Security Department will have an extraordinary and unrealistically large set of duties, which inevitably will lead to disappointing results. There is simply too much work to be accomplished by a single department. The Information Security Department in today's organizations doesn't have the political power, the organizational vantage point, the resources, or the technical tools to be in all the places where it needs to be to ensure effective information security throughout an organization. Only by an orchestrated definition of an information security team can empower an Information Security Department to achieve the information security goals sought by top management.

Such a team can achieve things that could not be achieved if Company X relied exclusively on specialists. For example, when terrorists attempted to commandeer an airplane over western Pennsylvania on September 11, 2001, the passengers took over. The passengers, apparently working without direction from the crew, determined that if the terrorists who had hijacked the airplane were going to be stopped, they were going to have to do it themselves. These passengers fought with the terrorists, which in turn caused the plane to crash, but this is much better than the terrorists' apparent intention, which was to crash the airplane into a large building full of people. This example shows the extraordinary things that ordinary people can do when they know what's happening and when they take personal responsibility. Through the definition of information security roles and responsibilities, we can empower rank-and-file workers to be important information security team members. There are a number of threats, such as social engineering (where imposters pose as authorized personnel), where users are on the front lines, where they must call the shots, where they must personally fight in the information security battle. In many of these same situations, there is not time analyze the options, to get management approval, and then to take action - the users must instead act immediately.

Over the years, many organizations have tried to organize the information security function with an all volunteer army. At the same time they skimped on training and awareness efforts, so it should be no surprise that the all volunteer army was not motivated. When it came time to do something important, they did not fight as management hoped they would. Information security has become too important to modern business to continue with this informal and uncommitted approach. What Company X needs now is a team of motivated individuals who understand the roles each member of the team plays and how they all work together. What Company X needs now is both accountability and mandated responsibility for information security as reflected in clearly defined roles and responsibilities.

I have provided below a list of the job titles that I believe have some role or responsibility in the information security area. Please authorize me to speak with these people, either in person or by phone, so that I can get their perspective about the roles and responsibilities that they should have in the information security area. While I will do my best to incorporate their comments about the unique ways in which Company X does business, the specific roles and responsibilities that I will recommend will primarily be a function of the prevailing standard of due care.

The specific job titles at Company X which I believe have an important contribution to make to the Company X information security effort are:

- Information Security Department Manager
- Access Control System Administrator
- Internal Information Security Consultant
- Information Security Engineer
- Information Security Documentation Specialist
- Information Systems Contingency Planner
- Local Information Security Coordinator
- Chief Information Officer
- Chief Technology Officer
- Information Systems Analyst/Business Analyst
- Systems Programmer
- Business Applications Programmer
- Computer Operations Manager
- Computer Operator
- Data Librarian
- Information Systems Quality Assurance Analyst
- Help Desk Specialist
- Archives Manager/Records Manager
- Telecommunications Manager
- Systems Administrator/Network Administrator
- Web Site Administrator/Commerce Site Administrator
- Database Administrator
- Data Administrator
- Data Administration Manager
- Physical Security Department Manager
- Physical Asset Protection Specialist
- Building And Facilities Guard
- Office Maintenance Worker
- Mail Room Clerk
- Internal Audit Department Manager
- Information Systems Auditor
- Internal Intellectual Property Attorney
- Ethics Officer
- Chief Knowledge Officer
- Chief Privacy Officer
- Chief Security Officer

- Chief Governance Officer
- Human Resources Department Manager
- Human Resources Consultant
- Receptionist
- Outsourcing Contract Administrator
- In-House Trainer
- Insurance And Risk Management Department Manager
- Insurance And Risk Management Analyst
- Business Contingency Planner
- Public Relations Manager
- Chief Financial Officer
- Purchasing Agent
- Chief Executive Officer

Please sign (with a date) below indicating your approval that I proceed to contact these individuals to discuss information security roles and responsibilities.

_____

[*insert your manager's name here*]

Chapter 4 BEFORE YOU DOCUMENT ROLES & RESPONSIBILITIES

There are many dependencies in the information security field, and this chapter describes those that relate to the development of roles and responsibilities documentation. This chapter discusses the efforts which should be completed to ensure that information security roles and responsibilities documentation will be read by those involved, will be taken seriously, will be used appropriately, and will be updated periodically. This chapter also discusses the efforts that will lay the foundation for a successful information security roles and responsibilities development project. These will, for example, ensure that interviewees will be cooperative, that middle management will review draft documents, and that top management will be willing to approve the final documents.

One essential prerequisite to any information security documentation effort is top management appreciation that information itself has become an asset or an organizational resource. Sometimes called Information Resource Management (IRM), this way of looking at modern business activity (including the activity in governments and non-profits) suggests that the factors of production have been expanded to include information. Traditional factors of production included labor, land, and capital. People were added to this list recently. Most recently, progressive managers are coming to appreciate that information itself is used to produce whatever products and/or services an organization offers. This perspective is essential because it implies that special tools and techniques are needed to manage information, just as special tools and techniques are required to manage people. When management adopts this modern perspective, an information security roles and responsibilities effort is likely to naturally follow.

Another important prerequisite to information security documentation efforts is management appreciation that they could be held personally liable for information security problems. In the United States, laws such as the Foreign Corrupt Practices Act define the circumstances under which managers can be held personally responsible for lapses in internal controls, including information security problems. This type of discussion is perhaps the single most influential way to get top management support for information security projects that you may propose. Putting together a presentation on management liability is also a great opportunity for you to establish a good working relationship with internal legal counsel, if that relationship does not already exist. Legal issues are addressed in Appendix E.

Although popular publications will have partially done it already, you should also get management to appreciate that the old techniques for managing information security are no longer sufficient. For example, the use of locking file cabinets and shredders is no longer sufficient to achieve true information security. More sophisticated tools like virus screening software, intrusion detection systems, and web traffic blocking software are necessary. To get management to admit this critical point, you may need to talk about recent cases, particularly cases that dealt with problems in the organization's industry, organizations in the same geographical area, and organizations with similar information systems technology. Clippings from newspapers and magazines with hand-written notes like "Could it happen here?" are additionally recommended if management still does not understand information security.

Information security roles and responsibilities should be documented as soon as possible after management support is obtained. Management support typically goes up and down over time in a fairly predictable fashion. Figure 4-1 illustrates this phenomenon graphically. Over time, management awareness will gradually die away because concern about information security unfortunately is often an "out of sight, out of mind" situation. Then an information security incident occurs that causes management to become concerned again. Such an incident might be an internal computer fraud, a hacker break-in to a competitor's system, or simply a widely-publicized information security problem. Shortly after things have been brought under control, management should be approached with a proposal to document information security roles and responsibilities. In Figure 4-1, a security related incident occurred at points A and C, and therefore a good time to propose a roles and responsibilities project would be at points B and D.

Figure 4-1: Level of Management Awareness Over Time

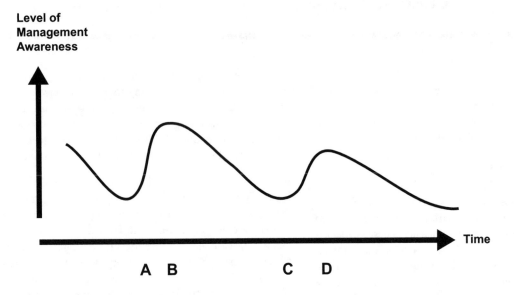

While serious information security incidents are happening with greater frequency these days, they are a mixed blessing. For example, not knowing what else to do after a serious security incident, senior management at some organizations will terminate the Information Security Department Manager. Each incident -- if not handled so that there's no damage -- will make it look like the information security unit is not doing its job. If there are no recent incidents, management will wonder whether they should cut back on the information security function in order to save money. Rather than relying on unpredictable incidents, many Information Security Department Managers are hiring independent consultants to perform penetration attacks. Using technical information security consultants - hopefully consultants whose ethics are clearly aligned with those of the organization - can help to rapidly increase the level of management concern. In effect, a risk assessment can take the place of an incident in terms of raising the level of management awareness. For instance, a penetration attack could show how easily a disgruntled ex-employee or a competitor could gain system access, and at this point you may be in a good position to propose to write information security roles and responsibilities documentation. Of course, other less dramatic ways to perform a risk assessment will also be effective in raising the level of management awareness. These techniques include scenario analysis, standard of due care comparisons, as well as quantitative estimates of threat probabilities and the associated expected losses.

After management support has been obtained (through a serious security incident, a lawsuit, a bad audit report, an alarming risk assessment, or some other method), management must buy into a centralized initiative to formalize roles and responsibilities. A centralized initiative is necessary because the defined roles and responsibilities will be issued by a certain executive, a certain committee, or a certain department. While a centralized focus for a role and responsibility development project is necessary, in no way does this prevent or discourage the establishment of a partially decentralized information security organizational structure. For example, Local Information Security Coordinators may be an important part of the proposed organizational structure. Similarly, having a centralized group put together a clear definition of roles and responsibilities in no way prevents or discourages input from workers in other groups. In fact, the role and responsibility statements that you develop are much more likely to be successful if they have been reviewed by all the people at your organization who have a vested interest in information security. The issue of centralization is discussed at length in Chapter 19.

Before an information security role and responsibility documentation effort gets underway, other roles and responsibilities critical to the organization's mission should already be documented. For example, within a software company, the roles and responsibilities for the Chief Executive Officer, the Chief Technology Officer, and the Chief Information Officer will need to be clear before the roles of information security staff are developed. Information security is a support and service function, and with the exception of companies specializing in information security, it is not the main focus of business activity. The nature of the information security roles and responsibilities will vary from organization to organization, and these roles and responsibilities cannot be adequately defined unless the roles and responsibilities that they support have been previously clarified. An exception should be made in the case of a brand new organization, such as a business to sell goods or services through the Internet, in which case all roles and responsibilities can be defined at the same time. Even in this relatively rare case, it will be important to know the roles and responsibilities of other organizational functions at the same time that the roles and responsibilities of an information security group are defined.

The performance of an information security function is critically dependent on the fit between its organizational structure and the organizational structure of the larger organization. For example, if top management has been intent on empowering individuals, and has distributed decision-making to many different workers, then a completely centralized approach to information security is likely to be problematic (this topic is further explored in Chapter 19). To ensure that the information security roles and responsibilities you propose will fit with the larger organizational structure, you should research the existing information security roles and responsibilities. In the process of conducting this research, you are likely to encounter certain patterns that are likely to be reflection of management's vision for the organization, of the organizational culture, and of other unique circumstances affecting the organization.

For example, one increasingly common pattern is the preferred use of consultants and contractors over full-time employees whenever possible. These patterns should in most cases then be used to modify the templates provided in this book (outsourcing is discussed in Chapter 16 and Chapter 18.) In some cases the patterns will be dysfunctional from an information security standpoint, in which case they should be changed and not used to modify the templates provided in this book. For example, if users are permitted to buy their own computer hardware and software, without any standardization or approval process, this is likely to be dysfunctional from an information security standpoint, and most likely should not be carried forward into a new information security organizational structure. Chapter 14 explores other factors which affect the extent to which these templates need to be modified.

When researching the existing information security roles and responsibilities, as mentioned immediately above, it is important that you involve those workers who are currently attending to information security matters. This can be accomplished through interviews, direct observation while they do their jobs, and customized questionnaires. Even though these people may not yet have job descriptions or other roles and responsibilities documentation to assist them, these workers are nonetheless more familiar with the jobs to be done than anybody else in the organization. So you should be sure to spend a good deal of time with them, getting their list of tasks, their list of objectives, and their list of problems associated with the work that they do. The more you involve these workers with your project, the more likely they are to accept and work with the roles and responsibilities that you document. This is especially true in those cases where job descriptions are used in a process to determine pay levels, annual vacation time, exemption from overtime pay, and related matters.

Also needed before an information security roles and responsibilities project gets underway is an organizational method to capture, store, and disseminate roles and responsibilities documents. These days this is accomplished most often through an intranet server that provides roles and responsibilities for all authorized users to view. In organizations that don't yet have an intranet, there may be a documentation repository where this information is filed, and there may be a group whose job it is to archive, index, distribute, and otherwise manage this type of information. If you are not yet familiar with your organization's approach to documenting and handling organizational design documents, you should become acquainted with that process before a roles and responsibilities development project begins.

Another thing needed before a roles and responsibilities project is initiated is a clear and documented management approval process. Roles and responsibilities documentation that is prepared only for the consumption of those within the Information Security Department will be very much less effective than documentation that is widely dispersed throughout the organization, especially if this documentation contains the approving signature of a top executive. Most often this approval process will have been defined by others who have gone through similar initiatives, but occasionally you will be required to clarify who approves and at what step in the process. One very important benefit of clarifying this management approval process in advance is the identification of certain criteria that must be met before the final management approval can be obtained. This topic is addressed at greater length in Chapter 7.

Before roles and responsibilities related to information security are documented, it is advisable for you to get a clear picture of what happened to the information security function in the years gone past. If the people working in information security made fools out of themselves because they took an unsupportable stand, you should know that. If the people working in information security were generally viewed as technically incompetent, that too should be known. If these same people did a great job, but were lured away to other firms offering higher salaries, this should also be known. In general, you should learn how the information security function is viewed by the rest of the organization, the extent to which the internal information security function has been a success, and the extent to which management supports the information security function. This internal politics information should be kept in mind and subtle changes reflecting this information should be made to the roles and responsibilities templates included in this book (factors affecting changes to the templates are discussed in Chapter 14. While some of this political information can come to light when conducting data gathering interviews, it is far better to have it before the project begins (interviews and related data gathering activities are discussed in Chapter 3.)

Another important thing to do before you assign roles and responsibilities related to information security, is to analyze the information security related knowledge and skills of existing technical and management staff. This effort is formally called a skills assessment. A skills assessment will help you to understand specifically what skills management thinks, or at least thought at one point in time, were important for information security. In some cases, the skills assessment will provide you with additional ideas for roles and responsibilities that you may not have previously considered. A skills assessment will also allow management to see whether the existing staff can do the work that needs to be done, as reflected in the roles and responsibilities documentation that you will prepare. Often the bottom line result of a skills assessment, in conjunction with a set of new information security roles and responsibilities, is that management clearly sees that the people they now have can't do the work that needs to be done. This means that they need to either outsource some work, hire consultants and/or contractors, or else hire additional permanent staff. Doing a skills assessment will also help you to definitively advise management about who should play what information security roles, as defined in the new documentation you will have prepared. A skills assessment will furthermore help management with IT project planning, technical training planning, career development planning, outsourcing, and downsizing. A skills assessment will additionally help management to understand that information security is a very complex field, a field which requires the work of bright and experienced people if it is going to be adequately addressed. See Appendix B, Appendix C, and Appendix D, for further discussion on this topic.

Chapter 5 UPDATING ROLES & RESPONSIBILITIES

Since it's fundamental to so many other activities related to information security, writing roles and responsibilities documentation should be one of the first things that an organization does in the information security area. Having proper roles and responsibilities documentation is part of the foundation for information security-something on which many other tasks will be built. For example, this type of documentation will be useful background for information security policy development projects, information security awareness and training projects, information security architecture projects, and many other initiatives. A list of internal documents that are supported by clear information security roles and responsibilities can found in Chapter 10.

In most organizations, some information security efforts have already taken place and information security roles and responsibilities have not yet been sufficiently clarified. Perhaps management has noticed that the efforts were not as successful as they could be. Perhaps some of the problems described in Chapter 2, "Reasons To Establish Clear Roles & Responsibilities," are beginning to be noticeable (these problems included confusion about who should be doing what jobs). When these problems become evident, it's time to write the initial version of, or update the existing version of information security roles and responsibilities.

If the problems discussed in Chapter 2 are not yet painful enough to get management to allocate sufficient resources to develop clear roles and responsibilities documentation, often a security related event will raise management's awareness to the point where they take action. These events include a major computer fraud written up in the newspaper, a serious hacker intrusion that disrupts operations, a massive computer virus infestation, or a serious privacy related customer relations problem. The larger the financial loss, the more the adverse publicity, and the more the liability exposure that is associated with such an event, the more effective it will be when it comes to raising the level of management awareness. You should exploit the times when management awareness is high, and if needed, make a proposal to revise or update information security roles and responsibilities at that time. A graph found in Chapter 4 depicts this timing.

If management is considering the outsourcing of any significant portion of information systems activities, this is also a great opportunity to revisit the existing information security role and responsibility documentation. Before any outsourcing agreements are struck, the specific roles and responsibilities of the two firms need to be very specifically defined. The author has direct knowledge of a number of horror stories where outsourcing firms did not respond well to break-ins, virus infestations, and other pressing information security problems because the outsourcing firm's mitigation and recovery services were not specifically defined in the contract. The risk to your organization goes beyond a slow response to security relevant events-now experts in the information security industry are talking about the reputation risk associated with outsourcing contracts. Many other risks of outsourcing information security are discussed in detail in Chapter 17.

Another important time to revisit and formalize information security roles and responsibilities is when new business partnerships are being considered or when they are actually being established. Suppose your organization is building a new product or service with an outside firm, and management wants to establish linked firewalls with encrypted channels over the Internet (alias Virtual Private Networks or VPNs). Management may also want to establish a certain level of trust between the computers found in both firms, perhaps through file/directory loading mechanisms like Network File System (NFS) used for UNIX. Before all this gets implemented, management needs to clarify not only network security policies, but also information security roles and responsibilities. For example, who is going to decide which users obtain what privileges associated with the communications link between the two organizations?

Information security roles and responsibilities are most useful for repetitive tasks that are performed on an ongoing basis. There are a large number of repetitive tasks that workers perform to achieve a satisfactory level of information security. These tasks, however, often require creativity as well as innovative approaches to problems that may never before been encountered at your organization. One example involves determining what applications should be allowed to tunnel through an Internet firewall; even when the roles, responsibilities, policies, procedures, and other aspects of this activity are documented, there will still be a variety of new challenges and questions. When repetitive tasks change, you will need to change the associated roles and responsibilities. If organizations don't promptly make these changes, there is a risk that workers will engage in what's called malicious compliance. Malicious compliance takes place when a worker knows that inappropriate results will be achieved if he or she is in compliance with documented roles and responsibilities, but he or she proceeds as documented in order to cause trouble for management. This abusive behavior points to the need to emphasize that results are more important than compliance, although certainly the ends should not blindly be used to justify any means. Some professional judgement should be involved to avoid trained incompetence where workers blindly follow orders, not thinking about what they are doing. This notion of trained incompetence was used widely as a war crime courtroom defense strategy. At your organization, if there is a reasonable chance that workers will engage in malicious compliance or trained incompetence, then roles and responsibilities must be changed promptly after either the underlying business processes or the underlying technologies change.

Unlike information security policies, role and responsibility documentation does not need to be modified every 12 to 18 months as business activities and information systems technology change. On the other hand, role and responsibility documentation will often need to be modified in response to organizational changes whereas information security policies often will not. For example, a merger or acquisition will generally require roles and responsibilities documentation to be changed, but it may not require policies to be substantially changed. You should expect your information security role and responsibility documentation to be modified every few years. You shouldn't think that the first set of documentation must last a long time, or that it must cover every conceivable situation and every question that someone might ask. As your organization adjusts to the initial assignment of roles and responsibilities, it is customary and expected that adjustments will need to be made. Likewise, when you notice that changes are required to the roles and responsibilities documentation that you recently worked so hard on, you should not take these changes as an indication that you necessarily did a poor or incomplete job.

In general, if there are no significant changes within an organizational structure, information security roles and responsibilities should be reviewed and most likely modified once every two years. In the business world, many significant changes are happening at an accelerating pace. This means that, in the years ahead, this time frame for regular updates will probably be reduced. This compressed update tomfooleries will especially be found in those industries undergoing substantial technology-induced change.

Looking at the update process from a different angle, certain events will require that roles and responsibilities documentation be revised. Organizations with recent documents that describe information security roles and responsibilities may need to have these documents reviewed, and most likely updated, if any one or more of the following events have taken place since the documents were prepared:

- The organization has gone through a merger or acquisition process, or has gone through a major reorganization (such as a significant layoff or a multi-departmental reengineering project),

- The organization has had a significant change in the nature of products or services currently offered (for example, a major new product was introduced),

- The methods used to market the existing products or services have gone through a major change (such as a shift of marketing efforts from direct mail into Internet commerce),

- A markedly different new working arrangement with an important business partner, customer, or supplier has been established (such as electronic data interchange or an extranet),

- The local or international laws or regulations related to information security (which includes privacy), laws and regulations which are also relevant to your organization, have changed significantly,

- It is clear that those working in the information security area are not doing the work that needs to be done (for example, a serious hacker break-in demonstrated the need for better access controls),

- A "white hat" (ethical hacking) penetration attack project or a vulnerability identification software project indicates that essential work in the information security area is not being performed,

- A third-party information systems audit or risk assessment has indicated that changes in information security roles and responsibilities are necessary,

- A benchmarking study which compared the in-house information security function with that of a comparable firm indicated there are major deficiencies in the current in-house roles and responsibilities documentation,

- A scandal or some other public relations problem related to information security has recently developed (for example, a customer has sued your organization alleging an illegal privacy violation),

- A member of the top management team has decided that he or she will become personally involved (in an intensely focused way) in matters related to information security,

- There has been a high-visibility internal dispute over who is responsible for certain important aspects of information security,

- Those responsible for certain aspects of information security have complained to top management about inadequate roles and responsibilities documentation,

- The documented roles and responsibilities of workers in departments or groups related to information security have gone through a major change (for example, the systems development group has dramatically changed the way it performs program design, testing, and documentation),

- Internal legal counsel has openly expressed concerns about the potential liability of management to information security related claims,

- The way in which the worker performance evaluation process is performed internally has gone through a major change (for example, project completion bonuses have been widely adopted),

- A consulting firm has evaluated incentive systems at your organization, and as a result, has concluded that workers are motivated to act in ways which are not supportive of information security,

- A significant number of those working in the information security area have taken jobs elsewhere in part because they didn't feel that they could meet management's expectations as reflected in current role and responsibility documentation,

- The number of people working in the Information Security Department has recently increased or decreased in a significant way, or

- A new manager has taken over the Information Security Department, and he or she wants to ensure that the Department's performance will be evaluated according to realistic goals and objectives.

Chapter 6 WHO SHOULD WRITE ROLES & RESPONSIBILITIES DOCUMENTS

From the start of any roles and responsibilities project, you should be clear about who will write the first and subsequent drafts, who will review these drafts, who will make modifications in response to comments received, and who will approve the final draft. If you fail to do this from the project's inception, you are running the risk of being accused of not "practicing what you preach" (because you may advocate the need for clear and defined roles and responsibilities, but you did not take the time to prepare them for your own project). So before interviewing interested parties, before writing the first draft document, and before doing anything else described in this book, you should make sure that the project roles and responsibilities are clear and documented. This chapter discusses who should write the actual documents, while Chapter 7 discusses the review and approval process.

As is discussed in Chapter 11, an Information Security Management Committee is a group, typically composed of middle level managers or their delegates, which prioritizes and supervises information security projects as well as provides policy guidance. While this committee may sound like a logical group to develop role and responsibility documentation, the use of any committee to write such documentation is strongly discouraged. Those who have attempted it before will acknowledge that writing with a committee, no matter how smart and motivated the participants may be, is very difficult, unnecessarily time-consuming, and generally a waste of organizational resources. An Information Security Management Committee should, of course, review, modify, and approve of roles and responsibilities documentation that has been developed.

Instead of a committee, a single individual who knows the organizational structure and the organizational culture within your organization should write the first draft. This individual should also have significant business experience so that the resulting document will be clearly grounded in practical day-to-day business activities. This person should furthermore have an overall understanding of information security including generally accepted practices found at other organizations in the same industry. These qualifications will help ensure that the resulting roles and responsibilities document is realistic and grounded in the real world.

At first blush, some people may consider it prudent to have a professional writer compile the roles and responsibilities documentation. While it's highly desirable to send the first draft of the documentation to a professional writer for polishing after it's been prepared, a professional writer is not the appropriate person to generate the first draft. To have a professional writer compile the first draft would be like asking an automobile mechanic to design a new car. An auto mechanic, like a professional writer, doesn't have the appropriate background to do the job in question. With all due respect to professional writers, if a professional writer does compile the first draft, it will probably be too high-level as well as contain a large number of technical inaccuracies, impractical ideas, and inadvertent inconsistencies.

The person who generates the first draft roles and responsibilities document should nonetheless be a decent writer. For example he or she should be able to quickly generate clear and direct sentences. Being a decent writer in this case will require that the individual also be able to envision the big picture, as well as separate the essential from the irrelevant. The individual should ideally be able to sense what is best for the organization as a whole, and then write the roles and responsibilities document from that perspective rather than be swayed by internal political pressures. Certainly nobody is going to be perfect when it comes to all of these objectives. Keep in mind that it is primarily the review and approval process that will help to correct significant deficiencies on the part of the writer of the initial draft.

The best person to write the first draft is most often a senior member of the Information Security Department at your organization. This could be the manager of the information security function, or it could simply be a seasoned and highly experienced technical staff person. Nonetheless, sometimes this approach is not feasible or appropriate. For example, if an information security function is just getting underway, there will be no senior member to write the initial roles and responsibilities documentation. Likewise, if the current members of an existing Information Security Department are all relatively new to the field, then it may be best to use an experienced external party to write roles and responsibilities documentation.

If an employee is not going to write the first draft, it is preferable to have an external technical consultant (or contractor) prepare information security role and responsibility documentation. Such a consultant should go through all the same steps that an employee would, such as interviewing interested parties within your organization. While a consultant should not skip any steps, a consultant often works faster and in a more focused way because he or she has significant experience in this area. A consultant may also be able to produce a result faster than an employee would because the consultant can devote all of his or her working hours to this task. A consultant may additionally be able to work more independently with many different groups throughout an organization than internal information security staff person can due to existing relationships and internal politics.

Another advantage to having a consultant do this work is that he or she doesn't have a conflict of interest, or at least a perceived conflict of interest. If an information security specialist who is also an employee prepares roles and responsibilities documentation, he or she stands to benefit through the resulting assignments. In spite of potential conflicts of interest, many organizations designate employees who are senior information security specialists to write roles and responsibilities documentation. If employees write the documentation, they should be ready to justify the choices they made based on best practices for the industry in question, published descriptions of the standard of due care, the opinions of technical experts, management's stated intentions, as well as existing laws and regulations. If the reader is an employee, keep this justification process in mind, and keep detailed notes that can be referenced at a later date. These notes will help to ensure that any future accusations of conflicts of interest can quickly be shown to be unfounded.

Some organizations may believe that it is prudent to use an outsourcing firm to prepare roles and responsibilities documentation. Although there are some excellent outsourcing firms that can do this type of work, this approach introduces a number of potential problems. In the first of these, management should be concerned about delegating too many tasks associated with information security to an outsider. There are some tasks that should always be performed only by the management at your organization. For example, the final approval of methods to protect and conserve organizational assets (including the definition of roles and responsibilities) should always be performed by internal management. For management to do otherwise would be dereliction of their duty to manage these assets.

In the second of these problems involving outsourcing firms, management needs to look at potential conflicts of interest. For example, by structuring roles and responsibilities in a certain way, an outsourcing firm may directly or indirectly give itself more business when top management never intended to send the business to that particular outsourcing firm. In a similar fashion, an outsourcing firm that writes roles and responsibilities could create an organizational structure which places undue reliance on outsourcing firm personnel, and not enough on internal management. This could be a problem after a hacker break-in takes place; outsourcing firm personnel may be designated as the decision makers when internal management should instead be the ones calling the shots. Likewise, in an effort to keep costs down, outsourcing firms may not incorporate sufficient cross-training, technical expert back-up, and separation of duties into the roles and responsibilities that they write-up. Additional discussion about conflicts of interest that may be encountered with outsourcing firms can be found in Chapter 17.

If the person who is going to be writing information security roles and responsibility documentation is an employee, you should be sure that the writer is expected to stick around the organization for a significant period of time. The writer of this documentation should not be given this project because they had nothing else of consequence to do, as would be the case with someone who management has recently placed on administrative leave with pay due to disciplinary problems. Likewise, the writer should not be expecting to retire in a few months. In these and similar situations, the writer is probably unmotivated, and as a result, will in all likelihood not devote the time and effort required to prepare a document uniquely tailored to your organization's business and technological needs. This is too important a task to give to somebody who isn't motivated to do a good job with it. One motivating reason to use a senior information security specialist, who has been at the organization for a considerable period of time, is that he or she is going to have to live with the document's consequences. This helps to ensure that he or she does a good job, because he or she knows that a poor job will come back to haunt the Information Security Department.

A provocative study performed by the Meta Group in 1996 indicated that 48% of the information systems budget is currently controlled by departments other than the Information Technology Department. This percentage was expected to grow to 70% by the year 2000. Even though the study is now a bit outdated, the major shift of power to user organizations continues. The statistics indicate that user departments are increasingly calling the shots when it comes to information technology. This does not, however, mean that someone from a user department should put together documentation for information security roles and responsibilities. A clear definition of roles and responsibilities should instead come from a centralized organizational unit such as the Information Technology Department (alias the Data Processing Department or Information Systems Department). Since the roles and responsibilities will apply to many different departments across the organization, they should be developed by a centralized group with clear authority to specify roles and responsibilities. The merits of centralization over decentralization are discussed in greater detail in Chapter 19.

It is very important that the person who is writing the new and/or revised information security roles and responsibilities be recognized as the designated person to perform this task. Out of frustration, memos will often be prepared in an attempt to clarify the often-murky domain of roles and responsibilities. These memos typically come from a wide variety of people including the Chief Information Officer (CIO) and Information Systems Auditors. While these memos may help or hinder, they will not be definitive unless top management recognizes the author as the designated person to write information security role and responsibility documentation. While clarifying the person to write roles and responsibilities may seem obvious to some, it is woefully missing in many organizations.

Top management recognition of responsibility to develop information security roles and responsibilities can be implied, for instance with the title Senior Vice President of Information Security. Alternatively, this recognition can be explicit, for example, through a project memo. If you do not have responsibility for roles and responsibilities implied by your title, or already expressly-mentioned in your job description, then a project memo is strongly recommended (see Chapter 4 for more details). A project memo simply defines what will be done, who it will be done by, how it will be reviewed and approved, the schedule, and the resources to be consumed. The memo should be issued by the Chief Executive Officer, the Chief Information Officer, or another member of the top management team. To save time, you, in many cases, should prepare a draft of this project memo and then submit it to the executive in question for signature. If you cannot get these members of the top management team to issue the memo, it will often suffice to have top management approve a memo that you develop.

Whoever it is that will be compiling the draft documentation should not chop-up the work and dole it out to various groups. While this task segmentation approach may at first seem like a good way to gain grass-roots support and reduce the burden on the primary writer, it is not recommended. Inevitably this approach leads to inconsistent material that must be extensively rewritten to get a finished product that is professional in appearance, internally consistent, and pitched at the right level of detail. The task segmentation approach is furthermore ill-advised because it involves a significant amount of time to facilitate communications and resolve disputes between the parties involved, and thus will often seriously delay the delivery of a first draft. Instead, you should go out and interview all the people who have a significant vested interest in information security (Information Systems Auditors, Systems Administrators, etc.) and get their ideas about roles and responsibilities. Then these notes should be merged with the templates provided in this book to yield a customized document that is truly responsive to the unique needs of your organization. Through the latter approach, or through a similar approach managed by a single person, you can achieve a consistent and high-level view that would not otherwise be possible.

Chapter 7 REVIEW & APPROVAL OF ROLES & RESPONSIBILITIES

Chapter 6 discussed the best individual to write the initial draft (or a revised draft) of an information security roles and responsibilities document. That same chapter discussed a project memo which defines what will be done, who it will be done by, how it will be reviewed and approved, the schedule, and the resources to be consumed. This chapter provides input to that memo, specifically it addresses the document review and approval process.

Because so many different people are involved with information security, it is important to understand the different perspectives of each person. You should interview a good number of them to get their views on the work that should be done, who it should be done by, and related considerations. This type of initial data gathering is also advisable because it gives the interviewees an opportunity to indicate whether they would be interested in the subsequent review and editing process. This interviewing approach is additionally advisable because it can be used to generate "grass roots" (widespread) support for the project. This support will be important when the time for implementation of these roles and responsibilities comes around. As a by-product of a roles and responsibilities effort, the interviewing process can additionally be used as an opportunity to increase the level of awareness about information security.

Determining who should be interviewed is a straightforward task with the aid of information in this book. A simple review of the Table Of Contents entry for Chapter 12 will reveal the job titles of those who would be good interview candidates. Certain third parties such as the partner of the external auditing firm who reviews your organization's books (see Chapter 16 and Chapter 17 for additional ideas), may also make good interview candidates. Beyond these lists, there will always be other people who can provide valuable input. These people often work in user departments that rely on one or more information security measures (for example the Telemarketing Department may rely on access controls to maintain the integrity of the sales contact manager database). In other cases, these people have prior experience with information security activities in other organizations, have worked within the

information security unit at your organization, or in some other respect have relevant experience which may be helpful in a roles and responsibilities project.

To help identify these supplementary interviewees, you should prepare a brief announcement of the project and have it issued by a member of the top management team via broadcast e-mail or traditional paper memo. The announcement should identify the project manager and should solicit support for the activity. This statement will encourage interviewees to give you their time for an interview. The announcement should also ask interested parties to get in touch with the project manager. After an e-mail exchange or a telephone conversation, the project manager can readily determine which of the people who have expressed an interest should receive an interview. For those people who expressed an interest but did not get an interview, there can still be an opportunity to respond to the first draft roles and responsibilities document.

To conserve time, you should only interview those who express an interest if they would offer an important perspective that no other interviewee could provide, if they have significant management roles, and/or if they have hands-on experience with information security activities. More than any other aspect of the effort to develop a first draft roles and responsibilities document, the interviewing process has the potential to significantly extend the project completion date into the future, and also to significantly inflate project expenses. Accordingly, the number of interviews should be strictly limited, and a list of interviewees should be approved by your manager prior to embarking on the interviewing process. For an organization of over 1000 employees, 15-20 interviews, each lasting 20-30 minutes, should be sufficient.

Questions to ask during these interviews include:

- Are you currently playing any role in the information security area? (Note: a concise definition of information security may be necessary.) If so, what is that role?

- If the answer to the previous question is yes, for information security purposes, what are the names of the other people you interact with, and what is the role each of these people play?

- With respect to information security, what other roles are you aware of within Company X, and who plays those roles?

- In your opinion, what would you say are the essential information security tasks that need to be performed?

- Here at Company X, are there some information security tasks that are not currently being done - tasks that nonetheless should be done? If so, what are they?

- Are there some information security tasks currently being performed, that are being done with insufficient resources or with insufficient expertise? If yes, please explain.

- Are there some information security tasks that are currently being done, but should be abandoned? If so, what are they?

- In your opinion, which departments or other organizational units should be primarily responsible for information security here at Company X? Why is that the best way to do things?

- Which information security tasks should be performed by outsiders such as outsourcing firms, consultants, contractors, and temporaries? Why is that the best way to do things?

- Where in the organizational hierarchy do you think the information security function should report? Why?

- To what extent do you think that information security responsibility should be decentralized or centralized? With this opinion in mind, how would the organization best be designed in terms of roles and responsibilities?

- Have there been any major security incidents which indicate that information security work is not being adequately handled here at Company X? (This might include a hacker intrusion, a widespread virus infestation, or some other major security-relevant events.) If so, what types of work were not being done adequately?

- Are you aware of any major law or regulation that specifies the information security work that Company X must perform? If so, what are these requirements?

- Are you aware of any major law or regulation relevant to Company X which specifies that certain job titles, like a Chief Privacy Officer, must be assigned?

- Are you aware of any contract with a supplier, a customer, or a business partner that dictates that certain information security tasks must be performed? If so, what are these tasks?

- Do you believe that Company X must perform the information security activities dictated by the standard of due care in our industry, by generally accepted ethical standards, or by some other source? If so, what are these activities?

- In your opinion, for Company X, what do you think is the most important contribution to be made by an Information Security Department?

- What do you think is Company X's greatest weakness when it comes to the information security area?

- Are you familiar with the information security distinctions called owners, custodians, and users [see Chapter 15 for details]? (Note: a concise definition may be necessary here.) If so, do you think that these distinctions could work well here at Company X? Why or why not?

- Are there any other organizational design models or structures that you think Company X should be using to organize its information security roles and responsibilities?

- Would you like to review an initial copy of the roles and responsibilities document?

- Who else should we interview regarding information security roles and responsibilities, and why are they important to this effort?

- What documentation are you aware of that defines existing information security roles and responsibilities here at Company X? If you know of any such documentation, where could I go, or to whom could I go, to get a copy of that documentation?

- How do you see the roles and responsibilities of the information security function changing over the next five years here at Company X? For example, do you believe that information security will become something that is viewed as a competitive advantage or even a competitive necessity? If so, what would be the organizational design implications of this new attitude?

- What methods do you suggest for communicating these roles and responsibilities once they have been developed, edited, and approved?

• What types of resistance to change in the organizational structure for information security do you anticipate here at Company X?

After the interviewing process is complete, you will want to use the information that you have gathered to customize the templates found in Chapter 11, Chapter 12, and Chapter 13. This template editing process ordinarily involves only a word processing program such as MS-Word, and optionally a graphics program such as Visio. After you have edited the templates in light of specific Company X information gathered via the interviewing process, a review and approval process begins. Note that the specifics of the review and approval process should have already been specified in the project memo mentioned in both this chapter and in Chapter 6.

To save time, a bottom-up review and approval process is recommended. This involves obtaining the support and feedback of people on the lower levels of the organization and then submitting the roles and responsibilities document to the middle level of management for review and approval. After the middle level of management has approved, then the material is submitted to top management for final review and approval. In smaller organizations, there will typically be fewer middle managers, and as a result this stage in the process can be abbreviated. The bottom-up approach allows you to gather important technical details about information security roles and responsibilities earlier rather than later in the documentation development process. The sooner these technical details can be integrated into the draft documentation, the faster the final product will be produced and approved.

Review of the first draft roles and responsibilities document by the managers in certain departments is mandatory. These departments include Internal Audit, Information Security, Information Technology (Information Systems), Human Resources, Legal, and Physical Security. Managers in other departments are optional but often useful. These departments include Accounting & Finance, Training, Sales & Marketing, Public Relations, Risk Management, and Strategic Planning. All of these department managers are the bottom level approvals of the organization and their support is very helpful when making a case for approval with the members of the middle and top management teams. Often no formal documented approval is required at this level; it is often sufficient to get some feedback and to incorporate some of this feedback into the documentation. By the way, the mark-up features in MS Word or a similar word processing program allow

reviewer comments to be quickly embedded in the document itself, and then sent back to you as an email attachment. Because this mark-up feature saves so much time, you may wish to encourage all reviewers to submit comments to you in mark-up form.

In an effort to standardize job descriptions and other human resources related documents across the organization, many organizations have established a single person as the coordinator through which all material of this nature must be funneled. This person may be situated in the Human Resources Department, or perhaps in a Strategy & Planning Department. If such a person exists within your organization, his or her review and approval is essential before you take the roles and responsibilities material to higher level management. If no such person exists at your organization, you should have nonetheless done your best to have the written materials you prepared look similar to, and be consistent with similar documents already published within your organization. As discussed in Chapter 4 before writing these documents, you should have identified the criteria that this coordinator will be using when he or she is reviewing and approving your documents.

Next, you should take your roles and responsibilities documentation to the Information Security Management Committee. This Committee may have been established for the purpose of generating an information security infrastructure including clear roles and responsibilities, or it may be a permanent committee that supervises and oversees all information security activities. The Committee will provide stamp of approval, validating the practicality of your documentation. The provision of such an approval will go a long way towards getting additional middle management and top management approvals. If your organization doesn't have such a committee, you may wish to establish one so that they can support you in your efforts to clarify information security roles and responsibilities. The specific tasks of this Committee are described in Chapter 11.

For a medium to large-scale organization, the next review process typically involves selected members of the middle management team. These include Chief Operations Officer, Chief Information Officer, Chief Marketing Officer, Chief Privacy Officer, Chief Legal Officer, and Chief Financial Officer. To provide background and to answer any questions they may have, a brief presentation may be given at a monthly meeting for the middle managers. If it can be shown that the support and acquiescence (if not approval) of many other managers at lower levels of the organization has already been obtained, then review and approval at this level will be accelerated significantly. This step in the review and approval process constitutes the middle level approvals of your organization.

Assuming that all required changes have been made, and that the resulting documentation has been approved at both the bottom and the middle levels, it is now time to submit the documentation to the upper levels of management. This may involve the Chief Executive Officer, the President, the Chairman of the Board, and members of the Audit Committee on the Board of Directors. A presentation is often necessary to explain why the project has been initiated and why top management support is needed. The existence of support and input from both lower level and middle level managers will make approval at the upper levels move along rapidly. In many cases, top managers will trust the other managers who are, after all, closer to the issues, and will then approve of the roles and responsibilities with only perfunctory review. The author is not encouraging top managers to deal with this important topic in a perfunctory manner. He is instead only acknowledging the many other pressing issues that top managers must deal with on a regular basis.

The signature of one or more of the top managers is needed to bring credibility and influence to those people and groups that will be performing the tasks defined in the roles and responsibilities documentation. Top management should be asked to go beyond a signature, to support the project in other ways, such as mentioning the new document in its quarterly speech to employees. Top management will also be asked to allocate resources to support the work defined in the roles and responsibilities document. Note that a specific budget may also be needed before top management approves of the roles and responsibilities document. Prerequisites for a roles and responsibilities document are further discussed in Chapter 4.

The whole area of roles and responsibilities is fraught with internal politics. Certain managers will, for example, want the function to be within their division. Other managers will want nothing to do with it, fearing that it is a thankless task and not part of their path to the executive suite. To have a roles and responsibilities document that is truly in the best interests of the organization, it will often be necessary for the person writing the policies to politely say no to influential and powerful managers. This should not be taken lightly because there may be personal repercussions associated with saying no. A "no" such as this needs to be well-justified and documented, not to mention communicated in a polite

and respectful manner. If this approach is adopted, you may later be surprised how the managers who received such a "no" are strong supporters later in the project.

Another important aid that you should employ to protect yourself from an internal political standpoint is a log of all suggested modifications accompanied by the reasons why these modifications were adopted or abandoned. To make this log work effectively, you should only accept written suggestions. This log should also indicate the date when memos were sent back to those people who submitted suggestions, explaining what was done with each of their suggestions. These memos can also be good way to thank people for taking the time to review the roles and responsibilities documentation. Such a log will enable you to effectively defend yourself from later being accused of forgetting an important topic that a manager supposedly suggested some time ago. The log can also be an important way to organize the review and revision process, making sure that there has been some action taken for each suggestion received.

If consolidating comments in a log sounds like too much work to you, you should at the very least be sure to save the handwritten reviewer comments in addition to the word processing files with reviewer mark-up comments embedded. These should include your own written remarks about the comments received, as well as why you made the suggested changes, or not, as the case may be. These working papers may be important to auditors looking over your work, as well as to lawyers defending against allegations of management negligence. Most importantly, these working papers will be useful a year or two in the future, when someone needs to update the documentation. Perhaps the best reason to keep a log or detailed working papers is that this someone making the document modifications may be you. Without detailed notes, you may have, several years later, forgotten many important points.

Given the politicized environment surrounding the clarification and documentation of roles and responsibilities, it should come as no surprise that some people will attempt to sabotage the process. Perhaps the most insidious way to do this is to hold up the process by not approving or reviewing a certain version of the document. To prevent this type of abuse, and to accelerate the project progress (perhaps there is no malicious intent, perhaps the reviewer is simply overwhelmed with other tasks), you can insist that all suggested changes be communicated by a certain date. If that date comes and goes, and feedback from certain parties was not received, then you should assume that there was no problem with the roles and responsibilities documentation.

Reminders can be sent to all the reviewers who have not yet responded, and these reminders can arrive just before the due date to reinforce the fact that you intend to take this same due date seriously. A series of reminders can also be used, but that runs the risk that you will be perceived as obnoxious and pushy. The reminder that you employ should ideally include words informing reviewers that no response has been received, and that the lack of a response by a certain date implies consent. Such a reminder is also good practice because it often allows previous communications problems (such as e-mail deleted by spam filters) to be overcome.

Another thing that people may do to sabotage or delay the review and approval process is to claim that they never got a copy of the draft document. An objection of this nature coming from a reviewer may mean that the reviewer wants the original project schedule to be abandoned and replaced by a schedule entirely dependent on them. A convenient way to prevent this type of manipulation and delay is to get an acknowledgement of receipt. Many electronic mail systems provide a return message indicating that a message has been examined. Likewise, couriers such as Federal Express have delivery services which indicate that a package was received on a certain date and by whom. In those organizations where there are a lot of internal politics related to a roles and responsibilities project, these acknowledgements of receipt are highly recommended.

In large organizations there may be a formal process for the generation, review, approval and dissemination of documents dealing with roles and responsibilities. Where this process exists, you should attempt to follow it as much as possible to help ensure rapid progress in the direction of a final approval by top management. The entire process often takes months, so you shouldn't take it personally if you get bogged-down in review, revision, and approval efforts.

Chapter 8 RESOURCES REQUIRED TO DOCUMENT ROLES & RESPONSIBILITIES

Inevitably, management will ask anyone who proposes to write information security roles and responsibilities how much it will cost. This query is really two questions that should be dealt with separately: (1) how much will it cost to develop, edit, and approve information security roles and responsibilities documentation, and (2) how much will it cost to implement the new ideas embodied in the documentation. This chapter can only do justice to the first of these because the second will always be a function of your organization, the extent of the changes that have been proposed, the time frame for implementing these changes, and other unique factors. This chapter also provides a detailed listing of the resources needed to develop, edit, and approve roles and responsibilities documentation, as well as a template for calculating the cost of the time involved in this same documentation process.

To compile professional-looking roles and responsibilities documentation that truly responds to the needs of a particular organization, very few resources are required. Specifically you will need:

- A personal computer that has a web browser, a word processing package, a printer, and a CD-ROM drive

- Access to a phone to conduct interviews with people at remote locations

- Access to an electronic mail system to schedule appointments with interviewees, and to shepherd the document review and approval process

- Pens, pencils, and writing paper to take notes during face-to-face interviews

- Manila file folders and a file cabinet to organize your papers and notes

- This book and the accompanying CD-ROM containing role and responsibility templates

- The time of at least one information security specialist (you are assumed to be this person) to plan the project, interview relevant people, compile initial drafts, edit subsequent drafts, and make management presentations

- The time of various interviewees to provide relevant background information and to review draft versions of the roles and responsibilities documents

- The time of management to review and approve of the documents that have been prepared and/or revised

Before you attempt to estimate the costs of these resources, you should make a distinction between *incremental costs* and *sunk costs*. Incremental costs are costs that require an additional outlay, such as the retention of an information security consultant to help write roles and responsibilities documentation. Sunk costs are costs that would have been incurred anyway due to existing commitments, or that have already been incurred. Sunk costs are not relevant to a decision regarding the initiation of a role and responsibilities project because they do not change. An example of a sunk cost would be this book and CD-ROM -- if you are in possession of the book and the CD-ROM, and the cost has already been incurred. In most organizations, management is most interested in incremental costs because these are above and beyond the costs that have already been budgeted or committed. From an incremental cost standpoint, in most cases, all that is required to write roles and responsibilities documentation is the time of the individuals involved plus communications costs such as telephone, e-mail, and courier services.

Another concept which is useful when answering management's question about costs is called *opportunity cost*. Technically, an opportunity cost is defined as the maximum alternative earnings or profit that might have been obtained if a productive resource was used for some other purpose. In this situation, the most important opportunity cost is associated with workers, because these people could be working on other projects which, hopefully, would benefit the organization. For example, middle and top management may have been able to negotiate a new deal with a supplier if they were not attending to a roles and responsibilities document development project. Just what this opportunity cost happens to be is often difficult to estimate because it is based on speculation and subjective opinion rather than specific transactional data. If management in your organization is interested in opportunity costs, it is often sufficient only to provide the number of hours of the three types of people that are involved on the project: the information security specialist, various interviewees, and middle and top management. The rest of the items on this same list are inconsequential, or as the accountants would say "immaterial," when compared to the time of people in these three categories. Accordingly, the balance of this chapter will be devoted to a process for estimating the time required to develop (or revise), edit, and approve information security roles and responsibilities documentation.

Before specific estimates of the time required are presented, it is important to discuss a few factors that will reduce the average estimates. For example, if your organization already has information security roles and responsibilities documentation that has been formally approved by management, and this documentation has been prepared within the last five years, then the estimates can be reduced by approximately 20%. If this documentation exists, but has not yet been approved, the estimates can be reduced by approximately 10%. If the documentation is over five years old, whether or not it has been formally approved, then no discount on these estimates is generally warranted.

The size of the organization will have a lot to do with the complexity of the effort to develop, edit, and approve roles and responsibilities documentation. The following estimates are based on an organization with 1,000 full-time equivalent workers. This means that 1,000 people work full-time, or alternatively 2,000 people work half-time. The estimate of the number of workers on staff includes employees, outsourcing firm personnel, contractors, consultants, and temporaries. Table 8-1 provides a very rough estimate of how the hourly estimates can be modified to reflect the size of the organization. You can simply change the number of hours by the inflator or deflator factor to arrive at a rough estimate applicable to your organization. As is the case with all numbers in this chapter, these numbers are not based on statistical studies, but they are a reflection of the author's consulting experience. As a result, your actual experience may vary considerably from these estimates.

Table 8-1: Factors to Estimate Development Time

Full Time Equivalent People	Inflator or Deflator Factor
10,000	+150%
5,000	+50%
1,000	no change
500	-10%
100	-20%
50	-30%
25	-40%

Next you will find estimates of the number of hours required to work on roles and responsibilities documentation for the three categories of people involved on the project. The hours shown in Table 8-2 are broken into three specific phases of the work, respectively develop (or revise), edit, and approve.

If you are ambitious, you can multiply the hours for each type of worker by a certain hourly rate to develop estimates of the personnel resource costs associated with the project. The actual real world hourly rates will vary considerably by organization, and so are not presented here. Actual hourly rates should include payroll taxes, fringe benefits, and other costs associated with retaining workers, not just the straight hourly rate paid to the involved workers.

Table 8-2: Estimated Hours to Complete Roles & Responsibilities Documentation

Category of Person	DEVELOP	EDIT	APPROVE	TOTAL HOURS
Information Security Specialist	60	35	15	110
Information Security Specialist	60	35	15	110
Total by Phase of the Work	90	50	17	157

Table 8-2: Estimated Hours to Complete Roles & Responsibilities Documentation

Category of Person	DEVELOP	EDIT	APPROVE	TOTAL HOURS
Interviewees	25	10	00	35
Middle and Top Management	05	05	02	12
Total by Phase of the Work	90	50	17	157

Table 8-3: Unadjusted Opportunity Cost to Complete Roles & Responsibilities Documentation

Table 8-3: Unadjusted Personnel Cost to Complete Roles & Responsibilities Documentation Category of Person	TOTAL HOURS	COST/HR	PERSONNEL COST
Information Security Specialist	110	$50	$5,500
Interviewees	35	$60	$2,100
Middle and Top Management	12	$100	$1,200
Total Personnel Opportunity Cost	157	$56.05 (avg.)	$8,800

To provide an integrated example how all of these numbers can be used to quickly come up with an estimate of personnel costs, consider the situation at a fictitious Company X. This firm has role and responsibility documentation that has been approved by management within the last five years, so we can reduce the time required by 20%. At the same time the organization has 10,000 full-time equivalent workers, so we need to increase the estimates by 150%. Combining these two adjustment factors, this means that in overall terms we need to increase the estimates by 130% (+150% - 20% = +130%). At this company, the fully loaded cost (including fringe benefits, income taxes, pension costs, etc.) for information security specialists is $50/hour, for interviewees is $60/hour, and for management is $100/hour. This means that the opportunity cost for developing, editing, and approving role and responsibility documentation is $8,800. The calculations are briefly sketched in Table 8-3.

Note this personnel cost calculation is not necessarily a reflection of the opportunity cost. If there are no other significant contributions that these people were expected to make in the time involved to work on the roles and responsibilities project, then the personnel costs are equal to the opportunity costs. But if their contribution to the organization was expected to be much larger, then the amount of that net contribution should instead be used as the opportunity cost. For example, if middle and top management could have been closing a deal with a new supplier, if that deal will have been otherwise lost, and if that deal had a net benefit to the organization of over $1,200, then the net amount of that deal should be used as the personnel opportunity cost for middle and top management. Continuing with the example, we assume that there is no such opportunity cost greater than the personnel cost, so we proceed simply with the personnel cost.

Adding the totals for these three types of worker we have $8,800, which needs to be inflated by 130% for the reasons described above. Stated another way, multiplying $8,800 by 130% and then adding the result to $8,800 we come up with $20,240. Reflecting the fact that these calculations are only rough estimates, this number should probably be rounded to $20,250 and some sort of significant error factor should be attached (for example +/- 20%). You may want to explain why such a wide range of error is included (such a project has never been done at Company X before, the involved individuals have never before worked on such a project, the information security area has gone through major changes over the last few years, you anticipate a significant amount of internal politics, etc.).

Before you get engrossed in detailed cost calculations, it's important to ask what is the opportunity cost of not writing or updating information security role and responsibility documentation? This will be significant in almost any organization. The numbers in most instances will be several orders of magnitude larger than the opportunity costs for the three types of workers described immediately above. In some cases, these numbers are available in a recently-performed risk assessment. If you have made a persuasive case about the need for formal information security role and responsibility documentation, the detailed numbers discussed in this chapter in most cases will not need to be calculated. But if management at your organization insists on cost estimates, you can get more ideas for the opportunity costs associated with not writing roles and responsibilities documentation by reviewing Chapter 2, "Reasons To Establish Clear Roles & Responsibilities."

Chapter 9 TIME ESTIMATES TO DOCUMENT ROLES & RESPONSIBILITIES

This chapter discusses the schedule for an information security roles and responsibilities project including project tasks and milestones. The estimates assume that your organization is not going through a major internal change such as a significant reorganization, a merger, a large acquisition, a management buyout, or an initial public offering (IPO). If a major internal change is underway, the elapsed time to complete the project should probably be extended by 50% or more.

Taking the opposite perspective, if management is especially motivated, perhaps due to a recently publicized system penetration, the project can be accelerated. Such motivation may also come from an audit report, a lawsuit in process, an upcoming government regulator investigation, or an imminent buyout. In these cases, the elapsed time to complete the project can be compressed 25% or more. Such an acceleration of the project requires that more people get involved, and these additional people must communicate with each other. This in turn imposes some additional overhead that would not ordinarily be required if only one information security specialist (assumed to be you) acts as project manager and document writer.

In general, consider allocating two and three-quarters months for the completion of the whole project. Smaller organizations can move considerably faster, and larger organizations inevitably move more slowly. This estimate for the entire roles and responsibilities project is based on an organization with 1,000 full-time equivalent workers (including employees, contractors, consultants, temporaries, etc.). This two and three-quarters month estimate also assumes that no other up-to-date internal information security roles and responsibilities documentation exists.

While at first two and three-quarters months may sound like a long time, it really is not when you appreciate that the majority of the elapsed time is consumed by the review and approval process. It is certainly advisable to prepare a schedule in advance, but in the real world, you are at the mercy of the schedules of both top management and middle management. The review and approval process can, however, be accelerated by periodic friendly reminders, by agreements about the dates when certain tasks will be completed, and by default approval mechanisms (for example, if there is no objection, then approval is implied).

A typical roles and responsibilities project schedule with tasks to be completed is presented in Table 9-1. The author suggests that you simply copy this set of tasks into a memo which discusses the project schedule. The list of milestones, which appears later in this chapter, can also be copied and used in this same manner.

All references to days involve business days rather than calendar days. Due to weekends, holidays, etc., the actual number of days that you work on the project will, in most cases, be considerably fewer than the total elapsed days. Typically a single project manager and document writer (assumed to be you) will need about 12-15 days of focused work to complete the project. This estimate assumes that you have no prior experience developing this type of material, and that English is your native language. This estimate also assumes that there will be three versions of the roles and responsibilities document (rarely fewer versions will be required, and often additional versions will be needed).

Project Milestones

- Complete project proposal management memos
- Receive management authorization to proceed
- Review related internal documentation
- Complete interested party interviews
- Complete first draft of document
- Deliver presentation to the Information Security Management Committee and/or lower level managers
- Complete second draft of document
- Complete third draft of document
- Deliver half-hour top management presentation
- Receive top management approval for document
- Publicize document within the organization

The estimates in this chapter assume that the prerequisites to a roles and responsibilities project, such as a risk assessment, have already been handled. These items were discussed in Chapter 4. If any of these tasks must still be accomplished, this will further delay the completion of a roles and responsibilities project because additional remedial work will be required. Similarly, the schedule presented below does not acknowledge any pressing projects that an Information Security Department might be currently engaged with, and these in turn are likely to further delay the completion of a roles and responsibilities documentation project.

The estimates in this chapter also assume that it will be straightforward and relatively easy for you to schedule time to meet with top management. At an organization which is highly motivated due to a recent information security incident, this will indeed be the case. In a less motivated organization, it may be some time before top management agrees to give you the time to deliver a presentation about your information security roles and responsibilities document. The wait may be months until the next top management meeting with an open agenda, or until all the relevant top managers are simultaneously in the office. If you anticipate this type of delay, because your organization is less than highly motivated, or for other reasons, then the estimate of elapsed business days provided below should be extended accordingly.

Table 9-1: Estimated Days to Complete Project Tasks

Task Description	Elapsed Time (days)
Review this book and CD-ROM and prepare project memos	2
Gather and review related internal documentation	2
Prepare and deliver talk to Information Security Management Committee	2
Select interviewees and make appointments for interviews	2
Perform interviews and document/analyze results	5
Write first draft roles and responsibilities document	3
Circulate first draft for comments and feedback	15
Write second draft roles and responsibilities document	2
Circulate second draft for comments and feedback	15
Write third draft of roles and responsibilities document	1
Develop and deliver half hour presentation to top management	2
Make additional adjustments requested by top management	1
Internally publicize new roles and responsibilities document	3
Total number of elapsed business days for project (no holidays or vacation included)	55
Assuming an average of 20-business days per month, total months required for project	2.75 months

Chapter 10 KEY INFORMATION SECURITY DOCUMENTS

No matter how little work has actually been done in the information security area at your organization, and no matter how small the budget for information security happens to be today, every organization with over 50 workers should at the very least prepare and issue three basic role and responsibility documents: job descriptions, mission statements, and reporting relationship diagrams. Words and diagrams that you can use for each of these three documents are provided in Chapter 11, Chapter 12, and Chapter 13, respectively.

Moving beyond these three basic documents, this chapter assists you in identifying the other documents that should include mention of information security roles and responsibilities. These other documents may already exist within your organization, or they may still need to be compiled. In general, as the number of different documents containing information security roles and responsibilities rises, workers will view information security more seriously. The more seriously that workers take information security, the more they will perceive it to be a regular part of modern business, just like accounting and marketing. The more workers consider information security to be just a part of modern business, the greater the compliance, support, and alignment with information security objectives. Thus one major objective of documenting information security roles and responsibilities is to make information security a part of your organization's corporate culture.

To prepare an abbreviated list of other documents that should include mention of information security roles and responsibilities, you can cut-and-paste the subheadings for Chapter 10 found in the Table Of Contents. If you seek a list of other documents with descriptions for each, you can simply copy the list found later in this chapter. In either case, you should delete mention of those documents that do not seem appropriate at this point in time, and use the balance as the basis for a memo to management. Management's review of this list may also trigger a conversation about the merits of further revisions to these documents - revisions above and beyond the inclusion of more specific information security roles and responsibilities.

When making a decision about the other documents that should include mention of information security roles and responsibilities, you should keep in mind that information security deals with many intangible matters-things that cannot be specifically touched and

felt. For example, privacy is a psychological, social, and legal issue that cannot be tangibly manifested without some documentation. This documentation takes the form of laws, policies, and procedures. In many areas of the information security field, security cannot be said to exist unless it is reflected by an official written document. For example in a court of law, the fact that management exercised due diligence can be evidenced by an up-to-date information security policy manual. You are urged to consider the many ways in which the following documents may be needed to tangibly manifest an information security effort.

When looking over the list of documents shown below, you should also bear in mind that the number of different documents, the length of these documents, and the level of detail found in the documents is largely a function of the level of information security sophistication at your organization. For example, a commercial bank will typically have more information security documents, of greater length, that provide more detail than a manufacturing firm. This situation is a reflection of the fact that a bank has typically spent considerably more time and resources focusing on information security than a manufacturing firm. But even within the same industry, two different organizations can have quite different levels of information security sophistication. Larger organizations are generally more sophisticated because the complexity of their operations requires more formal structure. Likewise, information intensive organizations (like a research institute) will tend to be more sophisticated than those that are not information intensive (such as a chain of restaurants). Similarly, those organizations that rely heavily on information systems as a mechanism to achieve competitive advantage will typically have a greater investment in information security, and will accordingly be more sophisticated.

When you review the list of information security documents that can include some mention of roles and responsibilities (shown below), you should attempt to define just how sophisticated your organization is. If your organization is very sophisticated, roles and responsibilities will probably appear in a vast majority of these documents. If your organization is just beginning its serious information security work, roles and responsibilities words may appear in just a few of, or perhaps none of these documents. If the latter situation prevails at your organization, the first step should be to write the basic three role and responsibility documents: job descriptions, mission statements, and reporting relationship diagrams. In the latter case, you may want to skip the rest of this chapter until the time when these three basic roles and responsibilities documents have been prepared and approved.

If your organization has information security words in less than every one of the documents found on the list, you should consider how you can further the cause of information security by adding roles and responsibilities words to these same documents. To do this, you should consider which of the documents without roles and responsibilities words are highly regarded, which are often referenced, and which are considered authoritative. It is those documents which should soon be modified to include information security roles and responsibilities. Because they do not make such a significant contribution to the adoption of information security as a part of your organization's corporate culture, the documents on the list shown below which do not fall into this "change soon" category should nonetheless still be amended to include roles and responsibilities material. This latter type of document change should however take place at a later date.

Although outside the scope of this book, it should be mentioned that there are a variety of dependencies between the documents mentioned below. For example, it will be difficult to develop a systems administration procedures manual if an information security policies manual has not already been developed. This is because the latter document is a higher-level document, which establishes the general rules that are then in part implemented via the former document. In general, to save time and to minimize trouble with dependencies, you are urged to write the general documents before the detailed documents are prepared. Beyond the basic three roles and responsibilities documents mentioned above, the most important general document is an information security policy manual. For pre-written words that can be included in an information security policy manual, the reader may wish to consult another book written by the author entitled "Information Security Policies Made Easy" (see Appendix J, "Sources and References").

The author acknowledges that, in the real world, the actual situation within a particular organization most often is not so clear-cut, and that you often inherit a hodge-podge of incomplete and conflicting documents with various degrees of obsolescence. Nonetheless, to economize with your time, and also to provide the greatest contribution with limited resources, revisions to these existing documents can still follow the general to detailed approach mentioned immediately above. This

general to detailed approach will also allow you to start with the big picture and then to apply this big picture in a consistent and logically straight-forward manner.

The following list of documents is meant to be illustrative rather than comprehensive. Within your organization there will undoubtedly be other documents where information security roles and responsibilities are mentioned. If an important type of document has been left off this list, the author would appreciate hearing about it via e-mail. A brief discussion of the nature of each of these documents is provided below as well as an example of how information security roles and responsibilities could be included in these documents. The actual words to include in these documents can be found in Chapter 11, Chapter 12, and Chapter 13.

Information Security Department And Other Department Missions

An Information Security Department mission statement specifies, in overall terms, the charter of the Information Security Department (the reasons why management has created this organizational unit). The document will typically cover the objectives of the department and how it fits in with the organization's business or strategic objectives. The inclusion of this type of roles and responsibilities information in an Information Security Department mission statement is of course required, but information security roles and responsibilities also need to be incorporated into the mission statements of other departments. For example, information security related objectives could be included in the mission statement of the Computer Operations Department. Detailed words for a wide variety of department mission statements can be found in Chapter 11.

Information Security Staff And Other Staff Job Descriptions

Job descriptions provide the specific tasks and duties of a certain job or position. For example, the activities of an Access Control System Administrator on a day-to-day basis would be specified in a job description. While there is likely to be little objection to including information security tasks and duties in the job descriptions for staff in the Information Security Department, there may be some push back for inclusion of these same tasks and duties in job descriptions for staff in other departments. For example, information security tasks and duties can be included in the job descriptions of Business Applications Programmers. Likewise, progressive organizations are now starting to include information security tasks and duties in the job descriptions for rank-and-file end-users. Detailed words for all types of job descriptions can be found in Chapter 12. Note that job descriptions may include verbal descriptions of reporting relationships, just as they may include standards of performance.

Information Security Department Reporting Relationships Diagram

This document graphically depicts the organizational units that report to the Information Security Department as well as the unit to which the Information Security Department reports. These reporting relationships can be dotted line (advisory) as well as straight line (manager/direct report). For example, an Information Security Department may have a dotted line reporting relationship to the Audit Committee on the Board of Directors, and it may have a straight line reporting relationship to the Legal Department. If specific roles and responsibilities information is included (perhaps in bulleted form), this document includes only a few words. In many cases reporting relationships are not diagrammatically represented, but are instead described in words. In the latter cases, the words may be integrated with job descriptions and/or mission statements. Detailed words and diagrams for information security reporting relationships are found in Chapter 13.

Information Security Awareness Pamphlet

This booklet, pamphlet, or manual covers the basics that every worker should be aware of when it comes to information security. The organization's basic philosophy about information security is typically presented, as are some essential policies (such as never share a fixed password with any other person). Other topics include who to contact when there is a question or a suspected information security problem. These contact points include the Help Desk (for trouble reporting), the Information Security Department (for security problem reporting, system access control, and contingency planning), Physical Security Department (for theft of equipment, access to buildings, and other physical security issues), and the Information Systems Department (for systems development, testing, and change control reasons). This pamphlet can also describe the distinctions between information Owners, Custodians, and Users. The latter distinctions are covered in Chapter 15.

Information Security Awareness Reminder Memos

These brief memos are typically broadcasted to all workers via electronic mail or internal physical mail. They remind people to attend to a certain aspect of information security, such as backing-up data on portable computers. A contact point is always provided should a worker need additional information. URLs on an intranet may also be included. A brief mention of the roles and responsibilities of the Information Security Department is often included at the end of these memos. Such memos can also be provided on coffee mugs, on mouse pads, on log-in banners, and in other places.

Information Security Policy Manual

This manual defines the rules which will be used to manage information security throughout an organization. An example of such rules involves user-chosen fixed passwords, which may be restricted to strings of characters that are at least eight characters long and composed of both numbers and alphabetic characters. This policy manual typically includes an introductory section which, in a high-level way, addresses who is responsible for information security, who to contact if there are questions, and who to contact if a security problem exists. A policy manual also covers who is responsible for implementing the rules (such as a systems development group within the Information Technology Department). Aside from job descriptions, mission statements, and reporting relationships, this document is one of the most likely places to find statements of information security roles and responsibilities. For example, department managers may be required to make sure that someone in their department prepares and maintains a departmental information systems contingency plan. To help with the preparation of a policy manual, the author has written a reference book and CD-ROM entitled "Information Security Policies Made Easy", which contains sample policies. (see Appendix J).

Information Security Standards Document

This document specifies the technical standards for selecting, implementing, and configuring information security systems. In the encryption area, for example, a standards manual will typically cover algorithms and key management systems. A web site, for instance, may be required to employ an encryption standard called SSL (Secure Sockets Layer). Brief comments about responsibility for enforcing these standards and the approval process for changing the standards are typically found in a document like this. Standards documents may also include mention of the authority for preparing and issuing such standards, and this may require a brief statement about information security roles and responsibilities. Additional words about the persons responsible for implementing standards may also appear in this document.

Information Security Architecture Document

This document provides a broad overview of the control measures which will be observed throughout an organization or a multi-organization networked community. Such a document typically includes a description of centralized information security management systems as well as interfaces between information security systems (such as between logging systems and intrusion detection systems). Examples of the controls described in an architecture document include digital signatures and dynamic password access control. These control requirements will have no effect unless management specifically assigns responsibility for integrating these controls into systems, compliance checking, administering the controls, and the like. Mention of these responsibilities is recommended, although pointers to other documents may additionally be used, especially if this document appears on an intranet. An architecture document may also include mention of the authority for preparing and issuing the document, and this may require a brief statement about information security roles and responsibilities.

Information Security Action Plan

An information security action plan is a list of projects to be attended to in the near future. The ideas for projects often come from a risk assessment or an information systems audit. Action plans typically include mention of the results to be achieved, the person or group that will spearhead the projects, the persons or groups that will assist, the resources that will be required, and the estimated schedules. If the participating individuals and groups are not included in an action plan, management will still need to identify these individuals and groups before the work gets underway. These individuals and groups are sometimes discussed in an implementation details memo that goes along with an action plan. Whatever the documents needed to initiate these projects, management will need to work with existing mission statements and job descriptions. Reference to the relevant mission statements and job descriptions may reveal that they need to be modified or expanded. Until these changes to existing job descriptions and mission statements can be made, new roles and responsibilities may appear only in action plan memos. Note that action plans often have temporary roles and responsibilities assignments, while job descriptions and mission statements have permanent roles and responsibilities assignments.

Information Security Forms

Information security forms are paper or electronic blank forms with structured questions and answers. They are used to achieve a variety of results, such as request approval for a user-ID, and later approve certain privileges which go along with that same user-ID. Forms are increasingly being provided via HTML, and sent through the Internet or an intranet. Forms will often make mention of the person to contact if there is a question, as well as who is responsible for certain steps in a process. For instance, a form may indicate that the Owner of the information in question must approve access before a Systems Administrator actually grants access. Forms may also provide emergency information security responsibilities. For example, on the "contact us" form provided with some web sites, there is a notice at the bottom that security problems or issues should be directed to the Web Site Administrator.

Systems Administration Procedures Manual

A systems administration procedures manual discusses the steps that Systems Administrators need to take to maintain the systems they have been charged with managing. These steps include running vulnerability identification software to quickly illuminate security weaknesses, as well as the process of installing the latest operating system release to minimize the threat of intrusions. Systems administration procedures manuals not only discuss the very important role that Systems Administrators play on the information security team, they also refer the Systems Administrators to other people on the information security team for assistance with a variety of circumstances. For example, if an intruder has compromised the security of an organization's network, the Physical Security Department will typically get involved with the investigation. The roles and responsibilities of these other people can be covered in abbreviated fashion to help ensure that these other people are consistently engaged when they are needed. The job description for "Systems Administrator/Network Administrator" in Chapter 12 provides ideas for this manual.

Risk Acceptance Memos

A risk acceptance memo (sometimes called a risk accountability memo) is evidence that a middle level manager has approved of a situation where a system, a department, or an individual is out of compliance with an information security policy or standard. This middle level manager accepts personal career risk and personal responsibility for being out of compliance. When faced with the risk of seriously damaging their careers, as a result of taking on the responsibility defined in this type of memo, many middle level managers decide they will fix the security problem after all. If they do take the career risk and personal responsibility for the variance, this memo is completed and approved for a brief period of time, such as six months or a year. After this period ends, another risk acceptance memo is needed, or else the situation needs to promptly come into compliance. Risk acceptance memos often mention who is responsible for compliance checking, issuing policies and standards, revising policies and standards, and approving variances from these same policies and standards. Typically a memo with standardized language is developed and used repeatedly, and this stock memo can include statements about several management-related information security roles and responsibilities. The career risk and personal responsibility (not financial risk) that the middle level manager takes on by signing such a memo also needs to be specifically described in the memo.

Information Systems Contingency Planning Manual

An information systems contingency planning manual provides a methodology for the development, testing, and revision of contingency plans. These plans typically focus on information systems, although sometimes they include business processes. Alternatively, a separate business contingency planning manual may be issued. Both of these manuals need to define who is responsible for writing, testing, and revising contingency plans, as well as who is responsible for auditing and approving of these same contingency plans. For example, many organizations specifically place responsibility for business contingency plans on the shoulders of user department managers. Likewise, exactly who will approve a finished contingency plan should also be specified in a planning manual. Separately, these manuals can include pointers directing the reader to various groups within the organization that can provide supporting goods and services. For example, the Information Security Department may provide consulting assistance in the development of contingency plans. These internal pointers typically summarize a variety of roles and responsibilities related to the preparation of, testing of, and revision of contingency plans. Contingency plans additionally include pointers which direct the reader to external organizations for things such as replacement equipment and data recovery services.

Divisional Or Departmental Contingency Plans

Divisional or departmental contingency plans define the ways in which work groups will respond to certain types of problems such as the loss of electricity, the explosion of a bomb, or the unavailability of a centralized computing resource such as a network. The Information Technology Department should also have such a plan, except in this case the plan would apply to the networks and systems (like an Internet commerce site) which that department manages on behalf of users. These plans will vary considerably based on a variety of factors such as the technology employed, the business activities performed, the technical proficiency of the people in the relevant organizational unit. In order to define how to recover either an information system or a business process, the plans will need to define who is responsible for various activities. Although security and privacy matters may be a lower priority than recovery of the network or system, security and privacy roles and responsibilities should nonetheless be defined in the plan. For example, if a disaster has caused the Information Technology Department to move production processing from your organization's data center to a third party hot site, the plan should specify who will be handling access control for the hot site systems (third party staff or in-house staff). As is the case for information systems contingency plans (mentioned in the paragraph above), divisional or departmental contingency plans also include pointers to various internal and external groups that can provide a variety of relevant goods and services that could assist with a recovery effort.

Computer Emergency Response Team (CERT) Manual

A computer emergency response team, defined at length in Chapter 11, provides a trained and highly-technical response to a variety of problems including computer virus infections and hacker intrusions. The manual defines how the multi-departmental team works together, how to investigate and document information security incidents, how to keep damage from an incident to a minimum, and related matters. In this manual, responsibility for specific information security related tasks should be defined. For example, the principal investigator of a certain information security incident will be the only contact person for all reports to management, and the Information Security Manager will be the sole information security contact person for all discussions with outsiders such as news reporters and concerned customers. A CERT team can be provided by an outsourcing firm, although in most organizations this is not the case.

Help Desk Quick Reference Guide

A help desk quick reference guide is a compressed procedure manual which lists the essential steps to take in a variety of different situations. For example, if a user calls to report a virus infection inside his or her personal computer, the steps to eradicate the virus can then be referenced, and having this material on hand will assist with the expeditious handling of the problem. Besides defining the steps to be taken, these quick reference guides should include the names, job titles, and phone numbers of the people to be contacted in various security-related situations. For instance, if a system intrusion is believed to be underway, the help desk staff member should immediately alert the Computer Emergency Response Team (CERT). Although a quick reference guide can cover many other topics than information security, certainly information security should be one of the most important topics covered in this document.

Organizational Code Of Conduct

An organizational code of conduct is an ethics statement which defines the ways that an organization does business. Among other things, it covers conflicts of interest, such as an in-house buyer who receives personal gifts from an external supplier. Codes of conduct often overlap slightly with information security policy manuals, for example, in the area of disclosure of sensitive information only to those who have a demonstrable need to know such information. At the end of the code of conduct there may be mention of the internal departments that can answer questions. In this context, the Information Security Department may be mentioned as may the Legal, Internal Audit, and Human Resources Departments. Words in the code of conduct may also cover how violations will be handled, which group will perform investigations, which group will handle disciplinary actions, which group will receive anonymous complaints, etc.

Standard Operating Procedures (SOP) Manual

A standard operating procedures manual covers the regular business procedures needed to conduct day-to-day activities. For example, an SOP manual will often define how to prepare and submit a travel expense reimbursement claim. As the number of internal processes that are computerized continues to increase for most organizations, the number of procedures that involve some aspect of information security will also rise. For example, an SOP manual could outline standardized ways to protect paper-based information stored in offices. An SOP manual may also reference an information security policy manual as well as procedures that deal with information security topics (such as a systems administration procedures manual). An SOP manual will also point you in the direction of internal groups that can assist with various tasks and processes, and these should include the Information Security Department. A brief mention of the roles and responsibilities of the Information Security Department can appear at this point.

Department Or Division Head Manager's Manual

A manager's manual defines the special responsibilities of organizational unit heads, for example those who manage a department. These responsibilities include making sure that staff within that unit receive adequate training on topics like information security. These responsibilities can optionally include the notion of Owners, Custodians, and Users. Discussed at greater length in Chapter 15, this distinction defines specific responsibilities for people who fall into one or more of these three categories. Unit heads would often fall into the Owner category, and thus will often be called upon to do things such as (1) approve specific worker requests for access to certain data, (2) define the controls which are to be applied to information used by the involved organizational unit, and (3) define the ways in which this type of information will be backed-up and stored off-site. A manager's manual may also include words about other information security related manager responsibilities. These include allocating sufficient funds for various information security activities, setting a good example for staff within the department or division, and ensuring that staff complies with information security policies such as periodically backing-up their portable computers. A variety of explicit information security tasks to be performed by department heads or division heads, tasks which might be covered in this type of a manual, can be found at the end of Chapter 15.

Systems Development Process Manual

A systems development process manual discusses the steps that various people must go through to plan, analyze, develop, test, and deploy a new or modified business application system. This manual helps to ensure that serious errors are not made, that the application system will be responsive to business needs, and that it will be secure, reliable, and stable. Ideally, this manual mentions specific points in the systems development process where the Information Security and/or Internal Auditing Departments will review the work done to date to ensure that adequate controls are being incorporated into the new or modified application system. Likewise, the Quality Assurance Department may be used to test the application system before it is moved into production. The responsibility of the user department manager who approves the final system is also typically described in this manual. Typically, one of the most important aspects of a system ready to go into production, one of those aspects that a user department manager needs to approve, is the existence of adequate security measures.

Application System Requirements Documents

Application system requirements documents define the functionality of a proposed business application system. The proposed application may be brand new or it may be a major enhancement to an existing application. In either instance, the role of the Information Security and/or Internal Auditing Department can be at the very least implied by approving signatures at the end of the document. A more specific statement, perhaps only a sentence or two, can define the roles of either or both of these departments in the development process. The information security role of the user department manager who approves the final system can also be defined in a sentence or two. For example, "I have performed a detailed review of this requirements document, and to the best of my knowledge, all required functionality, including security and privacy measures, has been described herein." The results of an application-specific risk analysis can also be incorporated into such a requirements document, and the responsibilities for conducting a risk analysis, and for making changes based on the results of the risk analysis, can additionally be noted.

User And Computer Operations Application Manuals

These manuals provide specific instructions in the operation of business applications such as an accounts payable system. The manuals define the detailed actions that both end-users and those in the computer operations group within the Information Technology Department must take to achieve certain business results. These manuals are application specific, and in that respect differ from Standard Operating Procedure (SOP) manuals. These manuals should include mention of the user's information security responsibility, such as never sharing a personal fixed password with others. They can also define the responsibilities of the computer operations group, for example, to back-up the application's database on a nightly basis. These manuals can furthermore define the role of the Information Security Department (administering system- and network-based security systems on which applications rely), as well as other groups on the information security team (for example the Help Desk could answer questions about security, such as questions about application system password resets). When an Application System Provider (ASP) provides application-specific services, the manual is likely to be considerably more specific about security responsibility. In this case, who to contact for various types of information security problems, will generally be specified. Additional information about outsourcing firms can be found in Chapter 17.

Records Management Policies And Procedures Manual

A records management policies and procedures manual will, among other things, discuss the rules for designating certain information as an official archival record, as well as the procedures for granting access to this information, and the procedures for safeguarding the information against unauthorized modification. These policies and procedures are meant for both those working in the Records Management Department as well as all other workers who must interface with these same people. This manual discusses the responsibilities of users to pass along records that should be archived, as well as the responsibilities of other groups involved with the handling of this information. The roles and responsibilities of the Records Management Department and the Information Security Department are often mentioned in these manuals. The ways in which essential records (sometimes called critical information) are passed between groups is additionally specified in this manual, and some mention of the responsibilities of those involved in this process should also be found in the manual.

Worker Performance Reviews

Most organizations have worker performance reviews that ask a variety of questions, such as "Did this worker consistently show up for work on time?" Most do not make specific reference to information security. But those few progressive organizations which do ask questions like "Did the worker consistently observe information security policies and procedures?" are finding that workers take information security considerably more seriously. Even if no such broad question is included in the standard worker performance review form, much can be accomplished by modifying mission statements and job descriptions to include specific information security words. This is because the manager reviewing a worker's performance will consider these specific words when writing the review. The net effect will be that workers pay greater attention to information security, instead of saying "It's not my job." This topic is addressed in greater detail in Appendix C.

Systems Usage Responsibility Agreements

Systems usage responsibility agreements, also known as user compliance agreements, are typically signed when a worker is first hired, or when they are first given a user-ID and password. Some organizations require that workers sign such an agreement annually, although many people consider this to be overkill. The implication of this agreement is that the worker gets a job and/or system privileges in return for agreeing to abide by the existing information security policies and perhaps other information security requirements as well. In this document, the user's information security roles and responsibilities are covered in outline fashion, but reference is made to a document that contains the full list of roles and responsibilities (generally the information security manual). A standard set of words for this type of agreement is provided in Appendix F, "Sample User Responsibility Agreement."

Outsourcing And Consulting Agreements

Outsourcing and consulting agreements define the work to be done by a third party such as a facilities management outsourcing firm, a management consulting firm, or a technical contractor. Sometimes these agreements incorporate specific standards for performance, also called service level agreements (SLAs). Outsourcing and consulting agreements define the ways in which a third party must protect the information belonging to your organization, as well as the specific tasks that the third party will perform. These tasks include backing-up the data, performing network management services such as monitoring for intrusions, and conducting risk assessments. It is very important that these agreements are explicit about information security because the third party may not perform anything that is not specifically stated in the contract, and may disclaim all responsibility for doing things that are not expressly mentioned therein. Note that explicit delineation of information security roles and responsibilities is typically not necessary for temporary workers, which are treated more like employees (and who should be subject to similar requirements as employees, as would, for example, be defined in the information security policies manual). Chapter 16 and Chapter 17 discuss the roles of outsourcing firms and other third parties in greater detail.

Confidentiality And Non-Compete Agreements

Confidentiality agreements (sometimes called non-disclosure agreements or NDAs) are legal agreements which define the way that sensitive information will be handled after it has been disclosed to trusted third parties. Non-compete agreements also talk about how sensitive information will be handled, but are focused primarily on how the information must not be used to launch or support a business competing with the organization that disclosed the information. Both types of agreement can be used with employees as well as contractors, consultants, outsourcing firms, and temporaries. The role of these parties in terms of protecting the information in question is typically explicitly defined in these agreements (for example, sensitive information must not be disclosed to third parties without the express permission of the original source). If you are not satisfied with the specificity found in the current versions of these agreements at your organization, you can take this matter up with an Internal Intellectual Property Attorney. Further discussion about the roles and responsibilities of third parties can be found in Chapter 16 and Chapter 17.

Human Resources Manual

This document covers pension eligibility requirements, sick time policies, vacation policies, and other matters related to being an employee at your organization. Human resources manuals also typically discuss the information that the Human Resources Department keeps on each worker, how to access a copy of this information, and to whom this information will be disclosed. Other privacy issues related to worker-provided information (such as who can examine background check reports) may also be found in this manual. The information security responsibility of the Human Resources Department is accordingly covered as it relates to this information. The role of other individuals who may become involved with an employee's situation, such as an Ombudsman or Internal Intellectual Property Attorney, may additionally be described. These other individuals or groups may, for example, get involved if an employee is being investigated or disciplined for a violation of information security policies. Separately, progressive organizations are now extending the scope of human resources manuals to include contractors, consultants, temporaries, and other third parties. If your organization is embracing this broader audience, be sure to include mention of confidentiality agreements, non-compete agreements, and the like (these are mentioned immediately above).

Physical Security Pamphlet

This flier or pamphlet typically describes an identification badge system and a process for gaining access to buildings and other facilities during regular business hours, as well as after hours. It often also covers issues related to information security such as theft of computer equipment and use of shredders. The physical security responsibility of the worker will typically be covered, and so will the responsibilities of the Information Security and Physical Security Departments. For example, whom to contact in the event of a computer theft will typically be covered in this pamphlet. In many cases, also covered in this pamphlet are user department manager responsibilities pertaining to both physical and information security matters within a department's office area. These include management of building access keys, file cabinet keys, shredders, etc. A more complete discussion of department manager responsibilities is taken up in Chapter 15.

Chapter 11 ORGANIZATIONAL MISSION STATEMENTS

This chapter provides specific words that you can use to quickly prepare mission statements (also called charters) that define the work that needs to be done in the information security area. A complete mission statement is provided for a centralized Information Security Department. Partial mission statements are provided for other organizational units that, in one way or another, play an important role on the information security team. When a partial mission statement is provided, it deals only with information security. All the other words that describe the objectives of these other organizational units have been omitted from this book to keep the focus strictly on information security. This non-information security material is likely to already exist in written form within your organization, and if it does not, then many organizational design textbooks can be consulted for suitable words.

As an example of this approach, the Legal Department's responsibility to deal with employment discrimination issues is not addressed in this chapter because it is not directly related to information security. Nonetheless, the Legal Department's responsibility to assist with investigations of hacker intrusions, computer frauds, and other information security problems is discussed in this chapter. As this illustration implies, to minimize the time required to affect appropriate organizational design changes, you should restrict your inquiry and work only to matters that directly relate to information security. This approach also prevents you from being placed in the awkward and dangerous position where you are making organizational design suggestions to people working in a certain functional area, but you do not know exactly what that functional area does on a day-to-day basis.

You should make sure that the draft mission statements that you develop are no longer than a single page, and preferably no longer than a half page. People throughout the organization will examine mission statements, and they don't have time to go through a long list of all the many activities that an organizational unit performs. In many cases these people will simply want to determine whether they should call members of the unit in question for help with their problem. Rather than being covered in a mission statement, a detailed listing of activities should instead go into various job descriptions (see Chapter 12.) If a mission statement goes beyond 250 words, chances are that it's becoming a job descrip-

tion, which is generally only examined by a candidate for that job, the worker who currently fills that position, his or her manager, and occasionally an auditor.

At this point, a clear distinction between a mission statement and a job description should be drawn. A mission statement is a brief statement of objectives that describes what top management expects from the involved organizational unit. Although a broad-brush overview of activities is often helpful in a mission statement, specifics about these activities should instead appear in one or more job descriptions. A mission statement should deal with a whole department or similar multi-person organizational unit, and should not talk about the objectives for a specific job title (the latter should be handled in a summary section appearing at the beginning of a job description). Likewise, a mission statement should not use any technical language, acronyms, or other jargon that will not be immediately understood by non-technical workers or top management.

Prior to publication within your organization, every new or revised mission statement must have received top management approval. Certainly drafts can and should be circulated for discussion, but the final version must not be released in any form until written top management approval is obtained. Many Information Security Departments seek only the approval of the Chief Information Officer, or the Manager of the Information Technology Department. Stopping the approval process after the approval of these middle level managers is ill advised because information security is much more than just a technological issue. Getting the approval of other middle level managers, managers who are responsible for the people side of the organization, is also important. Stopping the management approval process after the approval of certain middle level managers has been obtained is strongly discouraged because middle level managers have jurisdiction over only part of your organization. Without top management approval, people in other parts of the organization can legitimately claim that their departments have not agreed, and this means that they need not observe the dictates of new roles and responsibilities documentation. Mission statements are read by more people than any other roles and responsibilities document, and for this reason should be completely approved, at the highest levels of management, prior to posting on an intranet web page or distributed in any other form. The approval process is discussed at length in Chapter 7.

You are also warned that suggesting changes to the mission statements of organizational units other than the Information Security Department is a tricky and highly politicized process. Before the suggested changes to information security roles and responsibilities are submitted to top management for approval, the managers in charge of the affected organizational units will need to approve of and support the suggested changes. Before they even consider these suggestions, top management will often ask whether the approval of these lower level managers has been obtained. To ensure that the suggestions are well grounded and supportable by those who will be affected, the information gathering, decision-making, and approval processes should all

move from the bottom of the organizational ladder to the top. This bottom-up approval process is further discussed in Chapter 7.

The balance of this chapter will be devoted to specific examples of mission statement wording. As is the case with all information security roles and responsibilities documentation, you are strongly urged to mark all documents with the date they were prepared, as well as the words "unapproved draft" until such time as the approval of top management has been obtained. At that point, you can delete these words and add the name of the approving manager and the date. Before you develop mock-up words for mission statements and other roles and responsibilities documents, be sure you have obtained the necessary agreement about the review and approval process to be used for your new words (this topic is also covered in Chapter 7.)

INFORMATION SECURITY DEPARTMENT

[Also known by a variety of other names including: Information Systems Security Department, Information Protection Department, Data Security Department, Computer Security Department (antiquated terminology), Systems Security Department, Information Technology Security Department, IT Security Department, InfoSecurity Department, InfoSec Department, and Information Resources Security Department.]

The Information Security Department is charged with identifying, assessing, and appropriately managing risks to Company X information and information systems. It evaluates the options for dealing with these risks, and works with departments throughout Company X to decide upon and then implement controls that appropriately and proactively respond to these same risks. The Department is also responsible for developing requirements that apply to the entire organization as well as to external information systems in which Company X participates (for example, extranets) [these requirements include policies, standards, and procedures]. The focal point for all matters related to information security, this Department is ultimately responsible for all endeavors within Company X that seek to avoid, prevent, detect, correct, or recover from threats to information or information systems.

These threats include, but are not limited to:

- unauthorized access to information
- unauthorized use of information
- unauthorized disclosure of information
- unauthorized diversion of information
- unauthorized modification of information
- unauthorized destruction of information
- unauthorized duplication of information
- unavailability of information

[As an aside, many organizations like to use the old-fashioned "CIA" terminology - confidentiality, integrity, and availability - but the author discourages the use of this acronym because the word "integrity" is ambiguous. For example, in this context, does integrity mean strength of character? The author instead suggests words such as: In support of these objectives, the Department additionally establishes, administers, and manages a variety of computer/network security systems that apply to the entire organization (password-based access control systems are the most common example)].

PHYSICAL (INDUSTRIAL) SECURITY DEPARTMENT

[Mission Statement Relevant To Information Security]

The Physical Security Department is responsible for protecting all Company X tangible assets including raw materials, finished goods inventory, company transportation vehicles, and office buildings. The Department is responsible for identifying, assessing, and managing risks to Company X tangible assets, no matter where these assets may be located, and no matter whose possession they may be in. In support of efforts to manage these risks, the Department is required to establish and manage physical access controls to Company X offices and facilities [*These include closed circuit TV, magnetic card badge readers, etc.*]. The Department is addition-ally charged with investigating all violations of laws, regulations, and company policies, as well as acting as the liaison with the law enforcement community. [*Due to its importance to Company X and its technical nature, information security is handled by a separate group; note that the focus of the Physical Security Department is not on information but on tangible assets.*]

INTERNAL AUDIT DEPARTMENT

[*Mission Statement Relevant To Information Security*]

The Internal Audit Department is charged with providing the Board of Directors and top management with objective reports on the effectiveness of internal controls, the accuracy of records, the reliability of information, and the safeguarding of assets. The Department acts as an instigator, urging management to establish processes and/or begin projects to improve internal operations. The Department also provides compliance checking services where it determines not only whether workers are following management's instructions but also whether the organization employs the same generally accepted practices found at other firms in Company X's industry. The Department additionally reviews the efficiency and effectiveness of business activities performed by internal organizational units [*Including the Information Security Department*]. The Department furthermore periodically follows up with various levels of management to determine the extent to which they have taken action in response to previously-delivered audit findings and reports [*These findings and reports can include problems with information security*].

INFORMATION SYSTEMS AUDIT UNIT

[*Mission Statement Relevant To Information Security*]

Located within Internal Audit Department, the Information Systems Audit Unit, also called the Electronic Data Processing (EDP) Audit Unit, provides specialized technical services in support of the performance of a wide variety of information systems audits. These technical services include reviewing the adequacy of controls accompanying business application systems in development, determining the adequacy of security measures provided with third-party software, checking that workers are performing their computer-related jobs in accordance with internal requirements (policies, standards, procedures, etc.), as well as performing statistical tests of computer-based records to determine whether they are accurate, up-to-date, and free from material error.

ETHICS AND COMPLIANCE UNIT

[*Mission Statement Relevant To Information Security*]

Part of the Legal Department, the Ethics and Compliance Unit is responsible for the development and implementation of an organization-wide program to ensure the consistent operation of Company X business in an ethical and moral manner that is compliant with all relevant laws and regulations. The Ethics and Compliance Unit regularly conducts reviews of Company X operations to ensure that they continue to be fully consistent with these requirements. The Unit additionally drafts and proposes policies and procedures to ensure ethical and moral business operations as well as compliance with external requirements. This unit furthermore conducts reviews of internal business operations to assure that the operations are fully in compliance with the above-mentioned requirements. [*An Ethics and Compliance Unit may deal with privacy violations; it may also in handle right-to-know issues, for example, notices to workers about the presence of workplace hazards, such as dangerous chemicals in the workplace.*]

EXTERNAL AUDITING FIRM

[Mission Statement Relevant To Information Security]

The External Auditing Firm is charged with testing the internal controls used to create financial records to ensure that the involved information systems are reliable and free from material error [*Note that the External Auditing Firm is not responsible for doing a information security related risk assessment on these same systems unless separately engaged to do so*]. The External Auditing Firm is additionally responsible for bringing to management's attention those information systems control deficiencies that come to its attention. The Firm is furthermore charged with delivering to management a professional opinion stating whether the financial records fairly represent the current financial status of Company X. [*If an "unqualified opinion" (clean bill of health) is not obtained, this could be an indication that there are serious control problems*]

[*While in-house documentation describing the information security responsibilities of external auditors is generally not prepared, it is nonetheless useful to clarify their roles and responsibilities. These are often stated in an engagement contract or proposal defining the work to be done by external auditors. Beyond the roles and responsibilities mentioned immediately above, external auditing firms (as well as many other consulting firms) also provide specialized information security related "management advisory services" or MAS consulting. These MAS consulting services can be used to provide specialized technical support, including information security support, when this support is not readily available within your organization. Separately, often in-house workers have exaggerated expectations about the tasks that an External Auditing Firm performs. For example, unless specifically engaged for this purpose, the Firm is not responsible for detecting fraud, although it may discover fraud in the course of doing financial auditing work. An External Auditing Firm or an outside information security consulting firm can also separately be engaged to evaluate the effectiveness of an in-house information security effort.*]

RECORDS MANAGEMENT DEPARTMENT

[Mission Statement Relevant To Information Security]

The Records Management Department is charged with establishing and operating a system of policies, procedures, and records for the designation and safe handling of archival Company X records. To achieve this goal, the Department trains workers about the need to designate and maintain archival records. It also establishes and maintains administrative systems used to access, protect, and keep track of these same archival records. The Department is additionally responsible for providing technical advice to the entire organization on backup systems that effectively ensure that these critical and/or archival records continue to be available in the event of a disaster, theft, or some other serious problem. [*Note that Records Management is not responsible for all backup systems, just those for archival records.*]

INFORMATION TECHNOLOGY DEPARTMENT

[Mission Statement Relevant To Information Security]

The Information Technology Department is charged with planning, specifying, designing, developing, acquiring, modifying, testing, and operating shared information systems and related communications networks needed to accomplish Company X business goals. These information systems and networks are intended be available on a continuous, predictable, and secure basis so that Company X's reputation for reliable products and services can be enhanced. The Department is also responsible for providing technical and operational management support for a wide variety of information systems projects and activities, including user database development, outsourcing firm processing, and connection to external information resources such as the Internet. [*Note that responsibility for information security is not ideally allocated to the Information Technology Department for conflict of interest reasons; it should instead be allocated to the Information Security Department, which should not report to the Information Technology Department (additional details can be found in Chapter 13.*]

HELP DESK UNIT

[*Mission Statement Relevant To Information Security*]

As part of the Information Technology Department, the Help Desk Unit provides immediate telephone assistance to users who are experiencing problems with any Company X information systems or networks. This type of 24 X 7 X 365 technical support is intended to facilitate users' efforts to promptly perform critical business tasks in a manner that is fully consistent with existing Company X information systems requirements including policies, standards, and procedures [These, of course, include security]. The Unit provides ad-hoc training as well as a variety of solutions to problems that users encounter [*Such as forgetting and resetting a password*]. This unit is additionally responsible for first level user technical support dealing with a wide variety of information systems matters, including those related to information security [*First level technical support for information security matters, for example providing instructions for the construction of a difficult to guess password, could alternatively be allocated to the Information Security Department.*] The Unit is furthermore responsible for notifying the Computer Emergency Response Team (CERT) if a serious information security event has taken place [*as would be the case with a virus infection*].

NETWORK OPERATIONS UNIT

[*Mission Statement Relevant To Information Security*]

As part of the Information Technology Department, the Network Operations Unit [*sometimes called the Telecommunications Department*] is charged with operating internal networks such as wide area networks (WANs) and local area networks (LANs) so that all communications links necessary for business activities remain available, so that user response time stays within acceptable limits, and so that only authorized users utilize Company X networked resources. Operation, in this instance, includes monitoring network management systems, running diagnostic software when problems occur, notifying information security personnel if suspicious activity is detected, and dynamically reconfiguring the network to minimize cost and maximize throughput. This unit is additionally responsible for the design, construction, operation, and maintenance of voice communications systems such as voicemail and telephone systems. [*Note that this group is responsible for detecting toll fraud on long distance networks, such as the fraud perpetrated via the DISA(direct inbound system access) feature in PBX (private branch exchange) phone systems.*]

COMPUTER OPERATIONS UNIT

[*Mission Statement Relevant To Information Security*]

As part of the Information Technology Department, the Computer Operations Unit is charged with operating multi-user computer systems so that all critical business activities are performed on schedule, so that computer response time stays within acceptable limits, and so that the security of these multi-user systems is not jeopardized. Operation, in this instance, includes monitoring the activities of users and applications, loading and unloading information storage media as necessary, handling backup storage media, distributing printed management reports, initializing production application software jobs, and reconciling the results of these software jobs. This unit is additionally responsible for immediately notifying the Computer Emergency Response Team (CERT) if it has determined that an information security incident is underway or has recently taken place. [*A Computer Operations Unit or a Network Operations Unit may additionally be responsible for monitoring an intrusion detection system*]

SYSTEMS ADMINISTRATION UNIT

[*Mission Statement Relevant To Information Security*]

As part of the Information Technology Department, the Systems Administration Unit is charged with configuring and updating workstations, servers, networks, firewalls, and other information systems equipment used in support of Company X business activities. The Unit is additionally responsible for configuring and updating systems software on these same information systems so that all applications critical to the business are supported, so that response time is within tolerable limits, and so that security vulnerabilities are minimized. [*This includes monitoring notices about patches and fixes, as well as applying patches and fixes,* *but activities about these patches and fixes is often mentioned only in job descriptions, not a mission statement*] The Unit is furthermore in charge of establishing and maintaining user access control systems for those multi-user information systems that are not handled by the Information Security Department. [*Access Control System Administrators within the Information Security Department may handle some of these duties; see Chapter 12 "for further details*]

DATABASE ADMINISTRATION UNIT

[*Mission Statement Relevant To Information Security*]

As part of the Information Technology Department, the Database Administration Unit is charged with designing, configuring, organizing, and maintaining Company X computer-resident databases so that the information contained therein is accurate and up-to-date. The Unit is also responsible for maintaining the database privileges of both users and systems, so that these privileges are allocated only when justified by business needs and approved by designated managers. [*Each working day, specialists known as Database Administrators, or DBAs, help to ensure that systems are consistent with the policies and other requirements issued by the Information Security Department. This policy related role is not generally mentioned in a mission statement, but would be appropriate to mention in a job description*]

DATA ADMINISTRATION UNIT

[*Mission Statement Relevant To Information Security*]

As part of the Information Technology Department, the Data Administration Unit is charged with creating metadata databases, information inventories, as well as information models and architectures that unify and standardize both information collections and information flows throughout Company X. These new tools and systems are intended to facilitate the development of new applications, new management reports, new products and services, and new relationships with third parties. In the process of centralizing and normalizing information throughout Company X, the Data Adminis- tration Unit is also charged with fostering standardization efforts that maintain or enhance the accuracy, currency, relevance, usefulness, and security of the information involved. [*Data Administration or Database Administration may be responsible for a datamart, a corporate data dictionary, or a data warehouse; the security administration tasks for these systems are then the responsibility of the involved group, and therefore may be mentioned in the mission statement if your organization supports these types of systems*]

INSURANCE AND RISK MANAGEMENT DEPARTMENT

[*Mission Statement Relevant To Information Security*]

The Insurance & Risk Management Department is charged with identifying and analyzing the strategic business risks faced by Company X. These include mergers and acquisitions, new product introductions, product liability lawsuits, and changes in macroeconomic conditions within Company X's markets. The Department is responsible for ranking the risks on a cross-organizational basis, as well as suggesting strategies and other high-level approaches for dealing with these risks. For identified risks, the Department is charged with presenting management with the pros and cons regarding risk retention (do nothing), risk reduction (add controls), or risk transfer (buy insurance). [*This Department is an important strategic ally of the Information Security Department, and both departments should work together to identify the types of insurance that Company X needs (the options include records reconstruction insurance, computer crime insurance, business interruption insurance, professional* errors and omissions insurance, directors and officers liability insurance, fidelity insurance, credit card fraud insurance, property (theft) insurance, etc.)]

CONTINGENCY PLANNING UNIT

[*Mission Statement Relevant To Information Security*]

The Contingency Planning Unit is charged with developing, testing, and maintaining practical and cost-effective plans, processes and systems that will allow critical Company X business activities to continue even though an emergency or a disaster has taken place. The Unit is responsible for identifying the nature of the business interruption threats facing Company X, analyzing the options for preventing or mitigating losses from these threats, and organizing internal staff so that they can expediently deal with these threats if they do occur. [*This mission statement is written broadly to include business contingency planning and information systems contingency planning, but some organizations*

break these activities into separate units. If the two are separated, the business contingency planning unit may report to the Insurance And Risk Management Department, while the information systems contingency planning unit may report to the Information Security Department. see Chapter 13 for further details on reporting relationships (including the six diagrams showing different options).] The Unit is additionally responsible for fostering an enterprise-wide contingency planning effort so that best practices can be shared, so that systems may be shared and interconnected, and so that business processes can be readily moved from one area of the organization to another.

COMPUTER EMERGENCY RESPONSE TEAM (CERT)

[*Mission Statement Relevant To Information Security*]

The Computer Emergency Response Team (CERT) is a group of Company X employees who respond immediately to a variety of information systems emergencies such as virus infections, hacker intrusions, and denial of service attacks. Team members are drawn from a wide variety of departments, but the following organizational units must be represented: Help Desk, Information Security, Internal Audit, Computer Operations, and Legal. Immediately stopping their normal work activities, the CERT members devote their efforts to quickly reestablishing a secure, reliable, and stable information systems environment. CERT members also act as the primary technical liaisons with consultants, contractors, and others who are needed to reestablish this trusted information systems environment. The CERT additionally develops and/or deploys tools, procedures, and

other mechanisms so that financial losses, business interruptions, and damage to Company X's reputation associated with such incidents are all minimized. The CERT is also responsible for documenting all alerts, all official declarations, and all actions taken to restore a trusted information systems environment, so that insurance, legal proceedings, and disciplinary actions can be fully supported. [*Note: A CERT is sometimes called a Computer Security Incident Response Team (CSIRT) or simply an Incident Management Team (IMT). The management of a CERT usually is allocated to the Information Security Department, even though the CERT team members come from many departments. This means that the CERT may properly be considered to be a sub-unit of the Information Security Department - see Chapter 13 for additional details.*]

DISASTER RECOVERY TEAM

[*Mission Statement Relevant To Information Security*]

The Disaster Recovery Team is a group of Company X employees made up of senior managers, computer and network technicians, logistical and procurement specialists, safety technicians, physical security staff, information security staff, and others who have a role to

play when responding to major disasters or security incidents. These major disasters and security incidents include floods, hurricanes, tornadoes, and other severe weather, as well as fires, bombings, hazardous material spills, serious infectious disease outbreaks, and acts of major sabotage. Working part-time on this team, these employees act much like the members of a CERT in that they are immediately mobilized, and stop performing their other duties, if and when circumstances warrant. The team is charged with ensuring continuity of Company X's critical business functions, including but not limited to the continuation of service with computers and networks. The team develops strategies for responding to serious threats, as well as procedures and methodologies that will ensure the continuity of critical business functions. The team monitors the work of others who prepare recovery plans, and also tests these same plans to ensure that they will in fact be useful in the time of a disaster. During a recovery, the members of this team perform specific predetermined functions in order to promptly recover, minimize losses due to the incident, document the loss for insurance purposes, and preserve evidence for investigation, prosecution, and disciplinary purposes. [*Note: A Disaster Recovery Team helps to spread this time-consuming and complex work to people outside the Information Security Department; this team may also be called a Contingency Management Team, or a Crisis Management Team*]

LEGAL DEPARTMENT

[*Mission Statement Relevant To Information Security*]

The Legal Department is charged with providing the expert legal advice necessary for management to conduct Company X business activities in a manner fully in keeping with existing laws and regulations. [*Software copyright laws are a good example relevant to information security*] The Legal Department is also responsible for providing expert advice on the ways that laws, regulations, and contractual relationships can be used to further Company X business interests, including negotiating business deals, drawing-up contracts, resolving disputes, investigating crimes against Company X property, and defending against legal actions such as lawsuits. [*Obtaining agreements not to compete from business partners is an information security example*] The Legal Department is additionally charged with providing management with advice about the ways to appropriately protect Company X assets, resources, and staff against a variety of legal risks. [*Management's exposure to lawsuits for not adequately protecting computer resident information is an information security example*]

HUMAN RESOURCES DEPARTMENT

[*Mission Statement Relevant To Information Security*]

The Human Resources Department provides guidance to all workers in the interpretation of legal and policy requirements that relate to employment, performance evaluation, career paths, succession planning, pay scales, and related staffing matters. [*Human Resources may thus have something to say about separation of duties, backup personnel for critical information systems positions, etc.*] The Human Resources Department additionally provides administrative support to keep the records needed to be in compliance with all human resources related laws, regulations, and internal policies. [*These records are an important resource for information security activities such as system access control decisions. These records are also often the subject of privacy laws and policies, and thus the Human Resources Department often gets involved in discussions about the controls over these records*] The Department furthermore coordinates the retention of, work with, and termination of consultants, contractors, and temporaries by department managers using standard procedures, contracts, and other tools. The Human Resources Department is additionally responsible for training new and current staff about the business practices, internal management policies, and organizational culture found at Company X. [*This includes training for new hires (so-called orientation) which should incorporate some basic information security matters; this type of information security training may alternatively be provided by the Information Security Department*]

INFORMATION SECURITY MANAGEMENT COMMITTEE

[*Mission Statement Relevant To Information Security*]

The Information Security Management Committee provides oversight, management direction, and a sounding board for the internal Company X information security efforts. The Committee helps to ensure that these efforts are appropriately prioritized, appropriately supported by the involved organizational units, appropriately funded, and realistic given Company X's business needs. The Committee is also charged with instructing the Information Security Department in those cases where a compromise between competing information systems objectives needs to be struck. These objectives include cost, response time, ease of use, ease of maintenance, flexibility, scalability, and time-to-market with a new product or service. The Committee is additionally responsible for designating specific individuals as responsible for various aspects of information security, approving proposals for organization-wide information security initiatives (such as awareness training), and coordinating the work of various departments so that information security goals can be achieved. [*Sometimes an Information Security Management Committee is called an Information Security Committee, an Information Protection Council, or an Information Security Advisory Committee*]

PRIVACY OVERSIGHT COMMITTEE

[*Mission Statement Relevant To Information Security*]

The Privacy Oversight Committee provides direction and guidance for all privacy enhancement and privacy maintenance efforts at Company X. Chaired by the Chief Privacy Officer, this Committee is responsible for managing all internal efforts to establish, improve, and implement privacy policies, procedures, and other requirements. The Committee is charged with evaluating, approving, and monitoring all projects which enhance the privacy protections afforded personal data which is in the possession of, or otherwise under the control of, Company X. The Committee additionally reviews all complaints about privacy violations or deficiencies received by Company X, and helps to ensure that internal staff are diligently acting to correct the problems revealed by these complaints. The Committee is furthermore responsible for clarifying privacy-related roles and responsibilities internal to Company X, as well as managing all efforts to bring Company X into compliance with relevant privacy laws and regulations. Membership on the Committee is limited to five representatives drawn from those Company X departments which handle, or have a stake in the proper handling of, private information. [*Sometimes a Privacy Oversight Committee is called a Privacy Committee, or a Privacy Management Committee; separately, in many organizations, particularly those which are not heavily regulated, there is no need for a separate Privacy Oversight Committee because the functions it performs are performed by an Information Security Management Committee*]

INFORMATION TECHNOLOGY STEERING COMMITTEE

[*Mission Statement Relevant To Information Security*]

The Information Technology Steering Committee is made up of managers drawn from the ranks of senior management, major user departments, as well as the Internal Audit Department, the Information Security Department, and the Information Technology Department. The Committee is charged with developing a strategic vision for the deployment and evolution of information technology at Company X [*The Committee supports and oversees the Information Technology Department in its efforts to develop a three to five year Information Technology Plan; then this plan is used by the Information Security Department to develop an information security action plan, an information security architecture, and other documents*]. The Committee is also responsible for establishing priorities for, arranging necessary resources for, defining appropriate trade-offs between competing objectives for, and approving major capital expenditures related to the realization of the strategic information technology vision. Although the Committee is not involved in day-to-day information technology operations, it will review, approve, and prioritize all major information technology projects and initiatives including: significant changes to hardware and software, major system conversion plans, development/refinement of contingency plans for shared system resources, and arrangement of information technology related insurance coverage. The Committee furthermore reviews and issues final approval for all policies, standards, and guidelines that relate to information technology at Company X. [*The Committee could, for example, approve information security policies, although policies should also have the personal signature of the Chief Executive Officer. The*

emphasis of this committee is strategic, while the emphasis of the Information Security Management Committee is more technical and more narrowly-defined. A small amount of information security related duties overlap between the Information Technology Steering Committee and the Information Security Management Committee may desirable in an effort to get support for information security.]

CHANGE CONTROL COMMITTEE

[*Mission Statement Relevant To Information Security*]

The Change Control Committee is composed of representatives from the Information Technology, Information Security, Quality Assurance, and Internal Audit departments, as well as selected user departments. The Committee is charged with evaluating software and hardware acquisitions, vendor-supplied patches and upgrades, as well as all internally developed software and systems, to determine whether these systems are ready to be moved into production operation. [*This sign-off process ordinarily would additionally involve user department managers, as well as the Information Security Manager*] The Committee furthermore evaluates and approves changes to all multi-user production computer and network systems; these

changes include firewall configuration standards, server configuration standards, backup processes, and system access control points. The Committee evaluates the adequacy of internal management planning efforts, internal testing and quality assurance efforts, and related internal documentation, to determine whether information systems changes are ready for the production environment. The Committee is additionally responsible for the establishment and proper operation of change management procedures, and related operational methods, which allow internal technical staff to follow Committee policies as well as make immediate emergency changes in the production information systems environment. The Committee meets weekly.

WEB SITE COMMITTEE

[*Mission Statement Relevant To Information Security*]

The Web Site Committee is composed of representatives from the Marketing, Public Relations, Information Technology, Information Security, and Legal Departments. The Committee is charged with defining standards and procedures for ensuring that the Internet web site, the Internet commerce site, as well as intranet web sites, are consistently professional in appearance, fully consistent with Company X business purposes, as well as secure, reliable, and up-to-date. [*Although not recommended, in some organizations, this Committee may only have jurisdiction over Company X Internet web sites and Internet commerce sites; this limited scope*

may be a reflection of management's intention to place greater emphasis on public appearance and reputation] The Committee defines the circumstances under which web site content and/or design are modified, the approval procedures associated with these modifications, the requirements which must be met before any new content or design is used on a Company X web site. [*These requirements should include security matters such as testing of software like JavaScript applets, privacy policy postings, and cookies*] The Committee meets monthly to review, and perhaps approve, all major changes that have been proposed according to these same stipulations.

BOARD OF DIRECTORS - AUDIT COMMITTEE

[*Mission Statement Relevant To Information Security*]

The Audit Committee is a subcommittee of the Board Of Directors composed of directors who are independent of the management of Company X, and who are free of any

relationship that, in the opinion of the Board Of Directors, would interfere with their exercise of independent judgement. The Audit Committee provides oversight and direction for the work of external financial auditors, internal auditors, external security consultants, information security specialists, physical security specialists, and others who are concerned with internal controls at Company X. The Audit Committee is charged with ratifying the existence and continued operational effectiveness of internal controls. [*Which, of course, include information security measures*] The Committee is additionally reponsible for ensuring that the organization keeps adequate records in a manner consistent with generally accepted accounting principles. The Committee is also responsible for monitoring and analyzing the results of examinations that review the extent to which Company X is in compliance with laws and regulations. [*These laws and regulations of course include information security and privacy issues*] The Committee is furthermore charged with monitoring the adequacy of management's responses to examinations and audits, the performance of internal auditors, the adequacy of insurance coverage, and whether Company X is living up to its contractual obligations. The Audit Committee thus helps to maintain transparent and open communications between the Board Of Directors, the independent auditors, and the management of Company X. [*This communication path can be essential in order to change those circumstances where an Information Security Department is not getting the financial support or moral support it needs from upper management*] In addition, the Audit Committee is responsible for the establishment and maintenance of an anonymous worker complaint reporting system which helps bring problems with internal controls to light.

BOARD OF DIRECTORS - GOVERNANCE COMMITTEE

[*Mission Statement Relevant To Information Security*]

The Governance Committee is a subcommittee of the Board of Directors, appointed by the Board annually, and composed of non-management Board members who, in the opinion of the Board, have no conflict of interest that would prevent them from exercising independent judgement when serving in this capacity. (This independence is required for compliance with the Sarbanes-Oxley Act.) The Governance Committee is responsible for all matters relating to the establishment of, implementation of, and monitoring of policies and processes regarding organizational governance. These matters include recruitment and nomination of candidates for the Board, its positions (Chair, Vice Chair, Committee Chairs, etc.), and its subcommittees. [*These tasks point to why the Committee is sometimes called the Nominating And Governance Committee*] These matters also include reviewing and making recommendations to improve the Board size, composition, and structure, member recruitment practices, and member compensation. The Committee is furthermore responsible for monitoring the ways in which the Board is in compliance with its fiduciary duties to Company X, its stockholders, its customers, the public, and other stakeholders. [*This fiduciary duty angle can be one way to sell top management on the need for more budget for information security*] The Committee also assists the Board of Directors in assessing its performance as a decision-making body, as well as assessing the individual performance of its members. The Committee gathers information on the governance structures used at comparable organizations, as well as the governance structures used within Company X, and then uses this information to make recommendations about the changes that need to be made at Company X. The Committee is additionally responsible for overseeing management's efforts to improve organizational governance, including clarification of internal decision-making processes, assignment of accountability and responsibility, and establishment of appropriate performance expectations. [*The information security function can be viewed as one of several internal functions that assist with organizational governance*]

INTERNAL CONTROL COMMITTEE

[*Mission Statement Relevant To Information Security*]

The Internal Control Committee is charged with bringing Company X in its entirety into a state of internal control. Chaired by a member of the top management team, and drawing on middle management from critical departments such as Human Resources, Internal Auditing, Physical Security, Information Security, and Accounting, the Committee coordinates, fosters the adaptation of, and follows-up with internal managers to convert Company X into an organization with an internal control mindset. The Committee also coordinates internal control relationships with outside parties such as external auditors, regulators, and others. The Committee stimulates and promotes synergy, which is intended to lead to compliance with internal requirements, high performance and correct operation of internal business systems, and continued security of business transactions. [*An Internal Control Committee generally works closely with the Board of Directors - Audit Committee, but its work is* *more hands-on and detailed than the Board of Directors - Audit Committee. An Internal Controls Committee would generally coordinate organization-wide initiatives such as the development of a code of conduct.*]

FACILITIES MANAGEMENT OUTSOURCING FIRM

[*Mission Statement Relevant To Information Security*]

The Facilities Management Outsourcing Firm is charged with operating Company X information systems, and providing other technical services that may from time to time be requested by Company X management, in a manner fully consistent with Company X policies, procedures, and other documented requirements. [*And these include information security requirements*] The Firm acknowledges that all policy, procedure, and system design decisions regarding the security or privacy of Company X information or information systems will be made solely by authorized Company X management. The Facilities Management Firm is also responsible for

processing, storing, and safeguarding the information assets of Company X in accordance with generally accepted information systems management practices. [*These should include security*]

[*The responsibilities of an outsourcing firm are not generally written-up in internal organizational design documents, but are instead often found in an outsourcing firm contract. Their responsibilities were included in this chapter as an indication that outsourcing firms have an important role to play in the information security area. Chapter 16 and Chapter 17 discuss outsourcing firm responsibilities in further detail.*]

Chapter 12 JOB DESCRIPTIONS FOR SPECIFIC TEAM PLAYERS

To save you time, this chapter provides specific words that can be copied and internally published when preparing first draft job descriptions. The chapter includes full job descriptions for all those positions that are ordinarily found within a centralized Information Security Department. Examples include Information Security Department Manager, Internal Information Security Consultant, Access Control System Administrator, and Information Systems Contingency Planner. This chapter anticipates that, for these people, you will be writing job descriptions from scratch. These job descriptions come first in the chapter and are easy to spot because the second paragraph of text in the relevant description indicates that the position is found in the Information Security Department.

This chapter also contains specific job description words dealing with information security for those individuals who are a part of the information security team, but who are not customarily part of a centralized Information Security Department. Examples of these positions include Local Information Security Coordinator, Systems Administrator, Network Administrator, and Database Administrator. This chapter anticipates that, for these people, you will be adding information security responsibilities to existing job descriptions. These partial job descriptions come later in the chapter. The second paragraph of text in the relevant description indicates that the position is part of a department other than the Information Security Department.

This chapter does not cover the words that should go into a job description of a rank-and-file user who does not fall into either of the above-mentioned categories. Examples of this type of user would be a Career Development Consultant in the Human Resources Department, or a Maintenance Engineer in the Manufacturing Department. Their omission from this chapter doesn't mean that they don't have an important role to play on the information security team. For instance, all users must abide by information security policies and procedures, and it is desirable to explicitly state this in job descriptions. Additional words that could be included in less-senior user job descriptions can be found in Chapter 15, in the section entitled "Role Of Users".

The material in this chapter does not cover certain things that may be included in job descriptions at your organization. For example, the ideal psychological profile and the professional qualifications needed are not covered. These are, instead, covered in Appendix B, "Personal Qualifications" and Appendix D, "Professional Certifications." Likewise, this chapter does not cover educational requirements, experience requirements, language skill requirements, mathematics and reasoning ability requirements, prior supervisory experience requirements, continuing professional development requirements, or physical movement requirements. These unmentioned requirements are a function of the business that your organization performs, as well as relevant local laws and regulations, in addition to prevailing expectations in the local labor market. In most organizations with over fifty employees, these additional requirements have already been developed by an in-house Human Resources Department, and therefore can be quickly added to a job description once you have come up with a version of the material much like that found in this chapter.

While the tasks listed below for each job are in many cases extensive, it is important to note that a job description is not generally intended to be completely specify exactly what a particular person in a certain job will do. Instead a job description is intended to highlight the major responsibilities, conveying a clear sense of what is required in order to keep the job. Just as a job description is not a legally-binding contract with a worker, so too there should be some words in each job description that make it clear that, in order to stay at a minimum performance level, the worker will be required to do other tasks above and beyond those defined in the job description. It is also wise to add words to the effect that management may change the job description, including the addition of new duties and expectations, at any time.

Although common reporting relationships are mentioned in the following job descriptions, these designated relationships are certainly not the only effective way to structure an information security team. For a discussion about the best ways to structure reporting relationships including conflicts of interest, separation of duties, cross training, and personnel backup, you should consult Chapter 13, which also contains a number of diagrams that show suggested reporting relationships for the positions described in this chapter.

Often the first piece of information on a job description is the job title, also known as a position title. People working in the information security field go by a lot of different titles such as Information Security Evangelist as well as more traditional titles such as Systems Analyst. The latter approach, which forces information security people to use more general titles, is undesirable because it doesn't really describe what these people do. Rather than something cute or obscure, it is better to have titles that genuinely describe the tasks performed. Instead of Information Security Evangelist, it would be better to use the title Information Security Training & Awareness Coordinator, and in place of Systems Analyst it would be better to use the title Information Security Technical Consultant. The more descriptive the title, the more people will understand from a cursory review of the employer's internal telephone directory, and from a quick glance at the individual's business card. It is not a good idea to try to increase the level of security by hiding the identity of the individuals who work in the information security area. Although super-secret government agencies may use this approach, for the vast majority of organizations, the difficulties and confusion that this approach engenders are not worth the marginal incremental security which is achieved.

Some organizations have a philosophy about job descriptions that essentially says that workers should fit into broad and vague categories such as "Technical Staff Member." Job descriptions are then written, on an individual-by-individual basis, to clarify and individualize these broad and vague positions. These organizations rely on the individual's immediate manager to define the specific work that each individual performs. This approach is acceptable as long as the immediate manager has documented the roles and responsibilities of each of his or her direct reports. If this doesn't happen, then the individuals involved will have very little reference material to direct their efforts, and their managers will have scant reference material for fair and accurate performance evaluations. If you are in a position where you can suggest an approach for the preparation of job descriptions, this two-tier approach is generally not recommended. The two-tier approach can be confusing for outsiders and others who have not seen the local manager's specific roles and responsibilities, or who don't know that a two-tier approach is employed. The two-tier approach to job descriptions is additionally not recommended because two job description documents will be needed when traditionally only one

was required. The two-tier approach is furthermore not recommended because, in spite of the best intentions, in far too many situations only the vague high-level description is prepared. Nonetheless, if such an approach has already been adopted by your organization, the detailed material in this chapter can be generalized to compile high-level job descriptions, or used as it is to prepare the low-level job descriptions.

The job titles described below are standard and customary job titles. Because the information security field is still embryonic, in the real world you will encounter a wide variety of different job titles. One recent Internet job posting survey noted over sixty-five different information security job titles, when there are only about seven different basic job descriptions for workers in an information security group. The author strongly discourages the use of quirky or unusual job titles such as Ethical Hacker. He instead encourages titles which are clear and consistent with standard business terminology, such as Information Systems Security Architect. Using this same criteria, other good job titles would include: Information Assurance Specialist, Information Systems Risk Management Specialist, Forensic Investigations Analyst, Information Security Trainer, and UNIX Security Specialist. The tasks for these job titles can be readily derived from the standard and customary job descriptions listed below.

Separately, this chapter discusses who interacts with whom to achieve what information security results, who does what information security activities, and who passes what information to other people in support of information security. All of these roles and responsibilities are permanent and ongoing in nature. While all organizational structures will need to be adjusted periodically, the following job descriptions are meant to help organizations establish information security as an activity that has been integrated into the existing organizational structure, and is recognized as an on-going business function. In far too many organizations, information security continues to be seen as a project or a temporary effort (see Chapter 5 for further discussion). On a related note, there will be temporary efforts, such as a task force to upgrade information security, so that your organization can do business with another firm that has higher security standards, but these temporary efforts should not be reflected in the job descriptions. Responsibilities for these temporary efforts will instead be reflected in project planning memos.

Even after you have prepared job descriptions and other documents reflecting roles and responsibilities, you may wish to use the CD-ROM version of this chapter as a reference. One common ad-hoc reference usage of this material would be to determine who should be responsible for certain information security activities. This information could be employed after a major information security event. For example, suppose a customer sued your organization for privacy violation. You could then search the CD-ROM version of this book to quickly identify the job titles that have some responsibility for "privacy." This information could then be used in a post-mortem memo describing the ways to prevent privacy problems in the future -- a memo which hopefully suggests changes in the ways that roles and responsibilities are assigned.

Given the significant demand for experienced workers in the information security field, it is not surprising that management at many organizations seeks to lower costs by delegating information security tasks to less-experienced and/or less-busy workers. While this makes sense for certain narrowly-scoped routine tasks, such as assigning user-IDs and issuing default (temporary) passwords, it is dangerous for more complex non-routine technical tasks. An example of the latter would be configuring a firewall so that it could protect the organization's internal network from attacks launched via the Internet. Thus staff in the Human Resources Department may appropriately be called upon to set-up user-IDs and passwords for new workers, but the investigation of suspected break-ins is something best left to technical specialists. While all of the tasks mentioned in the following job descriptions are conceivably potential candidates for delegation, great care should be taken when delegating information security tasks. Delegated tasks should be clearly documented in procedures, and the involved individuals should be adequately trained to competently perform the work in question. In addition, the delegation must not create a conflict of interest or otherwise put the organization at unnecessary risk (this topic is discussed at greater length in Chapter 13.)

INFORMATION SECURITY DEPARTMENT MANAGER

Job Title: Information Security Department Manager [*Also known as Information Security Manager, Information Systems Security Officer (ISSO), Chief Information Security Officer (CISO), Chief Security Strategist (CSS), Vice President of Information Security, or in high-tech firms, simply Chief Security Officer (CSO)*]

Department: Information Security

Reports To: Chief Information Officer (CIO) [Most common but least recommended option], Chief Operating Officer (COO), Chief Financial Officer (CFO), Chief Executive Officer (CEO) [*Most desirable option - see Chapter 13 for an explanation*], or Chief Legal Counsel [*The latter option is more likely in health care and other highly-regulated industries*]

Dotted Line: Board of Directors Audit Committee

Summary:

The Information Security Department Manager directs, coordinates, plans, and organizes information security activities throughout Company X. He or she acts as the focal point for all communications related to information security, both with internal staff and third parties. The Manager works with a wide variety of people from different internal organizational units, bringing them together to manifest controls that reflect workable compromises as well as proactive responses to current and future information security risks.

Responsibilities and Duties:

The Information Security Department Manager is responsible for envisioning and taking steps to implement the controls needed to protect both Company X information as well as information that has been entrusted to Company X by third parties. The position involves overall Company X responsibility for information security regardless of the form that the information takes (paper, blueprint, CD-ROM, audio tape, embedded in products or processes, etc.), the information handling technology employed (mainframes, laptops, fax machines, telephones, local area networks, file cabinets, etc.), or the people involved (contractors, consultants, employees, vendors, outsourcing firms, etc.).

Threats to information and information systems addressed by the Information Security Department Manager and his or her staff include, but are not limited to: information unavailability, information corruption, unauthorized information destruction, unauthorized information modification, unauthorized information usage, and unauthorized information disclosure. These threats to information and information systems include consideration of physical security matters only if a certain level of physical security is necessary to achieve a certain level of information security (for example, as is necessary to prevent theft of portable computers).

- Acts as the central point of contact within Company X when it comes to all communications dealing with information security, including vulnerabilities, controls, technologies, human factors issues, and management issues

- Establishes and maintains strong working relationships with the Company X groups involved with information security matters (Legal Department, Internal Audit Department, Physical Security Department, Information Technology Department, Information Security Management Committee, etc.) [*Note that the Information Security Department Manager is, in most cases, the chairperson of the Information Security Management Committee*]

- Establishes, manages, and maintains organizational structures and communications channels with those responsible for information security; these responsible parties include individuals within Company X departments (such as Local Information Security Coordinators) as well as Company X business partners (outsourcing firms, consulting firms, suppliers, etc.)

- Assists with the clarification of individual information security responsibility and accountability so that necessary information security activities are performed as needed, according to pre-established procedures, polices, and standards

- Coordinates the information security efforts of all internal groups that have one or more information security-related responsibilities, to ensure that organization-wide information security efforts are consistent across the organization, and that duplication of effort is minimized [*The Physical Security Department Manager does the same duty, but for physical security efforts*]

- Coordinates all multi-application or multi-system information security improvement projects at Company X [*A good example would be converting all operating system access control systems to a standard minimum password length*]

- Represents Company X and its information security related interests at industry standards committee meetings, technical conferences, industry specific on-line chat rooms, and similar public forums [*Smaller or less visible organizations will generally dispense with this duty*]

- Completes, obtains management concurrence on, and formally files government forms and questionnaires dealing with information security [*Generally, this task this would appear in a job description only in those industries which are highly-regulated, such as financial institutions and health care providers*]

- Investigates the ways that information security related technologies, requirements statements, internal processes, and organizational structures can be used to achieve the goals found in the Company X strategic plan [*This effort should include consideration of the long range information systems plan, which in turn should be an intermediate link between the business strategic plan and the information security plan*]

- Creates a strategic information security plan with a vision for the future of information security at Company X (utilizing evolving information security technology, this vision meets a variety of objectives such as management's fiduciary and legal responsibilities, customer expectations for secure modern business practices, and the competitive requirements of the marketplace)

- Understands the fundamental business activities performed by Company X, and based on this understanding, suggests appropriate information security solutions that adequately protect these activities

- Develops action plans, schedules, budgets, status reports and other top management communications intended to improve the status of information security at Company X

- Obtains top management approval and on-going support for all major information security initiatives at Company X (or supervises others in their efforts with these proceedings)

- Brings pressing information security vulnerabilities to top management's attention so that immediate remedial action can be taken (this includes consideration of reputation risk and damage to Company X's brand image)

- Performs and/or oversees the performance of periodic Company X risk assessments that identify current and future security vulnerabilities, determines the level of risk that management has currently accepted, and identifies the best ways to reduce information security risks [*In a general sense, the Information Security Department Manager performs information security risk management or else establishes a management structure that has others (such as line managers) perform this function*]

- Examines information security from a cross-organizational viewpoint including Company X's participation in extranets, electronic data interchange (EDI) trading networks, ad-hoc Internet commerce relationships, and other new business structures, and makes related recommendations to protect Company X information and information systems [*The prior paragraph discussing risk assessments deals with internal information systems, while this paragraph is advisable whenever new multi-organizational networks are contemplated or deployed*]

- Directs the development of, or originates self-assessment questionnaires and other tools that assist user department managers and other members of the management team in their efforts to determine the degree of compliance with information security requirements within their respective organizational units

- Periodically initiates quality measurement studies to determine whether the information security function at Company X operates in a manner consistent with standard industry practices (these include customer satisfaction surveys, competitor benchmarking studies, industry baseline controls comparisons, peer review comparison efforts, and internal tests)

- Coordinates and directs the development, management approval, implementation, and promulgation of objectives, goals, policies, standards, guidelines, and other requirement statements needed to support information security throughout Company X as well as within Company X business networks (such as extranets)

- Provides managerial guidance to user department staff on the development of local, system-specific, and application-specific information security policies, guidelines, standards, procedures, and responsibility designations

- Assists with the establishment and refinement of procedures for the identification of Company X information assets as well as the classification of these information assets with respect to criticality, sensitivity, and value [*The availability of this asset inventory information allows appropriate controls to then be chosen by management; see Chapter 15 for further details*]

- Coordinates internal staff in their efforts to determine Company X information security obligations according to external requirements (contractual, regulatory, legal, ethical, etc.)

- Closely monitors changes in society's information security related ethics, values, morals, and attitudes with an eye toward changes that Company X should make in response to these developments

- Designs and manages business processes for the detection, investigation, correction, disciplinary action, and/or prosecution related to information security breaches, violations, and incidents [*These efforts would for example include an intrusion detection system, also known as an IDS*]

- Manages internal Company X activities pertaining to the investigation, correction, prosecution, and disciplinary action needed for the resolution of information security breaches, violations, and incidents (whether actual or alleged)

- Prepares post mortem analyses of information security breaches, violations, and incidents to illuminate what happened and how this type of problem can be prevented in the future

- Directs the preparation of information systems contingency plans and manages worker groups (such as Computer Emergency Response Teams or CERTs) that respond to information security relevant events (hacker intrusions, virus infections, denial of service attacks, etc.)

- Works with the Public Relations Department and top management to develop suitable public responses to information security incidents, violations, and problems [*These responses should be scripted and ready-to-go, and well as ad-hoc*]

- Acts as an external representative for Company X in the event of a hacker break-in or some other information security relevant event [*This may involve news media interviews, discussions with concerned customers, etc.*]

- Acts as an expert witness in information security related legal proceedings involving Company X

- Provides technical information security consulting assistance for Company X staff disciplinary measures, civil suits, and criminal prosecutions, if and when needed

- Initiates and manages special projects related to information security that may be needed to appropriately respond to ad-hoc or unexpected information security events

- Provides technical support consulting services on matters related to information security such as the criteria to use when selecting information security products

- Performs management and personnel administration functions associated with Company X's Information Security Department (coaches employees, hires and fires employees, disciplines employees, reviews employee performance, recommends salary increases and promotions, counsels employees, establishes employee task lists and schedules, trains staff, etc.)

- Acts as the primary liaison and decision-maker regarding the work of information security consultants, contractors, temporaries, and outsourcing firms

- Stays informed about the latest developments in the information security field, including new products and services, through on-line news services, technical magazines, professional association memberships, industry conferences, special training seminars, and other methods

ACCESS CONTROL SYSTEM ADMINISTRATOR

Job Title: Access Control System Administrator
Department: Information Security [*In rare situations, such as when the Information Security Department cannot get adequate resources, this position may report to the Help Desk Department. Such an approach is not recommended because Help Desk staff may use the system privileges granted to the individual in this position for other purposes. This approach is additionally not recommended because prompt customer service may overshadow security objectives like granting access privileges only to those with a legitimate business need.*]
Reports To: Information Security Department Manager

Summary:

An Access Control System Administrator manages the user access control privileges associated with shared computer systems and networks that are otherwise managed by the Information Technology Department. The Administrator is responsible for maintaining accurate and up-to-date computer-resident records that reflect user contact information, current user privileges, and management authorization for these same user privileges. The Administrator is additionally responsible for immediately terminating user privileges when workers change jobs, go on leaves of absence, or otherwise leave their current job at Company X. In a general sense, the Administrator is responsible for promptly updating access control records so that workers have only the access to Company X computers and networks needed to perform their jobs.

Responsibilities and Duties:

- Processes requests to grant computer and/or network access privileges that have been approved by designated members of management [*Often this will, in many organizations, include approval by information Owners; see Chapter 15 for further details.*]

- Regularly obtains reauthorization from management that the granted privileges on Company X computer and networks are still appropriate for the workers involved [*Often this will, in many organizations, include approval by information Owners; see Chapter 15 for further details*]

- Modifies the system privileges of users in response to employment status notices sent by Department Managers and/or the Human Resources Department Manager [*For example, if an employee was terminated due to fraud, the system privileges for that individual would need to be immediately turned-off*]

- Establishes and refines procedures and other business processes to promptly update the computer-resident privileges used by computer and network access control systems (these privileges are sometimes called access control lists or ACLs)

- Establishes and refines procedures and other business processes to detect errors and inconsistencies in the computer-resident privileges used by computer and network access control systems [*A procedure to identify user-IDs that have not been used in 90 days, sometimes called dormant user-IDs, would be an example*]

- Monitors logs kept by computer and network access control systems to detect attempts at unauthorized use, and notifies the Computer Emergency Response Team (CERT) as necessary [*Note that Systems Administrators do this as well, but for remotely managed systems, while Access Control System Administrators do it for centrally managed systems*]

- Develops or supports the development of automated mechanisms that analyze the security violations found in access control logs to discover patterns and evidence of problems [*This work may involve writing scripts to catch certain abusive activity, or it may involve refinement of the rules used to initiate the alarms triggered by an Intrusion Detection System, also known as an IDS*]

- Provides technical assistance to Systems Administrators, Network Administrators, Commerce Site Administrators, Web Site Administrators, and Database Administrators in their efforts to monitor computer and networks under their control so that unauthorized use will be immediately detected and acted upon

- Integrates the Human Resources Database with computer-resident records of user privileges so that privileges will increasingly be changed exactly at the time when a worker's status with Company X changes

- Maintains and updates computer-resident records that support encryption related processes (such as line encryption devices, virtual public networks (VPNs), digital signatures, and digital certificates and other components of a public key infrastructure or PKI) so that Company X business operations can be securely automated

- Assists users in their efforts to use Company X information systems including handling password resets, smart card deactivations, private encryption key revocations, and the like [*Note that this work is primarily administrative in nature; the Information Security Engineer handles the technical aspects associated with the design, configuration, and ongoing management of these security systems*]

- Preserves all records indicating changes made to access control lists to facilitate investigations, disciplinary actions, and prosecutions

- Provides filing, typing, word processing, database entry, and related support needed to process requests for changes in user access privileges

- Performs other support activities in service of the mission of the Information Security Department

- Attends occasional conferences or training seminars to remain familiar with the latest tools and techniques in the information systems access control area

INTERNAL INFORMATION SECURITY CONSULTANT

Job Title: Internal Information Security Consultant [*Also known as Senior Information Security Advisor*]

Department: Information Security

Reports To: Information Security Department Manager

Summary:

An Internal Information Security Consultant provides business and technical advice on a wide variety of information security issues, concerns, and problems. A Consultant makes sure that all business applications developed in-house or developed by outsiders on behalf of Company X include adequate control measures. Working on committees and task forces throughout Company X, an Internal Information Security Consultant is an in-house subject matter expert who diligently assists with the improvement of security on information systems at Company X. A visible internal spokesperson of the Information Security Department, such a Consultant is charged with gaining widespread support of and compliance with information security requirements. [*Larger organizations may have several Internal Information Security Consultants, each with a specialization in a certain area, such as Internet commerce, desktop machines, telecommuting and mobile computing, or secure systems development. If this position is split into several different jobs, the tasks should likewise be split. The hands-on technical implementation work is generally done by an Information Security Engineer]*

Responsibilities and Duties:

- Provides in-depth technical advice for investigations of information security incidents including internal frauds, hacker break-ins, and system outages

- Assists with the documentation of information security incidents as well as the analysis of the circumstances enabling or permitting these same incidents to take place

- Participates on a Computer Emergency Response Team (CERT) that responds to various security incidents such as denial of service attacks, virus infestations, and internal frauds

- Analyzes selected commercially-available information security products and services to determine which of these should be adopted by, or tested by Company X

- Provides users and management with technical support on matters related to information security such as the criteria to use when selecting information security products (answers a wide variety of questions about information security)

- Acts as a technical information security reviewer of requirements statements, feasibility analyses, operating procedure manuals, and other documents produced during the systems development process

- Reviews proposals to significantly enhance or modify the configuration or functionality of intranets, firewalls, servers, applications, databases, and other important parts of the Company X information systems infrastructure

- Provides special technical guidance to the Information Technology Department staff about the risks and control measures associated with new and emerging information systems technologies

- Acts as a technical resource to users, user department management, and others within Company X who are seeking more information about information security

- Participates in, and acts as a technical leader in, periodic information systems risk assessments including those associated with the development of new or significantly enhanced business applications

- Reviews the cost-effectiveness and practicality of existing information security procedures and systems, and makes suggestions for the improvement of these same procedures and systems

- Develops detailed proposals and plans for new information security systems that would augment the capabilities of, or enable new capabilities for Company X networks or shared information systems [*For example, develop a proposal for implementing digital certificates within Company X*]

- Prepares and periodically updates draft information security policies, architectures, standards, and/or other technical requirement documents needed to advance information security at Company X

- Interprets information security policies, standards, and other requirements in light of specific internal information systems, and assists with the implementation of these and other information security requirements

- Assists with the selection, installation, and adoption of automated tools that enforce or monitor the compliance with information security policies, procedures, standards, and similar information security requirements [*Compliance checking should be the responsibility of the Internal Audit Department, but an Internal Information Security Consultant should provide technical advice on the selection, operation, and implementation of these systems*]

- Conceives of and proposes new approaches that will allow greater standardization and more effective management of information security measures [*Integrating a stand-alone intrusion detection system with a 24 X 7 X 365 network management system would be an example*]

- Provides technical advice to those who install, administer, and update computer-based access control systems [*The most common example involves systems which employ fixed passwords and user-IDs*]

- Guides developers, users, and other internal staff in their efforts to establish and maintain adequate audit trails so that sufficient evidence of computerized business activities exists to reconcile accounts, to detect frauds, to quickly resolve problems, and to otherwise maintain secure and reliable information systems within Company X

- Works with the Internal Intellectual Property Attorney and the Physical Security Manager in the development of procedures which capture and securely preserve evidence of computer related crime and/or abuse, so that this evidence may later be used for legal or disciplinary purposes

- Assists with internal efforts to inventory and control intellectual property (including restricting unauthorized copying of software)

- Develops and/or periodically refines a data classification system that allows workers to make quick decisions about the procedures they should use to protect information that has been marked with the designations described by this system

- Designs, develops, delivers or oversees the delivery of, classroom training and/or other information security awareness programs (videos, memos, computer-based training, etc.) for users, technical staff, and management [*A special training program for Local Information Security Coordinators is recommended*]

- Working in conjunction with the In-House Trainer, periodically determines the effectiveness of information security awareness programs, and quantifies this effectiveness [*The Internal Information Security Consultant should not be the only one checking the effectiveness of his or her own work; that's one reason why an In-House Trainer is involved*]

- Monitors current and proposed laws, regulations, industry standards, and ethical requirements related to information security and privacy, so that Company X is warned in advance and is ready to be fully compliant with these requirements [*If the organization has a Chief Privacy Officer, privacy may be handled by the Legal Department, and references to privacy may then be removed from all job descriptions related to the Information Security Department, but the author recommends that these references remain (perhaps with downplayed emphasis) to ensure that this important area is adequately addressed*]

- Stays informed about the latest developments in the information security field, including new products and services, through on-line news services, technical magazines, professional associations, industry conferences, training seminars, and other information sources

- Participates as a technical advisor for a variety of ad-hoc information security projects that will be dictated by current business and technological developments

- As needed, acts as an expert witness in information security-related legal proceedings involving Company X

INFORMATION SECURITY ENGINEER

Job Title: Information Security Engineer
Department: Information Security
Reports To: Information Security Department Manager

Summary:

An Information Security Engineer provides technical assistance with the design, installation, operation, service and maintenance of a variety of multi-user information security systems such as virtual private networks (VPNs). A hands-on technical specialist, an Engineer handles the complex and detailed technical work necessary to establish security systems such as firewalls and encryption-based digital signature software. An Engineer configures and sets-up information security systems such as firewalls, or else trains Access Control System Administrators, Systems Administrators, Network Administrators, and/or Database Administrators to do these tasks themselves.

Responsibilities and Duties:

- Provides hands-on technical consulting services to teams of technical specialists working on the integration of centralized and/or networked systems [*Examples of such systems include an active data dictionary, a data warehouse, and a data mart*]

- Provides technical assistance with the initial set-up and secure deployment of systems that support information security including virus detection systems, firewall content filtering systems, web site blocking systems, intusion detection systems, intrusion prevention systems, and software license management systems [*Other systems of this nature include single sign-on systems, centralized multi-platform access control databases, and enterprise security management systems*]

- Offers technical information security consulting services to distributed personnel who are responsible for one or more information security systems; these people include Network Administrators, Systems Administrators, and Database Administrators

- Evaluates information system bug reports, security exploit reports, and other information security notices issued by information system vendors, government agencies, universities, professional associations, and other organizations, and as needed, makes recommendations to internal management and technical staff to take precautionary steps [*An example of these notices involves the periodic reports issued by the CERT at Carnegie-Mellon University*]

- Acts as the primary technical support liaison in charge of distributing and loading updates to anti-virus systems, intrusion detection systems (IDSs), firewalls, and other deployed security systems within Company X

- Configures and tunes one or more Intrusion Detection Systems (IDSs) and Intrusion Prevention Systems (IPSs) to ensure that only authorized personnel have access to Company X systems and networks, and that only authorized activity is taking place on Company X systems and networks [*The monitoring of an IDS should be done by computer operations staff and/or network operations staff; note that a Systems Administrator may manage a host-based IDS and IPS, while this Engineer or another technical staff person in the Information Security Department may manage a network-based IDS and IPS*]

- Runs or works with others that periodically run vulnerability identification software packages and related tools to immediately highlight errors in systems configuration, the need for the update of software with fixes and patches, and other security related changes [*To leave this task solely to Systems Administrators introduces a conflict of interest because the results of such software will often indicate that Systems Administrators need to perform additional work*]

- Runs, or works with others that periodically run, fixed password guessing software, unauthorized wireless network access point detection software, unprotected dial-up modem identification software, and similar tools, and then informs those responsible about the need to change their systems to improve security [*The first clause in this task may not be necessary if the organization in question has gotten away from user-chosen fixed passwords (and user-chosen encryption keys), perhaps through the use of dynamic passwords along with digital certificates*]

- With management authorization, collects, securely stores, and utilizes software that is able to decrypt encrypted files, automatically guess user passwords, copy software that has been copy-protected, or otherwise circumvent information security measures

- Collects, maintains, and documents a collection of software that is able to trace the source of and otherwise investigate attacks on Company X systems

- Acts as a technical consultant on information security incident investigations and forensic technical analyses [*An example of such a forensic analysis would be determining whether a certain user had been downloading pornography with Company X computers, and then deleting these files from his or her desktop computer*]

- Conducts selected tests of information security measures in accordance with specific instructions provided by the Information Security Department Manager [*This effort usually includes penetration attacks*]

- Interprets information security policies, standards, and other requirements as they relate to a specific internal information system, and assists with the implementation of these and other information security requirements

- Redesigns and reengineers internal information handling processes so that information is appropriately protected from a wide variety of problems including unauthorized disclosure, unauthorized use, inappropriate modification, premature deletion, and unavailability

- Serves as an active member of the Computer Emergency Response Team (CERT) and participates in security incident response efforts by, among other things, having an in-depth knowledge of common security exploits, vulnerabilities and countermeasures

- Regularly attends conferences, professional association meetings, and technical symposia to remain aware of the latest information security technological developments [*An example would be digital rights management (DRM) systems*]

INFORMATION SECURITY DOCUMENTATION SPECIALIST

Job Title: Information Security Documentation Specialist [*Sometimes called an Information Security Department Administrative Assistant or Information Security Department Administrative Coordinator*]

Department: Information Security

Reports To: Information Security Department Manager

Summary:

The Information Security Documentation Specialist is an administrative coordinator of information security documents. Somewhat akin to a librarian, the Specialist updates and maintains policies, procedures, standards, architectures, forms, and other documents that facilitate information security activities. He or she organizes this material on an intranet site, as well as in internal paper-based files, and otherwise helps to ensure that the most up-to-date version of these documents is distributed to and used by those who have need for the documents. The Specialist does not act as the leader in the identification of new or evolving information security requirements. Instead, the Specialist provides administrative and organizational support that assists the Information Security Department Manager, and others within the Information Security Department, with such decisions. To this end, the Specialist provides limited research in order to answer questions like "which vendors offer firewall products?" [*Note this position does not independently make substantive changes to the content of information security documents such as an information systems contingency plan; the person(s) who prepared such documents, such as a Local Information Security Coordinator, would typically make these updates*]

Responsibilities and Duties:

- Maintains an inventory of all information security documents, with the exception of informal memos, that have been issued by Company X (this inventory should include selected documents issued by other departments such as the Information Technology Department) [*Note that documents can take any form such as paper, fax, html, etc.*]

- Maintains the master copies of, updates, and maintains critical information security requirements documentation such as policies, guidelines, standards, procedures, so that new business activities, new business relationships, and new technologies are reflected therein [*The Administrator would not generally initiate the request for technical changes, only handle the documentation reflecting these ideas*]

- Maintains a collection of information security awareness and training materials used by Company X including films, pamphlets, manuals, and computer-based training software

- Distributes information security documents so that those who need such documents have copies or can readily locate the documents via an intranet site

- Maintains an intranet site that reflects the current version of all information security requirements such as policies, standards, and procedures, etc.

- Assists various workers throughout Company X with the acquisition and use of information security documents [*The Information Security Documentation Specialist would not generally provide technical assistance, only administrative assistance*]

- Securely manages the paper and other types of files of the Information Security Department with the intention that only authorized workers gain access to these files (including past risk assessment projects, analyses of information security products, etc.), and with the intention that copies of all critical files be stored at a secure off-site records storage facility [*The handling of essential or critical records at an off-site records storage facility may alternatively be managed by a Records Management Coordinator*]

- Researches the continued usefulness, relevance, and currency of information security documents used at Company X and makes recommendations to the Information Security Department Manager that are intended to improve information security documents

- Complies and publishes a periodic report which includes information security metrics such as the number and type of attacks experienced, the percentage of attacks which were successful, and the elapsed time between the beginning of an attack and the time when a response was initiated

- Maintains an up-to-date log reflecting those in possession of sensitive information, the movement of this information from person to person, and the copying and destruction of such information consistent with data classification system requirements [*The types of "sensitive information" subject to this process should be defined in a data classification policy*]

- Acts as a coordinator of meetings and events that involve the Information Security Department so that the right people are brought together to create specific results defined by the Information Security Department Manager

- Manages the software escrow related interactions with software vendors in those cases where Company X has determined that escrow is required [*Software escrow involves the storage of source code and other proprietary development documentation with a third party in case a third party software developer goes out of business or otherwise fails to meet its obligations to Company X*]

- Establishes and maintains organized files containing invoices, contracts, and other agreements with information security vendors, such as those that offer virus detection software, software license management software, single sign-on software, and paper document destruction services

- Coordinates the development, issuance, and decision-making activities relevant to requests for proposals (RFPs), vendor bid solicitations, consulting contracts, and other documents describing products or services provided by third-party information security vendors

- Coordinates the shipping, receipt, inventory, and fixed assets control associated with information systems equipment and office equipment used in the Information Security Department

- Maintains a library of information security technical publications used by the Information Security Department [*These materials are published by government agencies, consulting firms, and additional organizations other than Company X*]

- Maintains a sufficient inventory of paper, pencils, staples, fax paper, copier paper, and other office equipment and supplies such that members of the Information Security Department can get their jobs done efficiently and effectively

- Acts as the primary administrative contact for the Information Security Department with the Human Resources Department, the Accounting Department, and other staff departments within Company X [*Typically this would involve distribution of certain handbooks, forms, time reports, etc.*]

- Documents Information Security Department internal procedures so that new members of the Department can be quickly and expeditiously trained and so that essential tasks can be performed even if critical staff are unavailable

- Makes suggestions to the Information Security Department Manager about the ways that administrative activities within the department can be improved

INFORMATION SYSTEMS CONTINGENCY PLANNER

Job Title: Information Systems Contingency Planner
Department: Information Security
Reports To: Information Security Department Manager

Summary:

The Information Systems Contingency Planner acts as the primary focal point for all efforts to design, develop, and test information systems contingency plans at Company X. Providing technical expertise to a wide variety of people throughout Company X, the Planner is a subject matter expert who brings best practices found in the industry and in the high-technology field to bear on the information systems contingency planning challenges faced by Company X. The Planner also coordinates efforts to integrate information systems contingency plans with business contingency plans. The planner does the necessary groundwork so that critical business transactions can continue to be processed by Company X information systems, even if an interruption or problem of some sort has occurred.

Responsibilities and Duties:

- For shared multi-departmental information systems and networks, develops and maintains up-to-date and practical contingency plans that assist Company X in quickly restoring operations after an emergency or a disaster

- Makes advance arrangements with a wide variety of vendors that will be needed to support a recovery effort in the event that multi-departmental information systems and/or networks are unavailable, unexpectedly too slow, or seriously malfunctioning [*These vendors include electric utilities, telecommunications service providers, Internet service providers (ISPs), application service providers (ASPs), and computer hardware manufacturers*]

- Evaluates commercially-available contingency planning tools, such as those that run on a desktop computer, and makes recommendations about the packages that would best support Company X information systems contingency planning efforts

- Participates in information security risk assessments to determine the impact of various threat events including sabotage, industrial espionage, fraud and embezzlement, errors and omissions, natural disasters, and privacy violations

- Performs periodic business impact analyses (BIAs) which examine the potential problems that would be caused by major outages or other serious problems associated with critical information systems at Company X

- Conducts periodic benchmarking studies or baseline controls comparison projects to determine where Company X stands, when it comes to information systems contingency planning, vis-à-vis other organizations in the same industry

- Prepares budgets, cost/benefit analyses, and other financial evaluations of the currently available information systems contingency planning options

- Develops and applies procedures that prioritize applications, systems, and networks within Company X so that limited resources can be devoted to the most critical information systems resources [*These procedures may, for example, include a framework for information Owners to rank production business applications by criticality; see Chapter 15 for details.*]

- Leads or simply participates on a Computer Emergency Response Team (CERT) that responds to various security incidents such as denial of service attacks, virus infestations, and internal frauds

- Develops, implements, and refines management decision-making processes that facilitate a rapid and appropriate response to information systems emergencies and disasters [*A problem escalation process would be an example of this type of decision-making process*]

- Develops customized damage assessment and reporting methods to be used after an information systems emergency or disaster, and periodically performs "post mortems" to determine the degree to which these methods are accurate and useful

- Assists with information systems related insurance claim investigations that are necessary in order for Company X to receive the proceeds from insurance policies [*This work would be done along with the Insurance And Risk Management Department*]

- Periodically performs analyses that seek to establish the rough value of information owned by or in the possession of Company X [*This valuation is important to make sure that contingency planning measures, and for that matter other information security control measures, are cost-effective*]

- Develops, or assists in the design of, information system asset inventories that will assist with information systems recovery efforts (these include data dictionaries, computer equipment inventories, and the like)

- Works with Systems Administrators, Computer Operators, and others to document and maintain an up-to-date description of system configurations, system settings, and system components so that these same conditions can be readily replicated in a back-up system or network

- Advises Systems Administrators, Computer Operators, and others about the selection, installation, configuration, and operation of digital signatures other tools that readily show what has changed on a system believed to have been compromised by an intruder [*Although they are decidedly inferior, checksums could also be used to detect unauthorized changes to files*]

- Defines the types of systems-related activity logs that Company X needs to keep in order to see what has changed on a system believed to have been compromised by an intruder, or a system which has been modified without explicit management authorization [*Of course these logs should be protected by digital signatures too*]

- Works with Systems Administrators, Computer Operators, and others responsible for production information systems, conducting drills that show whether these systems are ready to promptly recover from an intrusion, a power outage, and other problems

- Assists with the development and refinement of conceptual and organizational structures which help ensure that Company X is prepared for various information systems related threat events [*An example would be a departmental contingency planning testing process which illuminates whether a department has or has not developed an adequate local contingency plan*]

- Develops methodologies and instructional material that assist Company X workers with the preparation of their own local contingency plans to deal with decentralized or single department information systems such as a departmental server

- Provides expert technical assistance related to contingency planning to departments throughout Company X who are preparing, testing, and updating their own information systems contingency plans

- Trains Information Technology Department staff, and other workers who are responsible for managing production information systems, in contingency planning concepts, contingency planning best practices, and the use of contingency planning documentation relevant to multi-departmental information systems and networks

- Plans, supervises, participates in, and reports to management on the success of tests to information systems contingency plans

- Develops and documents contingency plan testing methodologies which best respond to the business issues facing Company X

- Compiles status information reflecting the completeness, accuracy, effectiveness, efficiency, and currency of information systems contingency plans at Company X, and then periodically communicates this information to management

- Reviews the contingency plans developed by departments and other organizational units to ensure that they meet Company X standards, and also to ensure that they have integrated all applicable Company X contingency planning practices

- Works with computer and network performance and capacity analysts to ensure that adequate excess capacity and bandwidth exists to realistically support information systems contingency plans

- Researches and stays abreast of all major threats that could adversely impact Company X's information systems including virus infestations, denial of service attacks, hacker intrusions, fires in computer centers, hurricanes, tornadoes, and earthquakes

- Attends several conferences or training seminars per year to become acquainted with the latest tools and techniques for information systems contingency planning [*It is desirable to write this training into a job description to help ensure that management will allocate sufficient funding and time for the training*]

- Maintains a good working relationship with, as well as open lines of communication with, contingency planning professional organizations as well as local emergency response organizations

- Coordinates information systems contingency planning efforts with the Business Contingency Planner's activities

LOCAL INFORMATION SECURITY COORDINATOR

Job Title: Local Information Security Coordinator [*Also known as Regional Information Security Coordinator, Distributed Information Security Coordinator, National Information Security Coordinator, Departmental Information Security Coordinator, Divisional Information Security Coordinator, or Departmental Information Security Advisor*]

Department: [*Insert a user department or division name*]

Reports To: Manager of [*Insert user department or division name*]

Dotted Line: Information Security Department Manager

Summary:

A Local Information Security Coordinator is familiar with local conditions including prevailing laws, organizational culture, management style, and business activities. A Coordinator uses these local conditions to interpret and implement the information security requirements issued by the Information Security Department. A Coordinator serves as a liaison between the Information Security Department on one hand, and the users and management in his or her own local organizational unit on the other. Most often not a full-time information security specialist, the Coordinator is ordinarily responsible for other information systems activities such as systems administration.

Responsibilities And Duties In Information Security:

- Introduces new information security issues and requirements to management within the department [*The Coordinator could alternatively work with another organizational unit, in which case all subsequent references to "department" in this job description would need to be changed*]

- Works with local department management and staff to assist them with efforts to come into compliance with information security requirements such as policies, procedures, and architectures [*Note that this position is not an enforcer or an auditor, but instead an advocate for information security as well as a liaison with centralized information security staff*]

- Interprets information security policies, standards, procedures, and other requirements in light of local needs, and assists user department staff in the implementation of these and other information security requirements [*These include data classification systems, application criticality ranking systems, and other models for coming to terms with information security needs*]

- Provides information security advice and perspective to users and management within the department, and when questions or issues cannot be resolved locally, acts as a liaison with the Information Security Department Manager

- Coordinates the activities of users, local Systems Administrators, and local Network Administrators to help ensure that all documented information security requirements have been met [*Note: Web Site Administrators could be added to this list*]

- Lobbies to change the organizational culture so that information security is embraced as a normal and customary way to do business, is supported by all workers in the department, and is increasingly embraced as a departmental responsibility

- Represents the needs and wishes of the department at Company X information security meetings [*These meetings typically take place every few months, and give the Coordinators a chance to meet and talk with each other as well as with members of the Information Security Department*]

- Provides a first level information security review of IT feasibility studies, IT upgrade proposals, business application development proposals, new IT implementation plans, operating system conversion plans, IT outsourcing plans, and related information systems change documents

- Brings local department information security issues, vulnerabilities, and compliance problems that have not been adequately addressed to the attention of the Information Security Department Manager

- Immediately reports to the Information Security Manager all security incidents and violations, and ensures that these same incidents and violations are properly investigated and correctly resolved [*Some organizations will want to restrict this reporting to "significant incidents and violations" but this task description deliberately avoided those words, thereby allowing the Information Security Manager to determine what is, and what is not, significant (Coordinators generally will not be adept at making this judgement)*]

CHIEF INFORMATION OFFICER

Job Title: Chief Information Officer (CIO) [*Sometimes this job title is called Vice President of Information Technology*]
Department: Information Technology
Reports To: Chief Executive Officer (CEO) [*In some cases the CIO may report to the Chief Operating Officer (COO), or the Chief Financial Officer (CFO), but generally these options are considerably less desirable than reporting to the CEO*]

Responsibilities And Duties In Information Security:

- Assigns information ownership duties to departmental managers who are most likely to benefit from, and/or be adversely affected by the information in question [*See the Chapter 15 for details.*]

- Allocates sufficient resources and manages Information Technology Department staff so that internal information systems are designed, built, and operated in a manner that is secure, reliable, manageable, and consistent with Company X business objectives

- Reviews and approves significant purchases for a wide variety of information technology projects [*This includes information security technology, information security consulting projects, etc. - this organizational structure is common but not recommended, that is to say that the Information Security Department Manager should not report to the CIO, in which case the CIO would not have this responsibility as it relates to information security*]

- Takes steps to ensure that all workers in the Information Technology Department are conducting their daily activities in a manner that is in compliance with established policies, standards, procedures and other management directives [*Compliance, in this case, could for example involve assuring that systems developers integrate information security requirements into the systems they build*]

- Educates top management about the need for reliable, secure, well managed, and well maintained information systems [*The CIO will be the conduit for information security information if and only if the CIO has the Information Security Department Manager reporting to him or her; see Chapter 13.*]

- Conceives of new information systems architectures, strategies, and processes that are intended to advance Company X's business objectives [*These architectures and strategies may include the use of information security tools; for example, an electronic forms system will rely heavily on digital signatures*]

CHIEF TECHNOLOGY OFFICER

Job Title: Chief Technology Officer (CTO) [*In the past, this job title was sometimes known as VP - Engineering*]
Department: Information Technology

Reports To: Chief Information Officer (CIO) [*In some cases the CTO may report to the Chief Operating Officer (COO), Chief Financial Officer (CFO), or the Chief Executive Officer (CEO), but since this job is so new, there is great variation from organization to organization*]

Responsibilities And Duties In Information Security:

- Creates, documents, and maintains an information systems architecture which takes as input the technology-related business requirements established by the Chief Information Office (CIO) [*Ideally this organization-wide IT architecture would embrace or reference an information security architecture, or at least in some way acknowledge information security policies and standards*]

- Conceptualizes and sells management throughout the organization on the merits of information technology related policies, standards, and governance measures [*This role will in some respects deal impact information security, for example, the establishment of a desktop configuration standard will have significant implications for information security*]

- Conceives of the ways that Company X could use the latest information systems technologies and innovations in order to achieve strategic advantage, greater profitability, and better customer service [*The objectives mentioned here will need to change based on the type of business, non-profit organization, or government agency involved; note that the CTO may be pushing the latest and greatest technologies and innovations, while the Information Security Department Manager may be trying to temporarily prevent the adoption of these same technologies and innovations*]

- Directs and manages on a day-to-day basis all internal research and development, if this work deals with information technology and information systems [*This research and development may involve new information security related technologies such as radio frequency ID tags*]

- Formulates, plans, and directs projects which create and enhance Company X information systems infrastructure [*Many of these infrastructure projects may include security features or security systems; for example, an infrastructure project could involve the move to adopt a public key infrastructure (PKI) encryption system*]

- Reviews the technical design of all major information systems projects, especially those with strategic or competitive implications, and provides technical consulting advice to those who work on the relevant project teams [*This advice will be brought to bear on information security projects, such as the installation of an intrusion prevention system, and the CTO's support can be very important in terms of selling top management on these projects*]

- Manages information systems technology vendor relationships and approves all major purchases of information technology systems and services [*Depending on the financial decision-making responsibilities of the Information Security Department Manager, the CTO's role as gatekeeper for major technology vendor purchases can mean that the CTO stands in the way of major information security purchases; at the same time having the CTO as gatekeeper can help bring order to the chaos that reigned when user departments all made their own information systems purchasing decisions independently*]

INFORMATION SYSTEMS ANALYST/BUSINESS ANALYST

Job Title: Information Systems Analyst/Business Analyst
Department: Information Technology
Reports To: Manager of Systems Development

Responsibilities And Duties In Information Security:

- Utilizes Company X systems development processes to ensure that all necessary steps have been performed prior to bringing up an application in a production operating environment [*These steps include consideration of security at several phases such as in the generalized systems design phase*]

- Evaluates user department security and privacy needs (in conjunction with staff from the Information Security Department) and includes suitable controls in all proposed information systems solutions

- Documents the ways to, and teaches user department staff to, employ clear decision-making criteria so that management can appropriately choose between conflicting objectives such as information integrity, information availability, information timeliness, and information security [The *decision-making process is exemplified by the criticality ranking process that information owners would use when deciding the type of back-up a certain application and/or a certain type of information requires; see Chapter 15 for further details. To the extent that these trade-offs involve security, the Information Systems Analyst would ordinarily work with the Information Security Department in the development of the decision-making process.*]

- Provides technical support consulting services to users and user department managers so as to allow them to achieve business goals, while at the same time ensuring that the envisioned system is adequately secure, reliable, manageable, and supportable

- Assists the In-House Trainer in the development of training materials for user departments, or else develops training materials for user departments, for those systems that the Analyst helped to design [*Training in many instances should include security*]

SYSTEMS PROGRAMMER

Job Title: Systems Programmer
Department: Information Technology
Reports To: Manager of Systems Development

Responsibilities And Duties In Information Security:

- Installs and maintains security-related systems software, such as fixed password access control systems, smart card systems, and user activity logging systems [*Included here would be extended user authentication systems such as dynamic password systems and biometric systems*]

- Provides in-depth technical support consulting services to the Computer Operations Manager, Business Application Programmers, and Information Systems Analysts to help them understand the systems software issues associated with achieving certain performance, reliability, and security goals

- Documents all systems software that has been developed in-house, according to existing documentation standards, to facilitate future maintenance and enhancements, as well as to quickly diagnose problems

- Maintains accurate records reflecting the current and historical configuration settings, the justifications for these settings, and the configuration option decision making process, for every multi-user system managed by the Systems Programming Group

- Develops computer operation scripts, job control language routines, and other programs to control operating system and application system software [*These programs often involve special security routines, such as a link between a system log, a log analysis program, and intrusion detection system (IDS)*]

- Informs the Information Security Manager of improper configurations, dangerous internal practices, and other matters which might jeopardize the security of production computer systems, to the extent that these matters come to the Systems Programmer's attention in the course of performing other duties [*Systems Programmers have a technical perspective about large production systems security that very few other people have, and for this reason they need to be an acknowledged source of vulnerability information for the Information Security Department*]

BUSINESS APPLICATIONS PROGRAMMER

Job Title: Business Applications Programmer [Sometimes called simply Applications Programmer]
Department: Information Technology
Reports To: Manager of Systems Development

Responsibilities And Duties In Information Security:

- Employs the risk assessment methodology issued by the Information Security Department to determine specifically which controls are needed for business application software being developed, significantly enhanced, or externally provided (the latter includes packaged software written by vendors, development work outsourced to contractors, and services supplied by an Application Service Provider (ASP))

- Builds appropriate controls into business application software so that the resulting business activity will be stable, secure, and reliable

- Follows the systems development process conventions published by the Information Technology Department to ensure that all important steps in the development process have been adequately performed

- Performs alpha tests of his or her own application software to ensure that it operates according to functional specifications before releasing it to other programmers, or to the Quality Assurance Department for further testing

- Diligently and clearly documents all application systems developed in-house to facilitate future maintenance and enhancements [*This is important from a contingency planning standpoint*]

- Helps the In-House Trainer to develop user-training materials which assist workers in properly operating the business application software that he or she developed

- Notifies management about potential problems associated with the application systems that they have been working on, problems which are not adequately addressed by existing control mechanisms [*These problems include potential privacy violations*]

COMPUTER OPERATIONS MANAGER

Job Title: Computer Operations Manager [*Sometimes called Technical Services Manager*]
Department: Information Technology
Reports To: Chief Information Officer

Responsibilities And Duties In Information Security:

- Manages electrical power, telephone, air conditioning, humidity control, fire detection and suppression, and other environmental systems that are necessary for the smooth and continuous operation of computer-center-based information

systems resources such as servers, hubs, routers, and firewalls [*Perhaps most importantly among these systems is an Uninterruptible Power System or UPS*]

- Establishes and refines operating procedures for computer center staff to follow to ensure that all production applications are run on time, in a manner that is secure and reliable

- Defines, documents, and directs the enforcement of controls which clearly separate the privileges and abilities of users in three different multi-user computer environments: production, testing, and development [*This work would ordinarily be done in conjunction with Access Control System Administrators, who would handle the day-to-day administrative changes in support of this activity*]

- Manages the work of Computer Operators, Network Operators, Computer Performance Analysts, and others who tend the operations of the information systems and networks managed by the Information Systems Department, so that reliable, secure, and cost-effective service is provided to internal users

- Declares an emergency or disaster, as necessary, at which point a predefined set of procedures must be followed to recover those production information systems and/or production networks which are managed by the Information Technology Department [*The responsibility to declare such an emergency or disaster should be restricted, and for more serious emergencies or disasters the approval of the Information Security Department Manager may be required. For example, the Computer Operations Manager may shut down the inbound E-mail gateway for up to half an hour without getting the Information Security Department Manager's consent.*]

- Supervises the change control process for equipment, facilities, and software such that only changes authorized by management are made (an exception may be made if an emergency exists) [*Although an exception should be permitted in cases of emergency, all emergency changes should be followed-up by a justification memo and other relevant documentation*]

- Plans and supervises hardware and software conversions for those information systems managed by the Information Technology Department so that information system reliability, availability, and security are maintained

- Prepares budgets, project plans, and other proposals that would enhance the reliability, cost-effectiveness, manageability, and security of the information systems managed by the Information Technology Department

- Maintains an up-to-date inventory of shared information systems equipment including routers, hubs, servers, firewalls, and monitors [*If an organization doesn't know what equipment and systems it has, securing them will be very difficult, if not impossible*]

- Performs in-house technical consulting to assist Business Application Developers and users with their efforts to best utilize the equipment and computer center environmental systems managed by the Information Technology Department

- Evaluates proposed technological changes to the centralized information systems managed by the Information Technology Department, identifying potential incompatibilities and other implementation issues prior to cut-over to production status [*This evaluation process would apply to proposed information security systems*]

- Performs analyses of the capacity and performance of the equipment, facilities, and software located in the computer center [*These analyses may highlight unusual conditions which could indicate that a security problem exists; alternatively, this job could be performed by a Computer Performance Analyst if such a person exists at your organization*]

- Keeps checks, customer statement stationery, and other valuable forms used by the data center in a secured location and grants access only to those who have a genuine business need

- Defines who will have what type of physical access to the data center, and updates this privilege list based on changes in the job status of the individuals who have access privileges [*Defining a closed shop, where programmers and users are not allowed in the data center, is recommended, and would be an example of this activity*]

- Designs and regularly refines workflow and foot traffic movement patterns so that only authorized personnel are permitted to enter the data center

- Establishes and supervises a system of printed output distribution such that sensitive reports, negotiable materials (such as paychecks), and other output is seen by and received by only authorized parties

- Supervises the work of information system vendor personnel when they are in the computer center

COMPUTER OPERATOR

Job Title: Computer Operator
Department: Information Technology
Reports To: Computer Operations Manager

Responsibilities And Duties In Information Security:

- Monitors the status of multi-user computers including system load, available disk space, and response time to ensure that all activities are in keeping with management intentions [*This monitoring is often an important first line of defense for noticing hacker intrusions, denial of service attacks, and other security-relevant events*]

- Monitors daily computer operations with an eye toward unusual events, and notifies the Computer Emergency Response Team (CERT) immediately of any suspected intrusions, virus infestations, denial of service attacks, and other abuses; also notifies the Information Security Department Manager of all other suspicious activities (suspected fraud, sabotage, etc.)

- Maintains and reviews logs, audit trails, and other shared information systems records indicating the activity that took place, and as necessary, promptly notifies others of unusual or suspicious events [*These logs can be essential for break-in investigations and problem resolution efforts*]

- Monitors Intrusion Detection Systems (IDSs) which identify suspicious activity, and immediately notifies designated staff members if the conditions and/or events so warrant [*This type of monitoring could alternatively be done by the Information Security Engineer, or else another technical staff member in the Information Security Department*]

- Adjusts the applications running, users logged-in, system configuration, data media loaded, and other aspects of multi-user computers so that business activity on shared information systems proceeds in an efficient, recoverable, and reliable manner [*These adjustments sometimes involve terminating the session of a hacker and revoking all privileges associated with the involved user-ID; these adjustments also involve loading tapes and other data media needed for backup processes*]

- Assists with and monitors the movement of new software into the production environment to ensure that only duly-authorized software is used to process production Company X information

- Restricts physical access to the licensed application program library and back-up tape library to authorized personnel

- Manages the secure handling of backup tapes, diskettes, cartridges, CDs, and other data recording media such that only authorized people are permitted to have possession of these media

- Confirms that backup processes are running properly, that data may be fully restored according to management's intentions, and that backup processes have been creating appropriate operational logs

- Maintains the physical security of all information systems equipment contained in computer centers, permitting only authorized personnel into the facility, and as necessary supervising the activities of outsiders such as vendor maintenance staff

- Follows documented instructions for the production operation of application systems software, including comparison of batch control totals, digital signatures, and other audit and security parameters [*Information security instructions should be written-into computer operations procedures*]

- Runs, and enters input data into, job control management systems which monitor and schedule production application programs [*These management systems can be used to significantly reduce errors and omissions, thus enhancing the likelihood that production applications will execute as management intends*]

DATA LIBRARIAN

Job Title: Data Librarian [*May also be called Data Storage Librarian or sometimes Program Librarian*]
Department: Information Technology

Reports To: Computer Operations Manager

Responsibilities And Duties In Information Security:

- Organizes, categorizes, monitors, and maintains computer files on production computer system storage media such as tapes, disks, CD-ROMs, and cartridges [*This is an important part of a contingency planning effort; note that files can contain both production programs and production information*]

- Watches to ensure that adequate data media storage capacity is available in order to uneventfully service on-going production system computer operational needs [*This activity may alternatively be done by a Computer Performance Analyst*]

- Manages the rotation of production computer storage media to/from a remote site so that all storage media are accounted for, physically secured, and if necessary properly encrypted [*This is an important part of a contingency planning effort*]

- Checks storage media to make sure that it is still in serviceable condition, and as necessary transfers computer files to newer media to ensure data integrity [*For example, magnetic tapes will "grow" errors over time as the media degrades; regular checking will ensure that the data is not unduly corrupted thereby*]

- Physically guards storage media housed in the media library and checks the media out to authorized computer operations personnel so that they may perform the duties assigned by management [*This duty may be at least partially automated with hierarchical storage management systems and related operating system utilities*]

- Checks-in and checks-out data storage media from the production library, making sure to maintain up-to-date records indicating the names of authorized individuals who are in possession of production storage media [*This process of checking-in and checking-out storage media may be partly automated in some shops that use robotic storage devices*]

- Uses established information security procedures to destroy or obliterate production data recorded on storage media, prior to the disposal of such media [*In some organizations, this activity may alternatively be done by specialist staff in the Physical Security Department; this activity may involve the use of specialized equipment such as degaussers, which obliterate magnetic data on magnetic tapes and cartridges*]

INFORMATION SYSTEMS QUALITY ASSURANCE ANALYST

Job Title: Information Systems Quality Assurance Analyst
Department: Information Technology
Reports To: Manager of Systems Development [*Although uncommon, a better reporting relationship would be to another manager who does not have a stake in what the Information Systems Quality Assurance Analyst discovers. Candidates include Internal Audit Department Manager or Information Systems Security Department Manager*]

Responsibilities And Duties In Information Security:

- Researches the latest testing techniques that will cost-effectively determine whether hardware and/or software will perform in a manner consistent with specifications [*It is at least ten times more expensive to fix security problems after an application has moved into production than if this fixing process was performed before an application went into production, so security mechanisms need to be properly tested before conversion to production takes place*]

- Compiles and documents clear-cut and specific testing criteria to determine whether a particular hardware and/or software system performs in a manner that matches its documented specifications [*This testing includes testing of security mechanisms built into hardware and/or software systems, although people working in this position do not generally perform penetration attacks or other highly-specialized information security tests (those could be performed by an Information Security Engineer, or better yet, by an external consultant)*]

- Manages and documents selected tests of business application software, systems software, and other information system components, so that conversions of these same components from test to production status can take place; these tests also provide the background information allowing lawsuits, personnel actions, and other significant events based on system performance to be justified [*The source of these components is deliberately not specified here, so the quality assurance process should therefore be applied to software developed by both inside and outside parties*]

- Evaluates externally developed software packages as well as packages developed in-house to ensure that they perform in accord with specifications and that they will have, so far as can be readily determined, no damaging or disruptive impact on the computing environment into which they will be placed [*This evaluation can be part of the due diligence process prior to purchasing or leasing a software package*]

- Performs post-implementation quality testing to determine whether the new system components are operating in a manner consistent with requirements and related documents [*Based on this type of testing, security lapses may be discovered, and then should be reported to the Information Security Department Manager*]

- Notifies management about potential problems associated with the system components that have been in testing [*These problems include inadequate documentation, insufficient user training, overly optimistic deployment schedules, and insufficient user access controls*]

- Declares software and/or hardware systems that are soon to be placed in production mode either "in compliance" our "out of compliance" in terms of existing Company X technical standards and requirements [*This can include determining whether systems are compliant with information security policies, standards, and architectures; alternatively this task can be performed by a technical staff member in the Information Security Department*]

- Where cost-effective, utilizes testing software such as simulators to automate and formalize the testing process

- Periodically reviews staff use of the production application change control system and the systems development methodology to determine whether they are being followed according to management instructions, and reports findings and recommendations to project managers and the Internal Audit Department Manager, as necessary [*A change control system is essential to the whole quality assurance process, and if it is compromised, then there is little point in having a quality assurance process*]

- Periodically reviews entries in the Help Desk's trouble ticket system to determine the specific nature of problems encountered by users of production systems, and then uses this information when designing future tests of system components

HELP DESK SPECIALIST

Job Title: Help Desk Specialist
Department: Information Technology
Reports To: Computer Operations Manager

Responsibilities And Duties In Information Security:

- Promptly documents and creates trouble tickets for all reports of information systems problems including system unavailability, unacceptable response time, unauthorized access, missing files, and virus infections [*Proper documentation is very important for prompt problem resolution, training of new staff, prosecution and disciplinary action, as well as insurance claims*]

- Immediately notifies Computer Emergency Response Team (CERT) members if an information security incident meets the escalation criteria established by the team

- Remains familiar with the current Company X organizational structure and the information systems related activities performed by other organizational units, so that users can be quickly referred to the appropriate organizational unit and/or contact person(s)

- Remains familiar with the current version of information security policies and procedures so that quick answers to users with simple questions can be provided [*More complex questions should be referred to the Information Security Department*]

- Prepares and updates reference documentation so that others working on the Help Desk can quickly and practically respond to users reporting difficulties and problems [*These quick reference guides should include security matters, such as what to do when a virus infects a user's personal computer*]

- Notifies information security staff of chronic information security difficulties and other indicators that information security problems may exist

- Resets fixed passwords, reissues smart cards, reinstalls virtual private network (VPN) software, and otherwise re-initializes user access control mechanisms, after the involved user has adequately authenticated his or her identity [*This task may alternatively be performed by Systems Administrators, Network Administrators, Database Administrators, and/or Access Control System Administrators*]

- Attends classes, reads manuals, and otherwise becomes familiar with the user perspective needed to operate computers, networks, and other information systems utilized at Company X [*This training provides the technical background that can enable a Help Desk Specialist to identify information security problems*]

ARCHIVES MANAGER/RECORDS MANAGER

Job Title: Archives Manager/Records Manager [*Sometimes called Records Retention Manager*]
Department: Information Technology
Reports To: Chief Information Officer

Responsibilities And Duties In Information Security:

- Develops, applies, and occasionally enhances a policy that clearly designates certain types of Company X information as either an archival record or vital information [The latter is sometimes called an essential record, and when it comes to this same type of information, the Archives Manager works with the Information Systems Contingency Planner]

- Maintains an up-to-date and complete listing of all document types that need to be retained as archival records or vital information [Web site pages are an important example of archival information that many organizations often don't retain; separately, the listing of document types could be provided on an intranet site]

- Defines a data retention schedule for archival records by periodically working in conjunction with the Internal Intellectual Property Attorney

- Assists information Owners in the process of determining whether information under their control should be designated as an archival record, determining for what period of time different types of information should be retained, and determining who should be allowed to access this type of information [See Chapter 15 for more information on Owners]

- Receives, categorizes, catalogs, and otherwise prepares information submitted from people throughout Company X for insertion into the Company X archival records

- Designs and manages information systems which facilitate the rapid retrieval of archival records, and assists in the design of systems which facilitate the rapid retrieval of vital information

- Assists workers throughout Company X with efforts to retrieve both vital information and archival records in support of business continuity, litigation support, dispute resolution, and various other business objectives

- Trains Systems Administrators, Network Administrators, Database Administrators and other workers who operate information backup systems about the need for and procedures associated with archival records

- Periodically disposes of (or destroys) archival information in accordance with existing policies and procedures [*The most important of these policies and procedures would be a data retention schedule; this destruction process would be particularly important if there is a threat that archival electronic mail could be used in discovery proceedings by an opposing side's attorney*]

- Periodically checks archival information storage media (such as magnetic tape) to make sure that the information stored thereon continues to be readily retrievable [*Certain data storage media like magnetic tape "grow" errors over the years and thus must be checked, or else the data recorded thereon needs to be migrated to more permanent storage media, such as CD-ROMs*]

- Transfers information from existing archival storage media to new and more permanent archival media if and when the information contained thereon is in jeopardy

- Maintains an inventory of tape drives, floppy disk drives, zip drives, and related data storage and data retrieval equipment needed to access archival records, in addition to a collection of necessary documentation for the use and repair of this equipment

- Maintains an up-to-date inventory of all archived files and vital documents, and manages computer-readable media that allows this information to be readily retrieved

- As needed, maintains a history of the movement and current location of archival records and/or vital information

- Establishes, maintains, and enhances environmental systems (humidity control, air conditioning, etc.) so as to keep archival records from prematurely deteriorating

- Designs, contracts for the installation and maintenance of, and periodically checks the operation of fire, water, and other detection systems for those areas where archival records are stored

- Manages the activities of vendors who are in possession of, or who otherwise handle Company X archival records

- Ensures that physical access controls over all archival records is sufficient to prevent unauthorized access and damage to the information stored therein

- Establishes and maintains authorization and documentation systems so that only authorized personnel can access and/or remove information contained in the archival records

- Establishes and maintains a reliable and permanent audit trail which shows who has gained access to which archival records on what dates

- Researches the latest innovations and commercial products for indexing, cataloging, organizing, storing, locating, and protecting archival records, and makes recommendations to the Chief Information Officer as warranted

TELECOMMUNICATIONS MANAGER

Job Title: Telecommunications Manager
Department: Information Technology
Reports To: Chief Information Officer

Responsibilities And Duties In Information Security:

- Periodically reviews commercially-available voice and data communications technology to determine whether it is cost-effective for Company X to upgrade its internal networks to improve reliability, improve quality of service, or reduce cost

- Periodically reviews, modifies, and renegotiates contracts with long distance service providers, toll fraud detection system firms, and other telecommunications vendors so that Company X's business objectives continue to be met at a minimum cost [*Two important business objectives that the Telecommunications Manager needs to keep in mind are uninterrupted service and secure service*]

- Acts as the primary liaison with voice and data network providers, such as Internet Service Providers (ISPs), or else establishes other communications paths between these same vendors and internal Company X staff [*An alternative communication path would be needed for a Computer Emergency Response Team (CERT)*]

- Manages contractual relationships with telecommunications vendors including long distance vendors, Internet Service Providers, and others so that economical and continuously available high-quality service is provided to Company X

- Works with the Information Security Department Manager to ensure that voicemail, fax, intranet, and other communications systems that employ computers have adequate access control measures, contingency plans, and other necessary controls

- Plans for the future, and extrapolates current network usage and requirements so that appropriate contracts with voice and data network providers can be arranged in advance

- Monitors performance statistics about network traffic and usage so that Company X networks are available to meet business needs [This could involve monitoring Internet systems for overload conditions such as those that would be occasioned by a distributed denial of service (DOS) attack]

- Performs troubleshooting services to isolate, diagnose, and fix problems dealing with shared servers and connected equipment [*The Telecommunications Manager may be a member of the CERT*]

- Participates in the recovery of voice and/or data network services in the event of a disaster or an emergency

- Performs periodic inventories to determine the technological nature, the locations, and the connections of current communications networks used by Company X [*If users are able to independently establish their own data lines to their desks, they may be able to thwart access controls via dial-up connections; similarly, if users are able to set-up their own wireless network access points, then they may unintentionally compromise the security of Company X's internal network; this may be a shared responsibility with an Information Security Engineer*]

- Establishes, maintains, and periodically validates the accuracy of a database of telephone circuits including location, number, and jack type [*This is important for contingency planning purposes*]

- Provides technical consulting services and technical leadership to other staff engaged in the development and update of both business contingency plans and information systems contingency plans [*Although the Telecommunications Manager is a participant on several shared internal resources contingency planning committees, he or she is generally not the leader of these committees*]

- Assists with the establishment of usage policies for internal networks [*Such as the use of message broadcasting facilities on a public address system or the transmission of chain letters via electronic mail systems*]

SYSTEMS ADMINISTRATOR/NETWORK ADMINISTRATOR

Job Title: Systems Administrator/Network Administrator
Department: Information Technology
Reports To: Computer Operations Manager [*An Administrator may be physically stationed inside a user department or division even though he or she is part of a centralized Information Technology Department; an alternative, but less desirable, reporting relationship involves reporting to the head of the involved department or division*]
Dotted Line: Access Control System Administrator [*A strong argument can be made for off-loading all security administration tasks from the Systems Administrator to a centralized group's Access Control System Administrator. This eliminates a conflict which otherwise exists in that the Systems Administrator may be tempted to compromise information security in the interests of getting non-security work done. For example, the Administrator may issue the same temporary fixed password to all new users as a way to make his or her work easier; but this practice also increases the likelihood that an unauthorized person would gain system access. This topic is taken up in greater detail in Chapter 20.*]

Responsibilities And Duties In Information Security:

- Configures, installs, and connects computer and network hardware so that users will be able to perform business activities in accordance with

management's intentions [*The work of an Administrator includes setting-up printers, routers, hubs, local area network servers, and the like; just how these systems are configured has a profound impact on information security*]

- Periodically runs software that inventories the hardware resident on Company X networks, in part to determine whether hardware is still connected to the network [*That is to say that the hardware is still operational and has not been stolen, or perhaps redeployed elsewhere without management permission*]

- Installs, configures, and initiates the execution of software that has been legally purchased by Company X, or that is in the public domain but validated as reliable by a trusted third party [*Company X may wish to employ only software authorized for use by management, in which case the last part of this bullet will need to be modified*]

- Re-configure and reinstalls operating systems and other security systems according to established policies and procedures whenever there is clear evidence that the security of a system has been compromised

- Periodically runs and administers autodiscovery software license management systems that, in a user-transparent fashion, determines whether software resident on various machines is properly licensed

- Disables and erases all licensed software (except legal demo copies) that has not been legally purchased by Company X

- Runs auto-detection software routines to discover prohibited software which could be used to compromise systems security, and then removes all such software from Company X systems [*Examples of the software that could be used to compromise systems security include password guessing routines like L0phtcrack, encryption key brute-force discovery routines, war dialers (which scan for modems on dial-up lines), data interception software such as Sniffers (TM), and vulnerability identification software like SATAN and COPS, and a database of product serial numbers which will allow stolen software to be executed*]

- Runs automatic software distribution systems to periodically transmit and install the latest software updates on involved computers [*This automatic distribution software can be, for instance, an important aid in the distribution of the latest computer virus scanner software*]

- Evaluates/determines whether vendor-supplied operating system patches and fixes will cause software incompatibility trouble, system crashes, systems response time degradation, and/or other operational problems before installing these same patches and fixes [*This evaluation process may alternatively be done by a Change Control Committee which should have as a member at least one person from the Information Security Department*]

- Promptly installs all internal-management-approved operating system patches and fixes to those machines which handle production business activities as well as those which are located on the perimeter to Company X's network; these machines include departmental servers, firewalls, web commerce servers [*This is an absolutely critical security task, and some organizations may wish to put it at the top of the Administrator's task list, as a reflection of its importance; if this task is moved to the top of the list, the task immediately preceding it, dealing with an evaluation of these same patches and fixes, may appropriately be moved as well*]

- Upgrades/migrates systems software as needed to ensure secure, reliable, and stable operation of servers and related equipment (including migration to other operating system platforms, other network protocols, etc.)

- Maintains in a safe place an inventory of the original installation disks, CDs, and other data storage media for licensed software used on the systems that the Administrator manages

- Maintains a computerized inventory of all major pieces of computer and networking equipment used by workers within the Administrator's department or division (or other area of responsibility) [*This job may alternatively be done by local Property Administrators, or on occasion by Department Managers (although the latter is not recommended), as is further discussed in the job description below for Physical Asset Protection Specialist*]

- Issues user-IDs and fixed passwords, or other system access control mechanisms (such as smart cards), and otherwise assists users in the secure usage of systems (including handling password resets) [*The Help Desk may instead handle password resets; or this responsibility may be handled by the Help Desk only if the involved system is centrally managed by the Information Technology Department; separately, access control mechanisms in this case could include dynamic passwords, biometrics, and related technologies*]

- Establishes and maintains access control systems so that only one individual has access to each user-ID, so that individuals who have left Company X no longer have any system privileges, so that the privileges of dormant user-IDs are automatically revoked, and so that individuals who have switched jobs have only the privileges required to perform their new jobs [*An Administrator does this work for distributed systems, whereas an Access Control Administrator does this work for centralized systems; both should receive news of changes in the status of workers from a Human Resources Consultant or from the human resources database directly*]

- Configures and maintains access control systems so that users can access only those machines, software, and information that are needed to perform their jobs [*This work may include routers, hubs, firewalls, servers, and other equipment*]

- Promptly updates user access control privileges in response to management instructions, communicating to the requesting party when there will be a delay in posting a requested change

- Disables user-IDs and/or privileges immediately in those events where an employee is found guilty of a major crime, has seriously violated internal policy, or has left the organization (especially in duress terminations)

- Periodically revalidates the continued business need for users to have the privileges that they have been authorized to receive [*This is often handled with a memo sent to the relevant manager requesting confirmation that existing privileges are in fact still needed by the involved users*]

- Faithfully follows established procedures for all changes to access control systems and documents all such changes so that problems may be quickly resolved [*The maintenance of an archive of access control change requests, management approvals, and Administrator-initiated changes made is essential for problem resolution efforts, security incident investigations, as well as information systems audits*]

- Securely preserves all records indicating changes made to access control lists to facilitate investigations, disciplinary actions, and prosecutions

- Establishes and maintains network directories, router tables, and other information systems collections that are used to interconnect Company X networks and computers [*For example, Lightweight Directory Access Protocol (LDAP) is a directory-based approach to providing network access control services, and an Administrator should manage this system*]

- Periodically utilizes freeware and shareware vulnerability identification tools to determine whether systems are correctly designed and configured, and whether all necessary software patches and fixes have been applied [*Ideally this task would be expanded to include tools that your organization licenses, but at the very least, the Administrator should run freeware/shareware tools*]

- Monitors computer and network activity including system load, response time, available disk space, and user activities to ensure that all activities are in keeping with management intentions [*When certain suspicious activities are detected, an Administrator would ordinarily notify the Computer Emergency Response Team, or CERT*]

- When so requested by management, monitors electronic mail traffic, instant message system traffic, web surfing traffic, and other data communications sent over Company X's internal network to determine whether these communications are fully consistent with Company X policies [*This bullet may be deleted if the company doesn't perform such monitoring; alternatively, such monitoring may be performed by a manager such as the Internal Audit Department Manager*]

- Periodically reviews access control system logs and reports to ensure that the system is working properly and that no unauthorized activity is taking place [*Again, when certain suspicious activities are detected, the Administrator would ordinarily notify the Computer Emergency Response Team, or CERT*]

- Notifies management about potential problems associated with the systems under their control [*These problems include inadequate disk space, untested contingency plans, inadequate security systems, and insufficient training; Administrators should not be the only ones to detect and report these problems - Internal Auditors, Internal Information Security Consultants, and others should also do this to help ensure that management receives and acts upon all important information*]

- Participates on, or cooperates with, a Computer Emergency Response Team (CERT) that responds to various security incidents such as denial of service attacks, virus infestations, and internal frauds

- Notifies the Information Security Department Manager of all intrusions, violations, or other suspected information security problems [*Note: an Administrator is not asked to judge whether a particular intrusion or violation is indeed significant; this judgement call is left to the Information Security Manager (some information security problems at first appear to be insignificant but later turn out to be quite important)*]

- Establishes and administers software and information backup systems, including the procedures and transmission paths used to securely move both software and information to a secure remote location [*The latter may for example involve electronic vaulting where current production data is instantly sent to a remote location over the Internet*]

- Confirms that backup processes are running properly, that data may be fully restored according to management's intentions, and that backup processes have been creating appropriate operational logs

- Develops, tests, and maintains information systems contingency plans that allow the systems and networks under his or her control to be quickly regenerated and used for business purposes at a remote site [*This work should include both emergency response and also disaster recovery*]

- Performs troubleshooting services to isolate, diagnose, and fix problems dealing with servers and other equipment under the Administrator's control

- Responds promptly to user requests for technical assistance in efforts to get systems to operate in a manner that supports the achievement of user-specified business goals [*These requests for assistance could be caused by a virus infection or other security related problems*]

- Works with the Information Security Department Manager or his or her delegate to help ensure that all information security requirements have been met on the systems under the Administrator's control

- Closely monitors, and where possible, personally escorts, all third-party computer service personnel including representatives from hardware vendors, computer supplies vendors, outsourcing firms, and other outside organizations, if these personnel are working on information systems equipment that is physically located on Company X premises, and for which the Administrator is responsible

- Monitors developments in the information security field to be able to make suggestions for the improvement of systems/network security and reliability; these activities include periodically reviewing notices about new vulnerabilities relevant to the systems for which the Administrator is responsible [*You may wish to integrate this bullet with the bullet above which covers the evaluation of patches and fixes to operating systems*]

- Periodically attends technical training classes and conferences which augment his or her knowledge about those information systems matters relevant to the job of an Administrator [*These classes and conferences should include some information security classes and conferences*]

WEB SITE ADMINISTRATOR/COMMERCE SITE ADMINISTRATOR

Job Title: Web Site Administrator/Commerce Site Administrator [May also be called Web master, Web Technical Administrator, or Web Site Manager]

Department: Information Technology

Reports To: Computer Operations Manager

Dotted Line: Access Control System Administrator [*Note: This job description could be easily modified so that it's appropriate for an Intranet Site Administrator*]

Responsibilities And Duties In Information Security:

- Installs, connects, configures, and inventories firewalls, routers, servers, and other network equipment associated with web/commerce systems in a manner consistent with the Company X information security policies as well as Information Technology Department policies

- Re-configure and reinstalls operating systems and other Internet related security systems according to established policies and procedures whenever there is credible reason to believe that the security of a system has been compromised

- Installs and upgrades systems software, and migrates to new systems software, as needed to ensure secure, reliable, and stable operation of servers and related equipment

- Evaluates/determines whether vendor-supplied operating system patches and fixes will cause software incompatibility trouble, system crashes, systems response time degradation, and/or other operational problems before installing these same patches and fixes [*This effort may be done in concert with a Change Control Committee*]

- Promptly installs all internal-management-approved operating system patches and fixes to those machines which handle production business activities as well as those which are located on the perimeter to Company X's network; these machines include departmental servers, firewalls, web commerce servers [*This is an absolutely critical security task, and some organizations may wish to put it at the top of the Administrator's task list, as a reflection of its importance; if this task is moved to the top of the list, the task immediately preceding it, dealing with an evaluation of these same patches and fixes, may appropriately be moved as well*]

- Maintains in a safe place an inventory of the original installation disks, CDs, and other data storage media for licensed software used for the Administrator's web/commerce site activities

- Installs, maintains, and operates filtering software that screens inbound information flows for viruses, Trojan horses, and other unauthorized software, and screens outbound web traffic such that this traffic only connects to sites that are consistent with authorized business purposes [*If your organization doesn't restrict where users go on the Internet, or doesn't expect to do this in the near future, the last part of this bullet will need to be modified (perhaps logging of the sites where users go on the Internet will be employed instead); this task could also be performed by a Systems Administrator or Network Administrator*]

- Generates and distributes outbound Internet web browsing activity reports, including attempted but denied connections, for management review and remedial action [*If your organization doesn't monitor outbound web surfing activity, this highly-recommended bullet should be deleted; this task could also be performed by a Systems Administrator or Network Administrator*]

- Installs, maintains, and operates change detection software that immediately flags any changes to critical software or files on Internet connected systems [*Change control software, such as Tripwire (TM), will not only make the management of these systems more orderly -- it can also immediately detect changes made by unauthorized parties such as system intruders*]

- Installs, configures, tests, and as necessary trains users on applications and systems software that runs on Company X's web/commerce systems in a manner consistent with Company X information security policies as well as Information Technology Department policies

- Monitors and estimates current and future traffic loads, response time, and related capacity planning statistics on firewalls and other Internet network equipment and makes recommendations to upgrade or fine-tune this equipment as needed [*This may also be called capacity planning; in large organizations, this activity may be performed by a specialist like a Computer Performance Analyst rather than the Administrator*]

- Installs and fine tunes load balancing software that allocates traffic to various machines on the web/commerce systems [*This software can help deal with mail bombs and denial of service attacks*]

- Makes changes to the web/commerce site only after approval by the appropriate management representatives has been obtained (exceptions will be made in emergencies) [*In many organizations, this approval comes from a Web Site Committee - see the mission statement in Chapter 11 for further details; although this is rare, in some organizations, a separate position called a Pagemaster is employed to manage the content on the web site*]

- Immediately removes all unauthorized content or programs that have been placed on the web/commerce site to limit Company X liability and to thwart intruders [*If one or more machines managed by the Administrator have become a "zombie computer" (a remotely-controlled machine that is a participant in a denial of service attack), your organization may be held liable for damages that the zombie computer causes; likewise, if one or more of these computers is a temporary waystation for the transmission of stolen credit card numbers, your organization may be held responsible as an unwitting accomplice to a crime*]

- Establishes and securely maintains a permanent archive of all pages posted on the web/commerce site, including dates when the pages were used [*This task alternatively may be handled by the Archives Manager/Records Manager*]

- Establishes and administers web/commerce site software and hardware needed for back-up systems, including the definition of transmission paths used to securely move software and information to a secure remote location [*The latter is called electronic vaulting when the transmission is done automatically via data replication software over the Internet*]

- Establishes procedures and then follows these same procedures for the regular backup of files stored on Internet web servers and commerce servers [*These procedures should include off-site secure storage of backups*]

- Confirms that backup processes are running properly, that data may be fully restored according to management's intentions, and that backup processes have been creating appropriate operational logs

- Participates on a Computer Emergency Response Team (CERT) that responds to various Internet-based security incidents such as denial of service attacks, virus infestations, and credit card frauds

- Configures and monitors an Intrusion Detection System (IDSs) and Intrusion Prevention Systems (IPSs) to ensure that only authorized personnel have access to Company X systems and networks [*An Administrator would typically only manage a host-based IDS, leaving the management of a network-based IDS to the Information Security Department staff*]

- Performs troubleshooting services to isolate, diagnose, and fix problems dealing with shared servers and connected equipment (this work typically involves interactions with Internet Service Providers (ISPs), Application Service Providers (ASPs), credit card processing bureaus, and other third parties)

- Notifies management about potential problems associated with the systems over which the Administrator has control [*These problems include inadequate disk space, untested contingency plans, etc.*]

- Develops, tests, and maintains web/commerce site contingency plans that allow the systems and networks under the Administrator's control to be quickly regenerated and used for business purposes at a remote site [*This work should include both emergency response and also disaster recovery*]

- Periodically utilizes freeware and shareware vulnerability identification tools to determine whether the site is correctly designed and configured, and whether all necessary patches and fixes have been applied [*Ideally this would be expanded to include tools that your organization licenses, but at the very least, the Administrator should run freeware/shareware tools*]

- Assigns and distributes user-IDs and initial expired passwords to authorized users according to established procedures [*Alternatively, an organization can use more sophisticated technologies such as one-time passwords supported by smart cards*]

- Maintains access control systems on the web/commerce sites so that only one individual has access to each user-ID, so that individuals who have left Company X no longer have any system privileges, so that users have only those privileges needed to perform their jobs, and so that individuals who have switched jobs have only the privileges of their new jobs

- Promptly updates user access control privileges in response to instructions from top management or members of the Information Security Department

- Disables user-IDs and/or privileges immediately in those events where an employee is found guilty of a major crime, has seriously violated internal policy, or has left the organization (especially important for duress terminations)

- Periodically revalidates the continued business need for users to have the privileges that they currently possess [*This typically is handled via a memo to management, asking them to confirm the continued need for the currently enabled user privileges*]

- Securely preserves all records indicating changes made to access control lists to facilitate problem resolution efforts, security incident investigations, disciplinary actions, and related prosecutions

- Periodically reviews access control system logs and reports to ensure that the web/commerce site is working properly and that no unauthorized activity is taking place [*Under certain circumstances, the Administrator should notify the Computer Emergency Response Team (CERT) about these activities*]

- Faithfully follows established procedures for all changes to web/commerce site access control systems (including content changes), and documents all such changes so that problems may be quickly resolved

- Establishes and monitors automated time synchronization systems so that all web/commerce system logs reflect accurate time/date stamps [*Accurate system time references are essential for reliable logs and will additionally help with investigations and prosecutions*]

- "Assists with domain name registrations, server digital certificates, search engine registrations, and other Internet directory listing efforts [*Some of these marketing activities may instead be performed by the Marketing Department, while some of the contractual activities may instead be handled by a Purchasing Department*]

- Serves as Company X's first level of contact with Internet web/commerce vendors, suppliers, and outsourcing firms, and to these parties communicates Company X's technological needs [*This communication should include mentioning Company X's security requirements*]

- Works with the Information Security Department Manager or his or her delegate to help ensure that all information security requirements have been met on the systems under the Administrator's control

- Closely monitors, and where possible, personally escorts, all computer service personnel from web/commerce site hardware vendors, computer supplies vendors, outsourcing firms, and similar third-party organizations if these personnel are working on equipment that is physically located on Company X premises

- Monitors developments in the Internet security and privacy field to be able to make suggestions for the improvement of systems/network security and reliability; these activities include periodically reviewing notices about new vulnerabilities relevant to the equipment for which the Administrator is responsible [*You may wish to merge this bullet with the bullet, in this same job description section but quite a number of tasks above, which covers the evaluation of patches and fixes from vendors*]

- Periodically attends technical training classes and conferences which augment his or her knowledge about those information systems matters relevant to the job of an Administrator [*These classes and conferences should include some information security classes and conferences*]

DATABASE ADMINISTRATOR

Job Title: Database Administrator (DBA)
Department: Information Technology
Reports To: Computer Operations Manager
Dotted Line: Access Control System Administrator

Responsibilities And Duties In Information Security:

- Handles day-to-day management and operations of database systems, including the assignment and distribution of database user-IDs and initial expired passwords to authorized users [*A more sophisticated user authentication technology could alternatively be mentioned here, for example, smart cards that generate one-time passwords; many organizations will want to keep the access control technology employed out of job descriptions, and in this way prevent the need to update job descriptions when technology changes*]

- Resets fixed passwords or otherwise reinitializes user access control mechanisms associated with specific database applications after authorized users have failed to authenticate their identities to the system [*Again, a more sophisticated user authentication technology than fixed passwords could be used here -- this alternative is recommended*]

- Promptly updates user access control privileges at the database level in response to management instructions, communicating to the requesting party whenever there will be a delay in posting a requested change

- Identifies and proposes database management system access control mechanisms that Company X could use to control who gains access to shared production databases as well as what they do once they have gained such access [*These mechanisms include schemas or views, which allow users to see only the information they are authorized to access*]

- Follows information security policies, guidelines, procedures, and other requirements when assigning and updating the privileges of users in shared databases

- Securely preserves all records indicating changes made to access control privileges to facilitate investigations, disciplinary actions, and prosecutions

- Generates and analyzes reports indicating database activity to highlight potential performance problems, security violations, and other problems needing attention [*Certain suspicious activities need to be reported to the Information Security Department Manager and/or the Computer Emergency Response Team, but these activities and the reporting process would generally be specified in an information security policy document*]

- Installs, and monitors the performance of, mechanisms to maintain and enhance the integrity and availability of the data contained in shared production databases [*An example of such a technology is data replication*]

- Designs, maintains, and controls access to a production application data dictionary [*Business Application Programmers would typically design application data dictionaries, but Database Administrators would maintain and control such application data dictionaries*]

- Assists with internal efforts to integrate and standardize databases across Company X, and in some cases like an extranet, to achieve these same objectives on projects involving both Company X and its business partners [*This database integration effort is especially important in the area of privacy policy because it is only through consistent and integrated databases that privacy policies will be observed on a consistent and reliable basis*]

- Researches and explains to management the privacy, security, decision-making, and other implications of combining databases via database matching and database consolidation (as, for example, in a data warehouse, data repository, or data mart) [*The combination of previously separate types of information, through database matching or other techniques, remains one of the greatest privacy risks of the modern age*]

- Notifies the Information Security Department Manager about risks that may be encountered when shared production databases are used in new and different ways [*For example, if a new distributed database system is being contemplated, the Administrator can bring distributed data integrity issues to the attention of the Information Security Department Manager*]

- Maintains, in a safe place, an inventory of the original installation disks, CDs, and other data storage media for licensed software used in the Administrator's database related activities

- Monitors developments in the database technology and management areas so as to be able to make suggestions for the improvement of database activities [*These typically would include security and privacy enhancements*]

DATA ADMINISTRATION MANAGER

Job Title: Data Administration Manager
Department: Information Technology
Reports To: Chief Information Officer (CIO)

Responsibilities And Duties In Information Security:

- Develops a corporate data dictionary that reflects the critical information used throughout the organization [*This data dictionary could reflect data classification, data location, and access control restrictions defined by data type; a data dictionary will also be important for contingency planning efforts*]

- Develops a secure and reliable data warehouse that brings together current information from disparate Company X systems, and normalizes this data so that structured queries can be run against this same data, and so that regular management reports can be prepared [*Access control to the data warehouse is a major headache and many new issues are introduced by the process of building a data warehouse (such as mosaic theory problems); a data warehouse may also be called a data repository or a data mart*]

- Leads and/or collaborates in efforts to develop and refine an information management architecture for Company X [*This information architecture could define conventions and ways of organizing, collecting, and dispensing information that will assist in bringing both order and security to the information systems management process*]

- Works with the Information Security Department Manager on the refinement of information ownership policies and procedures to ensure that all Company X critical information has an identified owner, and that these owners are performing their assigned duties [*See Chapter 15 for more details.*]

PHYSICAL SECURITY DEPARTMENT MANAGER

Job Title: Physical Security Department Manager
Department: Physical Security
Reports To: Legal Department Manager

Responsibilities And Duties In Information Security:

- Acts as liaison with all internal groups that have one or more security-related responsibilities, so as to ensure that organization-wide security efforts are coordinated and that duplication of effort is avoided [*The Physical Security Manager alone may have this organization-wide security coordination role, or it may be a shared responsibility with the Information Security Department Manager. Alternatively, it may be the responsibility of a Chief Security Officer*]

- Acts as a permanent member of the Company X Computer Emergency Response Team (CERT), which quickly responds to a variety of events such as hacker break-ins, virus infestations, and computer frauds

- Establishes and refines a crisis management system which can assist top management in the decision-making process, assist the Public Relations Department with the words to publicly release, and assist internal staff in quickly resolving the crisis [*This system could be pressed into action with particularly severe information security problems such as a denial of service attack against an Internet merchant*]

- Acts as the primary liaison with law enforcement personnel including the local police force, the state police force, and the Federal Bureau of Investigation (FBI) on all criminal investigation matters pertaining to Company X [*If your organization is outside the US, replace the FBI with your local country's primary law enforcement agency*]

- "Investigates all alleged criminal activities that involved Company X resources, which took place on Company X premises, or were committed by people in the course of working for Company X [*Some organizations would include in this task alleged violations of organizational policy, but these could alternately be handled either by the involved organizational unit manager or the Human Resources Department Manager*]

- Investigates and immediately stops leaks and inadvertent disclosures of confidential information [*The Information Security Department Manager will often assist with this activity*]

- Establishes and maintains physical access control systems which help to ensure that all people who are present within Company X offices or facilities are authorized to be within these same areas, that the entrances and exits of these people through a secure perimeter are logged, and that all attempts to breach this perimeter are recorded for subsequent investigation

- Supervises the installation, maintenance, and operation of security systems including CCTV surveillance systems, burglar alarm systems, and time and attendance systems [*These systems help to determine who was in what location at what time, and can therefore provide important information for investigations as well as serve as a deterrent to the commission of abusive and criminal acts*]

- Periodically commissions bug sweeps to ensure that Company X senior management offices, the Board Room, and other locations where sensitive information is discussed do not contain eavesdropping devices

- Establishes and supervises a force of Guards that maintains the safety of Company X employees as well as protects Company X physical property [*Guards help to keep unauthorized people out of offices that might contain sensitive information; while guards are often outsourced, the Physical Security Manager still needs to manage the outsourcing firm*]

- Trains the force of Guards in appropriate responses to a variety of circumstances including burglary alarms, violence in the workplace, and theft of Company X property [*Property, as used here, includes portable computers*]

- Establishes and manages a team of personnel who collect sensitive information stored in locked containers and who then shred, burn, or otherwise destroy this sensitive information according to Company X policy [*Local off-site shredders may also be necessary for telecommuters. Separately, this document destruction activity may be outsourced, but the Physical Security Manager will still need to manage the outsourcing firm*]

- Writes and periodically updates policies and procedures for facility management, facility access control, facility security surveillance, facility environmental controls, facility layout and design, facility fixed asset inventory, facility maintenance, facility alarm responses, as well as personnel health and safety when in Company X facilities

- Develops and refines awareness material for all workers that deals with physical security and personal safety, and then provides this material to the In-House Trainer [*Personal protection ideas can also prevent theft of Company X property such as portable computers*]

- Provides consulting and technical assistance in the establishment and operation of secure inventory control systems to monitor and control valuable Company X property and negotiable instruments (examples include portable computers, blank check stock, and company credit cards)

- Offers advice and counsel about the ways that Company X should best protect itself against a variety of physical security risks including fire, wind storm, flood, earthquake, burglary, kidnapping, assault, battery, vandalism, and industrial accidents [*These physical security recommendations will often help with the protection of both information systems and information itself*]

- Organizes and periodically updates a background checking system to verify the representations of job candidates to ensure that stated qualifications, work experience, academic degrees, and references meet Company X standards [*This activity in some cases may instead be performed by the Human Resources Department*]

- Acts as a coordinator of the physical security for special events such as stockholders meetings and Board of Directors meetings [*These meetings may involve disclosure of significant sensitive information*]

- Provides executive protection consulting services to top management and key staff members, and thus helps to prevent these people or their family members from being kidnapped or otherwise hurt [*This activity helps to ensure that sensitive, critical, and valuable information in the possession of these people continues to be available to Company X; in many cases such information resides only in the heads of these people*]

- Researches the latest developments in physical security, worker safety, and executive protection, and recommends physical-security-related management strategies if these would be likely to benefit Company X or its staff

PHYSICAL ASSET PROTECTION SPECIALIST

Job Title: Physical Asset Protection Specialist
Department: Physical Security
Reports To: Physical Security Department Manager

Responsibilities And Duties In Information Security:

- Periodically performs physical security reviews to determine whether existing or proposed Company X facilities are adequately protected against burglary, vandalism, bomb explosion, fire, flood, earthquake, wind storm, and other threats [*Effective information security requires that effective physical security is already in place*]

- Designs and supervises the installation and operation of CCTV and other systems that monitor the physical security of Company X offices and facilities [*Including the data center and areas where sensitive information is stored*]

- Designs and supervises the installation and operation of environmental control systems for offices and other Company X buildings (air conditioning, heating, ventilation, drainage, electrical shock prevention, burglary prevention, etc.) [*There may be some overlap with the duties of the Computer Operations Manager when it comes to the physical security of a centralized computer center, but this overlap is desirable*]

- Valuates proposed changes to offices and facilities to ensure that adequate physical security measures have been included in the design of these offices and buildings [*If people can simply walk away with a server's hard drive, it doesn't matter whether users employed strong passwords or not*]

- Issues, updates, and revokes picture ID badges that control access to Company X buildings and facilities, in accordance with current worker duties and relationships [*Perhaps physical keys or cipherlocks are used instead, in which case the wording in this task would be changed*]

- Provides direction and advice to the Property Administrators so that they can periodically take inventory and also take steps to prevent damage to, or loss of, property within their departments [*Property Administrators keep track of portable computers, office furniture, overhead projectors and other equipment, some of which contain Company X information*]

- Manages an inventory of hardware that is intended to assist workers in the protection of Company X information (shredders, locking file cabinets, data media and document safes, etc.) [*The Information Security Department may also keep an inventory of hardware that can assist with the protection of information; for example, the Information Security Department may have an inventory of encryption devices, smart cards, and data backup devices*]

- Manages physical keys that protect Company X information and property such as those that control access to file cabinets, office doors, and closets (this includes issuing keys to authorized personnel, maintaining records reflecting key copies made and the people in possession of keys, ensuring that related locks are properly maintained, and rekeying locks as necessary)

- Maintains the secure working status of all safes, gun cabinets, door locks, company car locks, and other physical mechanisms used to protect both Company X physical property and sensitive information

- Manages and supervises the maintenance of fire detection and suppression devices and systems [*This may include those within the computer data center, or those may be managed by the Computer Operations Manager*]

- Maintains an ongoing history of security incidents including computer break-ins, theft of employee property, theft of Company X portable computers, vandalized cars, traffic accidents, and the like (including estimated dollar losses, staff time lost, and business consequences) [*This is also called a loss history*]

- Conducts investigations of alleged abusive acts, criminal acts, or violations of Company X policy, as instructed by the Physical Security Department Manager [*These acts include hacker break-ins, information systems equipment theft, and other information security loss events*]

- Monitors Company X's compliance with Department of Defense classified document handling procedures, and makes recommendations for changes where appropriate [*Use this bullet only if Company X handles national defense information*]

- Oversees efforts to dispose of Company X property including gifts to charity, scrap recovery, or refurbishment and reissue [*Computers that go through these processes must be purged of all Company X information*]

- Monitors the disposal of sensitive paper records through shredding, burning, or other authorized measures [*Confidential information in paper form can be easily and often legally scavenged from trash bins and needs to be properly destroyed prior to disposal*]

- Researches the latest developments in physical security and executive protection, and recommends specific products and services if these same products and services would be likely to benefit Company X or its staff

BUILDING AND FACILITIES GUARD

Job Title: Building And Facilities Guard
Department: Physical Security
Reports To: Physical Security Department Manager

[*A Receptionist is generally used to greet visitors in low security environments while Building And Facilities Guards are generally used for this purpose in high security environments; Receptionists can also be used to establish and maintain physically protected areas (like an executive suite) inside the perimeter maintained by Building And Facilities Guards*]

Responsibilities And Duties In Information Security:

- Signs for packages in the lobby and otherwise keeps delivery personnel and other third parties out of Company X offices unless they are escorted by an authorized Company X worker

- Politely greets all people who are not authorized Company X workers (employees, contractors, consultants, temporaries, etc.) and who seek to enter Company X offices, and then asks them to wait in the lobby until an escort takes them into a restricted access area

- Checks the identification of all parties wishing to gain access to Company X buildings and facilities without an escort, and if proper identification is not provided, prevents these parties from gaining such access [*Most often proper identification is by picture badge, in which case badges may be read by automated readers, and the flow of people through gates or turnstiles equipped with these readers may then be monitored by Guards*]

- Monitors and/or maintains access control logs of people entering Company X buildings and facilities including visitors, those seeking employment, consultants, contractors, temporaries, and regular employees [*In some instances, documenting or otherwise recording the people leaving a building may also be part of a Guard's duties*]

- Documents all security-relevant, unusual, or suspicious events in the guard's log [*These logs provide important evidence for investigations as well as important indicators of conditions that could soon turn into security problems*]

- Monitors the materials that people remove from Company X premises to ensure that all outgoing equipment is accompanied by an authorized property pass [*Although rare, in some instances, Guards may also monitor the removal of paper documents, floppy disks, and other computer media to make sure that sensitive information is not removed without proper management authorization*]

- Monitors the status of remote closed-circuit TV cameras, environmental sensors (such as fire detection systems), and other building and facilities control gear [*These systems will generally be integrated into a front desk console in larger organizations, and may be accompanied by video taping gear*]

- Tours Company X offices and facilities after hours to ensure that door locks remain secured, that security lighting remains turned on, and that environmental control systems (such as fire detection systems) remain functional

- Notifies local police, local ambulance services, local rescue services, and the local fire department as needed according to procedures defined by the Physical Security Department Manager [*Computer crimes should be reported to criminal justice authorities only after the approval of the Internal Intellectual Property Attorney and the Information Security Department Manager have first been obtained*]

- Immediately notifies the Physical Security Department Manager and other designated members of the Company X management team of any activity that could be reasonably expected to lead to a major loss for Company X (a leaky roof, loitering by suspicious people in a parking lot, car accident on Company X premises, etc.)

- Provides after-hours telephone operator services and otherwise assists authorized workers with their performance of authorized business activities [*It is desirable to have somebody who can act as a centralized contact point in case of after-hours emergency or disaster*]

OFFICE MAINTENANCE WORKER

Job Title: Office Maintenance Worker
Department: Physical Security
Reports To: Physical Security Department Manager

Responsibilities And Duties In Information Security:

- Maintains a "chain of custody" for confidential information in paper and other forms according to Company X policies and procedures [*In other words, no unauthorized parties have had possession prior to destruction of the information*]

- Destroys confidential information in paper and other forms according to Company X policies and procedures (employing shredders, burning, etc.) [*This task may alternatively be performed by staff in the Physical Security Department*]

- Disposes of general office trash via locked containers and other systems that prevent unauthorized persons from gaining access

- Works after hours and securely manages the doors to Company X offices so that unauthorized persons cannot gain access during non-business hours [*Maintenance Workers must not keep doors open while they do their work after hours because unauthorized persons may gain access thereby; this bullet can be eliminated if it is the policy of Company X to have maintenance workers perform their duties during working hours in order that their activities may be observed and more readily controlled by employees*]

- Alerts the Physical Security Department Manager when and if there appears to be sensitive information in the general office trash [*This is an indication that better worker training is needed*]

- Notifies the Information Security Department Manager if there appears to be sensitive information left out in the open during non-working hours [*This policy is consistent with a clean desk policy that requires workers to lock-up all sensitive information when the information is not in use; if no such policy is employed at your organization, this task can be deleted*]

MAIL ROOM CLERK

Job Title: Mail Room Clerk
Department: Physical Security
Reports To: Physical Security Department Manager

Responsibilities And Duties In Information Security:

- Maintains secure physical custody of all mail and packages received from the postal service as well as other delivery services [*This mail and these packages may include negotiable instruments such as checks as well as confidential information such as plans for new products*]

- Delivers mail and packages to designated recipients in a timely manner, and where required, obtains signatures of the receiving party to assure a chain of custody [*A chain of custody provides a reliable paper trail showing who had access to high sensitivity documents such as merger/acquisition proposals*]

- Screens incoming mail and packages so that junk mail and other solicitations which are obviously not business related are trashed before they reach employees, contractors, and other workers on the premises

- Maintains complete and reliable records of certified, registered, insured, and other high-value and/or critical mail and packages

- Selects the appropriate type of courier/transportation service for mail and packages so that Company X goals of low cost, adequate security, traceability, and adequate delivery speed are all met

INTERNAL AUDIT DEPARTMENT MANAGER

Job Title: Internal Audit Department Manager [Also known as Internal Audit Manager]
Department: Internal Audit
Reports To: Chief Executive Officer [*Sometimes this position reports to the Controller, Chief Financial Officer, or Vice President of Finance, although all of these are less desirable options than reporting to the CEO; also the Internal Audit Department Manager should have a dotted-line reporting relationship to the Board of Directors Audit Committee, as is more fully described in Chapter 13; separately, some organizations are outsourcing a large part of the internal audit function, in part to deal with the conflict of interest that arises when internal auditors must investigate the potential misdeeds of top management*]

Responsibilities And Duties In Information Security:

- Develops audit plans that rank the overall risks which Company X faces, and allocates internal audit resources in a manner consistent with these risks [*In the last few years, this risk ranking approach to the development of audit plans has meant that information security receives a lot of attention*]

- Appraises, evaluates, and reports to top management on the existence of, effectiveness of, and need for changes in internal controls such as computer password systems

- Researches, defines, and proposes corporate governance strategies as well as strategies for monitoring compliance with management requirements [*Governance strategies, in this case, include mechanisms like publishing written policies which define required staff behaviors; these strategies will then be applicable to information security, although not necessarily limited to information security*]

- Researches, defines, and proposes the adoption of appropriate risk management and control self-assessment tools throughout Company X [*These self-assessment tools could for example include questionnaires that help department managers determine whether they are in compliance with information security policies and standards*]

- Acts as the eyes and ears of top management, performing internal audits that determine whether workers are carrying out their duties in accordance with top management intentions (including confrontation of unethical, illegal, and questionable practices)

- Documents and follows up on all reported ethical problems, legal problems, policy violations, criminal behavior, and other matters anonymously reported in the Company X hotline's voicemail box

- Evaluates the degree to which Company X operations are in compliance with external requirements including contractual agreements, societal ethical expectations, laws, and regulations [*In some highly-regulated organizations, a group reporting to the Legal Department, called the Compliance Department, may instead perform this duty*]

- Serves as a liaison with both top management and the Board of Directors' Audit Committee, providing specialized advice and counsel about the need for changes in internal controls [*These internal controls would include information security measures*]

- Arranges for independent specialized third parties to periodically inspect, test, and provide suggestions for the improvement of internal control measures such as computer access controls [*This would, for example, include periodic third-party vulnerability assessments and penetration attacks; these two activities combined are sometimes called ST&E (Security Test & Evaluation)*]

- Orchestrates the appropriate use of a risk acceptance process whereby departmental managers and others jointly agree to temporarily approve and support a situation that is out-of-compliance with existing Company X policies or standards [*Chapter 10 defines risk acceptance memos in greater detail*]

INFORMATION SYSTEMS AUDITOR

Job Title: Information Systems Auditor [*Often called an IS Auditor, Electronic Data Processing Auditor, or EDP Auditor*]

Department: Internal Audit

Reports To: Internal Audit Department Manager

Responsibilities And Duties In Information Security:

- Researches and writes audit reports indicating the existence of, effectiveness of, and need for changes in, information technology related internal controls [*Such as computer password access control systems*]

- Determines whether in-house information systems are in compliance with existing policies, standards, architectures, procedures, laws, regulations, and other requirements [*These of course include information security requirements*]

- Determines whether in-house information systems policies, standards, architectures, procedures, organizational structures and other management tools are consistent with customary practices found elsewhere in the industry [*Also known as determining whether Company X is consistent with a baseline set of controls, or a standard of due care*]

- Determines whether information systems are designed, specified, configured, tested, operated, and managed in a manner that is efficient, reliable, secure, and consistent with organizational objectives [*As part of this activity, an Information Systems Auditor performs risk assessments although they are often called information systems audits*]

- Acts as the eyes and ears of top management, performing internal audits that determine whether workers are carrying out their information technology related duties in accordance with top management intentions (including confrontation of unethical, illegal, and questionable practices) [*This includes evaluating the Information Security Department Manager's effectiveness and efficiency*]

- Determines whether workers have been assigned specific responsibility and accountability for information technology related controls, and as needed, makes specific recommendations for clarifying and assigning both responsibility and accountability

- Evaluates and assesses the adequacy of information technology documentation and records, including the strategic information technology plan, the information technology architecture, and information technology job descriptions [*The Information Systems Auditor should also review information security documentation such as the information security architecture*]

- Evaluate and recommend improvements to the controls associated with information technology related business processes such as: acquisition of information systems hardware and software, application system development and testing, as well as systems change management [*Note that, with respect to this bullet, the Information Systems Auditor has a job which deliberately overlaps with the jobs of several people in the Information Security Department*]

- Examines both the input and output of various business application systems to confirm that input has been transformed according to management's intentions, and that the results of this intended transformation match the output [*Besides validating the correctness of the processing, this activity also confirms that application systems have not been modified by unauthorized persons*]

- Gathers statistically valid samples of the records at Company X, and analyzes these records to determine whether internal controls are operating effectively

- Periodically reviews compliance with information systems related contractual terms and conditions to ensure that both vendors and Company X remain in compliance with these same terms and conditions (software licenses, hardware leases, outsourcing contracts, etc.)

- Reviews proposals for outsourcing business activities to determine whether the benefits that the vendor alleges are likely to be achieved, whether the vendor is in a position to adequately handle Company X business, and whether controls would be compromised in the course of outsourcing the proposed activities

INTERNAL INTELLECTUAL PROPERTY ATTORNEY

Job Title: Internal Intellectual Property Attorney
Department: Legal
Reports To: Legal Department Manager

Responsibilities And Duties In Information Security:

- Monitors and evaluates new legislation, new regulations, and new case law in the jurisdictions where Company X does business, and provides management with recommendations about appropriate responses [*These include information security and privacy issues such as the trans-border data flow laws in Europe*]

- Periodically reviews the liability exposures of Company X management to a wide variety of threats including negligence, breach of fiduciary duty, and violation of various statutes, and then provides recommendations as needed [*These reviews can uncover the need for additional internal controls to protect information assets, violation of privacy statutes, etc.*]

- Acquaints management with its legal responsibilities as well as its exposure to liability allegations under prevailing laws and regulations (Foreign Corrupt Practices Act, Fair Credit Reporting Act, Sarbanes-Oxley Act, etc.) [*These examples are from the US; if your organization is based in another country, change them as need be*]

- Makes legal recommendations to prevent Company X from taking on undue risks as a result of its use of new technologies such as Internet commerce, handheld computers, and text-based pagers

- Stays informed about the latest technologies and business solutions for protecting intellectual property [*Examples include digital rights management (DRM) systems, and robot web spiders that search the web for the unauthorized posting of protected information containing digital watermarks*]

- Informs appropriate Company X staff about the legal data retention requirements for various types of information as well as other requirements that apply to Company X information

- Develops, periodically revises, and educates relevant Company X staff about procedures to protect evidence for an upcoming lawsuit [*This should include steps to prevent a backup system from automatically erasing electronic mail that had been archived for a certain period of time*]

- Works with the Information Security Department Manager in the creation and enhancement of a data classification system and related controls that protect sensitive information owned by or in the custody of Company X

- Drafts and reviews legal documents related to the handling of intellectual property including confidentiality (non-disclosure) agreements, agreements not to compete, software licensing contracts, and outsourcing agreements

- Identifies and specifies ways that management can preserve and protect Company X intellectual property rights (copyrights, patents, trade secrets, trademarks, etc.) [*This could for example come into play when a deal with a third party is being negotiated*]

- Supervises a staff member or outside service that monitors the information available on the Internet, as well as through other public sources, to ensure that no unauthorized use of Company X intellectual property is taking place [*The defense of intellectual property rights assumes that violations have previously been discovered; at the very least Company X may wish to ensure that it's name is not being used without permission*]

- Provides advice and guidance regarding periodic inventories of Company X intellectual property assets [*This could include advice on a corporate data dictionary*]

- Assists with the legal aspects of negotiations that deal with either third-party intellectual property entrusted to Company X, or Company X intellectual property entrusted to third parties

- Represents Company X in all legal and regulatory proceedings related to intellectual property including court appearances, preparation of court documents, and applications to government agencies

- Acts as a secondary liaison with district attorneys and other members of the criminal justice system when Company X is engaged in prosecutions and other legal actions [*The primary liaison is the Physical Security Department Manager*]

- Provides legal advice to investigations of alleged violations involving organizational policies as well as laws and regulations

- Provides strategic and tactical advice on civil and criminal proceedings, as well as internal disciplinary actions, associated with breaches of Company X policies as well as violations of various laws and regulations

- Provides internal management guidance on legal actions related to employee terminations, disciplinary actions, background checks, and related human resources matters

- Establishes and maintains a compliance program to ensure that the organization is in compliance with relevant laws and regulations, and that it can readily demonstrate this compliance [*In some industries, particularly those that are highly regulated, this is sometimes a separate organizational unit, called the Compliance Department*]

ETHICS OFFICER

Job Title: Ethics Officer
Department: Legal
Reports To: Legal Department Manager [*In some highly-regulated industries, a separate Compliance Department is typically established, in which case this position may report to the head of that department rather than the head of the Legal Department; in some cases the position may report to the Human Resources Department Manager*]

Responsibilities And Duties In Information Security:

- Maintain a current working knowledge of all laws and regulations, ethics, morals, and cultural expectations which pertain to Company X and its industry [*An Ethics Officer would thus be well aware of privacy laws and regulations, as well as related laws and regulations relevant to information security, and could assist in efforts to convince top management to take action to come into compliance with these same laws and regulations*]

- Develop, get management support for, distribute, and periodically update an ethics policy relevant to all workers at Company X [*This policy is occasionally called a code of conduct; a code of conduct is related to an information security policy, and the two documents should be aligned in their intention and delivery; this task may alternatively be done by the Human Resources Department Manager*]

- Develop, get management support for, and deliver training programs which highlight the meaning and implications of the ethics policy [*New employee orientation training is usually one place where this training is delivered; this training needs to dovetail with information security related training*]

- Provide confidential meetings for, and relevant advice about, the resolution of ethical concerns and questions held by employees [*These concerns and questions may have to do with conditions which involve information security, such as a fraud which is perpetrated via internal computer systems*]

- Provides a confidential and anonymous conduit for reporting violations of Company X policies, as well as abusive and/or illegal activity committed by workers at Company X [*These illegal or abusive situations can be information security related, such as the deliberate misuse of customer information for identity theft purposes; a confidential conduit for reporting these problems may also be provided by the Information Security Department*]

- Acts as one of the primary liaisons for, and an expediter of resolutions for, all reported policy violations, abuses and illegal activities

- Advises senior management on the ethics implications of various decisions and courses of action [*These decisions may involve postponement of efforts to come into compliance with laws and regulations, some of which will deal with information security*]

- Assists with the development of an organizational governance program which seeks to prevent and avoid problems, and when they do occur, promptly report them and promptly resolve them [*Governance in this case refers to monitoring those in power, having appropriate checks and balances, and having other internal controls which support the proper working of the organization; many of these same internal controls will support information security activities*]

CHIEF KNOWLEDGE OFFICER

Job Title: Chief Knowledge Officer (CKO) [Occasionally called Vice President - Knowledge Management, or Chief Learning Officer (CLO)]
Department: Information Technology [*Some organizations place this individual within the Human Resources Department, in which case the focus is primarily learning and training rather than information management*]
Reports To: Chief Executive Officer (CEO)

Responsibilities And Dues In Information Security:

- Envisions, plans, and manages internal knowledge management practices which foster the documentation, organization, and sharing of information critical to Company X [*A CKO fosters information sharing across an organization, and if the CKO is not working with information security staff working in the access control area, this effort may be perceived to be in opposition to information security*]

- Works with the Information Technology Department to develop networks, systems, processes, procedures, and other mechanisms to facilitate the transfer of skills and knowledge among internal workers [*The notion of cross-training, as well as documentation that will facilitate self-training, is an important part of knowledge management, and this effort bolsters information security*]

- Acts as a missionary and evangelist selling knowledge management concepts to workers across Company X with the intention of capturing, leveraging, and appropriately disseminating intellectual capital (knowledge and skills) [*The intention to prevent the loss of knowledge and skills when workers leave a firm is consistent with other security objectives*]

- Facilitates the transfer of both knowledge and skills from the heads of workers into more permanent repositories such as database management systems, groupware systems, document management systems, and knowledge management systems [*The effort associated with the transfer of non-computerized information into computerized systems is a major cultural shift for organizations and it has significant implications in terms of information security policies, such as restricting information based on the need to know*]

- Strategizes, plans, evaluates, and assists with the integration of Company X's disparate information systems, networks, and information collections [*Rationalizing and integrating islands of information is a very important task, especially at large organizations, and the effort has major implications for information security; for example, the matching of information from two separate databases might constitute a privacy violation*]

- Acts as the primary liaison between Company X and external providers of knowledge and skills so that these transfers are rationalized, streamlined, economized, and properly secured [*The person acting in this inter-organizational information management role must be cognizant of many information security issues such as exactly what constitutes a copyright infringement*]

CHIEF PRIVACY OFFICER

Job Title: Chief Privacy Officer (CPO) [*Occasionally called a Freedom Of Information And Privacy Protection Officer; note that this job title would ordinarily exist only in those organizations which have significant reputation risks associated with privacy violation, and/or those organizations which have significant privacy-related legal/regulatory requirements which must be observed; this person may be simply called a Privacy Officer*]

Department: Legal

Reports To: Chief Legal Counsel [*No standard chain of command exists for a CPO; alternatively the CPO could report to the CEO, the Ethics Officer, the Marketing Department Manager, or the Compliance Department Manager (the Compliance Department could be a smaller department associated with, or within the Legal Department)*]

Reponsibilities And Duties In Information Security:

- Investigates Company X's current and proposed policies, procedures, strategies, forms, notices, and practices related to the handling of personal and private information, and makes proposals to streamline, coordinate, rationalize, and improve these same activities [*This handling should include Company X information in the hands of third parties, and third party information in the possession of Company X*]

- Develops, or assists in the development of, documentation of organization-wide privacy-related policies, procedures, strategies, and practices, and also acts as the primary promoter of these same policies and procedures with top management [*This work would ordinarily involve close involvement with the Information Security Department Manager, the Internal Intellectual Property Attorney, and the Internal Audit Department Manager*]

- Assists internal units by providing consulting advice whenever staff are attempting to implement or otherwise come into compliance with privacy requirements [*This compliance assistance may include working with outsiders such as outsourcing firm staff; note that the CPO should not do compliance reviews, this should be left to the Internal Audit Department*]

- Assists business associates, such as outsourcing firms, in their efforts to improve the privacy protections applied to private data which has been provided by Company X [*This responsibility might be altered to refer to "private data for which Company X is responsible"*]

- Trains employees, contractors, consultants, temporaries and other members of the Company X information security team about privacy and how to achieve and maintain it

- Acts as the internal and external primary point-of-contact on all matters related privacy requirements [*Serving on the Information Security Management Committee may be one of the ways in which a CPO acts as a point of contact; some organizations have even established a Privacy Oversight Committee, which is very much like an Information Security Management Committee, but with a very restricted scope; see Chapter 11 for more information about these committees.*]

- Monitors existing and proposed regulations and legislation related to privacy and alerts management to the implications of these requirements [*This is a giant task, and it is especially challenging for those organizations with international operations and/or Internet commerce sites*]

- Periodically delivers reports to both top management and the Board of Directors Audit Committee about privacy requirements that the organization faces, how well the organization is doing in terms of meeting these requirements, and what privacy-related problems need management's attention and resources [*Note that nowhere in this job description does the CPO's job get restricted to internal data; externally-supplied personal data could be entrusted to Company X, in which case the CPO would need to help look after the privacy of that data as well*]

- Monitors Company X's privacy-related performance in terms of existing legal contracts, laws, regulations, policies, public representations, and standard industry practices; and then regularly informs management about Company X's status [*A great deal of personal information (such as a list of people who bought certain products) is shared between companies these days, and there are typically restrictive agreements on the use of that information; it is the CPO's job to monitor whether Company X is consistently in compliance with these contractual terms and conditions (the Information Systems Auditor should also provide a double check on the CPO's work in this area); some organizations will want to expand the CPO's work in this area to monitor business partners who are in possession of Company X information of a personal or private nature*]

- Monitors trading partners, business associates, outsourcing firms, and other third parties which are in possession of Company X private information to establish whether they are in compliance with both Company X privacy policies, and also the requirements of laws and regulations [*Fixing these problems with third parties is not the CPO's job; the CPO should also hire external auditors, or use internal auditors, to actually do the compliance checking of third parties*]

- Spearheads internal efforts to reassure customers and other data subjects that their personal data will be adequately protected, and where necessary, initiates communications with these same data subjects [*An example of a data subject who is not a customer would be a consumer whose credit and payment history is stored by, and distributed by, a credit bureau*]

- Serves as a primary point-of-contact and a primary investigator in those cases where a privacy-related complaint has been brought against Company X and the way that it handled private or personal data [*The complaint resolution process would involve the Internal Intellectual Property Attorney if it entailed a violation of a law or regulation; some organizations claim that the CPO is an ombudsman for the independent resolution of a complaint, but realistically the CPO cannot play this role because the CPO is an employee of one of the parties to the dispute, and is therefore not truly independent*]

- Establishes, administers, and oversees a business process for collecting, documenting, tracking, investigating, and resolving complaints about privacy

- Reviews all major feasibility studies, project plans, and project proposals that deal with production information system enhancements and expansions, to ensure that these studies, plans, and proposals include adequate privacy control measures

- Represents Company X's privacy interests with external parties, such as government agencies and industry standards making committees, when these parties undertake efforts to adopt/amend privacy legislation, regulations, or standards [*This representation may include lawmaker lobbying as well as giving testimony in hearings about privacy*]

- Prepares the draft version of official reports and government forms, when required, if these reports and forms deal with the privacy of personal data held by Company X [*Note that the approval of these reports and forms will probably be provided by someone else, such as the Intellectual Property Attorney and/or the Chief Information Officer*]

CHIEF GOVERNANCE OFFICER

Job Title: Chief Governance Officer (CGO) [*Occasionally called Vice President - Corporate Governance or Corporate Governance Officer; in some cases this job is being added to the existing duties of Corporate Secretary*]

Department: Legal

Reports To: Chief Executive Officer (CEO)

Reponsibilities And Duties In Information Security:

- Investigates how the organization is run and makes recommendations to top management to improve internal controls, checks and balances, transparency and appropriate disclosure, and the like [*In the course of performing this task, the CGO may review the current status of information security, and then determine that the function is not as effective as it could be; thus the CGO could be an important ally in the restructuring of the information security function, for example, elevating the Information Security Department Manager in the management hierarchy*]

- Works with top management to identify and change existing conflicts of interest, and establishes permanent organizational structures intended to prevent these and other conflicts from occurring in the future [*These conflicts not only involve personal worker objectives versus organizational objectives, they also involve the ways that certain organizational structures impede the effectiveness of certain organizational units; for example, if the Information Security Department Manager reports to the CIO, this will blunt the effectiveness of the information security function because the CIO then has conflicting objectives*]

- Reviews executive compensation, communications with shareholders, relationships with government regulators, the Board of Directors nomination process, the Board member reelection process, and related activities to identify governance issues and concerns, and then brings these same matters to the attention to both top management and the Board of Directors, suggesting appropriate remedies and responses [*This will typically involve an examination of certain threats such as insider trading of stock and breach of management's fiduciary duties*]

- Acts as a liaison with the public, the investor community, and the stock analyst community, conveying information about Company X's internal governance efforts, and helping to reassure these communities that Company X is well-managed [*This task puts the CGO in a position where he or she touts the organization's internal control structures, and information security is one of those structures*]

- Follows the latest developments in organizational governance and makes suggestions to top management if some of these developments appear to be applicable to Company X [*This effort would further help ensure that Company X is run in a manner in keeping with the legal notion of the "standard of due care"*]

- Benchmarks the organization's performance vis-à-vis other organizations in the same industry, and reports to management on the current status of organizational governance [*One data point in this benchmarking process is a code of conduct; note that the CGO could write the code, or it could be done by an Ethics Officer*]

CHIEF SECURITY OFFICER

Job Title: Chief Security Officer (CSO) [*Note that the CSO title implies different things based on industry; in a high-tech firm, the title may be the same as or similar to the Information Security Department Manager, whereas in other industries, the title often refers to a higher level manager to whom the Information Security Department Manager and the Physical Security Department Manager both report*]

Department: Insurance And Risk Management

Reports To: Chief Executive Officer (CEO) [*Sometimes reports to the Chief Operating Officer (COO); to report to the Chief Information Officer (CIO) would be a conflict because the CSO coordinates risk assessments which would potentially be less than complimentary about the performance of a CIO*]

Responsibilities Related To Information Security:

- Designs, promotes, and assists with the implementation of organization-wide security solutions which align the business objectives of Company X with its information technology infrastructure, its physical infrastructure, and its human resources

- Develops plans, goals, objectives, service level agreements (SLAs) and other project management aids for the coordination of all security efforts throughout the organization in a manner which is fully in support of business strategies, goals, and objectives

- Uses an integrated risk management approach to create executive level perspectives on, and status reports about, all of the security risks that Company X faces, including risks in the physical security, information security, human resources safety, facilities security, and contingency planning domains [*A member of the senior management team, the CSO must be articulate and persuasive, and additionally able to communicate technical matters in terms that top management can understand and support*]

- Champions the contribution to be made to Company X goals and objectives by information security and other new security disciplines, new security technologies, and new management thinking in the security field [*If your organization has no CSO, then the role of management champion for information security may be performed by the Chief Information Officer if and when an Information Security Department reports to the CIO; but as noted above, due to conflict of interest reasons, this organizational reporting relationship is not advisable*]

- Acts as the primary change agent who facilitates improvements in organizational design, organizational culture, business relationships, and other matters so long as these improve the security posture of Company X [*The Information Security Management Committee is one vehicle through which the CSO could perform this work*]

- o Oversees an organizational network of security staff which safeguards Company X's assets such as its intellectual property, computer networks, buildings, motor vehicles, employees, and visitors [*Some of these staff could be outsourced - for example, building guards are often provided by an outside company*]

- Represents the security interests of Company X in public forums such as industry professional association committees, hearings of government bodies, and industry standard setting groups

- Acts as the primary external contact person on matters related to security, maintaining good working relationships with local, state, and federal law enforcement agencies, as well as other government agencies concerned with security matters

- Spearheads the investigation of security breaches such as computer system intrusions, and acts as the primary contact point with outsiders about these same incidents

- Orchestrates integrated contingency planning and business resumption efforts throughout Company X so that all such efforts are truly responsive to Company X needs

- Arranges the work of, supervises the engagements of, and communicates the results of projects conducted by, outside security auditors and consultants (the primary objective of this work is to double-check the work of internal staff attending to security matters)

HUMAN RESOURCES DEPARTMENT MANAGER

Job Title: Human Resources Department Manager
Department: Human Resources
Reports To: Operations Vice President

Responsibilities And Duties In Information Security:

- Working in conjunction with other members of the top management team, defines and periodically revises a code of conduct for all workers [*This code often addresses a number of information security issues such as use of Company X information for personal purposes, right to know certain information (such as workplace hazards), and freedom of speech; alternatively, an Internal Control Committee may develop a code of conduct (see Chapter 11 for further details); if this Manager doesn't perform this job, it may be done by an Ethics Officer.*]

- Establishes, documents, and supervises the equitable application of a disciplinary process that has progressively more severe penalties for those who are not in compliance with internal policies, standards, and other requirements [*This can and should be used for information security policies, standards, and other requirements*]

- Supervises and/or participates in any major staffing decisions such as the duress termination of an employee [*This is where somebody is fired and escorted off the premises immediately when a serious offense is discovered and shown to be caused by the involved worker*] or the layoff of a group of workers [*A variety of information security issues are triggered by these personnel actions; these include retaliation against Company X by a terminated employee*]

- Establishes and supervises the use of a process for screening prospective workers to make sure that they are suitable employees prior to actually extending an offer of employment (or signing a consulting or contracting agreement) [*Contingent offers of employment can be extended, if the offer may be withdrawn due to the discovery of previously undisclosed negative information; this screening process may alternatively be done by the Physical Security Department*]

- Provides top management with observations about and suggestions for the evolution of organizational culture [*This area is sometimes called corporate culture rather than organizational culture; this task includes some information security issues such as the openness with which information flows between individuals*]

HUMAN RESOURCES CONSULTANT

Job Title: Human Resources Consultant
Department: Human Resources
Reports To: Human Resources Department Manager

Responsibilities And Duties In Information Security:

- Periodically reviews organizational culture and the ways that this culture supports or interferes with the accomplishment of business goals and objectives [*This culture review may uncover a problem with existing incentive systems, such that information security is compromised in favor of competing objectives*]

- Maintains the human resources database so that it accurately reflects the current status of all workers including full- and part-time employees, consultants, contractors, temporaries, and outsourcing firm personnel [*This database is increasingly being used as the source of input for computer access control systems, computer based training (CBT) systems, electronic mail systems, etc.*]

- Communicates all departures from Company X immediately to the Physical Security Department Manager, Access Control System Administrators, Systems/Network Administrators, Web/Commerce Site Administrators, Receptionists, Guards, and others with a need to know [*This will allow privileges to be revoked before fired or laid-off employees engage in vengeful acts*]

- Performs exit interviews for selected employee departures, and during those interviews-or immediately afterwards-recovers Company X property in the possession of departing workers [*This property includes portable computers, palmtop computers, pagers, cellular phones, and company credit cards; exit interviews may also reveal security problems such as an on-going fraud being perpetrated in the departing worker's department*]

- Checks the employment history, academic credentials, references, and other personal details associated with prospective workers (employees, contractors, and consultants) so that only appropriate people are working at Company X [*This activity may alternatively be performed by the Physical Security Department*]

- Performs special in-depth background checks prior to employment for those applicants seeking positions that entail access to sensitive Company X information, and/or provide powerful information systems privileges that could be used to disrupt or otherwise damage Company X business operations [*This activity may alternatively be performed by the Physical Security Department*]

- In conjunction with the Internal Intellectual Property Attorney, interprets privacy laws and regulations and submits suggested changes in internal systems and procedures to the Human Resources Department Manager as well as the Information Security Department Manager [*This task may alternatively be done by a Chief Privacy Officer*]

- Prepares government reports indicating compliance with human resources laws and regulations such as affirmative action, trans-border data flows (and other privacy regulations), and employee access privileges to their own records

- Administers worker counseling programs, short-term loan programs, and other employee benefits [*These will help prevent or alleviate problems that may, if not handled appropriately, later show up as computer crimes*]

RECEPTIONIST

Job Title: Receptionist
Department: Human Resources
Reports To: Human Resources Department Manager

[*A Receptionist is generally used to greet visitors in low security environments while Building And Facilities Guards are generally used for this purpose in high security environments; Receptionists can also be used to establish and maintain physically protected areas (like an executive suite) inside the outside perimeter maintained by Building And Facilities Guards*]

Responsibilities And Duties In Information Security:

- Politely greets all people who are not authorized Company X workers (employees, contractors, consultants, temporaries, etc.), who seek to enter Company X offices, and then asks them to wait in the lobby until an escort takes them into a restricted access area [*If outsiders are permitted to have physical access to information and information systems, security will be noticeably degraded*]

- Signs for packages in the lobby and otherwise keeps delivery personnel and other third parties out of Company X offices unless they are escorted by an authorized Company X worker

- Recognizes all parties wishing to gain access to Company X buildings and facilities, and if the person is unknown, asks this person to provide proper identification before he or she is permitted access to restricted access areas [*This low security approach is appropriate for smaller offices that do not require picture ID badges to be worn at all times*]

- Notifies local police, local ambulance services, local rescue services, and a local fire department as needed according to procedures defined by the Physical Security Department Manager [*Computer crimes should be reported to criminal justice authorities only after the approval of the Internal Intellectual Property Attorney and the Information Security Department Manager have been obtained*]

- Immediately notifies the Physical Security Department Manager and other designated members of the Company X management team of any activity or condition that could reasonably be expected to lead to a loss for Company X (for example, smoking in areas where combustible materials are stored)

- Provides telephone switchboard operator services to connect callers with authorized Company X workers in a manner that is consistent with information security policies (without disclosing private or confidential information, such as the home telephone numbers of employees) [*The Receptionist may also detect and report to the Information Security Department Manager those people who are attempting to use social engineering (also known as spoofing) to gain access to confidential information*]

OUTSOURCING CONTRACT ADMINISTRATOR

Job Title: Outsourcing Contract Administrator
Department: Human Resources
Reports To: Human Resources Department Manager

Responsibilities And Duties In Information Security:

- Maintains an organized collection of all contracts with outsourcing firms, facilities management firms, and other third parties retained by Company X to perform services on an ongoing basis [*Security requirements should be written into these contracts; see Chapter 17."*]

- Monitors the performance of outsourcing firms, facilities management firms, and other third parties to ensure that they meet the terms and conditions stipulated in the relevant contracts [*This includes receiving reports about the status of security and any incidents that took place*]

- Schedules periodic audits of outsourcing firms, facilities management firms, and other third parties to ensure that these organizations are living up to the terms and conditions specified in the relevant contracts

- Negotiates initial contracts, and renegotiates existing contracts when these contracts expire, with outsourcing firms, facilities management firms, and other third parties, to help ensure that essential Company X requirements are included in all contracts [*This would typically include service level agreements (SLAs), which in part should address security, such as how long will it take before an outsourcing firm will respond to a break-in by a hacker*]

- Establishes and periodically convenes advisory committees (made up of selected Company X employees) that provide advice regarding the use of outsourcing firms, facilities management firms, and other third parties [*The Information Security Department Manager would typically sit on these committees*]

- Performs due diligence investigations of outsourcing firms, facilities management firms, and other third parties that Company X is considering for the performance of critical Company X business activities [*This includes reference checks, review of financial condition, determination whether third-party staff have necessary knowledge and skills; see Chapter 17 for an extended list of these efforts*].

- Establishes efficient and effective communications channels with staff at outsourcing firms, facilities management firms, and other third parties working on behalf of Company X [*The Contract Administrator may or may not be a liaison; these communications channels should include a Computer Emergency Response Team, also known as a CERT (see the mission statement in Chapter 11 for a "Computer Emergency Response Team" for a full definition); these communication channels should also include privilege change processes, as well as problem reporting and resolution processes*]

- Advises user department managers, Human Resources Department staff, and other internal workers about the laws and regulations which pertain to the retention of outsourcing firms, consulting firms, etc. [*These laws and regulations involve some information security issues such as whether a third-party computer programmer's work is a "work for hire" and is therefore the property of the programmer or the property of the hiring firm*]

IN-HOUSE TRAINER

Job Title: In-House Trainer
Department: Human Resources
Reports To: Human Resources Department Manager

Responsibilities And Duties In Information Security:

- In conjunction with the Information Security Department Manager, designs, develops, and measures the effectiveness of information security training and awareness material provided to new hires, employees, contractors, consultants, and others who have access to sensitive information or information systems

- Conducts orientation classes to familiarize newly-hired workers with the various departments within Company X, the roles and responsibilities of each department, and the organizational culture [*This class should let new hires know who to contact in case there is an information security problem, how top management perceives information security (assuming they are serious), etc.*]

- Working with the Information Technology Department, provides ongoing information systems training so that workers can best utilize the available tools and technologies [*This activity is often outsourced to a training company; separately, the intention is to empower users to be able to spot problems such as virus infections and to then take appropriate action*]

- Researches new tools and methods for delivering training to Company X employees and makes suggestions for use of these new tools and methods as appropriate (these methods include computer based training or CBT) [*An intranet is one of the most cost-effective ways to deliver information security training*]

- Periodically conducts needs analyses to determine what types of training workers need in order to accomplish organizational objectives [*In many cases, this activity will include a determination that workers need more information security training and awareness material; some new CBT systems allow organizations to automatically test their worker's knowledge of policies and other security requirements*]

INSURANCE AND RISK MANAGEMENT DEPARTMENT MANAGER

Job Title: Insurance and Risk Management Department Manager
Department: Insurance and Risk Management
Reports To: Chief Operating Officer (COO)

Responsibilities And Duties In Information Security:

- Fosters an integrated risk management approach that generates periodic reports showing the nature of Company X's exposure across departments such as Finance, Information Technology, Physical Security, Legal, and Human Resources

- Coordinates business contingency planning and information systems contingency planning efforts so that an integrated contingency planning effort addresses all areas critical to Company X's business

- Remains familiar with the latest mechanisms to reduce risk, and transfer risk away from Company X, and also engages top management in a discussion about the suitability of these mechanisms where appropriate [*One example is insurance against Internet commerce credit card fraud*]

- Acts as a liaison with insurance companies for the determination of the adequacy of coverage, the acquisition of various types of insurance, as well as processing of claims [*Insurance against information security problems such as credit card fraud would be handled by this manager*]

INSURANCE AND RISK MANAGEMENT ANALYST

Job Title: Insurance and Risk Management Analyst
Department: Insurance and Risk Management
Reports To: Insurance and Risk Management Department Manager

Responsibilities And Duties In Information Security:

- Based on risk assessments or information systems audit reports, determines the nature and extent of the perils faced by Company X in the information systems area [*These perils include fraud facilitated by information systems and interruption of business activities due to information systems unavailability*]

- In conjunction with the Physical Security and Information Security Department Managers, monitors loss experience in the information systems area, including privacy violations, credit card fraud, and equipment theft

- Periodically reviews insurance coverage to determine whether Company X is adequately insured against information systems risks such as errors and omissions, business interruption, credit card fraud, identity theft, industrial espionage, equipment theft, and information systems sabotage

- Manages claims with insurance companies including the preparation of adequate loss reporting documentation, and descriptions of actions taken to prevent a similar loss [*These activities may be undertaken for computer crimes and other information security related incidents*]

BUSINESS CONTINGENCY PLANNER

Job Title: Business Contingency Planner
Department: Insurance and Risk Management
Reports To: Insurance and Risk Management Department Manager

Responsibilities And Duties In Information Security:

- Researches and stays abreast of all major threats that could impact Company X's business activities including mergers/acquisitions, earthquakes, and changes in economic conditions [*Some of this research may also be performed by a strategic*

planner; this research is important input to a risk assessment*]

- Performs periodic business impact analyses (BIAs) which examine the potential problems that would be caused by earthquakes, floods, bomb explosions, and other serious perils associated with business resources at Company X

- Prepares budgets, cost/benefit analyses, and other financial evaluations of the currently available business contingency planning options

- Evaluates commercially-available contingency planning tools, such as those that run on a desktop computer, and makes recommendations about the packages that would best support Company X's business contingency planning efforts

- Conducts periodic benchmarking studies or baseline controls comparison projects to determine where Company X stands, when it comes to business contingency planning, vis-à-vis other organizations in the same industry

- Assists with the development and refinement of conceptual and organizational structures (such as a business application criticality ranking criteria and a management escalation procedure) which help to ensure that Company X is prepared for various threat events

- Develops and maintains up-to-date and practical contingency plans which assist Company X in quickly restoring operations after an emergency or a disaster that affects centralized multi-departmental business resources, such as office buildings

- Develops, implements, and refines management decision-making processes that facilitate a rapid and appropriate response to business emergencies and disasters [*A problem escalation process would be an example of this type of decision-making process*]

- Trains user department staff in the proper use of contingency planning documentation relevant to business resources

- Develops methodologies and instructional material that assist Company X workers in preparing their own business contingency plans to deal with decentralized or single department business resources, such as a remote sales office

- Provides expert technical assistance related to contingency planning to departments throughout Company X who are preparing, testing, and updating their own contingency plans for decentralized or single department business resources

- Reviews the business contingency plans developed by departments and other organizational units to ensure that they meet Company X standards, and also to ensure that they have integrated all applicable Company X contingency planning practices

- Compiles status information reflecting the completeness, accuracy, effectiveness, efficiency, and currency of business contingency plans at Company X, and then periodically communicates this information to management

- Plans, supervises, participates in, and reports to management on the success of a variety of tests to business contingency plans

- Assists with the establishment of practical and integrated organization-wide contingency plans which combine information systems contingency plans with business contingency plans

- Develops customized damage assessment and reporting methods to be used after a business emergency or disaster, and periodically performs "post mortems" to determine the degree to which these methods are accurate and useful

- Assists with business loss event related insurance claim investigations that are necessary in order for Company X to receive the proceeds from insurance policies

- Attends several conferences or training seminars per year to become acquainted with the latest tools and techniques for business contingency planning

- Coordinates business contingency planning efforts with the Information Systems Contingency Planner's activities

PUBLIC RELATIONS MANAGER

Job Title: Public Relations Manager
Department: Public Relations
Reports To: Marketing Vice President (sometimes called Chief Marketing Officer)

Responsibilities And Duties In Information Security:

- Acts as a spokesperson or relay person for all news media communications including those occasioned by disasters, lawsuits, and interruptions in the provision of Company X products or services [*This could, in certain instances, include hacker break-ins, information systems outages, and other information security problems*]

- Coaches and trains internal management staff so that they may appropriately represent Company X in professional society conferences, television shows, newspaper story interviews, and the like [*It is important that management not inadvertently disclose sensitive information, unwittingly make the organization look bad, or otherwise appear to be uninformed or unprofessional*]

- Acts as the manager of the Web Site Committee, and in this capacity leads others in the establishment of checks and balances to ensure that all postings to the Company X Internet web site are professionally presented and consistent with existing presentation standards [*Standards for posting material on the web site or commerce site can include information security requirements; see the Web Site Committee mission statement in Chapter 11.*]

- Works with the Information Security Department Manager, the Physical Security Department Manager, and other members of the management team to identify when customers and other constituencies should be notified about internal problems

- Develops scripted pre-written responses to disasters, emergencies, and other major events which need to be communicated to the public, to customers, and to other significant constituencies of Company X [*This work proceeds with the Public Relations Manager acting as the primary coordinator of discussions through which scripts are developed; the Public Relations Manager works in this case in conjunction with the Information Security Department Manager, the Physical Security Department Manager, and other members of the management team*]

- Monitors Internet on-line chat sessions, Internet web pages, and other electronic and paper-based public forums to ensure that the good name of Company X is not being denigrated or eroded, and where necessary, take appropriate actions on behalf of Company X [*This increasingly important function may be outsourced or approached with special-purpose Internet search tools*]

CHIEF FINANCIAL OFFICER

Job Title: Chief Financial Officer
Department: Accounting & Finance
Reports To: Chief Executive Officer

Responsibilities And Duties In Information Security:

- Establishes and maintains a system of internal controls that accurately keeps track of transactions, and that fairly represents the financial status of Company X [*These internal controls include mechanisms which support information security*]

- Arranges the annual engagement of external auditors who examine the financial records of Company X [*The external auditors often provide a management letter that includes information security suggestions*]

- Establishes internal financial accounting systems that provide incentives for, and information about, the attainment of Company X goals and objectives [*A charge back system for information systems usage would be one such system, but information security consulting and related services should not be charged back to user departments because this would discourage usage; in this respect the CFO is in charge of changing incentive systems, such as bonus structures, to encourage the achievement of an appropriate level of information security; see Appendix C for further discussion*]

PURCHASING AGENT

Job Title: Purchasing Agent
Department: Accounting & Finance
Reports To: Chief Financial Officer

Responsibilities And Duties In Information Security:

Negotiates volume purchase agreements (VPAs) and other discount arrangements with software vendors, information content vendors, and other third parties in a manner that is practical from an operational standpoint, fully in keeping with applicable laws and regulations, and fully in compliance with the vendor's terms and conditions [*The Purchasing Agent can assist with software licensing and related information security matters*]

Screens all major information, software, hardware, and telecommunications equipment purchases to ensure that these are in compliance with established internal standards (such as the Desktop Configuration Standard issued by the Information Technology Department) and to block those purchases that are not consistent with standards unless a waiver has been granted by the

Purchasing Department Manager [*This approach will only be practical if local departments do not have the authority to independently purchase their own information systems hardware and software; some organizations may wish to delete the word "major" from the first line of this paragraph*]

Makes sure that all necessary paperwork for major acquisitions has been prepared prior to generating a purchase order or otherwise making any commitment to a vendor [*This paperwork, for information systems acquisitions, could include a risk assessment as part of the systems development process*]

Ensures that contracts with outsourcing firms, consultants, and contractors and other third parties include confidentiality agreements, agreements not to compete, and other legal requirements

CHIEF EXECUTIVE OFFICER

Job Title: Chief Executive Officer
Department: Executive Management
Reports To: Board of Directors

Responsibilities And Duties In Information Security:

- Establishes new organizational units and alters the functions performed by existing organizational units so that Company X can best respond to current and anticipated business needs [*This includes setting up an Information Security Department*]

- Directs others to establish and operate control systems that safeguard organizational assets from material loss and ensure that workers are following policies, standards, procedures, and other management directives [*The CEO is ultimately responsible for allocating sufficient resources for information security, as well as giving it the attention it deserves*]

- Directs others to establish and operate a system of accounting-related internal controls that accurately keeps track of transactions and fairly represents the financial status of Company X [*These internal controls include information security*]

- Reviews the decisions made by line managers to ensure that these decisions are consistent with both the business's strategic direction and internal control requirements [*In this respect, the CEO must make sure that managers are following the CEO's instructions in various areas, including information security*]

- Envisions the organizational culture and communicates this new culture to those who work at Company X [*One part of this new corporate culture should be valuing the security and privacy of information*]

- Provides clearly evident support and encouragement for those working on critical business activities [*Such as information security initiatives*]

- Sets the moral and ethical tone for Company X operations and as such is expected to operate with the utmost integrity in both business and personal areas [*For example, if the CEO isn't wearing his or her identification badge, the rest of the organization isn't going to be taking security seriously either*]

ജ്ഞെ‌യ്‌ഞ

Chapter 13 INFORMATION SECURITY REPORTING RELATIONSHIPS

This chapter covers the generally-accepted and frequently-encountered reporting relationships for an Information Security Department. The pros and cons of twelve options are explored and six reporting relationships are recommended. Because there are many places in the organizational hierarchy where an Information Security Department could be situated, you should review the list of pros and cons for each option, thinking about what is most important in your organization. You are urged to read this chapter in the hardcopy book with highlighter, pen, or pencil to indicate relevant objectives for the reporting relationship. You should then summarize these considerations in a memo, and after this memo is prepared, you will most likely be leaning in the direction of one of the six recommended reporting relationships. At that point in time, a clear and well-justified proposal for an Information Security Department reporting relationship can be formulated.

In any discussion about reporting relationships it is important to, first and foremost, recognize the existence of a separate information security group, generally called a department or unit. To have an information security function remain an embedded part of the Information Technology Department, or any other department for that matter, is to downplay its importance to the business and to force it to fit in with other functions that will often perform inconsistent and incompatible activities. An information security group is an important and different organizational function which needs to be separately distinguished with its own group name, its own group identity, and its own group mission statement (see Chapter 11 for an example). After management has agreed that an information security group should be a separately-recognized organizational entity, then you can have a more meaningful conversation with management about where it should report within the organization.

A good place to start a discussion about reporting relationships is to find a common characteristic of nearly every successful Information Security Department's organizational structure. In these successful organizational structures, the Department reports high-up in the management hierarchy. Reporting directly to a top manager is advisable for the Information Security Department Manager because it fosters objectivity and the ability to perceive what's truly in the

best interest of the organization as a whole, rather than what's in the best interest of a particular department (such as the Information Technology Department). A highly-placed executive in charge of information security will also be more readily able to gain top management's attention, and this in turn will increase the likelihood that the Information Security Department will obtain the necessary budget and staffing resources. An Information Security Department that reports high up on the management ladder will also be more readily able to force compliance with certain requirements such as a standard specifying consistent implementation of certain encryption technology.

In an increasing number of progressive organizations, being located high on the management ladder means that the Information Security Department Manager is a Senior Vice President who reports directly to the Chief Executive Officer (CEO). This is, for example, the organizational structure now found at a well-known credit card company. Those organizations which are less dependent on highly-visible and absolutely impecable information security will typically have the Information Security Department Manager reporting further down on the organizational ladder. Nonetheless, in the latter organizations, having an Information Security Department Manager who reports directly to the CEO may be appropriate for a short while until major improvements in the information security area have been made. This temporary reporting structure clearly communicates that information security is important and worthy of top management's attention.

Before you conclude that such a high-ranking reporting relationship is just a dream for your organization, consider that some 32% of over 1,000 respondents to an August 2002 survey conducted by CSO Magazine (the article was entitled "The Evolution Of the Chief Security Officer") indicated that they held senior-level titles such as vice president or Chief Security Officer. Of the survey respondents, some 17% indicated that they reported directly to the CEO or president. While only 40% of the respondents said their sole duty was information security, this is still good news indicating that information security is increasingly being elevated in the management hierarchy. Reflecting this same notion, in April of 2001, Gartner published another report predicting that fully half of the Fortune 2000 companies would establish a Chief Information Security Officer who had executive level responsibilities by the year 2004.

Nonetheless, for a medium to large-scale organization, the most common reporting structure involves one or two levels of management between the Information Security Department Manager and the CEO. In general, the smaller the number of intermediate levels of management, the greater the strategic importance of the information security function. Nonetheless, it is important that the distance between the CEO and the Information Security Department Manager be minimized. As famous management theorist Peter F. Drucker has observed, every time you insert another level of management in an organization's hierarchy, the noise is doubled and the message is cut in half. An information security function already has a difficult time delivering its new and different message to top management, so having a long line of intermediate managers will only make this more difficult.

Just who the middle managers between the Information Security Department Manager and the CEO should be is the topic of great debate. One perspective on this troublesome question is opportunistic, looking to see who these individuals are, rather than what their currently-assigned duties happen to be. With this perspective, you would choose, as your allies, sympathetic executives who understand the need for information security and are willing to fight for the necessary funds when departmental budgets are prepared. If you are establishing an information security function for the first time, or if a major reorganization is underway, you should seriously think about which middle managers would best serve as the conduit for messages sent to the CEO. Other desirable attributes are:

- openness to new ideas

- clout with top management

- respect in the eyes of a wide variety of employees

- comfort and familiarity with basic information systems concepts

- willingness to take a stand for those things that are genuinely in the long-term best interest of the organization

The ideal middle level manager, to whom you may wish to have the Information Security Department Manager report, should report directly to the CEO, or as high-up on the organizational hierarchy as possible. This middle level manager's organizational unit will also need a credible day-to-day relationship with, or a strategic tie-in with, the information security function. For example, a Risk And Insurance Management Department would have such a tie-in, but an Assembly Line Operations Department most often would not. The candidates are many, but some common choices are: the Executive Vice President Administrative Services, the Legal Department Manager (Chief Legal Officer), and the Chief Information Officer (CIO). The pros and cons of these and other options are discussed below.

This chapter makes reference to six diagrams labeled Option 1 through Option 6. These six reporting relationships are explored in that sequence. After that, six other options, which are not as frequently encountered, are then discussed. The six diagrams are illustrative of real-world organizations and are not in any way meant to be hypothetical or normative. Throughout this book, the author has attempted to be descriptive rather than to propose a new paradigm, and in that respect, because these options are based on real-world experience, you can be assured that any one of these six initial options could be effective within your organization. The diagrams are also meant to convey an indication of good practice on which you can rely. The fact that there are so many reporting options for information security reflect the fact that this is still a relatively new organizational function, and that most organizations are still tinkering with the function, trying to determine where best it should permanently reside.

Option 1: Information Technology

In the Option 1 diagram, you will note that in this organizational structure the Information Security Department reports to the Information Technology Department (the latter may also be called the Data Processing Department, the Information Services Department, or the Management Information Systems Department). Here the Information Security Department Manager reports directly to the Chief Information Officer (CIO), the Chief Technology Officer (CTO), or perhaps to the Vice President of Information Systems. In this option, you will find the most common organizational structure. Various statistical studies show that about 25% of organizations use this type of reporting relationship. This option is desirable because the manager to whom the Information Security Department Manager reports generally has clout with top management, and understands (in broad and general terms) various information systems technological issues. This option is also advantageous because it typically involves only one manager between the Information Security Department Manager and the Chief Executive Officer (CEO) - generally the CIO. The option is additionally attractive because the Information Security Department staff, on a day-to-day basis, must spend a good deal of time with the Information Technology Department staff. In that respect, this option is convenient, and it also allows information security staff and information technology staff to be readily aware of what the other is doing. Likewise, the Information Technology Department creates and operates information systems technological infrastructure, and the Information Security Department does the same, so there is some consistency in the nature of the work that is done.

Nonetheless, in spite of these advantages, this option is flawed because it includes an inherent conflict of interest. When confronted with resource allocation decisions, or when required to make tradeoffs, the CIO is likely to discriminate against the information security function. In these cases, other objectives such as cost minimization, enhanced user friendliness, or rapid time-to-market with a new product or service, will likely take precedence over information security. This conflict of interest is also evident in those not-hard-to-imagine situations where the Information Security Department Manager notices that the CIO instructs staff to do something that violates information security policies and standards. Under the latter circumstances, what should the Information Security Department Manager do? Confronting his or her boss could be a dangerous career move, but not confronting the boss would be bad for information security. Similarly, if security is breached when this reporting relationship exists, the CIO may be tempted to withhold this information from top management rather than pass it along, lest top management get the impression that the IT Department is doing a poor job.

Another drawback of this option involves the implied conclusion that information security is strictly a technological issue, which clearly it is not. Information security involves protecting information in all forms, including information in paper records and embedded in physical products, and these and several other areas where information resides are clearly outside the scope of influence of the Information Technology Department. Reflecting this broader mission for an information security function, it is important to note that modern information security has become a multi-disciplinary and multi-organizational effort, an effort which requires diplomatic coalition building, and at times this is more

important than technological expertise. To be successful, an information security function must bring together people from many other departments including Human Resources, Legal, Risk Management, Ethics, and Internal Audit. To be able to do this effectively, the information security function needs to be removed from the Information Technology Department, and the Information Security Department Manager needs to be elevated to a senior management level. Still another reason to get the information security function out of the Information Technology Department involves credibility in the eyes of the rest of the organization, especially the eyes of top management. As long as information security is seen as just another technological specialty, it will be treated as a routine technical matter, like data administration and other information technology sub-specialties. Although being part of the Information Technology Department is common, it is not as desirable as several of the other options listed below, and for that reason is not recommended.

Note that the Option 1 diagram does not have information security reporting to a Computer Operations Manager, the Management Information Systems Manager, the Information Resources Manager, or some other manager who in turn reports to the CIO or the Vice President of Information Systems. This one additional level of middle management can make a world of difference for the Information Security Department. The CIO is dealing with the business uses of information systems, for example, using these systems to achieve strategic advantage. At the same time, the Computer Operations Manager (or perhaps the CTO) is dealing with the bits and bytes of everyday computer operations and related technical matters. The CIO is more removed from the technology and is therefore better able to make appropriate trade-offs between security and competing objectives like response time. In contrast, because that's what he or she knows and is measured by, the Computer Operations Manager (or perhaps the CTO) in many cases will favor response time, ease-of-use, and other technical objectives rather than information security. Having an additional level of management also increases the likelihood that messages sent from the Information Security Department to the CEO will be corrupted in transit (the so-called "whisper down the lane problem"). Other reasons not to pursue this organizational structure are covered in Option 3.

Option 1: Information Security Reports To Information Technology Department

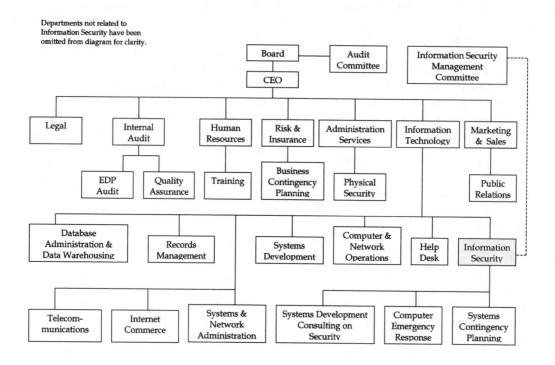

Departments not related to
Information Security have been
omitted from diagram for clarity.

In the Option 1 diagram, you should note that the Information Security Department Manager also has a dotted line reporting relationship with the Information Security Management Committee. Although they are highly recommended, both this dotted line relationship and the Committee can be omitted for smaller organizations. A Committee of this nature is a good idea because it provides a sounding board, a management direction setting body, and a communication path with the rest of the organization. A mission statement for the Information Security Management Committee can be found in Chapter 11. Because this Committee is relevant no matter where the Information Security Department reports, it has been shown on all six diagrams. In fact this Committee is relevant to every one of the options described in this chapter. A drawback of using a committee like this is that it may take longer to get management approval for certain initiatives, but the approval that is obtained is likely to be more lasting and more widely distributed throughout the organization.

As an aside, although it is not shown on the Option 1 diagram, another dotted line reporting relationship, from the Information Security Department Manager to the Board Of Directors Audit Committee, is also recommended. This dotted line relationship provides a way for the Information Security Department Manager to make sure that top management hears his or her

message, even if the chain of managers between the CEO and the Information Security Department Manager is not particularly receptive to this message. The Board Of Directors Audit Committee is discussed further in Chapter 11.

Option 2: Security

Another popular option, which again is not necessarily recommended, involves the Information Security Department Reporting to the Physical Security Department, or to a department which combines both information security and physical security. If the latter option is chosen, the manager of the department may be called the Chief Security Officer (as described in Chapter 12.) In this option, the information security function is perceived to be primarily protective in nature, and therefore comparable to the Physical Security Department as well as the Personnel Safety Department. Where this organizational design prevails, you may occasionally find the Information Security Department is instead referred to as the Information Protection Department. Shown in the Option 2 diagram, this approach is desirable because it facilitates communication with others who have both a security perspective and related security responsibilities. This proximity to physical security staff may help with information security incident investigations as well as reaching practical solutions to problems like laptop computer theft (which involves a combination of physical and information security). This option is also desirable because it brings a longer-term preventive viewpoint to information security activities, which in turn is likely to lower overall information security costs. This option is additionally attractive because many traditional security ideas from the phyiscal security area, like securing the perimeter of an important asset, have been successfully adapted by and applied to the information security field.

One of the most important reasons to adopt this reporting relationship involves management's coordination of activities with other departments involved with asset protection tasks. Because information security is fundamentally a multi-disciplinary field, it can significantly benefit from an organizational structure which acknowledges that it must rely on other related fields in order to be successful. This reporting relationship may thus also help to rationalize and standardize the organization's efforts to deal with all types of asset protection.

Option 2: Information Security Reports To Broadly Defined Security Department

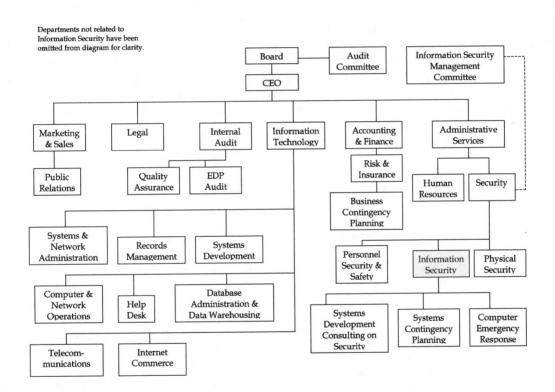

Nonetheless, there are some problems with this structure. Although the information security and physical security functions may at first seem to be philosophically aligned, there is a significant cultural difference between the two. For example, information security staff see themselves as high-tech workers, while physical security staff see themselves as participants in the criminal justice system. These cultural differences may cause some information security specialists to feel that it's not appropriate to be managed by a specialist in physical security, which will often be the background of a combined Security Department Manager. This option is additionally undesirable because, at most firms, the budget for physical security has not increased much over

the last few years, but the budget for information security has rapidly escalated. Thus by combining these two departments under a combined Security Department umbrella, top management may examine historical budget increases and thereby underestimate the resources that the information security function will need. Still worse would the distinct possiblility, with this organizational design, that the Information Security Department's budget should be cut when the overall business suffers a slowdown. Rationalizing that they are simply cutting fixed overhead expenses, management can and often does cut the budget to the Physical Security Department when business is slow, and with this organizational design, this same perspective may then be dangerously transferred to the Information Security Department.

Option 2 is furthermore undesirable because the Security Department Manager will often lack an appreciation of information systems technology, and so may be a poor communicator with top management. This option is furthermore ill-advised because it involves two middle managers in the communication path between the Information Security Department Manager and the CEO. To make it still less appealing, this option is likely to indirectly communicate that the Information Security Department is a new type of police; this perspective will make it more difficult for the Information Security Department to establish consultative relationships with other departments. Another reason why this organizational design may be problematic is that it prevents the Information Security Department from being seen as strategic, instead subtly communicating that the Department is instead just another operational department. To the contrary, the information security function is critical to many industries such as financial services, and if information security is done well, this can confer a strategic advantage. To summarize, this organizational structure is acceptable, but not as desirable as some of the other options described below.

Option 3: Administrative Services

Another way to do things, which is a significant improvement over both Option 1 and 2, is shown in the Option 3 diagram. Here the Information Security Department reports to the Administrative Services Department (which may also be called Administrative Support). In this case, the Information Security Department Manager reports to the Administrative Services Department Manager or the Vice President of Administration. This approach assumes that the Information Security Department is advisory in nature (also called a *staff function*), and performs services for workers throughout the organization, much like the Human Resources Department. When you closely examine what the information security function does (see Chapter 11), you will see that on balance, it provides services and not products. This option is desirable because there is only one middle manager between the Information Security Department Manager and the CEO. The approach is also advisable because it acknowledges that information and information systems are found everywhere throughout the organization, and that workers throughout the organization are expected to work with the Information

Security Department. This option is also attractive because it supports efforts to secure information no matter what form it takes (on paper, verbal, etc.), rather than viewing the information security function as strictly a computer and network oriented activity. This option is additionally recommended because it reflects the fact that information security is a multi-disciplinary function which brings together knowledge from many different areas. Still another reason to recommend this option involves more of a people focus rather than a technology focus. Because this option involves the combination of both Human Resources and Information Security in the same organizational unit, the human factors side of information security (training for example) will be emphasized more than it would be with most other options.

In many cases, depending on who fills the Administrative Services Vice President position, this option suffers because the Vice President doesn't know much about information systems technology, and this in turn may hamper his or her efforts to communicate with the CEO about information security. This option may also be ill-advised for those organizations that could severely suffer, or even go out of business, if major information security problems were encountered. An Internet merchant (a so-called "dot-com" firm) fits this billing. For these firms, this option doesn't give information security the prominence it deserves, nor does it give it the strategic and long-term focus that information security requires. Thus, with this option, the Information Security Department may be subject to more cost-cutting pressure from top management than it would with Option 4 or 5. This may not be an appropriate reporting relationship for your organization because it may subtly communicate that the information security function is primarily clerical or administrative in nature, when in fact there is a great deal of technology involved. On a related note, this organizational design in one way denies information security specialists the opportunity to feel special, to feel proud, to feel like they are futuristic technological priests and priestesses. From a coming to terms with reality perspective, this may be good, but from a personnel recruiting standpoint, this may be bad. On balance though, for organizations that are not highly information intensive, such as a chain of restaurants, this is a desirable and recommended option. For a high-tech firm or a financial institution, this option would downplay the information security function too much, as well as embed it too deeply in the administrative infrastructure.

Option 3: Information Security Reports To Administrative Services Department

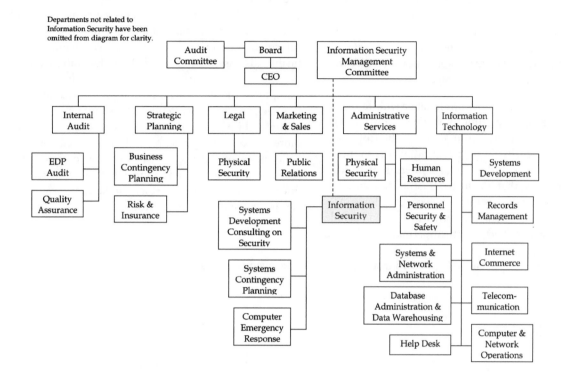

Departments not related to
Information Security have been
omitted from diagram for clarity.

Option 4: Insurance & Risk Management

The Option 4 diagram shows how the Information Security Department can report to the Insurance & Risk Management Department. With this approach, the Information Security Department Manager would typically report to the Chief Risk Manager (CRM) or the Vice President of Risk & Insurance Management. This option is desirable because it fosters what is often called an integrated risk management perspective. With this viewpoint, a centralized perspective prioritizes and compares all risks across the organization. The application of this idea typically involves assessing the extent of potential losses and the likelihood of losses across all functional departments including Information Security, Physical Security, Legal, Internal Audit, Customer Relations, and Accounting & Finance. The intention is to see the big picture and be able to allocate resources to those departments and risk management efforts that most need these resources. You are strongly urged to foster the integrated risk management viewpoint, even if the current or proposed organizational structure doesn't reflect it, because information security will thereby be shown to be a serious and largely unaddressed problem area deserving greater organizational resources and

greater top management attention. Beyond integrated risk management, this option is desirable because it involves only one middle manager between the Information Security Department Manager and the CEO. Another attractive aspect of this organizational design is that contingency planning will get a great deal of attention, and this in turn will allow the organization to be better prepared for a wide variety of contingencies like terrorist attacks. Yet another attractive aspect of this organizational structure involves the strategic perspective that this approach confers on the information security function. Specifically, the long-term nature of information security work, and also the potential to thereby achieve competitive advantage, are implied by this organizational approach.

The CRM is also likely to be prevention-oriented, to have a longer-term viewpoint, and to be able to engage the CEO in intelligent discussions about *risk acceptance* (doing nothing), *risk mitigation* (adding controls), and *risk transfer* (buying insurance). This option is thus desirable because the conversation generated by the CRM will definitely help top management understand their role when it comes to selecting adequate internal controls, including those controls which involve information security. A CRM is also likely to be comfortable thinking about the future and generating scenarios reflecting a number of different possibilities, including information security scenarios such as a distributed denial of service (DDOS) attack. This scenario analysis will help to show information security to top management in a strategic light, for example illuminating the ways that information security can contribute to competitive advantage.

The CRM, however, is often not familiar with information systems technology, and so may need some special coaching or extra background research from the Information Security Department Manager to make important points with the CEO. Another problem with this approach is that its focus is strategic, and the operational and administrative aspects of information security (such as changing privileges when people change jobs) may not get the attention that they deserve

from the CRM. This reduced attention may, however, be appropriate in those organizations with especially decentralized information security organizational structures. For example, if Systems Administrators and Network Administrators, and perhaps Decentralized Information Security Coordinators (see Chapter 12 for further discussion of these jobs), are handling many of the information security operational and administrative tasks, there will be little need for a centralized information security group to attend to these same matters. The centralized information security function can then play more of a consulting role. Nonetheless, in spite of these deficiencies, on balance this is a desirable option and is recommended for organizations that are information intensive such as banks, stock brokerages, telephone companies, and research institutes.

Option 4: Information Security Reports To Insurance & Risk Management Department

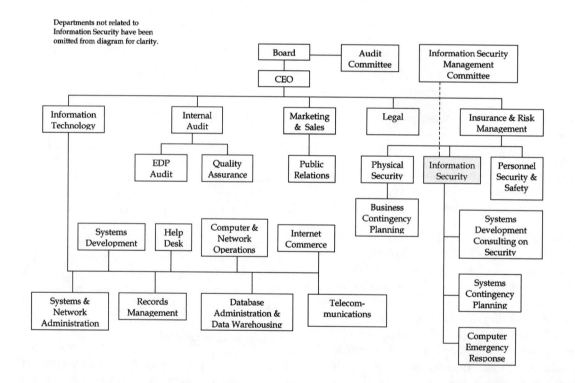

Option 5: Strategy & Planning

In the Option 5 diagram, you will find still another possible organizational structure found in the real world. Here the Information Security Department reports to the Strategy & Planning Department. In this case, the Information Security Department Manager reports directly to the Vice President of Strategy & Planning. This option views the information security

function as a proactive planning activity which is critical to the success of the organization. The option is thus desirable because it embraces the long-term integration of information security into feasibility analyses, business plans, project plans, and other management documentation. The option would be appropriate for an organization that sold products or services which in one respect or another involved information security. An example would appropriate for a credit card clearing house that processes credit card purchase transactions as well as purchase authorization requests. This option would also be appropriate for an Internet merchant (a so-called "dot-com" enterprise) or any other organization which is critically dependent on the success of the information security function. This option is also desirable because it involves only one middle manager between the Information Security Department Manager and the CEO. It is thus just one step down from the option mentioned within the introductory remarks for this chapter, where the Senior Vice President of Information Security reports directly to the CEO.

Option 5 is desirable because it underscores the need for documented information security requirements (policies, standards, procedures, etc.) that apply to the entire organization. Like Options 3 and 4, this reporting structure also acknowledges the multi-departmental and multi-disciplinary nature of information security tasks such as risk analysis and incident investigations. This option is also advisable because the Information Security Department works with others that share a scenario-oriented view of the world (they often ask "what if..." questions). Another desirable aspect of this approach is that it implicitly communicates that information security is very importantly management and people issue, not just a technological issue.

This same advantage can be a disadvantage if workers in the Information Technology Department consider the staff in the Information Security Department to be management-oriented, and out of touch when it comes to the technology (of course, the work of the Information Security Department can clearly communicate that this is a misperception). One problem with this approach is that the focus is strategic, and the operational and administrative aspects of information security (such as changing privileges when people change jobs) may not get the attention that they deserve from the Vice President of Strategy & Planning. As indicated for the discussion of the previous option, in some cases, like organizations with very decentralized information security organizational designs, this is a desirable option. On balance though, this is an advisable reporting relationship for the information security function, and should be something that the Information Department Manager is considering for the long-run even if he or she is not proposing it today. This option is especially encouraged for those organizations which are critically dependent on the success of the information security function (Internet merchants, banks, credit card companies, Internet Service Providers (ISPs), outsourcing firms, etc.).

Option 5: Information Security Reports To Strategy & Planning Department

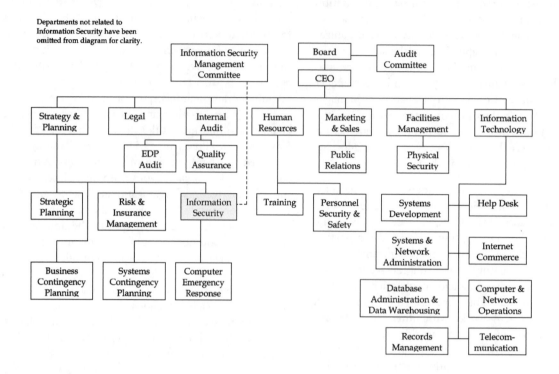

Option 6: Legal

The Option 6 diagram shows an unusual, but nonetheless increasingly-popular and highly-recommended organizational structure. In this case the Information Security Department reports to the Legal Department. This option correctly emphasizes that information is the asset of primary concern, not information systems. This option thus places great emphasis on copyrights, patents, trademarks, and related intellectual property protection mechanisms. It may thus be especially appropriate for those organizations, such as pharmaceutical firms, which spend a lot of money developing their own intellectual property. Separately, contracts-such as non-disclosure agreements (NDAs) and outsourcing agreements-will also get great attention with this organizational structure. With this option there is also great emphasis on compliance with laws, regulations, and ethical standards (like privacy). Having the Chief Legal Counsel act as a promoter of information security is an effective way to carry the information security message to both top management and the Board of Directors, and it is fully consistent with the fact that a lot of the exposure that top managers and directors face these days relates to legal liability. The fact that the Chief Privacy Officer is often a part of the Legal Department reflects this increasing emphasis on the legal and regulatory

issues associated with information security. This organizational design is furthermore desirable because lawyers are excellent and credible communicators, who are able to make good cases for important information security issues like management's fiduciary duty to protect organizational assets (and information itself these days is considered an organizational asset). Top managers and directors are therefore more likely to -- with this organizational structure -- be more interested in and concerned about information security.

In the years ahead, information security will increasingly be mandated by law, regulated, and affected by ethical standards, so Option 6 is really an organizational structure for the future. If your organization happens to be in a highly regulated industry, such as credit bureaus, hospitals, banks, or defense contractors, then this organizational structure could be appropriate today. This option is desirable because access to top management is provided through only one middle manager-the Legal Department Manager, sometimes called the Chief Legal Officer (CLO). This reporting structure is also advisable because the members of the Legal Department are comfortable with, and spend a lot of time developing, revising, and communicating documentation such as policies and procedures. Documentation showing that the organization is in compliance with the information security standard of due care is increasingly important, and is now essential for critical business tasks like the exchange of proprietary information that accompanies a new business partnership. One more good reason to adopt this option involves outsourcing. To the extent that your organization uses third parties to provide information technology services, this option will encourage the explicit treatment of information security matters in contracts and other official documents like non-disclosure agreements (NDAs).

On the downside of Option 6 is the potential overemphasis on compliance, with the consequential under-emphasis on other aspects of information security, such as the marketing and strategic importance of information security. This organizational structure might also inadvertently lead to the Information Security Department doing compliance checking work, which presents a clear conflict of interest (as explained in Option 7: Internal Audit.) Compliance checking

should be performed by an Internal Auditing Department, not the Information Security Department (see Chapter 11, Internal Audit Department mission statement for futher details). Another downside of this approach is the possibility that the focus will be on meeting the letter of law, the absolute minimum, and nothing more. With this organizational structure, top management may be reluctant to spend money on needed information security tasks if they are above and beyond what laws or regulations currently require. One more problem associated with this reporting structure is that lawyers may not know much about information systems technology, but lawyers are generally smart and pick things up quickly, so they can be easily-trained about important technical matters. On balance, although this organizational structure has much to recommend it, and will probably be encountered in an increasing number of organizations in the years ahead.

Option 6: Information Security Reports To Legal Department

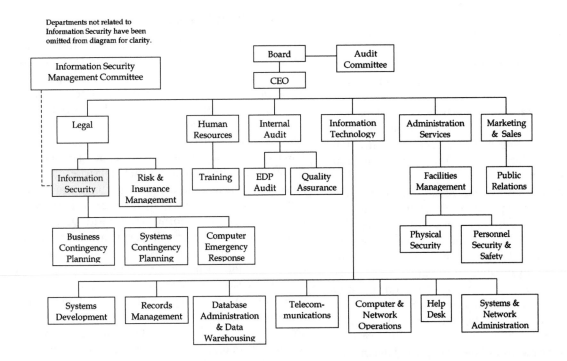

Option 7: Internal Audit

Even though the author has seen it in the real world, the Information Security Department should definitely not report to the Internal Audit Department. This is why you will not find a diagram for this option. In this case, the Information Security Department Manager reports

to the Internal Auditing Department Manager. An examination of the mission statement for the Internal Audit Department (see Chapter 11) reveals that Internal Audit is charged with reviewing the work done by other units, including the Information Security Department. If the Information Security Department were to report to the Internal Audit Department, a conflict of interest would then exist. Internal Audit would be tempted to exaggerate the good work of the Information Security Department so that the Internal Audit Department as a whole would look good. A controls-oriented Chief Internal Auditor may also be tempted to allocate more resources to an Information Security Department than are realistically warranted, and this in turn could create an undue security burden for the rest of the organization as well as a backlash that could take years to overcome. Reporting to the Internal Audit Department may also be contra indicated because Internal Audit often has adversarial relationships with other departments, and the perspectives that go along with those relationships could be unwittingly transferred to relationships between the Information Security Department and other departments. To foster smooth working relationships, an Information Security Department should instead be considered advisory and consultative in nature, and not a new type of auditor. The Internal Audit Department Manager may also lack sufficient technical expertise to understand what the Information Security Department is doing, and this may make it hard to convey messages from the Information Security Department Manager to the CEO.

On the other hand, one advantage of reporting to the Internal Audit Department is that the Internal Audit Department Manager has a controls perspective and will at least in theory support what an Information Security Department is trying to do. Another reason in favor of reporting to Internal Audit reflects the tremendous clout that this group has with top management and the Board of Directors. Nothing in this paragraph is meant to discourage the Information Security Department from establishing a close and mutually-beneficial working relationship with an Internal Audit Department, and such a good working relationship is characteristic of firms with successful information security efforts. One additional reason to try to create this type of organizational design has to do with the empowerment of people throughout the organization to be part of an information security team, rather than relying on a central group of specialists. If the Information Security Department were to report to the Internal Auditing Department, then the day-to-day administrative work should be done mostly by other groups, and the Internal Audit Department would be primarily concerned with checking the work of these other groups. In some very rare organizations, this approach may make sense because the information security day-to-day activities are pushed almost entirely out to user departments, and information security is seen as primarily a line function (part of local management's job), rather than a staff function (an advisory/consulting job). In this case, the centralized information security function would primarily provide consulting services, not so much technical administrative services.

Just because there is no direct reporting relationship to Information Systems Audit (or Internal Audit for that matter), doesn't mean it isn't a good idea to have a dotted line reporting relationship from the Information Security Department to the Audit Committee on the Board of Directors. As mentioned in the discussion for Option 1, this dotted line relationship is intended to be a periodic reporting relationship as well as a safety valve. The Information Security Department can provide quarterly reports about the status of information security to the Audit Committee. If this Committee doesn't like what they are hearing, they can then redirect the efforts of top managers. Likewise, if top management is relatively unreceptive to the Information Security Department's point of view, Information Security can take its concerns to the Audit Committee. This dotted line reporting relationship doesn't currently exist in many organizations, but there are many efforts now underway to establish this type of relationship.

Option 8: Help Desk

Another option involves having the Information Security Department report to the Help Desk Department. In this case, the Information Security Department Manager reports to the Help Desk Department Manager. As is the case with reporting into the Internal Audit Department, this option was not presented in a diagram because it is not advised. A Help Desk Department is a lower level technical group that does not get much top management attention or respect. Likewise, the Help Desk Department generally does not command many resources, and this scarcity of resources is likely to be carried over into the Information Security Department. If the Information Security Department reported to the Help Desk Department, there would be at least two levels of middle management between the Information Security Department Manager and the CEO, and this is likely to hinder management appreciation of the importance of information security as well as the acquisition of an adequate budget. Another reason not to establish an organizational structure like this involves the Help Desk Department's customer-focus and service-orientation. While this may at first be perceived to be a desirable characteristic, it may also force the Information Security Department to opt for quick response, ease-of-use, and other customer service objectives, at the expense of a high level of security. Still another reason not to report to the Help Desk involves getting away from the early days of the Information

Security Department. Several decades ago, the information security function in many large organizations running mainframes was a separate and often glorified administrative unit within the Help Desk group. The information security function has come a long way since then, and the reporting relationship should reflect its new importance, rather than provide an echo of the early days of information security.

Under certain circumstances, it could, nonetheless, be advantageous to report to the Help Desk Department. Mobilization after a system break-in or some other information security event could be expedited with this organizational structure. This is because the Help Desk is often the one to mobilize a computer emergency response team (CERT). This makes sense because a Help Desk is on the front lines, and is often first to hear about a problem. This also makes sense because many organizations have Help Desks which are staffed all the time (24 X 7 X 365). Separately, this reporting structure could also be beneficial because the Help Desk Department's trouble ticket system could be directly tied into logs of information security problems. Analysis of these logs could provide the Information Security Department with important insight into problems as they are occurring. Integration of these logs with intrusion detection systems may furthermore enable the organization to prepare sophisticated scripted responses to automated attacks such as Distributed Denial Of Service attacks (DDOSs). These scripted responses may in turn augment information systems contingency planning efforts.

On balance though, this reporting relationship, like reporting relationships to other lower level departments, is strongly discouraged. Similar remarks could be offered for organizational designs involving the reporting of an Information Security Department into other subgroups within the Information Technology Department. Examples include the Computer Operations Department, the Systems Development Department, and the Records Management Department. For additional discussion about reporting to the Information Technology Department, see the discussion under Option 1 above.

Option 9: Accounting & Finance through Information Technology

Yet another option involves the Information Security Department reporting to the Accounting & Finance Department through the Information Technology Department. This option is similarly not recommended and is therefore not shown in a diagram. This very traditional organizational structure is a reflection of the early days of information systems where, at least in the commercial world, the computer was applied largely to accounting and finance tasks. The uses of computers and networks have expanded dramatically over the last few decades, and so the Information Technology Department should now report higher in the organizational ladder, not through the Accounting & Finance Department.

This option is also undesirable for the reasons mentioned under Option 1 (notably security losing-out in trade-offs with competing objectives). This option is furthermore undesirable because the Information Security Department would be buried deep in the organizational hierarchy, and would be therefore unlikely to get the resources and top management attention that it needs. While the Information Security Department is a staff (advisory service) department like the Accounting & Finance Department, it is growing much more rapidly than the Accounting & Finance Department. Integration with the Accounting & Finance Department may thus conceal this rapid growth rate from top management, which in turn could lead to under-funded information security efforts. Reporting to the Accounting & Finance Department may also cause the needs of the Information Security Department to be lost within, and overshadowed by, the much more traditional and more prominent needs of the Accounting & Finance Department. If the Information Security Department is combined with other activities in the Accounting & Finance Department, top management is likely to see the information security function as a back-office operation, and not a strategic issue worthy of top management attention.

Reporting through the Accounting & Finance Department appears to some people to be advisable because the Accounting & Finance Department Manager is controls-oriented, and this may be true, but this in many cases does not compensate for the other deficiencies. In fact, reporting to the Accounting & Finance Department may put additional pressure on an Information Security Department to cut costs, a move that may pay-off in the short-run, but is most likely to spell serious trouble in the long-run. Some people may say that the same detail-oriented-mindset is appropriate for accounting and finance on one hand, and information security on the other. This mind set will be helpful, but it may be found in many other areas of an organization, and thus is a weak justification to place the information security function within an Accounting & Finance Department. On balance, this organizational structure is strongly discouraged.

Option 10: Human Resources

Still another possibility for the Information Security Department is reporting to the Human Resources Department. Because this option is not recommended, it has not been shown in a diagram. This relatively rare organizational structure places emphasis primarily on the people side of information security, and down-plays the technological side of information security. There is a certain synergy that could be achieved when the Information Security Department is part of the Human Resources Department. This synergy comes from both groups developing policies that must be followed by workers throughout the organization. For example, the Human Resources Department's disciplinary process is used to deal with those who are not in compliance with information security policies. If the Human Resources Department also handles the staff training function, this synergy can be magnified. Such an organizational structure may also be appropriate in industries where privacy requirements and other personal data handling issues are very important (credit reporting, insurance, medical services, etc.). In these industries, the Human Resources Department has expertise associated with the handling of private information held in a personnel database, and is also subject to laws and regulations regarding this sensitive information. The Human Resource Department's prior experience in the privacy area may thus be of assistance to the Information Security Department, at least in the short run.

Some people may think that the Human Resources Department is a good place for the Information Security Department because the HR Department is the source of critical information used by the Information Security Department. For example, the personnel database is, in some organizations, used as a reference point for various system access control database activities. If a worker were to resign, his or her name could be communicated automatically to Systems Administrators, who then should delete this person's name from various lists of authorized computer users. This sharing of certain types of information does not, however, in itself indicate that these two departments should be combined. For example, the Accounting & Finance Department shares certain financial data with the Legal Department in order to prepare quarterly shareholder reports, but this does not mean that the Accounting & Finance Department should be combined with the Legal Department.

To position the Information Security Department as part of the HR Department is generally not advised because the HR Department Manager often knows very little about information systems, and is therefore most often not a credible conduit for communications to top management. Another reason not to have the Information Security Department report to the Human Resources Department is that little of the day-to-day work of information security involves the people working in Human Resources. With this option, there is therefore much less of an opportunity for cross-pollination between groups than if the Information Security Department is part of the Information Technology Department. Reporting to the Human Resources Department is furthermore not advised because the strategic importance of the information security function is likely to be lost amidst the clerical, legal, and regulatory work that the Human Resources Department performs. This option is furthermore discouraged because it leads the rank-and-file staff to consider the information security function as something administrative rather than strategic in nature. Another reason to have the information security function report elsewhere involves the way people look at the human resources function. Most people have a "huggy-feely" view of human resources, a sense that they handle the soft side of the organization. Many managers consider this soft and personal attitude to be inconsistent with the clear, focused, and definitive security requirements that should be coming from an Information Security Department.

Option 11: Facilities Management

Yet another option for the Information Security Department involves reporting to the Facilities Management Department (sometimes called Buildings & Grounds). Since this option is not recommended, no diagram has been provided. This is a rare but occasionally-encountered organizational structure that views the information security function as something similar to the building guards who help prevent burglary, or the gardeners who tend to the grounds. With this organizational structure, the Information Security Department is seen by top management as an asset protection function much like the Physical Security Department. In fact with this organizational structure, Buildings & Grounds may report up through the Physical Security Department. This option thus implies no strategic importance whatsoever for the information security function. This option implies that the information security function is basically a low-level administrative and/or maintenance activity, which it has been in days gone past, but which it is no longer in progressive organizations. This option is also not a good idea because it typically involves an extra layer of management between the Information Security Department and top management (Option 3, where the Information Security Department reports to the Administrative Services Department, is preferable). This option is furthermore ill-advised because the Manager of the Facilities Management Department is often unfamiliar with information systems technology, and thus may not be a credible conduit of messages to top management. This option is also discouraged because it encourages rank-and-file staff to view the information security function as it would maintenance workers, and this may interfere with efforts to establish authoritative consultative relationships within your organization. Still another reason not to go with this organizational structure involves the fact that the Facilities Management Department is often preoccupied with cutting costs, and this same preoccupation can mean that important information security measures are foregone in the interests of keeping costs down.

Some people may say that this option is desirable because Facilities Management is taking on an increasing array of internal asset protection duties, such as physical security, and should therefore rightfully include information security as well. The information security and physical security functions were in fact combined in 19% of the organizations responding to a 2003 survey conducted by CIO Magazine. While this consolidation of related organizational functions is certainly desirable, it is best achieved with other approaches, such as Option 4. When this consolidation is achieved, it typically involves the establishment of a Chief Security Officer, and this could additionally be achieved through Option 3. If you want to achieve this type of integration and consolidation, then it is better to do it with more of strategic and higher-level-management organizational unit than Facilities Management. Thus, on balance, this option is strongly discouraged.

Option 12: Operations

The last option to be discussed involves reporting to the Operations Department. Under this approach, the Information Security Department Manager reports to the Chief Operating Officer (COO). This approach assumes that information security is a line management responsibility, and a topic that all department managers must consider in their day-to-day activities. For this option to be effective, information security duties would need to be very explicitly assigned to department managers (see Chapter 15 for examples of these duties). While it is certainly desirable to clearly assign management responsibilities, it is also true that information security is primarily a staff function, a function that provides advice and guidance to other departments. This organizational structure thus dramatically downplays the important staff nature of information security work, and as a result, it is not recommended.

Looking at this reporting relationship a bit differently, consider that information security is a strategic information handling function, not a production-oriented function (as is the case with assembly line manufacturing). The information security staff thus has little in common with workers who are in operating divisions of the organization. Information security specialists are often highly-paid technical professionals, while operations personnel typically earn considerably less and are often not technical.

The people in an Operations Department are typically focused on getting the work done, and anything that might impair their production objectives is likely to suffer. Thus, this organizational structure is likely to result in information security objectives which have been compromised in the interests of operating objectives like low cost, time-to-market with a new product, and meeting customer commitments. Although this organizational structure has only one manager between the CEO and the Information Security Department Manager, the COO in many cases will be physically-oriented rather than information-oriented. As a result, he or she may not be a credible or articulate conduit to carry messages from the Information Security Department to the CEO.

One reason that some people give, a reason for establishing such a reporting relationship, involves an attempt to get department managers and other local managers to take information security more seriously. The reasoning goes something like this: if these operational managers see information security as part of their job, then hopefully they will devote more resources to it, and then hopefully it will be more widely supported. Rather than establishing an organizational structure that reflects this strategy, it is preferable to clearly articulate local management's responsibilities in other ways. For example, a department or division head manager's manual (as discussed in Chapter 10) can explicitly state information security duties of local managers. In addition, departmental mission statements and worker job descriptions reflecting an increased role for local managers can be drawn-up. Thus, specifically-assigned local management responsibilities will be much more likely to achieve the desired result, rather than positioning the information security function within an Operations Department. On balance, this option is thus strongly discouraged.

Summary

The Information Security Department at many organizations has been handed back and forth between various organizational units, never finding a proper home.

Consider what happened to the information security function at a major commercial bank. The information security function originated in the Internal Audit Department. Over the course of twenty years it migrated to the Information Technology Department, primarily because the Internal Audit Department lacked in-depth technical expertise. Because certain security objectives were in conflict with other Information Technology Department objectives like ease-of-use and low costs, the information security function was then moved to the Insurance & Risk Management Department. While there were some synergies in the contingency planning area, the financial mind set of the Insurance & Risk Management Department was decidedly different from the technical and operational mind set of the Information Security Department. As a result, the Information Security Department was moved again to the Physical (Industrial) Security Department, where it remains to this day. At this bank, the Physical Security Department was considered to be a good home for the Information Security Department because the asset protection objectives are similar, and because top management acknowledges that Physical Security is a necessary business activity like Accounting and Marketing. This example shows that the Information Security Department often moves around the organization, and that today's reporting relationship may be quite different from tomorrow's.

The previous paragraph's story is intended to encourage you to suggest reporting relationship changes that would further the evolution of the information security organizational structure at your organization. While these organizational realignments are unquestionably disruptive, they are often very much worth the effort. For example, if the contingency planning side of information security is still relatively undeveloped at your organization, a move of the information security group, so that it then reports to the Insurance & Risk Management Department, may help this undeveloped area to rapidly expand.

Smaller organizations will want to have a part-time Information Security Coordinator or Information Security Department Manager (see Chapter 18 for more details). Small to medium sized organizations will often require at least one full-time person, and medium to large organizations will often require several full-time information security staff (see Appendix A for specific staffing ranges by organizational size). Since so few people are involved, in smaller organizations, the formal designation of a separate department will most often be unwarranted. But for all other organizations, no matter where the information security function happens to report, it is desirable to designate a separate department that has been formally recognized by top management. Words such as "Committee," "Project," and "Team" are discouraged because they don't convey a sense of permanency. Certainly the word "Department" is not essential-you could use whatever word the organization's staff is accustomed to, such as "Division," "Unit," "Group," "Section," or "Regiment." To designate a separate department is advisable because it is in keeping with general business practice whereby special needs are recognized with unique departments. For example, credit card processing companies typically have a Fraud Department that is separate and distinct from both the Information Security Department and the Physical Security Department. This is because credit card fraud is a serious problem that requires the use of different tools, techniques, and perspectives. To have a separate department for the information security function is to subtly communicate that this area is expected to grow, that this area deserves special consideration, and that this area is different. All these messages can be helpful to an information security effort.

While this chapter has examined the placement of an Information Security Department in the traditional notion of a hierarchical organizational structure, there are certainly other ways to do things. One common alternative is called a *matrix* or *networked organizational structure*, where individual workers have more than one immediate manager. In this case, the Information Security Department Manager reports to two or more managers. If you are one of the rare people who work with an organizational structure like this, you can combine the considerations mentioned above to come up with an appropriate spot for the Information Security Department. For example, the Information Security Department Manager may then report to both the Chief Legal Officer (CLO) and the Chief Information Officer (CIO).

Having more than one conceptual structure to clearly define roles and responsibilities is also advisable. This is different than the matrix organizational structure mentioned in the last paragraph. Here a traditional hierarchical organizational structure can be combined with other models like the owner, custodian, user (OCU) approach. The latter approach involves the placement of all workers into at least one of these three categories, and then defines the information security roles and responsibilities of each. For those organizations that are relatively sophisticated in the information security area, the use of more than one conceptual model is advisable. This is because it helps to create checks and balances that will ensure that critical information security tasks are getting done. More than one conceptual model is additionally desirable because it helps to foster a widespread appreciation that each worker who comes in contact with information or information systems has specific and assigned information security duties. The OCU model is discussed at length in Chapter 15.

Chapter 14 TEMPLATE CUSTOMIZATION FACTORS

Although this book attempts to make it very easy for you to prepare roles and responsibilities documentation, it is not possible to provide a single set of documents that will be uniformly applicable to all organizations. You will need to make adjustments to these templates so that the result is responsive to the needs of your organization. In an attempt to sensitize you to the changes that will need to be made, this chapter provides a list of customization factors. For each of these factors, your will find at least one specific action step that you can take to best learn how this factor affects the organization's information security roles and responsibilities documentation. The factors listed are shown in rough order from most to least important. The actual ranking of these factors will vary by both industry and organization.

Local Laws And Regulations

Certain countries have laws and regulations that dictate management activities with respect to information security. For example, western European nations generally take the privacy of citizens very seriously. Organizations in Western Europe must register all databases containing personal information with a government agency. In other countries, such as the United States, organizations are bound by no such sweeping laws or regulations. In the US, specific industries, such as health care, are subject to relatively-narrowly-defined privacy laws. Where these and other legal and regulatory requirements exist, you will need to add the appropriate words to the job descriptions of the Information Security Manager, the Chief Privacy Officer, and the Intellectual Property Legal Counsel. Separately, if your organization has operations in more than one country, you will need to consider the laws of each of these countries. For example, trans-border data flow (TBDF) laws affect the types of data that can be legally transmitted from one country to another. Likewise, various country-specific statutes affect the exportability of encryption software and hardware. Other countries restrict the use of encryption to protect data because the government wishes to reserve the right to read your communications. There are many other examples. The best way to learn about information security laws and regulations is to discuss these matters with the Intellectual Property Legal Counsel at your organization.

Industry Category

Certain industries have unique information security requirements. For example, in the commercial banking industry in the United States there is a requirement that contingency plans be documented and periodically audited by government examiners. As another example, the existing standard of due care in the United States dictates a higher level of privacy protection at consumer credit bureaus than it does at mailing houses that distribute junk mail, even though both organizations handle much the same information. In some industries, such as with commercial banks, the overall reputation of an organization will be highly dependent on customer confidence-and this confidence could be seriously damaged by publicly-known information security incidents. In other industries, such as high-tech firms, the impact may not be so serious. If you do not already know about them, the best way to learn about these industry differences is to talk to both the Director of Marketing and the Director of Strategic Planning at your organization. This type of information may also be available from industry associations such as the American Bankers Association. Going to industry-specific conferences and seminars, when these events are devoted to information security, will also be a good way to illuminate these requirements.

Criticality To The Business

If information security is critical to a business, then the roles and responsibilities documentation should incorporate supplementary organization-specific job description duties. One example of a supplementary duty could involve the Information Security Department Manager periodically meeting with the Strategic Planning Department Manager. If top management at a particular firm didn't think that information security function was all that critical, a periodic discussion with the Strategic Planning Manager would not appear in the Information Security Department Manager's job description. Separately, three attitudes are reasonably good indicators that top management thinks information security is critical. First, top management may see the information security as an essential function, something necessary for continued organizational survival. Second, top management may see the information security function as a competitive necessity, as something they must do to keep up with the competition. Third, top management may see the information security function as a strategy for achieving competitive advantage, as a way to distinguish themselves from the competition. If any of these three attitudes prevail at your organization, then information security will receive considerably more top management attention, and the job descriptions may warrant additional duties along these same lines. The best way for you to learn about management's perspective is to interview a few executives. This attitude information can be obtained from top management at the same time that you are conducting initial interviews for an information security roles and responsibilities project. Chapter 7 provides a list of questions that can be asked when conducting these interviews with top management. Note that just because management currently doesn't think information security is critical doesn't mean that this is true. You may need to engage in some awareness raising efforts with management before the true criticality to the business can be revealed.

Line Or Staff

This customization factor takes the notion of "criticality to the business" one step further by examining the way that management sees the information security function relative to other business activities. In most organizations, an Information Security Department will perform a *staff function*. In other words, the Information Security Department provides administrative support and expert advice that may be accepted or rejected by top management. As a staff group, the Information Security Department does not have the power to impose its perspective on the rest of the organization. This role is distinctly different when the Information Security Department is viewed as a *line function*. Line functions are concerned with the basic objectives of the organization, and line functions have decision-making power. In the vast majority of organizations, the information security function is still a staff function, but this is slowly changing in some industries. Organizations such as an Internet electronic bill payment service would probably be well advised to define the information security function as a line function. This is because the business is critically dependent on information security -- if the level of information security is inadequate, then the whole business can quickly disappear. If an Information Security Department performs as a staff function, then it typically will be lower on the management hierarchy than it would be if it were recognized as a line function. Likewise, if it's a staff function, the Information Security Department will generally not be directly involved with decision-making processes such as application change control. However, if it's a line function, it may be directly involved and may be able to force certain actions if the

result would be improved security. As you might expect, the roles and responsibilities documentation for a staff function will generally be less detailed than it would be for a line function. To determine the extent to which information security should be a line or a staff function, interview top management and ask for their opinions.

Organizational Culture

Organizational culture may be influenced by religious, spiritual, ethical, or other regional cultural norms. Organizational culture, in turn, will affect how roles and responsibilities will be documented. For example, certain organizations have recently adopted the notion of "open book management" as a fundamental way to run their business. Open book management suggests that all information, including financial data previously reserved for top management, should be available to all workers (of course, certain exceptions are made for information protected by law, such as staff medical treatment expense claims). This radically open approach to information security places a very different slant on the roles and responsibilities of an information security unit. Relative to other organizations, an organization with an open book management approach will have an information security unit that spends considerably more time on information integrity and availability, and considerably less time on information confidentiality. The best place to find information about organizational culture is to read the organization's code of conduct, its mission statement, its in-house newspaper, its recent press releases, and its annual reports. If a new hire orientation course has recently been compiled, this too could contain some information about organizational culture. You could also consult with the Director of Human Resources and the Director of Strategic Planning to get a better sense for the organizational culture relevant to information security.

Scope Of Information Security Function

Certain organizations have a very narrowly defined information security function, while others have a broadly defined function. (In an effort to make life easier for you, this book contains a broadly defined function because deleting functionality is always easier than adding it.) Exemplifying the difference in scope, in some organizations you will find an information security unit responsible for contingency planning whereas in other organizations the unit will not have this responsibility. In some organizations, compliance checking is the information security function's responsibility, whereas in others it is not (for conflict of interest reasons, the author advocates performance of this work by the Information Systems Audit Department). You need to clearly understand which functions management expects information security to perform before you write up roles and responsibilities documentation. The best way to learn about these scope matters is to consult with the Managers in charge of related Departments including Information Systems Audit, Physical Security, Quality Assurance, Legal, Human Resources, and Information Systems. In these interviews, you can go down the list of activities described in Chapter 11. Before these interviews, you should review the mission statements of each of the departments you will consult with, and this will thus allow you to define the scope of their current activities. To a large extent, the scope of an information security unit's duties will include what is not already specified in these mission statements.

Information Security Effort Sophistication

Certain organizations are just starting to get their information security efforts underway, while others have had an information security function in place for a decade or more. The extent of an organization's information security experience (which often correlates directly with the degree of sophistication) will affect the activities performed by an information security unit. For example, newly-minted information security units may not have the power and clout to prevent a new application system from being moved into production processing mode, even if this application system has inadequate controls. On the other hand, a well-established and well-respected information security function may have the power and clout to act in this manner. Accordingly, some of the words in the templates provided in this book may need to be diluted for a new information security function. For example, instead of "dictate virus screening standards" the documentation that you prepare might say "provide advice on virus screening standards." The best way for you to learn about the power and clout that the information security organization previously had and currently has is to examine all prior internal documentation dealing with information security roles and responsibilities. The level of sophistication is also discussed in Chapter 10, which deals with the different documents where roles and responsibilities could be mentioned.

Size Of Organization

Large organizations generally will have need for considerably more roles and responsibilities documentation than smaller organizations. This is simply a matter of complexity, since the larger organizations have so many more people and activities to coordinate than smaller organizations. This complexity can be seen, for example, in the computer hardware and software procurement process. In a large organization, the purchase of a computer may be subjected to several screening processes (internal network interface standards, information security standards, etc.). In smaller organizations, these screens are typically absent or abbreviated. The best way for you to learn about the role and responsibility implications associated with various processes is to trace the processes through to conclusion. Time constraints often don't normally allow you to do this, so a discussion with various participants may suffice. Each participant should be asked what they do, as well as which other participants are a part of the information security team. A set of questions that may help in this regard is provided in Chapter 7. Another approach, which is not recommended, is to circulate the draft templates in this book without any significant background investigation. In this case, you are simply saying to the recipients, "Alter this to suit our needs." The reason why this is not recommended is that the recipients will resent doing the work that should instead be done by you, and the level of participation will vary widely from person to person. Some investigation will then be needed anyway to fill the gaps in the material received as well as to compensate for the internal politics that will have been provoked by the material distributed for comment. If you use the latter method, the extra time and effort needed to put the feedback you receive into some sort of cohesive document will generally overshadow any benefits you might have received by giving the work to others.

Outsourcing

The complexity of information security roles and responsibilities documentation will be expanded whenever an organization has automated systems that are linked with other organizations (extranets, electronic data interchange networks, third-party credit card processing firms, third-party data entry firms, facilities management firms, outsourcing firms, etc.). The greater the number of business functions that are performed by these third parties, the more the need to formalize the information security roles and responsibilities, usually in the form of legal contracts. The greater the number of different third parties, the more the interactions between each of them will need to be formally managed and also documented. If any of these organizations are located in different countries or otherwise have significantly different legal jurisdictions, then still more attention will be needed to precisely define the third-party roles and responsibilities involved. Separately, the limitations of existing agreements may force you to define the information security roles and responsibilities of in-house staff in certain ways that would not otherwise be chosen. This topic is taken up in greater detail in Chapter 11 and Chapter 12. The best way for you to gather information about outsourcing is to review existing legal agreements. You may also wish to speak with the legal counsel involved in drafting these agreements as well as the Chief Information Officer (CIO).

Intended Audience

The intended audience for your information security roles and responsibility documentation should also be considered before writing gets underway. If only managers will see the documentation, then a number of lower-level and detailed considerations may in certain circumstances be eliminated. Note that this approach is not advised because it is desirable that all workers be able to read their own job descriptions, their own department's mission statements, as well as those same documents for other people within the organization. Alternatively, if the audience is familiar with high-technology terms, then certain definitions and explanations will not be necessary. If the audience doesn't speak English well (or if it's not familiar with the language used to publish roles and responsibilities statements), then the material may need to be considerably simplified. There are certainly many other audience-related adjustments that need to be made; these observations were offered only as examples of how the materials found in this book will need to be adjusted. You probably already know a good deal about the audience at your organization, but if you want to know more, the In-House Trainer (who often reports to the Human Resources Department Manager) is a good reference point.

Separation Of Duties

The organizational structure described in Chapter 11, Chapter 12, and Chapter 13 has been designed so that it already includes separation of duties. In other words, checks and balances have been incorporated into these job descriptions. For example, the access control systems established by an Access Control System Administrator should be periodically reviewed by an Internal Auditor. If you delete a number of the suggested positions, or delete a number of the duties for the suggested positions, you must take special care so as not to create a potential lapse of internal control. The best way to ensure that problems are not created when you adopt a streamlined

organizational structure is to clearly define the essential areas that must have separation of duties. These include, but certainly are not limited to, development vs. testing of new application systems, management authorization vs. systems administration of access control systems, specification of requirements vs. compliance checking to see whether people are following these requirements, and design of encryption systems vs. administration of the keys for encryption systems. After these essential areas are clarified, you can go back and make sure that the streamlined organizational structure you have developed has not inadvertently created a potential lapse of internal control. Additional strategies for dealing with separation of duties problems are found in Chapter 18 and Chapter 20.

Cross-Training And Staff Backup

Another factor to consider when streamlining the recommended organizational structure defined in Chapter 11, Chapter 12, and Chapter 13 is the need to have at least two trained and immediately-available information security experts. Suppose that the primary internal expert was to take a job with a competitor on one week's notice-would your organization have a difficult time replacing him or her? In this case, what would happen if a hacker broke in just after this person left the organization? The best ways to ensure adequate backup staffing is to do ample cross-training in the information security area, and also to accurately document the day-to-day procedures of people working in the information security area. The cross-training and documentation will also enable immediate response to security problems even though one of the staff members is away on vacation, taking sick leave, or attending an off-site conference. In terms of the organizational structure suggested in Chapter 11, Chapter 12, and Chapter 13, having adequate backup does not imply changes to the suggested roles and responsibilities. What is affected is the number of people who hold certain job titles such as Systems Administrator. Another approach to this same issue involves cross-training on essential duties, but not other things. Thus a part-time Local Information Security Coordinator might be able to step-in and fulfill some of the duties of an absent Access Control System Administrator. See Chapter 18 and Chapter 20 for additional details about stretching your staff to achieve these security objectives.

Formatting

Of course, you will also need to make various editorial changes to the templates provided in this book. Generic organizational names (like "Company X") will need to be replaced with the actual organizational unit names. Company logos and graphics will need to be added. Type fonts and margins will need to be changed. You may need to change the format of the word processing materials that come with this book, for example putting it in HTML format for use on an intranet site. You will likewise also need to reformat and repackage the material to suit the organization's internal documentation standards. For example, if a management approval date appears at the bottom of each job description found within your organization, a similar date should be applied to the material extracted from this book. Other organization specific information, such as a contact person's name and E-mail address, will additionally need to be added to the final document.

Chapter 15 Owner, Custodian, And User Roles

Just as the old-fashioned concept of "computer security" erroneously focused on the technology when the real issue was the information itself, so too have many businesses erroneously assumed that information security was solely the responsibility of the Information Technology Department. As time goes by, more responsibility for information security day-to-day decisions is now being passed to the user community-where it should have been all along. One of the most popular ways of clearly specifying the responsibility for user department managers, end-users, and those who have the day-to-day possession of information is through the roles of owners, custodians, and users. This chapter describes these roles and responsibilities as well as how best to implement a related organizational structure. These roles and responsibilities are often documented in an information security policy manual (a description of information security documents, including a policies manual, can be found in Chapter 10. You are additionally directed to Chapter 11 and Chapter 12, which contain mission statements and job descriptions for those working in the information security area.) Note that it is desirable to have several different ways to define the roles and responsibilities of workers, and that the use of several different methods helps to ensure that critical information security work gets done.

Role Of Owners

An Owner (sometimes called a Sponsor or Steward) is an employee who has been designated by the Chief Information Officer as the one responsible for the proper management and handling of a particular type of production information on behalf of Company X. An Owner's ultimate accountability cannot be delegated to anyone, but his or her responsibility may be delegated to a worker in his or her department or division. Under no circumstances can an owner's accountability or responsibility be delegated to external service provider. Owners do not legally own the information in question; they instead make decisions on behalf of Company X, which legally owns the information.

If an owner has not been officially assigned, the creator of the information (if this person is a Company X employee) must act as an interim Owner. [Interim owners are sometimes called Guardians.] Thus an employee working at his workstation becomes an interim Owner if he compiles a new type of information that will be used for production information systems at

Company X. Production information systems are systems that are repeatedly used in the normal course of business, such as an information system that evaluates the credit of potential customers.

Often a new information type is created when existing information types are combined. If any of the existing information types were previously in the possession of Company X, the Owners of these existing information types should determine who the Owner of the new type of information should be. If the sources of the new information are entirely external to Company X, or if the internal sources had no previously designated Owner, then the Chief Information Officer must promptly designate an Owner for the new type of production information.

Owners must understand how the information they are charged with overseeing is used inside and outside of the organization. Owners must also understand the potential security and privacy risks associated with this type of information. These risks include unavailability, unauthorized disclosure, unauthorized modification, as well as unauthorized deletion, plus the consequences that might take place when these and other problems occur. Owners must furthermore be aware of the relevant security and privacy requirements dictated by laws, regulations, contracts, and other agreements. For this reason, Owners are most often managers in charge of departments that use or otherwise manage the information in question.

Owners are responsible for classifying, and periodically reclassifying, Company X information based on its sensitivity and criticality. Generally there will be a scale for sensitivity, and in an increasing number of organizations, a scale for criticality as well. Typical positions on a sensitivity scale are *confidential* and *secret*. Typical positions on a criticality scale are *highly critical* and *deferrable*. Criticality scales can alternatively be defined based on the number of hours, days, or weeks that may elapse before the information or information services must be restored.

The categories that information is placed into, in terms of sensitivity and criticality, will imply certain basic control measures. For example, secret information may need to be encrypted when not in use. These requirements should be specified in policies and other information security requirements. Owners do not develop these requirements. The Information Security Department is responsible for developing and revising these requirements. Owners do, however, select an appropriate sensitivity and criticality level for the information that they have been charged with managing.

Beyond the controls automatically implied by certain levels of information sensitivity and criticality, owners are also responsible for selecting supplementary information security measures. These supplementary security measures are often needed because the basic requirements for most Company X information at that same level may not adequately protect the information in question. For example, the information in question may need to be handled in a manner that is in compliance with privacy regulations issued by a government agency. The Information Security Department and the Legal Department would, in this case, assist in the definition of possible supplementary controls. To help select supplementary information security measures, Owners may be asked to place a rough value on the information in question. These steps will help to ensure that only critical, sensitive, and valuable information is protected.

Owners are additionally responsible for developing manual procedures, operational documentation, and other things necessary to implement the information security requirements mentioned above. While Owners are, in most cases not personally doing this work, they are responsible for making sure it is done. For example, if an Owner designated certain information as highly critical, a separate policy may require that a departmental contingency plan be developed, tested, and regularly updated. It would then be the Owner's responsibility to ensure that a contingency plan to assure the continued availability of the highly critical information has indeed been developed, tested, and regularly updated.

Owners are also responsible for sharing their knowledge about the existence and nature of the control measures that have been adopted. This information must be shared with other members of the management team, Custodians, Users, and as necessary, interested third parties such as customers and business partners. The intention of this sharing is to assure these people that the information and the systems which handle it are adequately secured, and that management has paid attention to these matters.

Owners are additionally responsible for assigning custody for the information assets under their control, as well as all equipment and other resources used to manage these same information assets. Owners may thus assign custody for information assets, as well as the information systems that handle these information assets, to an internal Information Technology Department group or to an outsourcing firm. Owners must also prepare annual budgets which anticipate the costs of managing, updating, and protecting these same information assets and all related resources needed by the Custodian to properly handle these information assets.

Owners are also responsible for approving all requests for access to the information for which they are the designated owner. This access typically takes the form of privilege levels that are associated with a business application system such as a human resources database system. For example, data entry clerks may be able to see only the information they are entering, while department members may be able to see just enough to accomplish specified tasks, but the department head may be able to see all the data contained inside the database. These categories may be simplified if the Owner defines job titles or other categories of people who will be given certain types of access. Continuing with this same example, the HR Department Manager may be the Owner of human resources information, in which case he or she would decide who should be able to not just examine, but also to modify, delete, and otherwise use this human resources information. In addition, Owners must periodically review lists of authorized users to determine whether these same people still need access privileges in order to do their jobs. Note that the Owner does not usually handle the administrative tasks associated with access controls and privileges. These are instead handled by "Systems Administrator/Network Administrator" or "Access Control System Administrator" (see Chapter 12 for the specific duties of each).

Owners will most often employ standard forms and standard rules for making these access decisions. The development and refinement of these forms and standard rules are the responsibility of the Information Security Department. For the Owners, this access control decision-making is a relatively straightforward select-from-predefined-categories process, but it is more complicated these days because consultants, contractors, temporaries, outsourcing firm staff, and business partners need to have access. The need for a consistent approach to information security via a team of people is discussed in greater depth in Chapter 3.

Owners must be employees, and preferably members of the management team. This is because an Owner's decisions about information security requirements are essentially basic asset management and protection decisions. It is for this reason that many people believe these decisions should not be delegated. Management has a fiduciary duty to protect assets, including information, and this duty implies that they must be personally involved in these decisions. This decision-making contrasts with the development of procedures, documentation of these procedures, and other efforts to implement these decisions, all of which can be, and generally are, delegated to others.

Role Of Custodians

Custodians (sometimes called Stewards) are workers who have been entrusted with the safekeeping and secure processing of information that has been provided by either internal Company X Owners or third parties (such as business partners). Safekeeping can take many forms such as regularly backing-up the information. This safekeeping includes the provision of secure processing facilities, traditionally involving the administration of a fixed-password-based access control system. To securely process information entrusted to them, Custodians most often will need to provide general security systems that can be used for multiple data types.

Custodians are responsible for complying with the instructions provided by information Owners. Custodians are also responsible for complying with organization-wide information security requirements that are not specific to certain types of information (a policy regarding the prompt installation of operating system upgrades is an example). Custodians are responsible for the day-to-day handling of information that has been entrusted to them, including help desk assistance, in a manner that observes all of these instructions.

Custodians must provide Owners with periodic reports showing all people who have been granted access to the information in question. Custodians must also provide Owners with technical advice about the ways to best protect the confidentiality, integrity, and availability of the information that they have been charged to safeguard and process. This technical advice is supplemented by the organization-wide direction and consulting assistance provided by the Information Security Department.

Custodians are additionally responsible for immediately responding to all privacy, security, and/or availability problems that come to their attention so as to protect Company X information, information systems, workers, relationships, and reputation. In those cases where Custodians do not have the necessary expertise or resources to adequately deal with a privacy, security,

and/or availability problem on their own, they must immediately alert those who are in a position to assist them (most often a Computer Emergency Response Team; see Chapter 11 for a discussion of the duties of a CERT).

Custodians can be employees, contractors, consultants, temporaries or outsourcing firm staff. The job of Custodian is often outsourced to people who act as Systems Administrators, Computer Operators, and Data Control Specialists (the latter may, for example, manage data stored at an off-site location). The distinguishing characteristics of a Custodian is the fact that he or she is in possession of the information, that he or she has special information system privileges to manage this same information, and that he or she runs the systems that handle this information.

Role Of Users

Users are workers who have been granted access to Company X information and/or information systems to do their jobs. If they do not currently have authorization to access information and/or information systems, they must first request and receive permission from the relevant information Owner or the Owner's delegate. Users are forbidden from using any Company X information for purposes other than those expressly authorized by the information Owner or by their immediate manager. Likewise, Users must not disclose the Company X information in their possession to unauthorized parties (whether internal or external) without the prior permission of the information Owner.

Users must follow the information systems control requirements specified by Custodians and by the Information Security Department. An example of a Custodian-specified control would be the need to change passwords in response to a suspected break-in. An example of an Information Security Department specified requirement would be the need to construct a fixed password of at least ten characters that is made up of both numeric and alphabetic characters. The most important control requirements issued by the Information Security Department can be found in the "Information Security Policy Manual" described in Chapter 10.

Users are responsible for the secure handling of information in their immediate possession. For example, users must manage their desktop and portable computers in such a manner that unauthorized access does not take place. This includes keeping both a password-based access control package, a personal firewall, and a virus detection package enabled on these computers. Users must also securely handle sensitive information in other forms, such as shredding hardcopy reports rather than throwing them in the trash. Users are additionally responsible for safeguarding all storage media containing sensitive information (CD-ROMs, floppy disks, magnetic access cards, etc.).

Users must report all errors and anomalies in the information to which they have been given access to the Owner and/or their immediate manager. These include improper disclosure of the information to unauthorized persons as well as situations where the information has been lost or seriously damaged. Users must also report all suspected information security problems or violations to the Information Security Department. These reporting processes are a very important double-check that helps to ensure that other security measures are working as they should be.

Users can be full- or part-time workers, so long as they have business need to have access to Company X information. Users can be temporaries, consultants, contractors, or outsourcing staff. Users typically have a wide variety of job titles including Department Manager, Receptionist, and Data Entry Operator. The privileges of users must be turned off when they no longer have a legitimate business need for such access (for example when they quit the employment of Company X, when they go on a leave of absence, etc.).

Traditional Approach Summary

Within this three-way Owner-Custodian-User division of responsibilities there is a great deal of scripted, already-existent structure. This structure is intended to minimize the possibility that people in any one of these categories would make a decision that would jeopardize security. The burden on Users is deliberately light in large measure because there are so many of them. This approach minimizes the costs of, and productivity impacts of, information security measures. Another reason to have few responsibilities for Users is that the people in this category are often the least interested in, and the least knowledgeable about information security across all three categories.

Before your organization adopts an Owner-Custodian-User (OCU) assignment of roles and responsibilities, it should have several basic elements of an information security infrastructure in place. These include:

- a data classification system-for sensitivity, and ideally for criticality as well (both are strongly recommended)

- a list of basic information systems controls that go along with each of the categories appearing in the data classification system (for example, secret information must be encrypted when sent over a public network such as the Internet)

- a set of policies that define basic information security requirements for managers, technical staff and users (for example, do not share your fixed password with anyone, even if they say they need it in order to accomplish a business purpose)

- already installed computer-based information access control mechanisms (generally this means fixed passwords, but extended user authentication systems like dynamic passwords are recommended)

- a documented process for requesting and approving access to information systems (a specific type of manager must approve such requests, and then forward the request on to those who actually make the changes in computer-based access controls)

Note that the OCU roles and responsibilities are in addition to job descriptions, departmental mission statements, reporting relationship diagrams and other documentation defined in this book (see Chapter 10 for a list of other documents). While this three-way assignment of responsibility can often simplify discussions and allow projects to proceed in an expedited manner, it should be adopted after these other role and responsibility documents have already been endorsed by management and integrated into the existing organizational structure.

The OCU roles and responsibilities are information-oriented whereas job descriptions, departmental mission statements, and reporting relationship diagrams are duties oriented. This means that the two approaches are complimentary and not redundant. Information security is such a new and still embryonic field that every organization needs multiple models for roles and responsibilities to minimize losses to both information and information systems. Table 15-1 summarizes the duties for the OCU role.

Table 15-1: Summary of Owner, Custodian, and User Duties

Role	Duties
Owner	• Understand major risks to, and all internal uses of, a designated type of information • Share their knowledge about existence and nature of controls now used for the information • Select information sensitivity and criticality levels for this information, and periodically declassify/downgrade the these levels as necessary • Specify supplementary control measures to protect this information • Supervise the development of procedures, documentation and other local information security control implementation efforts • Designate Custodians for information and resources that handle this information • Establish annual budget for the management, update, and protection of this information • Approve user access requests to the information • Review user access control lists to determine which users should lose privileges
Custodian	• Safeguard and maintain physical possession of information • Follow Owner's instructions for information handling and processing • Provide Owner with periodic reports showing all users who have access to information • Make technological and procedural suggestions to Owner • Maintain secure access facilities for the information in question • Comply with other relevant information security requirements • Enforce controls specified by the Owner over user community • Immediately respond to all privacy, security and availability problems, and request technical assistance immediately if needed
User	• Request access to information and systems from the Owner • Refrain from using information or systems unless authorization is first obtained • Refrain from sharing information with unauthorized people • Employ secure access facilities provided by Custodian • Comply with controls specified by both Company X and the Owner • Report errors and anomalies in the information to the Owner • Report improper disclosure, damage, or loss to the Owner or immediate manager • Report vulnerabilities and security violations to Information Security Department

Role Of Department Manager - An Extension To The Role Of Owner

One of the most troublesome aspects of information security in many organizations remains the significant resistance that middle management has to adopting information security improvements. The reasons for this resistance are many, including local budgetary profit-and-loss systems which encourage belt-tightening that often causes managers to say "no thanks" when it comes to information security improvements. The reasons for this resistance are further explored in Appendix C. This sub-section explores another way to help garner the support of middle managers with an extension to the role of information Owners.

Many organizations are now holding department managers personally responsible for establishing and maintaining a certain level of information security within their department. If their departments fail internal audits, risk analyses, spot checks, or other tests to ensure that controls are in existence and functioning correctly, the involved department managers are held responsible. To specifically assign tasks to department managers, such as the development and testing of a departmental information systems contingency plan, is to hold them responsible to a degree that they had not been held responsible in the past. In years gone past, they could - and often did - say that these tasks were the job of the Information Security Department, and then they paid scant attention to information security.

As Chapter 3 explains in detail, information security within a particular organization will only be successful when a team of individuals have been clearly assigned various tasks and duties, and when all important members of this team feel as though it is their personal responsibility to support information security. Even though department managers may be assigned the job of Owner for certain types of information (as defined earlier in this chapter), they may still lack a deep and personal commitment to supporting and encouraging others to conform to information security requirements. Such a commitment is important because these managers set the tone, and establish the priorities, for the work performed by nearly all others throughout the organization. This is why a number of organizations are now assigning specific accountability to department managers.

This additional accountability is also necessary because not all department managers are information Owners. For example, the Public Relations Department Manager may not be an information Owner, yet he or she needs to make sure that everyone in that department consistently supports information security and privacy. Likewise, traditional assignments of ownership duties do not hold department managers accountable for things like: (a) sending all of the department's users to information security training, (b) taking steps to label all sensitive information in the department, (c) making sure that all labeled sensitive information has been properly locked up after hours, and (d) procuring shredders for all users in the department who need them at their desks.

Department managers may also be assigned specific duties such as acting as intermediaries for user reports of information loss, unauthorized disclosure, and unresolved error. Department managers can also be gatekeepers, rationing user requests to utilize certain powerful information system features, such as the ability to send a broadcast message to all internal users on an electronic mail system. Department managers can be the ones to approve or deny requests to perform information handling actions that could jeopardize information security, such as remove sensitive information from a physically-protected room within a secured office building. Department managers may also be

required to observe information security requirements when it comes to purchasing new hardware or software. Department managers may furthermore be used as a step in the approval process for user access control privilege requests. What's more, department managers can be an important adjunct to an internal disciplinary process, especially in those cases where a user in their department has violated an information security policy.

Department managers can also take on tasks which might have been performed by information security staff, for example, in some organizations they may be required to periodically monitor the web surfing habits of users within their department. Department managers, acting as surrogates for the user community, can additionally be assigned duties associated with the testing and approval for new application systems. For example, only if certain security and privacy requirements are met, will department managers be permitted to approve a new or significantly modified application system. Department managers can also be held responsible for recovering the property of the organization (credit cards, library books, portable computers, personal digital assistants, confidential information, etc.) when a user in their department is leaving the organization. Department managers can furthermore be accountable for making sure that users in their department follow information security policies and procedures, such as a requirement to back-up all portable personal computers at least monthly, if not more frequently. Of course, many of these duties will be delegated, but that's not to say that department managers shouldn't be fingered as responsible.

The assignment of department manager duties may be done through a set of information security policies, or it may be done through a department manager's manual (these and other related documents are described in Chapter 10.) Perhaps the most common way to assign these additional duties, a department manager's manual is a comprehensive reference guide, generally distributed only to department managers and higher level management. Job descriptions are also recommended, as are the written distinctions of Owner, Custodian, and User. All of these distinctions, in addition to the explicit assignment of department manager roles and responsibilities related to information security, are strongly recommended.

Chapter 16 ROLES & RESPONSIBILITIES OF PRODUCT VENDORS

Major Shifts In The Marketplace Now Underway

An important and evolutionary shift of information security responsibility from user organizations to vendor organizations is now underway. In the past, vendors would disavow all responsibility for security, claiming it was exclusively a user organization responsibility. This position was clear from the software contracts that user organizations were required to sign if they wanted to use a particular vendor's software. These days, new vendors like Managed Security Service Providers (MSSPs) are appearing, and these vendors are finding an eager clientele who wish to transfer information security responsibility from in-house staff to outside experts. Major software firms, such as Microsoft, have also recently announced that secure systems are now their number one priority. Vendors of both software and hardware are now looking to see how they can better respond to user organization security needs, and they now often tout new security features as a reason to buy their products.

What's happening in the information security marketplace happened in the automobile marketplace a while ago. When airbags were first introduced, they were offered in high-price cars as an option. Later they became standard in all high-priced models. Government regulations and increased consumer group pressure is increasingly causing airbags to be offered as standard equipment in all modern cars, regardless of the price. Likewise, Internet Service Providers (ISPs) have long offered cable modem and digital subscriber line (DSL) service without any security mechanisms like personal firewalls or anti-virus software. It has taken significant negative publicity and increased pressure on ISPs, but now some of them are offering these protections as an option. Soon we will see that they offer them as standard equipment on all connections that they provide. Vendors are slowly being forced to acknowledge that it is not sufficient to simply provide a bare bones service, that they must additionally provide the security measures which help to ensure that users are secure. For example, ISPs must ensure that user's personal computers don't become zombie computers participating in a distributed denial of service (DDOS) attack.

The shift in responsibility to vendors is necessary because historically the responsibility for information security has been disproportionately placed on the shoulders of user organizations. While there are many examples, perhaps the most obvious involves the way the software vendor community indirectly employs user organizations as beta test sites for bug-ridden code. Software vendors typically release products before they are adequately debugged or tested, and one result is that security problems are soon detected by hackers and others. This leads to a flood of upgrades (hot fixes, patches, service packs, etc.), many of which would have been prevented if the vendors had only done a diligent, conscientious, and secure job of creating the software before it was released to the marketplace. The constant stream of new viruses is in part attributable to this problem; if the operating systems of personal computers were designed with strong security in mind, viruses would never have been a problem. Likewise, many of the thousands of reported system vulnerabilities are attributable to poor programming practices (for example those that allow buffer overflows), and this has encouraged the rapid growth of a whole new type of business which focuses on intrusion detection/management. So this shift of responsibility is actually long overdue.

The problem with this shift in responsibility is that nobody seems to be talking about it, much less planning for it. One major reason why vendors aren't talking about it is that they don't want to inhibit their sales. They don't want to scare away potential customers or perhaps imply that there is something inherently dangerous or risky about their products or services. Vendors are also concerned that they might be held liable for security problems, and if they admit there is a problem, this might be used in court against them. But it is time to talk about it, and it is time for you to start planning how this shift in responsibility will manifest at your organization. This shift impacts Information Security Department mission statements, job descriptions, staffing plans, project plans, outsourcing contracts, systems architectures, and many other aspects of the information security management process. This chapter defines that shift and makes some suggestions about appropriate next steps.

Before we explore this trend in greater detail, a few definitions are in order. In this context, vendors include systems integrators, systems outsourcing firms, software publishers, and hardware manufacturers. When the words "user organization responsibility" appear below, reference is being made to the entire organization as a legal entity rather than specific user departments, such as Accounting or Marketing.

In the past, user organizations were responsible for performing risk assessments, identifying and implementing the controls needed to address their organization's unique risks, as well as administering and maintaining these controls. While these responsibilities will not disappear, in the future user organizations will orchestrate a team made up of both inside staff members and a variety of outside organizations (contractors, consultants, temporaries, outsourcing firm staff, etc.). Beyond these people, these outside team members will include information systems product vendors, software vendors, and information content publishers. Chapter 3 discusses the need for such a team in detail.

Not only is the law increasingly holding vendors and publishers responsible for incorporating adequate security into their products, but the technology itself is now making it possible for vendors and publishers to provide new and refined security mechanisms as standard functionality. Consider the toll fraud area related to private branch exchanges (PBXs). Carriers are being subjected to an increasing number of lawsuits alleging that they did not provide adequate controls, adequate training, or adequate notice of potential security problems. The recent introduction of new anti-fraud offerings, such as expert systems that examine calling patterns, clearly shows that vendors are feeling pressure from user organizations and responding to it. In addition, vendors like SPRINT are now offering insurance to help prevent devastating toll fraud losses. Telephone companies are also forming working groups such as the Toll Fraud Prevention Committee to help address this problem.

Another example involves unauthorized software copying. It is, in the long run, totally inappropriate for software publishers to hold user organizations responsible for looking after the publisher's copyrights. A host of new digital rights management (DRM) products now allow vendors to control unauthorized copying, executing, forwarding, and printing of software. Vendors will soon release their software accompanied by anti-copying security mechanisms, including built-in license management systems. This means that the copyright infringement audits performed by the Information Industry Association (formerly the

Software Publishers Association and the Business Software Alliance) are a temporary phenomenon. Several years from now, these user organization software license audits will be unnecessary. As a result, user organizations will need to spend much less time educating end-users about software licensing, issuing no-copying policies, performing compliance audits, and the like. In large measure, in the future, information systems will be required to take care of their own security.

Every year, organizations around the globe spend millions of dollars keeping their commercially-purchased software up-to-date through patches, fixes and updates. Many of these changes must be handled by user organization technical staff, and many are urgent because they handle what would otherwise be significant security vulnerabilities. To hold user organization staff responsible for the security lapses of vendor development staff is totally inappropriate. To preoccupy user organization technical staff with alerts about security problems, to force them to set other work aside so that they can clean-up the sloppy programming of vendors, all this seems inappropriate and in the long-run unsustainable. Vendors must stop treating their customers at user organizations as though they are beta test sites; vendors need to release products which have been securely designed and adequately tested, not repair problems after a commercial product has already been officially released. In the future, successful software vendors will only release software when it is truly really ready for commercial use, and then they will handle patches, fixes, updates and the like through automated software distribution methods such as "push updates" via the Internet.

Yet another example can be found in the information publishing field, specifically involving electronic document viewers, also known as secure content systems. These products allow multimedia documents to be published and viewed without requiring the user organization to be in possession of a copy of the software used to create the documents. The viewers are also, in many cases, able to accommodate multiple operating systems at the end user organization. Examples include Digital Envoy and Adobe Acrobat. These systems increasingly incorporate security measures allowing the publisher to define and enforce the rights it wishes to convey. For example, electronic documents can be made read-only, or users can be permitted to append annotations, or permitted to print the documents. These security features are incorporated into the document itself, and are not a function of the underlying operating system, an access control package, or some other software. In the future, whatever rights publishers choose to convey will be automatically enforced.

Why Vendors Should Take On More Responsibility

Nobody knows more about the complexities of their products and services than vendors and publishers. It only makes sense that they should fundamentally be responsible for the security of their systems and content. Of course, how a user organization installs, manages, maintains, and otherwise utilizes a product is still an important factor. For example, the user organization will still have its own responsibility for security, particularly when contributory negligence is involved. Instead, the field is evolving towards a more balanced situation where responsibility is shared in a manner commensurate with the actions that can be taken by the organizations involved. Vendors and publishers will be responsible for incorporating adequate security mechanisms into their products, for training user organizations in the usage of these mechanisms, and for making changes to maintain adequate security in light of new vulnerabilities. User organizations will continue to be responsible for the way they deploy, use, and rely upon these products.

If your organization is not already using these and other new tools whereby systems manage their own security, you should investigate their applicability. These and related products may hold the promise of significantly reducing the need for user training as well as administrative support for information security. For example if unauthorized software copying was prevented technologically, the need to train users not to make copies would be significantly reduced. To ensure the consistent application of security measures throughout an organization, and to reduce reliance on people who may not fully support information security, vendors will continue to automate many security activities that in days gone past were handled by humans. User organization management will also appreciate that it is in their own best interests to automate as many information security tasks as possible, so that reliance on individual users is reduced. When information security tasks are automated, they can readily be turned into packaged products, and then they can be transferred from user organization to both vendors and publishers. For example, if backups for all desktop machines on a local area network can be handled automatically at night, then security will be enhanced, user involvement will be reduced, and opportunities for vendors will be created.

If your organization is relying on end-user goodwill and understanding, to the extent that current technology allows it, an automated solution would be a preferable alternative. If your organization has been feeling like it has an undue burden for security, that vendors have not been shouldering their share, it is high time to enlist the cooperation of vendors so that a more equitable and more sustainable balance can be achieved. For example, when outsourcing contracts are up for annual review, the information security related responsibilities can be more clearly defined and perhaps some can be transferred from a user organization to an outsourcing vendor. (See Chapter 17 for further details). When new arrangements are made with consultants, contractors, and temporary support firms, information security responsibilities can be clarified and at least partially transferred to these outsiders.

In many cases, when a consultant, contractor or temporary is hired, that individual may sign a confidentiality agreement, but the individual does not typically go through new hire orientation. Likewise, that individual does not usually go through an information security training class. This is inconsistent since both new hire orientation and an information security class are generally required for employees. To have some members of an information security team receive this training, and some not (vendors often do not), is likely to lead to misunderstandings, and perhaps serious security lapses as well. All members of the information security team need to receive comparable training as well as receive clearly written descriptions of their responsibilities. The cost of providing this training and the cost of clarifying these responsibilities are now inconsequential relative to the risks that a user organization faces if it does not adopt this consistent approach.

Getting Vendors To Listen To You

One of the steps that your organization can take to establish a more equitable distribution of information security responsibilities includes leveraging the organization's buying power. If the user organization has some significant buying power, preference can be given to those vendors who have products that automatically take care of their own security. For example, some virus screening products automatically update themselves via Internet push technology. This preference for a certain vendor can also reduce costs for the user organization, as would for example be the case with a volume purchase agreement (VPA) or some other sort of long-term commitment. Requests for proposals (RFPs) can likewise be written so that vendors are required to take on a greater portion of the responsibility for information security. Similarly, organizations can complain to their vendors and make formal requests that additional security responsibilities be adopted by these same vendors.

Because they don't represent much potential revenue, smaller organizations will not, generally, be able to engage vendors in a serious discussion about sharing information security responsibility. These organizations will simply be presented with a license agreement or some other contractual document that they will be required to sign, that is if they wish to purchase or otherwise acquire a vendor's products or services. For these organizations, it will be sufficient to simply understand just what the license agreement or other contractual document says and to take action in light of this understanding. Far too many organizations don't pay attention to these documents. It is these same organizations that may find themselves in trouble with

the Information Industry Association, and the targets of a copyright violation audit. It is these same organizations that may find themselves in a stockholders' lawsuit alleging management's failure to adequately protect corporate assets.

This new-shared responsibility could be documented in renegotiated organizational-license contracts, outsourcing firm contracts, and consulting engagement contracts. The job description responsibilities shown in Chapter 12 are a good place to get ideas for responsibilities that could be off-loaded to vendors. Vendors in most instances have greater technical expertise and more extensive business contacts than most user organizations, so on balance the overall level of information security is likely to be improved. For further discussion about the pros and cons of using vendors, see Chapter 17.

Chapter 17 ROLES & RESPONSIBILITIES OF OUTSOURCING FIRMS

Chapter 16 addressed the ways in which third-party information security roles and responsibilities are evolving. If you have not yet read that chapter, the author suggests that you go back and read it before proceeding. This chapter discusses the risks of outsourcing an information security effort as well as the benefits of such an outsourcing endeavor. This chapter also covers the specific information security roles and responsibilities that an outsourcing firm could be called upon to perform. After that, you will find a section on the topics to be covered in a contract with an outsourcing firm as well as a discussion of the due diligence that should be performed before an outsourcing firm is retained to handle information security. All of these ideas can be used as input to the preparation of a contract, an agreement, or a memo of understanding. Throughout the chapter, the term outsourcing firm is used generically and it includes Internet Service Providers (ISPs), Application Service Providers (ASPs), Managed Security Service Providers (MSSPs), Internet web site or commerce site hosting firms, facilities management firms, and other similar organizations.

Risks Of Outsourcing

The decision to outsource an information security function, in whole or in part, should not be taken lightly. Far too many organizations are dazzled by the potential cost savings, the alleged access to third-party expertise, and the potential to refocus internal operations on activities considered to be strategic or critical to the business. While these are important objectives, management at your organization should not rush into an information security outsourcing deal without first having performed a risk assessment pertaining to the outsourcing effort.

Unlike other risk assessments, a risk assessment dealing with an information security outsourcing effort should not be performed by the Information Security Department. Instead, the work should be performed by an outside consultant (who doesn't work for, or have any other connection with one of the potential outsourcing firms being considered) or a member of the Internal Audit Department staff. For this type of a risk assess-

ment, the Information Security Department is likely to have a conflict of interest. Fearing that they may lose their jobs, members of the Information Security Department may paint an unrealistically negative and gloomy picture of the consequences associated with outsourcing information security work. Similarly, fearing that they may be shown to be doing a poor job, members of the Information Security Department may characterize the quality of service that they provide as excellent, when in fact it is not.

Although statistical studies, such as those from The Outsourcing Institute, indicate the popularity of outsourcing is unquestionably increasing, there are a number of serious risks associated with this new business arrangement. Although there are some overlaps, these risks fall into two broad categories covered below: (1) additional information security risks, and (2) additional business risks. Most of these risks are business risks, and all of them can be overcome through careful outsourcing firm contract planning, background checking, contract negotiation, and on-going contract management. In other words, if you have researched, planned, negotiated, and managed it well, outsourcing can work well. The same can be said for co-sourcing, where part of the work is done inside and part is done outside.

(1) Additional Information Security Risks

- Sensitive information may be disclosed to outsiders who should not have access to such information (this may take place because the outsourcing firm also processes the business transactions of a competitor)

- Critical or strategic information may be lost due to an error or omission on the part of outsourcing staff

- Access privileges may be exploited by outsourcing staff to perpetrate fraud, to violate privacy, or to commit other crimes and abuses

- Important customized controls that your organization developed to handle unique business circumstances may be abandoned because the outsourcing firm has a standardized approach that must be used by all of its customers

- Knowledge about outsourcing staff activities may not flow to your organization and this can in turn lead to a situation where your organization is unduly at risk (for example a high security server may have been improperly configured but this fact may not be revealed until the system has been compromised)

- Mechanisms that allow your organization to control the outsourcing firm staff may be insufficient and/or ineffective, and as a result, your organization may be unable to get the outsourcing firm to provide essential security products or services

- Total costs for outsourcing may be higher than necessary because your organization has been too strict in its definition of information security requirements, thereby eliminating or diluting one of the prime motivations for outsourcing (saving money)

- Intruders may exploit unknown information security exposures introduced because your organization did not sufficiently understand what security was needed, and thus an outsourcing contract did not require the outsourcing firm to implement adequate security requirements

- The outsourcing firm did not establish a contingency plan which reflects the unique needs of your organization, and thus your organization may suffer large and unanticipated losses from an interruption in service

- Your own organization's technical staff failed to establish a clear and well-thought-out contingency plan for bringing outsourced activities back in-house, and as a result your organization may suffer an extended period of service interruption when a contract with the outsourcing firm ends

(2) Additional Business Risks

- Management operational control may be lost because the outsourcing firm staff doesn't understand the complexities of internal systems at your organization, or perhaps because its staff doesn't care about these complexities

- Technical experts at your organization may leave because they think the interesting or important work is now being done by the outsourcing firm

- Technical experts at your organization may leave, in which case the organization would have nobody who could realistically evaluate whether or not the outsourcing firm is doing a good job in the information security area, nobody who can credibly determine whether the information security representations of the outsourcing firm are in fact true, and nobody who can credibly manage the work of the outsourcing firm staff (this risk is also known as loss of organizational knowledge)

- In-house technical staff may now have the impression that management doesn't care about them, only the bottom line, and this may lead to new or exacerbated loyalty and morale problems

- Outsourcing may foster an attitude among top managers that information systems are no longer critical to the success of your business, that they are non-strategic, and this may encourage budget cuts, reduced management attention, and related problems

- Outsourcing staff may not be motivated because your organization is just one of many organizations demanding service

- Inflexible outsourcing staff may refuse to take on additional information security tasks that are genuinely needed, but have not been explicitly defined in the outsourcing contract

- Tightly-defined contract and outsourcing arrangements may impose a level of inflexibility that makes it exceedingly difficult for your organization to rapidly respond to new products or services offered by a competitor

- Long-term contract provisions may lock your organization into a relationship that fundamentally doesn't meet the needs of your organization and can't be broken without considerable financial hardship

- Quality of service may erode because the outsourcing firm doesn't use sufficiently competent or technically trained staff to handle information security, or perhaps because they have experienced a wave of new customers and have not yet staffed-up to meet the demands of these new customers

- System response time and other system performance metrics may degrade because the outsourcing firm is substituting less expensive and slower firewalls, servers, and other system components for the components your firm previously employed

- Quality of service may be reduced because the processes involved are rapidly evolving or especially complicated and therefore better handled in-house

- You may encounter great difficulty changing the way activities are performed because the outsourcing firm has their own specific way of doing things, but your organization has discovered a preferred way of doing things after the contract has been signed

- Service from the outsourcing firm may degrade because the involved workers are complacent and don't appreciate how their work impacts your organization

- Communications problems with the outsourcing firm staff may delay appropriate responses to information security problems like hacker intrusions; these delays may be still longer when the outsourcing firm uses subcontactors (so-called daisy-chain delays)

- Outsourcing firm staff may be unavailable when heroic personal contributions would be forthcoming from in-house staff (for example after a disaster)

- Awkward and inefficient modifications to internal control processes at your organization may need to be made so that the work can fit into the outsourcing firm's internal processes

- Poor performance on the part of the outsourcing firm may cause financial losses, reputation degradations, or business disruptions to be suffered by your organization

- The outsourcing firm may go out of business without much, if any, advance notice, and your organization may not have an adequate contingency plan ready-to-go, thus causing significant business interruption

- You may have to make arrangements with more than one outsourcing firm in order to be assured that service for critical applications will continue to be provided, and this may significantly increase the cost of outsourcing

- Because the outsourcing arrangement did not meet your organization's needs, you may have to bear significant additional costs associated with the movement of oursourced activities from the outsourcing firm back to your own in-house operation

- Costs to transfer activities from your organization to the outsourcing firm may be significantly underestimated because the internal promoters of outsourcing were overly optimistic, and because they did not understand just how many adjustments are necessary in order to get two organizations to work seamlessly together

- Significant outsourcing staff overtime and additional consulting support may be required because a large number of adjustments are necessary to properly process your organization's transactions

- The costs for the outsourcing firm to act upon change orders and additional requests, matters which were not originally covered by the contract, far exceeds your organization's expectations, and thus also provides the outsourcing firm with a major source of additional profits

- Outsourcing firm management may have unanticipated disagreements with your organization's management due to fundamentally different information security philosophies, views, goals, policies, and/or procedures

- Outsourcing firm staff may consistently do a poor job which doesn't measure-up to your organization's standards, and it may take a significant amount of time and effort to determine that the only way to get the results your management wants is to terminate the contract

- Your organization may be adversely affected by human resources problems at the outsourcing firm such as hostile takeovers, leveraged buyouts, labor strikes, walk-outs, and layoffs

- Outsourcing firm management may unilaterally assign its rights and responsibilities to another party (such as a subcontractor), and with this transfer process significantly increase the performance risk that your organization faces because there are now more parties who must successfully act in concert with each other

- Through the outsourcing process your organization may lose its ability to perform certain functions in-house, and as a result your organization may now be at the mercy of its current outsourcing firm or a competing outsourcing firm

- Over time, your organization may gradually become estranged from the current technology used to perform certain tasks as well as the ways that business processes are performed, and your organization may thus face a significant additional cost to train internal staff and acquaint these internal staff members with these matters, all as a prerequisite to returning outsourced activities to your organization

- The good reputation of your organization may be degraded because it is indirectly associated with unsavory firms such as pornographic web sites, which are also run on the same equipment at the outsourcing firm

The performance of an outsourcing firm risk assessment should take place before an outsourcing vendor has been arranged and before a contract has been signed. The risk assessment can help define which tasks are suitably outsourced and which should remain in-house. For example, certain managers at your organization should maintain the ultimate decision-making responsibility for all information security requirements. Likewise, while an outsourcing firm or consultant can assist by preparing draft information security policies, an internal manager should be the one who ultimately makes the decision about the content and wording of these same policies. Similarly, while an outsourcing firm or consultant can propose the specifics of an information security architecture, an internal manager should be the one who ultimately determines which requirements will go into that same architecture.

In the course of clarifying the scope of the services that should be outsourced and those which should remain in-house, you should also define the nature of the decision-making relationship involving your organization and the outsourcing firm. For instance, you should clarify which decisions will be left to the outsourcing firm, and which will be reserved for your organization. If a hacker breaks into your organization's internal network, should the outsourcing firm initiate the response via a computer emergency response team (CERT), or should your organization do that? Similarly, if automated systems detect the fact that a specific user has unusual and suspicious computer usage patterns, should the outsourcing firm revoke that user's privileges or should the revocation be left to your organization? Likewise, if electrical power is interrupted in the data center, should the outsourcing firm determine when operations get moved to a remote site, or should that decision be reserved for in-house management?

Although firms that specialize in information security are likely to be an exception, many outsourcing firms have not paid enough attention to security. This is especially the case for organizations working in banking and other industries where excellent information security is a condition of continued business activity. Managers at customer organizations often think, "But of course information security duties will be handled, because after all, this outsourcing firm is a professional organization that seems to have its act together." You need to clearly articulate and diplomatically challenge this assumption via the risk assessment process. The risks of making this or a similar assumption need to be clearly articulated, and many questions need to be asked of those who are promoting the outsourcing effort. As a side effect of this questioning, managers involved in this discussion will be reeducated about the many valuable services that an internal Information Technology Department, an Internal Audit Department, and an internal Information Security Department can perform.

There is some merit to the old adage, "If it ain't broken, don't fix it." In many cases management does not fully realize the cost and disruption associated with the movement of the information security function from in-house personnel to an outsourcing firm, from one outsourcing firm to yet another, or from an outsourcing firm back to in-house staff. This disruption and cost can be prohibitive if the organization is frequently changing outsourcing firms and not seeking to establish a long-term mutually-rewarding relationship with an outsourcing firm. As an example, consider the relationships that staff in an internal information security group have developed over the years with others throughout the organization. These relationships are not readily transferable to an outsourcing firm-the outsourcing firm must start from the beginning with each of the people involved, developing new personal relationships, understanding the abilities of these people, understanding the assigned roles of these people, etc. Likewise, management may not appreciate that when they outsource information security they may need to buy new hardware or software in order to link in-house systems with outsourcing firm systems.

In a similar manner, you should challenge management's claims of special access to certain expertise that would come along with an outsourcing contract. The alleged experts may leave the outsourcing firm before the contract is signed, or the experts-even though they remain employed at the outsourcing firm-may never work on your organization's affairs. Depending on the situation, there are less expensive ways to gain access to expertise that are much less disruptive than outsourcing.

These include retaining expert consultants or contractors, or even hiring additional full-time information security staff. Consultants and contractors are often used as a way to obtain specialized technical services such as penetration attacks. Keeping some information security staff as employees at your organization is highly desirable because it helps maintain a continuity of operations that is less likely to be encountered when third-parties are used.

On another note, with the exception of legal problems and service disruption problems, nothing related to information security seems to get top management attention as much as reputation risk. Top management is often very concerned about the organization's image, specifically about the way the organization is perceived by various constituencies such as customers, suppliers, and business partners. The person performing an outsourcing risk assessment should be sure to examine the impact on the organization's reputation as well as the personal reputation of the managers who are promoting the outsourcing effort. Your discussions with management likewise should be sure to emphasize the reputation risk associated with an outsourcing effort.

While one or two information security outsourcing firms may be manageable, having more than this may quickly lead to breakdowns in communication. As the number of parties involved in dealing with information security increases linearly, the number of required communications between these same parties increases exponentially. Having many outsourcing firms will also require a greater commitment to training. For these and related reasons, many organizations are considering consolidating their outsourcing vendors with a smaller number of companies. These concerns argue for signing-up with an outsourcing company that handles many information security tasks, perhaps including physical security tasks.

Benefits Of Outsourcing Information Security

While you wouldn't want to outsource everything in the information security area, there are significant benefits to outsourcing some tasks. The major motivation to outsource for most organizations is to save money. For example, for many organizations, it doesn't make sense to have expert information security staff on-duty 24 hours a day, seven days a week, in case a hacker intrusion takes place. It makes much more sense, and is less expensive, simply to hire some other organization to monitor the network around-the-clock. By sharing an expensive resource, such as a team of information security experts, customers of an outsourcing firm can significantly lower their expenses.

A slight variation of the benefit mentioned in the last paragraph involves avoiding a major investment. If a well developed outsourcing market exists for the activity being examined, and if outsourcing firms can offer products and services which would cost the organization a great deal of money to create in-house, then going with an outsourcing firm is a justifiable and reasonable business decision. An example can be found in the network intrusion detection field. A variety of sophisticated outsourcing vendors can be found in this market niche, and they have advanced technology, specialized professional expertise, and a significant capital investment that would be difficult for all but the largest organizations to match.

Another reason to outsource is to obtain access to technical expertise that an organization can't consistently put to use. For example, an esteemed expert at intrusion detection systems may be underutilized if he is a member of your in-house staff, but his time would most likely be well-utilized if he were to work for a managed security service provider (MSSP). The same could be said of your medical doctor. You probably wouldn't hire the doctor full-time to wait around until you get sick; instead you would use the doctor only when necessary. Access to technical expertise is also an issue if the expert would not be somebody that your organization could hire due to limited salary ranges, geographical remoteness of the office, the worker's unwillingness to move due to family considerations, and other human resource issues.

Still another reason to hire an outside firm to handle one or more information security tasks is to be assured that you are getting assistance from people who have done this before. You certainly wouldn't want to get open-heart surgery from a doctor who had never performed such an operation before. Likewise, your organization shouldn't be the learning experiment for people who have never dealt with information security before. There is a certain amount of peace of mind that comes from knowing that you have a seasoned and experienced team addressing complex and important problems.

A related reason to outsource some or all of your organization's information security activities is an appreciation that it would take too long to teach existing employees to become proficient in this complex area. This perspective is prevalent in high-tech start-up firms that need to show results quickly. Any business that is under pressure to quickly change or to meet a deadline can also see that outsourcing is the preferred option if internal staff don't have sufficient knowledge, training, or expertise. In a more general sense, going outside rather than training insiders can be used to shorten the completion times for a variety of activities such as establishing an Internet commerce site and developing a new information security software product.

Another reason to outsource the information security function involves getting a quick understanding about what exactly has to be done in order to be in compliance with the standard of due care. For example, if you were to have a severe pain in your chest, you would typically be rushed to the hospital and a medical doctor would immediately examine you. There wouldn't be time for you to research all the possible causes of your pain -- you would want immediate expert advice about the next steps. The same can be said of many organizations considering the outsourcing of information security, especially those which have just suffered a significant information security loss. While it is definitely useful to get an outside firm's opinion about next steps, management shouldn't place too great a reliance on the advice of a single outsourcing firm. Just as you should get a second opinion regarding any complex and dangerous medical procedure like open-heart surgery, so too you should get other opinions about how to improve information security. The second opinion in the information security environment is most often obtained from expert consultants and external auditors. In this regard, there is a serious danger that organizations come to rely too much on an outsourcing firm, where management has in effect abdicated its responsibility. This topic is covered in greater depth in this same chapter, in the subsection below entitled Typical Areas To Outsource.

Still another reason to outsource information security involves management's perception that the market it serves has changed or will soon change. Most often this involves a sense that the business has gotten a lot more competitive. As a result, management believes that the firm must focus its efforts and resources on those matters which are it's core competencies. Said another way, it seeks to focus on what it does best, and then give the rest to outside firms.

Typical Areas To Outsource

The typical areas where information security activities are outsourced include:

- performing risk assessments including penetration attacks

- developing draft information security policies, architectures, and other requirements documents

- integrating security systems from various vendors into a turn-key system

- designing security systems to implement a predetermined security strategy

- developing and delivering training programs for in-house staff

- providing continuous intrusion detection, user activity monitoring, and intrusion response

- performing periodic vulnerability identification and notification in order to validate the level of security found in existing systems

- attending to systems security administration (establishing new user-IDs, changing passwords, etc.)

- managing complex security systems such as firewalls and virtual private networks (VPNs) on a day-to-day basis

- monitoring vendor announcements about patches, upgrades, and fixes, and informing customer about those which are relevant

- installing patches, upgrades, and fixes to software running on production systems

- performing computer crime forensic investigations

- providing expert witness consulting services for civil or criminal litigation

- recovering damaged or "lost" data resident on hard drives and other data storage media (sometimes called remediation)

- developing and revising contingency plans, most importantly information systems contingency plans

- testing information security products to determine whether they meet the vendor's advertised claims

While management may be excited about the prospect of using an outsourcing firm, it is your responsibility to ensure that your organization has precisely defined all the information security roles and responsibilities that the outsourcing firm is slated to perform. This will be difficult, if not impossible, if your organization has not first clarified its own internal information security roles and responsibilities. Accordingly, the prospect of outsourcing some or all of the information security work can, in fact, be a prime motivator for management-forcing them to get into action to specify what information security activities need to be performed.

Only after all of these activities are defined can management definitively determine which of them should be performed with in-house personnel and which should be performed with outsourcing firm personnel.

A spreadsheet or a word processing program table can be used to get the big picture about all of the information security activities that should be performed. The information security roles and responsibilities could, for example, be listed on the rows, and organizations that have one or more information security responsibilities could be listed on the columns. When preparing such a spreadsheet or word processing table, you can think of the outsourcing firm's relationship to your organization as something comparable to an employee's relationship to a department head. This means that the level of specificity brought to an outsourcing contract or an outsourcing performance measurement system should be comparable to, or even more detailed than the level of specificity found in a job description. For your convenience, a list of job description related roles and responsibilities can be found in Chapter 12.

In general, activities to protect physical assets (such as nighttime guard patrols) are much more likely to be outsourced than activities to protect information assets (such as computer access control administration). Mission-critical functions such as crisis management and contingency planning should generally be managed by full-time employees, although outside specialists can, and often do, assist with these activities. Those activities which require technical skills that in-house staff do not possess are also good candidates for outsourcing (Internet commerce security reviews, for example). Since employees are generally more loyal, more focused on the long-term needs of their employer, more familiar with the business needs of the employer, and more willing to provide extraordinary assistance in the time of a crisis, all other factors being the same, employees should be preferred over staff from an outsourcing firm.

Certain information security management activities, such as the development of an information security budget, the preparation of information security staffing plan, and the development of an information security strategy, are typically not outsourced to third parties. Likewise, the specification of information security roles and responsibilities is typically not outsourced. All these are important decision-making tasks that should be performed by internal management. Although the trend is to outsource an increasing array of information security tasks, the rationale behind keeping these and related information security management tasks under the direct control of senior employees is sound. This is because they are essential management functions, and

that to delegate them to third parties would be akin to the abdication of management's fundamental responsibilities to define requirements, allocate resources, establish internal processes and systems, and manage the work of those involved. You can, and should, anticipate that whenever these management tasks are outsourced, management may be accused of dereliction of duty to safeguard organizational assets (additional discussion about legal matters can be found in Appendix E.)

In addition to keeping the contract duration to a short period, you can play it safe by outsourcing only those information security tasks which are tactical and temporary tasks. For example, the administration associated with user-IDs and passwords might be outsourced. On the other hand, any information security activity which involves the protection of strategic assets should be kept in-house. For instance, the protection of the chemical formula used to manufacture a world famous soft drink like Coca-Cola would ordinarily not be outsourced. The latter would be too important, and if the outsourcing firm made a mess out of it, then the whole organization would be adversely impacted in a very big way.

Just as the outsourcing process is assisted by knowing what information security tasks need to be performed, so the process will be assisted by the prior performance of an organization-wide information security risk assessment (here we are talking about a general information security risk assessment as opposed to an outsourcing-decision risk assessment). An organization-wide risk assessment identifies the unique risks that the organization faces, and these unique risks in turn indicate tasks that need to be performed. For example, a photo bank that sells pictures over the Internet may have some unique risks associated with plagiarism that could be in part addressed with digital watermarks. Reflecting this unusual need, it may be a certain person's job to automatically scan Internet web pages to make sure that third-party uses of the organization's photos are all paid for and properly licensed. These unique information security tasks could alternatively be specified in a contract or agreement with an outsourcing firm.

Topics To Cover In An Outsourcing Contract

Joe Auer, President of International Computer Negotiations, a Florida-based consultancy which educates user organizations about high-tech procurement, has spent twenty years acting as an expert witness in court cases between vendors and user organizations. He says that in most instances where there is a dispute, the case revolves around who is responsible. In most of these cases contractual responsibility is either unclear or mutual, or else the vendor has disclaimed any responsibility through their standard form contract. The bottom line for user organizations is that if a contract does not clearly and completely assign responsibility to the vendor, then it is the user organization's responsibility. Hopefully your organization never finds itself embroiled in a legal dispute like this, but if it does, the case will critically depend on what if any words are written into the contract.

The author of this book has reviewed many outsourcing contracts in the course of his information security consulting work, and in far too many of these contracts there are only a few words about the outsourcing firm's information security roles and responsibilities. To foster a more explicit treatment of this area in contracts, this section lists information security topics that should be covered in an outsourcing contract. Further details of these responsibilities can be found in Chapter 11 and Chapter 12.

Checklist of items for outsourcing contracts:

- Who will perform background checks, and who at the customer organization will provide subsequent approval of the specific outsourcing firm workers who will handle Company X information and systems

- Who at the customer organization will provide advance approval of access privileges for all workers who are expected to gain access to information and systems entrusted to the outsourcing firm

- Who at the customer organization will provide advance approval for changes in the procedures or other operational details associated with the handling of Company X business applications or sensitive information

- Who at the customer organization will provide advance approval for changes in interfaces, system configurations, and network connections (for example, who makes decisions about firewall rules)

- Who at the customer organization determines acceptable responses to bring the outsourcing firm back within the acceptable range on target parameters (often handled via service level agreements or SLAs)

- Who will determine the circumstances when penalties and/or reductions in fees take place due to security-related failings or ongoing vulnerabilities (perhaps a third party), and likewise who will determine whether bonuses for good performance are warranted

- Who will determine when a contract may be terminated for cause, such as poor performance, and how this determination will be made

- Who is to perform monitoring of user access privileges that have been assigned as well as user activity (for instance through a network management system, operating system logs, and intrusion detection system)

- Who will provide customer management with quarterly or monthly reports about the outsourcing firm's finances whenever the outsourcing firm is going through financially troubled times

- Who will determine when the outsourcing firm's shutdown is imminent, and that the customer management can therefore hire key outsourcing firm staff without violating the terms of the contract

- Who at the customer organization and/or the outsourcing firm will specify and approve the operational policies and procedures to be used by staff at the outsourcing firm

- Who at the customer organization will specify the physical access controls to be employed at the outsourcing firm's data center and adjoining offices (if and only if these same facilities handle customer information and business activities)

- Who at the customer organization and the outsourcing firm will prepare and update of documentation describing the procedures used to process Company X information (including error detection and resolution procedures)

- Who at the customer organization and at the outsourcing firm will prepare and update information systems contingency plans

- Who at the outsourcing firm will provide advance customer notification of plans to install or upgrade hardware, software, and telecommunication systems

- Who at the outsourcing firm will make modifications to application software and operating system software in response to newly reported vulnerabilities

- Who at the outsourcing firm will place custom software source code in third party software escrow vault at regular intervals (in case the outsourcing firm goes bankrupt, refuses to provide service, or for some other reason cannot perform according to the contract)

- Who at the outsourcing firm will provide advance notice about imminent shutdowns, bankruptcy, and other conditions that may interfere with the continued provision of service

- Who will be the liaison for customer-sponsored audits of outsourcing firm workers to ensure they are in compliance with terms and conditions in the contract

- Who will run software that determines whether security measures are being followed and/or whether they are effective (software license management systems are an example)

- Who will take what response(s) to intrusions, outages, errors, and other security relevant events

- Who will respond to requests for password resets, smart card lock-out condition alleviation, and other help desk security problems

- Who within the outsourcing firm will manage a problem reporting and management system, and how this system will be run (a trouble ticket system is just one type of a problem reporting and management system)

- Who will provide troubleshooting, in addition to documentation of and resolution of service complaints (such as system down)-this may involve a trouble ticket system

- Who within the outsourcing firm will provide expert technical consulting assistance dealing with information security (providing advice on options, suggesting appropriate products, etc.)

- What liability and financial responsibility for information security problems the outsourcing firm is willing to assume, and who will be the point person for these matters

- What notification process takes place when the outsourcing firm does any work for competitors to your organization, and who will provide the notification

- What notification process takes place when the outsourcing firm causes any resources (servers, firewalls, database management systems, etc.) used to process customer information to be shared with a competitor to the customer organization (some customer organizations also want to be notified if they share resources with socially or morally questionable businesses, such as pornography-oriented Internet merchants), and who will handle this task

- When the outsourcing firm will generate and deliver status reports (including security incidents, changes in information security policy, changes in key personnel, changes in system or network configurations, suspected security weaknesses, and results of security testing activities) and who will handle this task

- Whether the outsourcing firm will return all information and software assets in its possession when the contract is terminated (including operational information such as operating system security logs), and who will handle this task

- Whether the outsourcing firm will grant the customer the first right of refusal if to buy IT equipment, in the event that the outsourcing firm shuts down and seeks to sell the equipment to raise cash, and who will handle this task

It is also important to structure a contract with an information security outsourcing firm such that a variety of ways are defined for dealing with problems. These include unilateral or mutually-developed problem correction plans, formal problem resolution processes, formal complaint processes, and restatements of performance levels. Another component of a good problem management system is a problem documentation process, such as a trouble ticket system. If an outsourcing firm allows the customer to access the trouble tickets related to his or her systems and activities, this will help to facilitate up-to-date communication as well as focused action to correct problems. Rather than relying on the outsourcing firm's boilerplate language in the contract, be sure to tailor these matters to your own organization's needs.

Better than dealing with problems that have already taken place are proactive approaches such as monthly reviews of service expectations and service level agreements (SLAs). SLAs are agreements between a service provider and a customer (SLAs can be between internal parties inside your organization, or used between your organization and an outsourcing firm). These agreements define the nature, quality, availability, and scope of the service to be provided. For example, if you have just terminated an employee who was in an information security related position of trust, you would want the outsourcing firm to immediately turn-off all privileges previously granted to this individual. In this case, an SLA can specify how quickly the outsourcing firm will respond to a so-called "duress termination." Included within the SLA would be details such as a definition of what it means to be in a state of non-conformance, relevant penalties and incentives, what corrective actions must be taken, dispute resolution procedures, problem reporting processes, and the conditions under which the contract could be terminated. It is also possible to specify outsourcing firm staff required skill sets, required security clearances, minimum training levels, and appropriate job titles within an SLA. On a related note, ideally an outsourcing contract is very specific about the ways to measure performance in the information security area, and SLAs are one increasingly popular way to do this. For example, an SLA could specify the acceptable time frame for a response to a hacker intrusion. Additional ideas for SLAs can be found in Appendix C entitled "Performance Criteria."

Due Diligence To Perform Before Outsourcing

Before any commitment is made to an outsourcing firm, an appropriate level of *due diligence* should be performed. The amount of due diligence is a function of several factors including: the dollar amount of the contract to be awarded, the duration of the contract, the number of vendors involved, the complexity of the transition, the importance of the activity to your business, and the maturity of the systems to which your firm would transfer its processing. A brief memo to interested internal managers, a memo detailing the reasons why you think a due diligence effort should be either abbreviated or expanded, will help to structure the due diligence project in a manner truly supportive of your organization's needs. This same memo will also help management to appreciate why it is important to invest money in a due diligence process.

Just as you would ask a good number of questions of a prospective candidate for employment, so you should also ask many questions of a prospective outsourcing firm. This questioning typically involves talking to existing customers of the best outsourcing firms to determine whether customers are satisfied with the services they are receiving. Ideally the customers should be selected at random or with some other method you choose, rather than just the customers that the sales representative at the outsourcing firm provides. This in turn will help you to get a realistic picture of the level of customer satisfaction. This customer interview process is also an important way to determine whether the outsourcing firm has gouged customers when it comes to requested additional services and change orders (many outsourcing firms make most of their money through these add-ons, keeping their profit margins low for the originally-contracted services).

Likewise, no matter how large and well-known an outsourcing vendor may be, people from your organization should visit the outsourcing firm's data centers and offices to confirm representations that were made in a proposal. This confirmation process may, for example, involve a check to see that an Uninterruptible Power System (UPS) is indeed installed and operational. A visit to the data center may also give you a sense for the motivation of the outsourcing firm's staff, the extent to which they are working according to established policies and procedures, and how seriously they take security on a day-to-day basis.

Due diligence also means checking the financial stability of the outsourcing firm by reviewing financial statements, examining credit reports, and searching legal records to see whether the outsourcing firm is in trouble with its customers, stockholders, or others. You should also look for early warning signs that the outsourcing firm is in financial trouble including layoffs, restructuring announcements, or the departure of the Chief Executive Officer. In addition, the financial stability of the firms on which the outsourcing firm critically relies should also be evaluated. While all this digging may seem to be going overboard, many outsourcing firms have recently gone bankrupt and left their surprised customers without the services promised. This is such an important area of due diligence that a US government regulation now requires staff at commercial banks to perform it periodically for all outsourcing firms on which their bank relies.

Another area to check during your due diligence effort is the management team at the outsourcing firm. Are they stable characters and are they likely to remain with the firm? Do they have the requisite experience to manage the outsourcing firm if the business grows substantially? Have they shown a genuine commitment to the information systems outsourcing industry by remaining in that niche for a certain period time? Are they genuinely mature enough to deal with an emergency or a disaster, or are they likely to make a mess of things in a situation like that?

As a prospective customer, you will probably want to confirm the level of training that outsourcing firm technical personnel receive as well as the qualifications of these same personnel. Many prospective outsourcing firm customers want to see the resumes of those who will be working on their systems. These potential customers are looking for relevant college degrees, extensive prior experience, and industry certifications (for a roster of relevant inform ation security professional certifications, see Appendix D.)

Besides checking the training and expertise of the outsourcing firm's staff, you should also investigate whether the outsourcing firm has experience in your industry and experience with organizations the same size as your organization. You can determine whether the outsourcing firm will be able to readily accommodate your organization's needs by looking over the firm's customer list. If most if not all customers are in a single industry, and that industry is not your organization's industry, there may be a problem. For example, if the outsourcing firm is accustomed to catering to airlines, and your organization is a bank, then there may be a problem in that the outsouring firm may place most of its emphasis on system availability rather than on fraud prevention. Similarly, an outsourcing firm accustomed to dealing with customers of a significantly different size than your organization may not provide the service or responsiveness that your organization requires.

Another important consideration is reputation. An outsourcing firm with a strong brand name built up over many years of strong customer service is important. You will probably not be able to ask all of the relevant questions before you sign a contract, so there's a lot to recommend going with a leader in the field (such an outsourcing firm is probably already doing whatever you forgot to ask about). These firms are also more likely to have a wide breadth of services, allowing you to add more services rather than having to engage several different information security outsourcing providers. These well-established firms are also more likely to provide rapid response time, 24 X 7 X 365 support, and best-of-breed technology solutions. But be sure to ask about these things anyway, even if the outsourcing firm has an excellent reputation. Perhaps the best reason to go with a well-known, proven, and reputable provider is reduction of risk to your own organization's reputation. Going with a reputable provider will significantly reduce the probability that management will be confronted by government regulators, news reporters, or stockholders with questions like: "What possessed you

when you determined that an inexperienced and ill-prepared outsourcing firm was going to be able to meet Company X's information security needs?"

Additionally, to the extent that the outsourcing firm is willing to disclose it, prospective customers should examine outsourcing firm documentation such as information security policies, an information security architecture, operational procedures (covering matters like facility access control, user authentication provisioning, data backup, and change control), an information systems contingency plan, the results of ongoing security assessments, job descriptions, employee confidentiality agreements, and prospective employee background checking procedures. This documentation should give you a "warm fuzzy feeling" that everything is under control and that the outsourcing firm has a great deal of experience with information security matters. If the outsourcing firm will allow it, you should make copies of these documents to be able to prove that you in fact examined the documents as part of your due diligence process.

Although your examination of internal documentation at an outsourcing firm will most likely give you an indication whether the firm has made the effort to establish internal infrastures, it is important to investigate what could happen if the outsourcing firm took on a whole lot more business. You may wish to investigate whether the present organizational design, and the information systems infrastructure, at the outsourcing firm seem sufficiently stabilized to rapidly scale to accommodate a great deal of new business? Is your organization likely to suffer if the volume of business rapidly expands at the outsourcing firm? Is the outsourcing firm willing to give you some assurances (perhaps in the form of SLAs) that their success will not damage your business?

Due diligence should also be performed after the contract is signed. For example, your organization should include words in the contract that allow either internal auditors or external auditors to review the outsourcing firm's operations. The use of internal auditors from your organization are preferred over external auditors because they are more familiar with your organization's specific business needs. In some instances, external auditors may perform what is known as a SAS-70 Review (Statement on Auditing Standards 70, issued by the American Institute of Certified Public Accountants). These SAS-70 Reviews may be too general in nature, and may not satisfy management at your organization who are trying to determine whether everything is being handled in a secure and reliable fashion. A more detailed type of SAS-70 review is now available from many Certified Public Accountancy firms, and this type of review allows your organization to specify the scope of the review. If your organization is going to use external auditors, in most instances, the latter will be a good way to provide you with due diligence information before a contract is signed, as well as after an outsourcing firm has already been engaged. Such a review can and often should include a penetration test to validate that the outsourcing firm has adequately dealt with security.

Another due diligence issue associated with the retention of third parties to handle information security tasks involves potential conflicts of interest. When retaining contractors, consultants, and other third parties, you should be sure to investigate: what products and services they are selling, what vendor marketing relationships they have, for which vendors they are a preferred provider, which vendors they have worked with, etc. These relationships may cause the outsourcing firm to recommend products or services which are not in fact the best for your organization, although they may be the best for sales commissions that the outsourcing firm earns. For this reason it is desirable to retain only those third parties who are truly independent, especially when it comes to engagements where the third party is providing advice and/or recommendations (a risk assessment, an information security architecture, etc.).

Investigating possible conflicts of interest is an especially important consideration because a surprising number of consulting firms will price their services very low in order to get a project which is subject to competitive bid, knowing that the real money will later be made through sales commissions rather than services rendered. Another way in which a potential conflict of interest may crop-up involves vendors who both sell and manage information security products. If they discover a vulnerability in their product, are they going to let you know about it, or will they quietly fix the problem and never inform you? And if you don't know about a serious vulnerability, are you going to be in a position to make realistic and appropriate decisions regarding the rest of your information security initiatives? So, before the contract gets signed, you should think hard about the ways in which the outsourcing arrangement may encourage the outsourcing firm to act in a manner which is not in your organizations's best interests.

A few other examples of the types of conflict of interest may help you to think about a wide variety of possibilties. For example, some people think that your firewall management outsourcing firm should not also provide intrusion detection services. This is because the latter acts as a second level of defense if the former should fail.

But if both of these services are provided by the same organization, will they tell you that the firewall has been breached? Would they risk your anger, and the possibility that you might take your business elsewhere? Other people will say that the convenience of a single outsourcing point of contact combined with the benefits of an integrated security system outweigh any potential conflict of interest problem. Along these same lines, you may not wish to use the same firm for both vulnerability analysis and penetration testing. The latter can show problems with the former. If you have both of these services provided by the same organization, then will they tell you that their vulnerability analysis software failed to detect a major problem? Don't you need to know this information in order to securely manage your systems? Additional discussion about separation of duties can be found in Chapter 18 and Chapter 20.

Your due diligence effort should also examine the circumstances and motivations of your internal management team promoting an outsourcing effort. Are they betting the company, taking unjustifiable risks, in order to get ahead in their careers? Are they setting up a sweetheart deal with an outsourcing firm that will lead to kickbacks or some other type of personal gain? Do they have personal relationships which could cause them to favor one of the outsourcing firms over the others? Are they pushing ahead with an outsourcing effort, without wanting to really take the time to examine the associated risks? If so, why are they in such a hurry to complete the deal? Could there be something going on behind the scenes that causes them to force the move to an outsourcing firm, even though it is not in the best interests of your organization?

One of the best ways to gather a good deal of the due diligence information your organization needs to make an informed decision is through a structured competitive bidding process. The process that your organization's management goes through to write a *request for proposal* (RFP) document will help a great deal to clarify what is needed as well as what yardsticks will be used to measure the relative desirability of vendors. The use of a competitive bidding process will also document management's decision-making steps, and this documentation may be important evidence if later there should be a stockholder lawsuit alleging management negligence or breach of fiduciary duty. Use of competitive bidding will not only help to assure that your organization gets a low-cost provider, it will also give you a sense for the reponsiveness of the outsourcing firms that received the RFP. A competitive bidding process will additionally help to assure that no "rigged" or sole-source deals are arranged between management and a single vendor. If your organization doesn't already have such a competitive bidding process, it is wise to develop one for any substantial outsourcing effort.

Chapter 18 ADJUSTMENTS FOR SMALLER ORGANIZATIONS

The descriptions of information security organizational structure found in this book will understandably be too expensive and complicated for some smaller organizations. This does not mean that these template materials should be abandoned. You should instead pare down the words found in Chapter 11, Chapter 12, Chapter 13 in a manner consistent with the customization factors defined in Chapter 14. Removal of inappropriate words is much faster and more efficient than compiling these documents from scratch. To assist with this editing process, this chapter offers some tips on an abbreviated and scaled-back approach intended to allow smaller organizations to cover all the essential information security areas. This chapter also includes quantitative reference points for budgets in the hope that this information will assist smaller organizations in their efforts to find the appropriate spending level for information security.

Human Resources Management Issues

The establishment of a formal Information Security Department is going to be too expensive for some smaller organizations, such as those with fewer than 100 employees. Typically these organizations have only one or two people working part-time on information security. Instead of a full-blown department, you should at least get management to designate a specific individual to be the Coordinator Of Information Security across the entire organization. Because information security is multi-disciplinary, multi-departmental, and increasingly multi-organizational, it is essential that one person bring it all together and provide management with the big picture. This person can have many of the duties that an Information Security Manager has (see "Information Security Department Manager" in Chapter 12 for a job description). Rather than having a staff to assist, such a Coordinator Of Information Security often works alone and reports to the Chief Information Officer or the Director of Physical Security (see the Chapter 13 for a discussion about reporting relationships). Reasons to have at least one centralized coordinator are presented in Chapter 19.

If you establish such a Coordinator Of Information Security position, it is desirable that this individual be focused on information security on a full-time basis. A full-time information security specialist is less likely to be caught in conflicts of interest that are present if a full-time worker devotes only part of his or her time to information security. For example, if a Systems Administrator, Database Administrator, or Computer Operator were to be assigned a part-time role as Coordinator Of Information Security, he or she would be confused about where to draw the line on a variety of trade-offs. More specifically, a Database Administrator may compromise access control security so that he or she doesn't need to spend so much time handling user-IDs and passwords. Likewise, a Computer Operator may compromise intrusion detection systems monitoring so that he or she doesn't need to spend so much time attending to the current operational status of systems. Full-time specialists will also be less likely to be "temporarily reassigned" to non-information security tasks when deadlines are fast approaching (the Y2K efforts of the recent past provide a good example).

In some small organizations, even a single full-time person is not going to be acceptable from a budgetary standpoint. These organizations can hire someone who works only part-time, and thereby avoid the conflict of interest problem. These organizations can also use outsourcing firms that increasingly are providing information security services. In many instances outsourcing firms will provide only a portion of the services that the Coordinator Of Information Security needs to handle. For example, one outsourcing firm may provide network intrusion detection monitoring services and break-in response team services. Another outsourcing firm may provide risk assessment and security administration services. Accordingly, if you are seeking outsourcing firm support, you are likely to find that several firms are required to meet the needs of the organization. Since employees are generally more loyal, more focused on the long-term needs of their employer, more familiar with the business needs of the employer, and more willing to provide extraordinary assistance in a time of a crisis, in these limited budget situations, an employee is to be preferred over an outsourcing firm. Employees are also more likely to be without time conflicts than consultants; these conflicts might cause consultants to attend to another organization's needs rather than the needs of your organization. For a more detailed discussion of outsourcing information security activities, see Chapter 17.

Whoever it is that's responsible for information security within a smaller organization, that person will have a very large impact on the success or failure of information security efforts. This person, or perhaps two people, will be doing nearly everything when it comes to information security. Rather than having a rigidly-defined specialty and narrowly-defined job duties, this person or persons must be a jack-of-all-trades type. Because this person or persons will have such a profound impact on information security, it is essential that this person or persons be both experienced and knowledgeable in the information security area. The more this person or persons is familiar with the many ways to achieve the same information security result, and the ways that things can be accomplished on a shoestring budget, the more successful the information security effort at the organization will be.

Another serious consideration for smaller organizations is separation of duties. For example, in a medium-sized organization, the person who writes the checks based on purchase orders is generally not the same person who signs the checks. The involvement of more than one person reduces the chances of fraud and errors. This same perspective should be brought to the information security area. For example, programmers should not be the only ones to test their own code, just as information security administrative staff members should not be performing information security compliance checks. Of course, if the organization doesn't have enough people to support separation of duties, in some cases certain people will need to have several roles-roles that certain other organizations would consider incompatible. In this case, you should consider how separation of duties is going to be maintained even though the number of people involved is restricted. This could, for example, be achieved through additional management approvals or review of work performed by other people. You can start to create a suitable down-scaled organizational structure by defining the areas in which separation of duties absolutely must be present. The roles and responsibilities documentation should then be compiled, all the while maintaining separation of duties in these same areas. The material provided in Chapter 11 and Chapter 12 already has separation of duties built into it. The topic of separation of duties is further discussed in Chapter 20.

Although not nearly as effective an option as having a single person who is designated as the organization-wide Information Security Coordinator, it is possible for small organizations to address information security by assigning specific tasks to a variety of existing personnel. While being concerned about conflicts of interest and separation of duties, you can, for example, assign information security administrative tasks to Systems Administrators, controls related consulting tasks to Internal Auditors, intrusion monitoring tasks to Computer Operators, etc. The important benefit of this approach is that the tasks have been clearly specified and assigned to individuals. Even with this approach, some additional effort will still be needed to coordinate the work of these individuals. If you choose this approach, you should be aware that there is a high risk that critical information security tasks will be overlooked or neglected.

Another option for smaller organizations is to assign various information security tasks to department managers. For example, department managers may be responsible for the physical security of sensitive business information, and may be expected to ensure that all the people in their department are using paper shredders, anti-virus software, computer lock-down devices (to prevent theft), and locking file cabinets. With this approach, responsibility is dispersed and localized, and only the bare essentials are covered. This approach still requires some coordination across the organization, and this coordination might be provided by an Information Security Coordinator or a Physical Security Manager. The use of department managers is discussed in additional detail in Chapter 15.

Small organizations should also consider cross-training and back-up for their information security personnel. To an increasing extent, information security is coming to be appreciated as an essential organizational function, a function that must be performed on a continuous basis. This trend argues persuasively for the existence of at least two people inside your organization who are fully-trained and ready to take over essential information security duties on a moment's notice. You can ask management, "What would happen if our Coordinator Of Information Security took a job elsewhere, but gave us only one week's notice?" With the continuing strong demand for experts in the information security field, this scenario is not just a remote possibility.

While a formal Information Security Management Committee is something that very small organizations can do without, there needs to be a formal assignment of certain basic responsibilities. For most organizations, these basics include information systems contingency planning, systems access control, controls in the systems development process, and information security user awareness. These basic duties must be clearly and definitively assigned to various individuals such as user department managers and Systems Administrators. Tasks related to information security still need to be included in other related job descriptions, such as those of the Chief Information Officer, the Internal Audit

Department Manager, and the Physical Security Department Manager (see Chapter 12 for more job descriptions).

An uncomfortable topic of discussion for many people is the issue of nepotism. Having a family member such as a spouse or child work in the organization is common for small businesses. The same issues come up when two people who work together are having a romantic affair (although this is certainly not an issue only applicable to small organizations). You may wonder how to adjust the templates found in this book for those circumstances where nepotism exists. In general, no reporting relationships should exist for people who have family or other ties. Thus the Information Security Manager, who may report to the Chief Information Officer, should not also be married to the Chief Information Officer. Likewise, where separation of duties is critical to the performance of a specific job, the two people supporting the separation of duties should not have a family or romantic tie. For example, the Information Systems Auditor should not be a brother of the Information Security Manager. In response to nepotism problems, it is better to move people around the organization, rather than create a dysfunctional organizational structure that will linger even after the people in question have moved on. In those cases where it is impractical to move people around the organization, additional checks and balances should be added to ensure that the people in question are doing their jobs as they should. These checks and balances most importantly include a strong internal audit function. Additional checks and balances are discussed in Chapter 20.

Small organizations also need to appreciate that information security is no longer a project that gets addressed periodically. At one time, an annual audit or risk assessment may have sufficed for those organizations that are not particularly information intensive. For example, a small manufacturing firm is not nearly as information intensive as a commercial bank, and as a result, the investment in information security in a small manufacturing firm will be a much smaller percentage of available funds. Instead of being addressed as an occasional project, information security has now become an essential and ongoing organizational function much like accounting and marketing. As such, for every organization with over 25 employees, it should be recognized in job descriptions as an ongoing activity.

Budgetary Issues

While the author is sympathetic to organizations that claim they don't have the budget for a significant investment in information security staff and tools, there is a grave danger that management will under-invest in information security. This can lead to a variety of problems such as unwanted hacker intrusions, excessive system downtime, privacy disputes with customers, and serious damage to the organization's reputation. These in turn may lead to the bankruptcy or untimely demise of the organization. While a focus on cash flow and increasing sales is certainly important for a small organization, top management also needs to focus on basic internal controls including information security in order to prevent the organization from getting into serious trouble. In other words, "If management isn't minding the store, there may soon be no store to mind." To ensure that management is investing sufficiently in information security, a statistical barometer of information security staffing is included in Appendix A. You should review this appendix to ensure that management is being realistic when they say, "As a small firm, we don't have the need, nor do we have the money for a significant information security effort."

This under-investment in information security in many instances means that those who do hold information security positions end up running around putting out fires, and otherwise attending only to those things that are the very most rudimentary (such as changing passwords when somebody leaves the organization). The Coordinator Of Information Security will need to have enough time to be able to take the pulse of the organization's information security status, to plan the changes that need to be made, to evaluate the merits of new products, etc. Management needs to understand that information security is an exceedingly complex field, not something that can be dealt with in a single afternoon once every few months. Additional tips that may be helpful when it comes to changing management's attitude can be found in Chapter 2 and Chapter 3.

Any specification of roles and responsibilities implicitly makes trade-offs that should be consistent with organizational culture, business objectives, available resources, and other organization-specific factors. You should engage top management at your organization in a discussion about the places where they wish to draw the line when it comes to these same trade-offs. This discussion in many instances will help top management to understand that they need to devote additional resources to information security. An example of such a discussion would entail the Information Security Department's ability to handle maximum demands, for example, during recovery from a hacker intrusion. While this may at first appear desirable, it may also mean that the Department is underutilized much of the time. Taking a different perspective on this same issue, the Information

Security Department could be fully utilized all the time, thus forcing certain departments to suffer occasional outages and delays, even if outsiders were used to handle occasional problems. There is no correct answer to this trade-off. A credit card processing firm would probably opt for the former approach, while a retail store chain would probably opt for the latter approach. The best answer has a lot to do with what's at stake, and an organization-wide risk assessment will provide the background that management needs in order to rationally make this decision.

As another point of reference to make sure that organizations are spending enough on information security, consider the one ratio that has gotten more attention than any other in the information security field: the information security budget as a percentage of the information technology budget. According to the 1994 survey of Fortune 1000 companies performed by Forrester Research, a Cambridge, Massachusetts information systems research firm, information security represents, on the average 9.0% of information technology budgets. This represents an increase of two percentage points over a similar study performed five years earlier. This Forrester survey is consistent with a 2002 survey performed by InfoSecurity Magazine, of Norwood, Massachusetts (published in the September issue). In the latter survey, information security budgets averaged 10.6% of the information technology budget. This is right in line with another study, performed by CSO Magazine in 2002, which found that information security was, on the average, some 9.5% of the IT budget.

In the InfoSecurity Magazine survey mentioned in the last paragraph, budgets varied by size of organization as well as industry. At the smallest organizations, budgets for information security generally constitute a higher percentage of the IT budget (19.9% on the average) than they do at largest organizations (5.5% on the average). This is apparently a reflection of the fact that there are some economies of scale when it comes to establishing and running an information security infrastructure. In terms of industry, as an example, consider that the information security budget was only 5.0% of the IT budget a real estate firm, while it was 43% at a managed security service provider (alias MSSP). The wide variance by industry is consistent with several surveys that the author conducted in conjunction with the Computer Security Institute, San Francisco, California. A summary of one of these surveys is provided as Appendix A.

When making these calculations about budget, note that as much or more of the budget for information security can come from the Physical Security Department as from the Information Technology Department. According to the CSO Magazine survey mentioned immediately above, some 42% of the information security budgets are lumped together with physical security budgets. But in most organizations, the information security budget is still a part of the IT budget. As a long term goal, it is desirable to break-out the information security budget as a separate line item, as a separate decision for top management to make. This helps to distinguish information security from both IT and also physical security, and it also helps management see that expenditures for information security have been rising (and need to continue to be rising) faster than they are for either IT or physical security.

While management at many organizations still thinks that information security is largely a technical issue, the budget figures revealed in a recent survey performed by Gartner Group indicate otherwise. The total cost of ownership (TCO) for IT systems, was between half to two-thirds labor and the balance technology. The author is aware of no reason to believe that information security is significantly different in this respect from any other area in the IT field. Accordingly, in your budget discussions, you should keep in mind that some half to two-thirds of the information security budget should be devoted to people (be they employees, temporaries, consultants, contractors, or outsourcing firms).

One dangerous approach that small organizations have adopted involves the perspective that they can't afford information security, and as a result they ignore the whole topic. To a much greater extent than in recent years, a new baseline of minimum controls is evolving. For example, if an organization (no matter what size) is going to support Internet credit card orders, it needs to offer SSL (secure sockets layer, a type of encryption) to protect the credit card data as it travels over the Internet. Other standards such as ISO Standard 17799 (entitled *Code of Practice for Information Security Management*) are defining a minimum set of controls that all organizations must subscribe to if they are going to participate in the modern computerized economy. This means that, as a percentage of total sales, smaller organizations may actually end up spending a higher percentage of their available cash on information security. This is because every organization must incur certain fixed costs to purchase and set-up these same essential controls. You can think of this as the cost to play the game (of Internet commerce, of electronic data interchange, etc.). A statistical study to support this conclusion for smaller organizations can be found in an article entitled "2003: Another Year Of Belt Tightening - InfoSecurity Budgets Are Increasing But At A Far Slower Rate Than Many People Assume," which can be found in the March 2003 issue of Information Security Magazine.

While your management may still be complaining that they don't have the money for anything sophisticated in the information security area, you should not think that management is going to be converted all at once. It is unfortunately a slow and painful process to get management to wake up to the importance of information security. All too often, major security losses or other painful events will finally force management to pay attention to information security. This is, and will continue to be, frustrating for information security specialists. For example, in 1993, the Computer Security Institute (CSI), an educational firm based in San Francisco, California, conducted a survey that found that only 40% of Information Security Managers consider their budgets to be adequate to meet the challenges posed by security risks. This is slowly changing for the worse. According to a survey of 700+ organizations written up in the July 1999 issue of Information Security Magazine, only 33% of respondents said that their information security budget was sufficient to meet the challenges they face.

Chapter 19 A CENTRALIZED ORGANIZATIONAL STRUCTURE

In addition to offering some advice about how best to implement a centralized organizational structure for information security management, this chapter explores the pros and cons of such a centralized organizational structure. As you go through this chapter, you should consider how your organization could be changed to better exploit the advantages of a centralized approach to information security management. In all organizations there should be at least some part of your organizational structure which should be centralized.

The author is a strong supporter of a hybrid approach to information security management which includes both centralized and decentralized components, an approach which includes a significant amount of centralized management. This support is born out of the author's consulting experience with over 125 different organizations. While an entirely centralized approach can be bureaucratic, slow, inefficient, and out-of-touch with the rest of the organization, an entirely decentralized approach leads to lackluster results and major control deficiencies. Most organizations can, however, significantly benefit from an increased emphasis on centralized information security management, and that increased emphasis is addressed in the balance of this chapter.

A Few Critical Distinctions

With the move to decentralized and distributed systems (such as personal computers and the Internet), centralized management of information systems acquired an undesirable image. When people think of centralized systems, they often think of bureaucracy, mainframes, and slow response time. While this image may have, in some cases, been justified for information systems management, it is not necessarily true for information security management. It is possible, and also desirable to have decentralized and distributed information systems management, and at the same time have a good deal of centralized information security management.

As covered in Chapter 3, the author believes that the information security field has become too complex and time-consuming for any one department to realistically handle everything. Accordingly, this chapter urges the adoption of an organizational structure that uses centralized information security management but decentralized execution of information security activities. For example, the information security policies and standards for developing business application systems

should be defined centrally, but these same policies and standards can be consulted by user department staff as they utilize a small database management system (such as Microsoft's Access) to develop their own applications. Likewise, the popularity of Local Information Security Coordinators is further testament to the merits of having decentralized execution of centrally-defined information security activities (a job description for these Coordinators is provided in Chapter 12.)

To make this discussion more real and tangible, the author has listed a variety of activities that should be performed on a centralized basis. The list is meant to be illustrative rather than comprehensive. The specifics of this list can be combined with the mission statement for the centralized information security function found in Chapter 11. Note that just because these activities are done centrally doesn't mean that they should all be done by an Information Security Group. For example, monitoring network activity ordinarily would be done by a network operations group within the Information Technology Department.

Information Security Activities That Should Be Centralized

Each of the following activities are ordinarily performed by a centralized Information Security Department unless otherwise noted in parenthesis. The significant number of activities that should be performed on a centralized basis argues strongly for the establishment and support of a centralized Information Security Department.

- Defining information security roles and responsibilities

- Developing network security architectures

- Issuing network security standards (such as encryption algorithms and encryption key management)

- Writing information security policies and guidelines

- Specifying organization-wide information security training and awareness material

- Developing systems development process security requirements

- Providing consistent information security consulting advice to those developing new systems including business application systems

- Ensuring systems acquisitions are compliant with security standards (usually done by Purchasing Department)

- Negotiating volume purchase agreements with security vendors (may be done by Purchasing Department)

- Compiling inventory of organizational intellectual property (may be done by Data Administration Department)

- Performing contingency planning related business impact analysis (may be done by Risk & Insurance Management Department)

- Issuing information systems contingency planning guidelines

- Conducting organization-wide risk assessments and information systems audits (may also be done by the Internal Audit Department or an external consultant)

- Interacting with the media about information security problems (may alternatively be done by Public Relations Department)

- Organizing and training a computer emergency response team, alias CERT

- Developing standardized confidentiality and non-compete agreements (most likely done by the Legal Department)

- Acting as a centralized point for all inquiries and reports about vulnerabilities and incidents (may also be performed by Physical Security Department)

- Collecting information about security-related incidents and analyzing these incidents for trends (may also be done by the Physical Security Department)

- Coordinating computer virus eradication efforts, hacker intrusion eradication efforts, and other information security related multi-departmental crisis management efforts

- Monitoring network security to immediately detect intruders (may also be done by a network operations group in the Information Technology Department)

- Analyzing external vulnerability reports and then determining what, if any, changes should be made to internal systems and networks (may also be done by Information Technology Department, Local Information Security Coordinators, or perhaps outsourced)

- Providing management with periodic reports which clearly indicate the status of internal efforts to improve information security

- Establishing and coordinating a permanent Information Security Management Committee and temporary project-specific information security committees

- Developing action plans, schedules, budgets, and related documents to coordinate information security work across the organization

Why Centralized Information Security Management Is Advisable

While the author may urge centralization of a wide variety of information security activities, he does not mean to imply that these same activities absolutely must be centralized. For example, consider the process of defining virus screening, blocking, eradication, and response efforts. The specification of these security requirements could be done by different departments on a decentralized basis. In this case, these efforts would be isolated and those doing the work would not share many, if any, of their ideas. Some departments may do a good job, and some may do a poor job. As a result, certain parts of an internal network may be well protected against a virus, and other parts may be unduly vulnerable. Because an internal network is a shared resource, the poor job done by some departments may adversely impact those departments that did a good job. This may mean that the departments that did a good job then establish additional controls, such as internal network firewalls that check for viruses, to protect themselves against the departments which have done a poor job. Costs for information security would then be expected to be higher than they would be if these same virus protection requirements were centrally dictated, and as a result consistently implemented. More staff virus eradication time and internal political squabbles may be associated with this decentralized approach, but it may still work relatively well. It's just not the optimal approach.

Some organizations have already gotten into trouble when they attempted to manage information security in a decentralized manner. For example, at a well-known semi-conductor manufacturer, the Research & Development Department was concerned about its latest chip designs "walking out the door." To protect this proprietary information, this department evaluated encryption products and established a standard to which every employee working in the department must subscribe. At the same time, the Information Security Department was worried about the same risks and they too were evaluating encryption products. When the Information Security Department learned that the R&D Department had already done this work, a dispute ensued about who sets the standards. Executive management intervention was required to settle the dispute, and after many heated words had been exchanged, eventually the job was delegated to the Information Security Department. A centralized approach to information security can help prevent these disputes from occurring. A centralized approach can also prevent resources from needlessly being wasted on redundant tasks. If the R&D Department had not been stopped from adopting an encryption system incompatible with the system that the Information Security Department selected, then the interoperability of internal encryption systems would have been seriously compromised. As we all move in the direction of networks supporting Public Key Infrastructure, also known as PKI (it uses digital certificates and digital signatures), it is increasingly important for organizations to adopt a standardized approach to encryption.

Left to their own devices, users are ordinarily not supportive of information security. Users, like local managers, often complain that they have other things to do, and that information security doesn't appear near the top of their to-do lists. Local managers will also complain that their people have no resources or time to attend to information security matters. To overcome these attitudes and anti-information-security pressures, a centralized group that has top management support should issue information security directives. An example of these directives is the use of extended user authentication systems for all inbound access to internal networks (dial-up connections, inbound Internet connections, wireless connections, etc.). Without a centralized approach to extended user authentication, some departments will use extended user authentication and some will not. If this departmental discretion approach is employed, because all departments share a network, the inevitable result will be that the security of every internal system will be needlessly jeopardized by those departments that refuse to adopt extended user authentication systems. Only through a centralized approach can across-the-board compliance be achieved. And only through consistent implementation of controls can an effective security system be established.

One of the perverse aspects of the information security field is the disproportionate amount of effort required by the "good guys" as compared to the effort required by the "bad guys." Hackers and others bent on compromising security need only find one major weak spot to achieve their goals. This is another way of stating the often-heard maxim where intruders need only discover the "weakest link in the chain." In many cases, these intruders don't even need to come up with the attack method; all they need to do is find the method (or software that executes the method) described on the Internet. On the other hand, those who seek to secure systems must have adequately dealt with all major threats to achieve a secure information systems environment. Thus the level of effort that the good guys must expend is disproportionately large relative to the level of effort that the bad guys must expend. Unless the good guys are addressing information security with a centralized approach, these efforts will be uncoordinated, and as a result, the likelihood that important areas are not being adequately addressed will be high. As information systems continue to get more complex, the amount of effort required by those attempting to ensure security will markedly increase. To manage the increasing amount of effort required to secure systems, only a centralized approach will prove effective. Modern automated information security tools, such as centralized access control system monitoring consoles, are a reflection of the efficiency and effectiveness that goes along with a centralized approach. Doing these same tasks manually is a reflection of the old-fashioned decentralized approach.

Networking is rapidly changing the nature of information security. Years ago, locking office doors, locking file cabinets, and shredding papers may have been sufficient for some departments. This was because the departmental collection of information was isolated from the rest of the world. Networks now interconnect the world and in the process they have created a shared information resource on which many people depend. For example, a single hacker could damage software, hardware, and information used by all the people connected to a wide area network. To prevent these types of problems, organizations need to adopt a minimum set of controls to which all people must subscribe (this standard is often called a *baseline*). For example, intrusion detection system (IDS) software, which is designed to spot the presence of a hacker, is often included in such a baseline. The most efficient way to define, publicize, and check compliance with a baseline is to use centralized groups such as an Information Security Department or Information Systems Audit Department. New compliance checking tools allow organizations to determine whether their systems are still in compliance with a centrally dictated baseline, and they can perform this task every night.

Perhaps the most significant force driving the movement to centralize various information systems functions (including information security), is the growing reliance on integrated systems. Closer links between applications and databases means that previously-encountered stand-alone systems are instead increasingly part of a tightly-knit web of data flows. Integration with the systems of outside companies, for instance via extranets, further accentuates this trend. The development of these integrated systems requires new roles to deal with organization-wide information systems that didn't exist before. An example is an organization-wide central point of contact for all emergencies or disasters related to information security (this person is also called a CERT team leader). Only through a centralized approach to information security can an organization ensure the security of the new integrated systems that are being established.

Another good reason to have a centralized information security organizational structure is to clearly show top management support. The fact that management has established a centralized organizational structure to formalize its communications related to information security shows a level of concern that will indirectly support information security efforts throughout the organization. A centralized structure will generally have greater control and influence than a decentralized structure, and this in turn will communicate in many subtle ways to the workers that management really is serious about information security. For example, a centralized information security function is likely to have more leverage with management and this will allow an information security group to influence policies, standards, much more persuasively than if the function were to be decentralized. This more serious management attitude towards information security, as evidenced by a centralized organizational structure, can also be helpful when it comes to defending management against allegations of negligence and failure to live up to a fiduciary duty to protect corporate assets (and information itself is now considered an asset).

A centralized approach to information security can enable a variety of new and innovative controls that would not otherwise be available. For example, with a centralized approach, an organization can negotiate special deals with vendors, such as VPAs (volume purchase agreements). A centralized approach can also enable certain technological solutions, such as an organization-wide user-ID database. Such a database

can be consulted when any worker leaves the organization, and it can be used to quickly identify the specific computers on which this worker had privileges. These privileges can then be quickly disabled. A centralized approach is also useful when adopting a variety of security tools such as software license management systems. Organization-wide technical standards, such as a minimum password length standard, are additionally very difficult to enforce unless a centralized information security management structure exists.

A survey conducted by InfoSecurity Magazine (published in the September 2002 issue) indicates that the information security organizations in larger firms are having a hard time dealing with the large scale and complexity found in their organizations. Nonetheless, smaller organizations spent more on security per user and per machine. Economies of scale allowed larger firms to markedly reduce the cost of security per user and per machine. They did this by adopting a centralized approach, which allowed them to get the greatest improvement in security for each additional dollar spent. Said a bit differently, only through centralization can a large organization hope to get security tools to scale to the size of their organization.

Local departmental management cannot and should not call the shots when it comes to information security. Departmental managers simply don't have the time or background to adequately research and weigh the many considerations involved. Specialists are needed to deal with the very complex information security field. Because these specialists are unlikely to be engaged full-time on information security issues if they are located in a user department, they should instead be situated in a centralized information security group. Only when the specialists are in a centralized information security group can their scarce time and attention be best devoted to the involved organization's information security problems.

Drawbacks Of Centralized Information Security Management

Some advocates of decentralized information security management will allege that a centralized approach will cause the information security function to be out of touch with business unit concerns. These people may have a fear that the information security group will dictate requirements which are unrealistic, too burdensome, or unduly expensive. This is quite possible, and in fact likely, if a centralized group has not made an effort to understand user department needs. But such a blatant disregard for user departments is rare. All well-managed information security groups will, for example, regularly conduct risk assessments which should illuminate these same user department needs. Similarly, the existence of Local Information Security Coordinator (see Chapter 12 for a job description) will help to ensure that a centralized information security group is indeed responsive to the needs of user departments. In a well-run information security group, other mechanisms to allow user departments to communicate to a centralized group should also be in place. For instance, a risk acceptance process can be used to highlight the fact that user department management doesn't agree with a security requirement dictated by a centralized group.

Some other advocates of a decentralized approach to information security management allege that when an organization doesn't have significant information security risks, then there is no need for a centralized group. For example, a small chain of restaurants typically doesn't have a great deal of information security risk (unless they are doing something quite unusual and high-tech such as taking orders via the Internet). In such an organization, there may only be one or two information systems specialists. While having a centralized information security group in this environment would clearly be unwarranted, it is still useful to designate one specific individual as the one responsible for information security matters. These low-risk organizations, especially if they are small organizations, can often do without a centralized information security function, in which case they could view information security as just another aspect of information systems management. Smaller organizations can find additional guidance along these same lines in Chapter 18.

Still other advocates of a decentralized approach to information secuirty management may claim that a centralized approach will concentrate too much power in a centralized group, and as a result this will slow down important projects. While it is true that information security considerations can slow down important projects, the truth is that management often makes a decision to pay the cost of security up-front or later, but either way they must pay. Various research studies show that it is far less expensive to build security into a system before it goes into production operation, than it is to add security after this same system has been in production operation. The reality is that information security can actually accelerate and expedite a wide variety of tasks if it is done right, done for an entire organization, and done on a centralized basis. As an example of this, consider the case of a large bank. This bank spent a good deal of time developing and documenting centralized

roles, responsibilities, policies, standards, and architectures related to information security. One of the areas where they did this was communications encryption. They selected a suitable vendor, tested the hardware and software, documented the system in the bank's standard ways, defined the interfaces, defined the key management system to employ, bought the products, and locked it all in a closet. With something akin to the notion of a software repository, this communications encryption system expedited the development of new business applications at the bank. Whenever a developer needed communications encryption functionality for a new application, he or she would go to the repository, instead of "recreating the wheel" on his or her own.

Resolving A Variety Of Implementation Issues

While some people can in theory agree that a centralized information security function should exist, they cannot specifically envision what this centralized group would do. If you fit into this group of people, you may want to read Chapter 11 and Chapter 12, which respectively deal with mission statements and job descriptions. The concept of a factory assembly line may also help here. As is the case in any manufacturing operation, a centralized group is needed to define the nature of the product, its quality, its specifications, its manufacturing process, and other specifics. There will always be a need for people to work on the assembly line, actually manufacturing the product. And these people, to get back to the information security field, could be Systems Administrators, Local Information Security Coordinators, department managers, users, and others. When confronted with a decision to centralize or decentralize a particular activity, you can think of how things are done in the manufacturing industry, and whether this analogy makes sense at your organization.

When some people encounter a proposal to centralize anything, they often get concerned about the development of an unresponsive and rigid bureaucracy. It is certainly possible for information security to evolve into such a bureaucracy, but in practice, the author has seen it only in civilian government and military organizations. In most cases, an information security group is so strapped for funds and so overwhelmed with important work to do that it cannot act as a rigid bureaucracy. Instead, it must be accountable to many constituencies, and it must work out appropriate compromises on a variety of difficult issues. These constituencies include top management, legal, internal audit, user departments, and other functions. A better way to characterize a centralized information security group is a flexible facilitator of desirable results. An example will clarify this role. If information security roles and responsibilities documentation exists, the internal response to a break-in can be much more rapid and effective than it could ever have been in the absence of such documentation.

No matter what type of structure your organization employs, it should have a single manager or executive who is responsible for information security throughout the organization. Only through a centralized manager or executive can the organization obtain a broad overview of an organization's information security risks and the appropriate controls to address these risks. As mentioned, many organizations are realizing that local solutions to information security problems are not sufficient, especially in the age of interconnected networks. This is why many have recently attempted to put together a network security architecture for the organization as a whole. Such an organization-wide information security effort is very difficult to achieve without a single manager or executive in charge of information security.

In a matrixed organization, a single manager or executive responsible for information security could have only a few staff members in his or her group. The bulk of the staff working on information security matters could be found in other groups such as the Information Technology Department. This structure would be quite different from a traditional hierarchical organizational structure, where a manager or executive could have many information security staff members all working in his or her department. In terms of a matrixed organization, to which departments these people are assigned is much less important than to whom they report when it comes to information security activities. Likewise, the use of a hierarchical or matrixed organizational structure is much less important than the clear, written, and management-approved definition of roles and responsibilities. Whatever the organizational structure, status reports, action plans, budget requests, and similar documents should regularly move between the involved staff and the single manager or executive responsible for information security. In other words, it is the coordination and communication that is essential, not the specific organizational structure. Consequently, the nature of this coordination and communication needs to be clearly defined in effective information security roles and responsibilities documentation. None of the recommendations found in this book is inconsistent with use of a matrixed organizational structure -- in fact the multi-disciplinary and multi-departmental

nature of a team working on information security (as discussed in Chapter 3) is absolutely consistent with the philosophy of matrixed organizational structures.

If the people actually doing the information security work are assigned to different departments, and physically located in different offices, it is important that formal coordination and communication structures be established. These structures go beyond the activities mentioned in mission statements, job descriptions, and reporting relationship diagrams. For example, at one high-tech firm, all the Systems Administrators got together once a month over lunch for a chance to share tools and techniques. In another example, an international consumer products company used encrypted video teleconferencing facilities to have quarterly meetings between a centralized information security group and the people working on information security matters who were located in different countries. Likewise, a financial services firm used quarterly meetings to bring everyone working on information security together for a day at the headquarters building. While face to face meetings increase trust between team members, formal communications can proceed in other ways, such as via a blog on an access-controlled intranet web page. Likewise, telephone conference calls may be used to periodically discuss problems and the best solutions. Even paper memos or electronic mail newsletters can be used to facilitate this coordination and communication. All such coordination and communication will be facilitated and made more efficient if it is centralized.

The technical support specialists working exclusively in the information security field should also be located in a centralized group. In even the largest of organizations, it is simply too expensive to have these individuals duplicated across business units. Typically these specialists will be reporting to the single manager or executive in charge of information security. These specialists include computer emergency response team (CERT) coordinators, network security architecture specialists, applications development security specialists, and other relatively expensive staff. With this approach, business unit managers do not need to recruit, train, supervise, or evaluate these technical specialists-something they may not know how to do anyway.

On the other hand, staff who are not specialists in information security, and who may have a designated information security role, will usually NOT be found in a centralized information security group. People falling into this category are Systems Administrators and Network Administrators. As the information systems work is increasingly being performed by user departments, it is not unusual to find Computer Operators, Application System Programmers, other traditional IT staff in decentralized user department groups. All of these staff members will typically spend most of their time addressing local needs, rather than organization-wide needs. If people are spending a significant amount of their time dealing with organization-wide needs, such as network security architectures, then they should be located in a centralized group.

The staff who are not information security specialists, who usually will not be located in a centralized information security group, should generally be trained by a centralized group. Likewise, users and others with some information security responsibilities should receive training from, or at least training developed by, technical specialists in a centralized information security group. This approach to training facilitates job rotation, that is, the movement of Systems Administrators and Network Administrators across groups thereby advancing their careers. More importantly, it fosters a consistent culture, and also a standardized set of tools and techniques for dealing with information security across the organization.

One important strategy that is relevant to information security role and responsibility specification involves minimizing unnecessary changes in the organization. The organizational structure that you develop should mirror the existing organization structure as much as possible. For example, if the organization is highly centralized, then the proposed roles and responsibilities for information security should also be highly centralized. If the organization is highly decentralized, then the

proposed roles and responsibilities for information security should include a scaled-down centralized group. But even in a highly-decentralized organizational environment a centralized information security group is still appropriate. Information security staff will have a difficult enough time working out suitable compromises on tough issues; you should not create unnecessary enemies by proposing roles and responsibilities that do not fit in with the existing organizational structure.

One way to make sure that information systems expenses are realistic and truly in the service of business needs is to adopt a charge-back scheme. Although widely used for IT services such as network connect time, charge-back schemes are not recommended for information security. This is because the people who pay the charge-back bills (local departmental managers) are often not supportive of information security, and generally very concerned about the financial results of their department. Instead, the budget for a centralized information security group should be organizational overhead, and shared by all organizational units. Besides, other mechanisms can be used to make sure that the centralized information security group is doing what needs to be done; the most recommended of these mechanisms are an organization-wide risk assessment and an Information Security Management Committee (see the section entitled "Information Security Management Committee" in Chapter 11 for a definition). Appendix C includes other approaches for evaluating the performance of a centralized information security function.

Chapter 20 WORKERS IN INFORMATION SECURITY RELATED POSITIONS OF TRUST

Nature Of The Problem

Ordinarily management doesn't think about it much, but there is in fact a special class of workers who can be referred to as those in "information security related positions of trust." In the past, the term used to be people in a "computer related position of trust," but that label isn't broad enough. This is because sensitive, valuable, and critical information may not be computer-resident, or even handled by computers at particular stage of its lifecycle.

People who are in information security positions of trust include those who can independently affect the confidentiality, integrity, or availability of sensitive, valuable, or critical information. This is to say that they are not tightly constrained by supervision, system controls, or separation of duties. If these people exist, your organization has given them the unilateral ability to do the organization great harm, and your organization needs to pay special attention to the actions taken by these people. Likewise, your organization needs to establish additional control measures which will deter, detect, avoid, prevent, recover from, and correct the problems which may be occasioned by this special type of trust.

An example should make this a bit more clear. In a traditional Accounting Department, you will typically find one person who makes out a check to a vendor, another who approves the check, and still another who signs the check. This is sometimes called maker-checker-signer separation of duties. With this approach no one person is able to write a check to themselves, their friends, or their family members. In this environment, there is no one person who is in an information security related position of trust.

With downsizing and budget pressures now experienced at so many organizations, this clearly defined type of separation of duties is becoming less common. What we have instead are at least a handful of workers who are in information security related positions of trust. For example, Systems Administrators at many organizations are in a position where they: (1) configure security systems, (2) administer security systems, and (3) act as a user of security systems. If we were to apply this notion to the area of encryption systems, the first of these would involve definition of the key length, the algorithm, and the initialization vector. The second of these would involve initiating key changes, setting-up privileges for new users, and terminating privileges for users who have left the organization. The third of these would involve utilizing the encryption system to protect information like electronic mail. The use of Systems Administrators for all three tasks allows Administrators to give themselves privileges to do harmful acts, as well as the privileges to destroy the evidence of harmful acts that they have done (by deleting logs for example). Better internal control would involve a Security Administrator who does the second type of job, while a Systems Administrator did the first type of job. Additional control could be obtained if neither a Security Administrator nor a Systems Administrator had the third type of job.

But why should you be concerned about those people who are in an information security related position of trust? These are often the people who have the knowledge, skills, and system access to do your organization great harm such as commit fraud, embezzle funds, fiddle with production data, sabotage systems, disrupt system operations, commit industrial espionage, etc. The worst part about it is that they can often do these things without anybody else knowing about it, and without having to be in collusion with anybody else, and without having to get anyone's approval.

Clearly, in the long run, as we progressively improve the level of security provided by information security systems, we want to reduce the number of people who are in information security related positions of trust. As we clarify who is doing what when it comes to information security (through the use of material in this book), we should be adding separation of duties, dual control, and other mechanisms to prevent these individuals from exploiting the privileges we have granted to them for nefarious purposes. By the way, dual control involves having two people be present, in the flesh, to perform a certain high-security task. For example, two officers of a bank need to be present first thing in the morning to open the vault where the cash and safe deposit boxes are stored. Likewise, to initially configure an Internet commerce system, it is wise to employ dual control to require at least two people to set-up the encryption key management system. Additional future developments related to separation of duties are further discussed in the last sub-section of Appendix H, "Role Based Access Control."

Suggested Strategies

But what should you do about this problem? So, first of all, management has to be informed which workers are in an information security related position of trust. In most organizations, management has no idea who these people are or how these people could do serious damage. This information could be produced as the result of a risk assessment or an information systems audit. Alternatively, it could be produced in the course of writing up new roles and responsibilities documentation. At any rate, management can't do anything to reduce the risk from this problem unless it knows who these people are, and in what positions they work.

The next step is try to give part of the jobs of these people in information security related positions of trust away to other people. For example, Business Application Programmers who test their own code could continue to do much of what they have been doing, but the testing activity could be outsourced to a third party. This double check on their work is likely to reduce the chances of undetected bugs in production software, and also likely to encourage them to do a higher quality job. The Programmers are likely to welcome this change because it allows them to focus on what they do best: design and develop programs.

If your organization is very small (see Chapter 18 for further discussion about options for small organizations), or if your organization just can't give away part of the jobs of these people, then there are other options. These include increasing supervision. Continuing the example of the programmers who test their own work, you could change the systems development process so that specific results needed to be demonstrated to management at discrete steps in the process of developing a new application. Or you could require Internal Auditors to review the work of the programmers at certain places in the systems development process. When people know that their work will be reviewed by a supervisor, they take extra care to ensure that everything is the way it should be.

If you can't give away part of their job to other people, then try to restrict the system privileges of these people in a position of information security related trust as much as possible. This will limit the damage that they can do, both accidentally and also intentionally. The policy of least privilege necessary to do the job should be the guiding principle as you restrict these privileges. Restricting privileges involves reducing the ways that these people can reach critical, sensitive, and valuable data (through dial-up lines, via a virtual private network through a firewall, over wireless networks, etc.). Restricting privileges includes narrowing the commands that these people can execute, the systems on which they have privileges, and the networks they can access.

Similar to restricting system privileges is another strategy called split knowledge. With this approach you can prevent people in information security related positions of trust from causing damage to the organization. Consider the case of information security specialists who enable the encryption processes inside Internet commerce servers. Rather than entrusting the master key to a single individual, each of these specialists can be given a key component. A key component must be combined with other key components (and there could be a total of two or more of them), in order to form the operational master key. The combination process is performed entirely inside secure hardware, away from prying eyes. Access to any one key component is not enough for an individual to compromise any of the servers so enabled, or the encrypted messages coming into or going out of these servers.

Similarly, continuing with the same example, you could add more logging and upgrade other methods to record what people do. Keystroke loggers could for example record the actions of programmers, and preserve them on archival CD-ROMs. If programmers know that their every keystroke is recorded, they will be reluctant to engage in fraud or in some other ways contravene internal controls. Because keystroke logging records a whole lot of data, it may be overkill for your environment. Perhaps logging only the powerful systems commands executed by these trusted people would suffice? And by the way, the logs you set up should be protected with a digital signature or a special change detection utility (like Tripwire) so that any tampering would immediately come to light.

To enhance the credibility of logs, as well as to increase their admissibility in court, you may wish to move from fixed passwords to a type of extended user authentication system (biometrics, smart cards, software-based dynamic passwords, etc.). Extended user authentication systems significantly reduce the risks that one user will be able to masquerade as another user. For example, with fixed passwords, it is easy to masquerade as another user if that other user has shared his or her password with you. But if biometrics are used, it is very difficult to masquerade as another user, unless that other user is in collusion with you. More definitively knowing who is on your system, for example via extended user authentication systems, also enhances the effectiveness of the access control privileges you have defined. It additionally discourages would-be perpetrators of criminal or abusive acts, some of whom may be in information sec

You can additionally monitor system access control logs to determine whether these people are attempting to do things for which they don't yet have privileges. Repeated log-in failures or system privilege violations associated with their user-IDs may be an indication that suspicious activity is taking place. You could also set-up scripts to automatically notify you or others on the Computer Emergency Response Team if suspicious activity was underway. Commercial intrusion detection systems (and now even intrusion prevention systems) are the most sophisticated way to immediately detect that an attack or an unauthorized activity is now underway.

You could also look to see what application-based security mechanisms could be used to detect abusive or criminal behavior on the part of those who are in information security related positions of trust. For example, if Wire Transfer System Operators have the ability to unilaterally initiate a wire transfer to any account at a bank, you could write software that detects whether transfers are to the personal accounts of the Operators, and if so, then block the transfers. Likewise, unusual patterns in the wire transfers made by Operators could be detected by neural network systems, and these could then automatically send a report to the Internal Audit Department. Of course, in a real bank, it would be very unusual to find an Operator with these significant privileges. That's because banks have thought a lot about security, particularly fraud and embezzlement, and they have broken-down the job of Operators, and parceled out the pieces to multiple people, so that these abuses are unlikely to happen.

Monitoring the workers in information security positions of trust can go beyond technical measures. Watch to see if they work irregular hours (perhaps an indication that they don't want to be detected when doing abusive or criminal acts). Notice whether they refuse to take time off for vacations (this may be an indication that they need to continue to be there to continue an on-going fraud or some other nefarious activity). You could also watch to see whether these workers are collecting information (such as programming manuals or printouts of data) which aren't really related to their jobs. This information may be necessary in order for them to perpetrate a computer abuse or computer crime. You could additionally notice whether those in an information security position of trust seem to be displaying some newfound wealth (perhaps they just bought a very expensive car, which is unlikely to be paid for out of their modest salary); this may be a tip-off that they are taking money from the organization.

Monitoring should also include a review of their morale and relationships with coworkers. If these people become disgruntled, this is a very bad sign (vengeful acts are a distinct possibility). If they are disgruntled, it may be time to transfer them to another position where they can do less damage, or else to give them time off (with or without pay) until things cool down. Your organization doesn't want to have an on-going dispute with a disgruntled employee who is in an information security position of trust (especially if they work in the Information Security Department).

Perhaps the most underutilized type of monitoring involves other workers. If you have trained your staff to spot unusual and suspicious situations, they can then immediately alert management so that defensive action can be taken to minimize losses. For example, end users are on the front-line when it comes to detecting social engineering (spoofing). End users can alert management to the fact that somebody keeps calling and asking for certain restricted information. Once management understands what type of information the social engineer is after, management can review the privileges of people who are currently in an information security position of trust. It could be that the information sought by the social engineer is a missing piece to the puzzle, a piece that will allow one of the people in an information security position of trust to commit a crime.

You could also look to see what could be done to correct and/or recover from a problem, should it be initiated by someone in an information security position of trust. An example of this in the banking industry would be a contingency plan to contact other banks and reverse wire transfers, should there be a problem. Likewise, for a Systems Administrator with many privileges, you might develop ready-to-go procedures to regenerate your production systems entirely without the involvement of this person who is in an information security position of trust. Of course, all the specific control measures you use will be a function of your industry, the technology your firm uses, prevailing laws and regulations, and the technology sophistication of the involved parties.

To summarize, most importantly, do everything you can to eliminate the presence of an information security related position of trust. If you can't do that (for political, contractual, cost, or other reasons), add more supervision and restrict system privileges as much as you can. You may also wish to segment sensitive information into different parts using the strategy called split knowledge. You should also add deterrent controls, particularly more logging, and be sure to let the people in these positions know that these logging systems exist (although you probably don't want to describe them in much detail so that they are kept in suspense, wondering whether they will be caught if they try something). You may wish to add extended user authentication systems to further bolster the effectiveness of your access control systems and your logging systems. You should also consider adding system-based or application-based controls which will detect any abuse or criminal activity. You may want to go one step further and add controls which will assist you in correcting and recovering from the problems that do occur. And don't forget to train your people to spot and immediately report unusual and suspicious situations. Using several of these control measures at once is strongly recommended. But prevention and avoidance, where you eliminate the existence of information security positions of trust, is by far the least costly of these options.

Chapter 21 COMMON MISTAKES YOU SHOULD AVOID

This chapter covers common mistakes that you will want to avoid when putting together information security roles and responsibilities documentation. While some of these mistakes may seem foolish and unlikely, the author has encountered all of them in real-life situations during consulting engagements. Topics in this chapter move from general and conceptual to specific and operational. Before you read this chapter, you are urged to skim Chapter 4, which deals with prerequisites to an information security roles and responsibilities project.

Management Has Not Been Sensitized To Information Security Risks

To start an effort to assign roles and responsibilities when management doesn't yet understand the need for information security is asking for trouble. If top managers aren't really concerned about information security, they will refuse to allocate the resources to develop specific roles and responsibilities documentation. If this sounds like your organization, you should back-up and deal with the basics first. In most cases, an organization-wide risk analysis (risk assessment) will be needed to clearly show how and where your organization is vulnerable. There is often merit to having an outside expert provide the risk analysis so that there can be no allegations of empire building (internal political advantage) or favoritism. An organization-wide information systems audit, performed by the Internal Audit Department or an external consulting firm, can generate much the same results. A less desirable yet often effective option is an intellectual property audit. In this process, trade secrets, patents, copyrights, trademarks, service marks, and the like are identified and inventoried. This type of an audit will naturally lead to discussions about the ways to protect the organization's intellectual property. When conducting this type of an audit, you should be sure to include intellectual property entrusted to the organization by other entities (such as business partners), as well as intellectual property owned by the organization and entrusted to other entities (such as outsourcing firms). For further discussion of management awareness raising efforts, see Chapter 4.

No Executive Sponsor For Information Security Has Been Arranged

To be successful with a roles and responsibilities clarification effort, you will need the support and encouragement of a member of the top management team. This top manager must understand the need for information security and be willing to take a stand for the establishment of formalized roles and responsibilities. If you don't have a top manager who meets this billing, it's best for you to postpone the roles and responsibilities clarification project until such a manager can be located. This is because top management will eventually need to formally approve the roles and responsibilities that you document. If you know that you can count on the support of at least one top manager, then the project will proceed a great deal more smoothly. Information security managers have been known to drop the name of this top manager when rounding-up support among the rank-and-file for a roles and responsibilities project. As an aside, it should be noted that reference to a "sponsor" in the title to this paragraph has nothing to do with an information "owner" (in rare cases called a "sponsor") who defines user access control privileges and who has additional duties described in Chapter 15.

Sufficient Management Approvals Were Not Obtained

Although an impressive information security roles and responsibilities document may have been developed, all too often this document doesn't go through the proper management review and approval channels. In some cases this is because the process is not clear to the persons who developed the document, while in other cases, these same people didn't want to risk a fight with certain members of the management team. Whatever the reason, anything less than full and complete approval by the very highest levels of internal management jeopardizes the future efforts of the information security function. If the proper approvals were not obtained, this fact will surface at the most inconvenient of times, for example, when a hotly debated issue is forced up the management chain for resolution. Any effort on the part of an information security group to engage in activities that have not been fully approved by all members of the top management team will be a major reason not to support information security's position on the issue in question. At times like these, the information security function needs all the support it can muster, and these are not the times to have arguments about roles and responsibilities. The management approval process is discussed in Chapter 7.

Positioning Of Information Security Conflicts With Organizational Objectives

For management to seriously support information security, it must clearly see the link between information security and the achievement of organizational goals and objectives. If information security is characterized (or "positioned" in marketing language) as adversarial or in conflict with organizational goals and objectives, a proposed roles and responsibilities definition effort is bound to fail. In most cases, this conflict in goals and objectives is implied or imagined, and never specifically articulated. In other instances, a promoter of information security is so forceful or strong-willed that he or she forgets that information security must play a supporting role, not a leading role (there are a few exceptions such as military and diplomatic organizations as well as information security consulting firms). For example, if management sees information security as an impediment to progress, perhaps an obstacle that may slow development of new applications, then it will be hostile to any efforts that appear to expand and strengthen related roles and responsibilities. On the other hand, if management appreciates that a clear definition of roles and responsibilities will speed business application development, it will be much more supportive. It's worth your time to identify management attitudes like this through a few interviews before actually releasing a draft roles and responsibilities document (this interviewing process is described in Chapter 4 and Chapter 7). Only when you know the objections that management harbors can you then deal with them effectively.

Top Management Believes Its Duty Is Discharged By Appointing Someone

To have an effective information security organizational function, it is critical that the people who work in the information security area have relevant experience, training, and skills. All too often management thinks that the totality of its duty has been discharged by simply appointing someone to a newly-created position of Information Security Coordinator or Information Security Department Manager. To the contrary, as explained in Chapter 12 there are a significant number of people throughout every organization who all have different roles to play on an information security team.

Likewise, top management's responsibilities in the information security area are not handled just because a person who knows very little about information security, who has no relevant experience, is now supposedly handling the issue. Sending these people to classes and conferences, and perhaps sending them to observe what happens at other organizations, in many cases will take too long to show significant results. When a new information security function is being created it is especially important to have seasoned and experienced staff who know what they are doing. Without this seasoned and experienced staff, a newly-appointed person is likely to make mistakes that significantly set back the information security effort, and it may take months or even a year to regain the ground lost in this way. Beyond the designation of an Information Security Manager, top management duties include allocating sufficient funds, reviewing progress, setting policy, and other tasks; these duties are described at length in Chapter 11 and Chapter 12 respectively.

Accountability Does Not Match Responsibility

In far too many cases, top management will blame and punish lower level managers for information security failings, even though these lower level managers were never given the resources to properly address information security. Often this unfortunate scenario takes place after a major publicly-known security breach. Management may not know what to do; terminating a manager who they think should have been more diligent often looks like the only justifiable reaction. If top management is going to hold these lower level managers accountable for information security, they should formally assign responsibility and allocate sufficient resources as well. The formal assignment of responsibility is best accomplished via mission statements, job descriptions, and the other documents described in this book (particularly those discussed Chapter 11, Chapter 12, and Chapter 13.) Some statistics to help you determine an appropriate budget for information security can be found in Appendix A as well as Chapter 18.

Staff Assumes Revenue Producing Activities Overshadow Information Security

For far too long, people have thought that information security is just an overhead cost. As such, information security activities are something to be minimized, perhaps even dispensed with in tough times. Information security in reality is much more than that. It can be a source of competitive advantage, a way to polish the organization's public image, a source of new features for existing products and services, and even a source of new products and services. In some industries, such as Internet commerce consumer product sales, information security is something more than a way to achieve competitive advantage-it is a competitive necessity. In some other industries, such as financial services, customer confidence critically depends on an image of good information security. For example, if your bank regularly made random errors on your bank statement it wouldn't be long before you found another bank. Top management has to appreciate the contribution that information security can make to the business before they will be willing to specifically define information security roles and responsibilities. This understanding will help them to see that revenue producing activities in addition to information security activities are all needed, that it is not a case of either one or the other. When management understands that information security is a necessity in modern business, then they will approve the budget for a wide variety of information security efforts.

Management Says Everybody Is Responsible

Some top managers will claim that every worker is responsible for information security, and that everyone must chip in. While it is true that information is handled by nearly every worker, and that every person must participate in one way or another, the "everyone is responsible" approach can make it appear as though responsibility has been assigned when in fact it has not. If remarks like this are all that top management says about information security roles and responsibilities, it will invariably cause perverse results. For example, this approach can cause all serious information security work to be postponed. In response, workers may say things like, "It's not my job," and "When management tells me to do something specific about it, I will." Accordingly, vague statements from top management about information security roles and responsibilities are not sufficient-they need to be accompanied by explicit documentation that assigns roles and responsibilities. Such vague statements can, nonetheless, be useful because they can underscore management's concern and reinforce the need for widespread participation. Just be sure that they are the beginning of an effort to clarify roles and responsibilities, not the final word.

Staff Takes A Reactive Approach To Information Security

You should ask whether your organization is primarily reactive or primarily proactive when it comes to information security. Most organizations have traditionally been reactive. Increasingly organizations are adopting a more proactive stance. The economics of information security clearly support a more proactive position. Recovering from the bad publicity and chaos surrounding an information security incident can take years and be much more expensive than correcting the immediate problems and thus preventing an incident. Similarly, research done at SRI International (formerly Stanford Research Institute) indicates that it's ten times more expensive to add controls to an application after it has gone into production than it is to build controls into the application while it is still in development. In addition, automated attacks like distributed denial of service attacks now take place so quickly that it's no longer viable to reactively mount a manual response. Instead, a proactive and scripted response to these attacks must be programmed into the involved systems. So if management is thinking that information security should be primarily reactive, they will minimize the roles and responsibilities of the function. On the other hand, if management appreciates what information security can really do for them, they will approve a considerably broader array of roles and responsibilities. In addition, one of the objectives behind a formal written definition of roles and responsibilities is to motivate staff to think and act in proactive fashion.

Management Relies On Voluntary Information Security Cooperation

Some things need to be dictated centrally, and information security roles and responsibilities are one of these things. Most users have no intention or motivation to understand the risks of information security, let alone what their role and responsibility is in terms of dealing with these risks. Most users are pressed by other objectives, rewarded for achieving results in areas other than information security, and likely to push information security projects to the end of their to-do lists. Thus reliance on the goodwill and voluntary cooperation of users and lower level managers is bound to lead to sub-optimal results. Even though an end-user empowerment approach is fashionable these days, workers still need specific instructions about roles and responsibilities related to information security. While information security decision-making can be pushed down the management hierarchy, in accord with the notion of empowerment, what's often missing is a clear description of the decisions that need to be made. That's where a clear articulation of roles and responsibilities is needed. Beyond clarifying the work to be done, there is a need to manage certain information security activities on a centralized basis. For example, network management systems, encryption standards, and dial-up user authentication standards all need a centralized organization-wide approach. Centralization is discussed at length in Chapter 19. User and department manager responsibilities are discussed in Chapter 15.

Contribution Made By Information Security Is Not Regularly Reinforced

To many people working in the field, the information security function feels like it's caught between the proverbial "rock and a hard place." If there has been a recent security incident, then management feels that information security isn't doing its job. If there has been no recent incident, management feels that they can cut information security's budget to save money. Sometimes this is called "damned if you do, and damned if you don't" (in this case it refers to experiencing a security relevant event). While this may sound discouraging, there is a way to avoid either of these undesirable alternatives. The preferred approach is to regularly communicate the contribution made by the information security function as well as others working in the information security area (Information Systems Auditors, Systems Administrators, etc.). This often takes the form of quarterly written status reports, although many other approaches can be used. For example, if you can show how superior information security is a factor causing new customers to do business with your organization, this will significantly advance the information security group's image in management's eyes. Likewise, if the Information Security Department can show how the latest strategic alliance critically depended on strong information security measures to protect the business partner's proprietary information, this should be trumpeted to top management. If these types of reinforcement are not periodically provided, management may downgrade and minimize the roles and responsibilities of information security. Another way to look at this is that good Information Security Department Managers must always be selling the contribution that their group is making to the organization.

Management Does Not Reinforce New Roles And Responsibilities

All too often information security roles and responsibilities are defined and approved, and then that's the end of the discussion so far as top management is concerned.

While these documents might be presented to outsiders like external auditors, they are often not periodically reinforced with insiders via staff training and awareness courses, information security manuals, system usage pamphlets, management memorandums, and the like (see Chapter 10 for additional documents). Likewise, at all too many organizations, management doesn't provide money for compliance checking to make sure that workers are in fact following the new instructions found in the information security roles and responsibilities documentation. In discussions with management, it is important to clearly communicate that the establishment of a formal organizational structure in support of information security is a major cultural change. To be truly effective, this cultural change must be periodically reinforced, repeatedly justified, regularly altered to reflect new circumstances, and periodically reevaluated. The most common place to communicate the new roles and responsibilities of the information security function is in new employee orientation. An information security policies manual is another favorite tool used to reinforce these same roles and responsibilities.

Major Projects Are Initiated Before Roles And Responsibilities Are Defined

This problem is sometimes referred to as putting the "cart before the horse." If a cart with wheels is placed in front of a horse, things don't work right. The horse has to come first and then pull the cart. Similarly, in the realm of application systems development, requirements must be defined before programming code is developed. The same is true with information security roles and responsibilities. Roles and responsibilities should be defined before major information security projects -- like the installation of and cut-over to an intrusion detection system -- are undertaken. Although management may say, "Just go do it," they may be unaware of the difficulties associated with major projects if roles and responsibilities are ill-defined. In the absence of clear roles and responsibilities, staff will typically spend an inordinate amount of time trying to figure out who is supposed to do what, attempting to get these people to attend to information security tasks, assigning blame to people who had no idea they were supposed to be doing something, etc. To avoid these problems, you should make sure that roles and responsibilities are clearly defined before major projects get underway. If roles and responsibilities are presently defined in a loose or informal way, you should fix them up so that people can work with focused effort and a clear understanding of who will do what. This topic and related dependencies are discussed in Chapter 4.

Scope Of Information Security Duties Are Too Narrowly Defined

Information flows quickly and relatively inexpensively from internal unit to internal unit, and increasingly back and forth with outside organizations like customers and suppliers. The widespread distribution of information makes information security a pervasive concern that should be on the minds of virtually every worker at your organization. Developments such as Internet commerce and extranets further underscore the need to adopt a broad view of information security roles and responsibilities. Nonetheless, in far too many organizations the roles and responsibilities of an Information Security Department are defined too narrowly. As a result, the Department is hampered from contributing to its full potential. For example, in some organizations privacy is considered outside the Department's mission. Similarly, in other organizations, contingency planning is considered outside the Department's mission. Both of these areas can and should be addressed, at least in part, by the work of an Information Security Department. The full range of activities for an information security function can be found in Chapter 12. While not all of these duties will be relevant to your organization, the list can help you move well along towards a fully-rounded definition of information security roles and responsibilities.

Scope Of Information Security Duties Are Too Loosely Defined

In many organizations, the roles and responsibilities of an Information Security Department are too loosely defined. For example, a one-paragraph mission statement may be all that exists. Job descriptions may be missing. This loose and fuzzy approach causes several undesirable results including: (a) excessive resources repeatedly consumed by ad-hoc role and responsibility definition work that could have been better spent actually doing project work, (b) surprise information security incidents because important duties had not been properly performed, (c) lack of results from the Information Security Department because the Department's authority to do certain things-such as block an application moving into production-was not clear. This book is intended to overcome these and related problems, and you should use the detailed mission statements and job descriptions to specifically define information security duties (see Chapter 11 and Chapter 12). The consequences of loosely defining information security roles and responsibilities are further discussed in Chapter 2.

Not Establishing Specific Enough Job Descriptions

In some organizations, management doesn't really understand the information security function, but management may nonetheless feel as though the people who work in this new area need job descriptions. To apply a quick fix, in these cases management often tries to pigeonhole information security specialists into the job titles and job descriptions for other jobs. For example, an Information Security Engineer may be given a Computer Systems Analyst job title and job description. This in turn causes problems, especially when it comes to staff performance. The criteria for success for a Computer Systems Analyst are typically very different from the criteria for success for an Information Security Engineer. This approach creates other problems, such as confusion for those using the organization's phone directory. The remedy is to create enough specific job titles and job descriptions for every one of the distinct jobs at the organization in question. This is why extensive information about the duties of different job titles is provided in Chapter 12.

Creating Job Descriptions Which Are Too Detailed

Job descriptions, especially information systems related job descriptions, can become unwieldy because they contain too much information. The form that this mistake most often takes is the inclusion of procedures, system design issues, or other technical details within job descriptions. A good job description should be in plain business language, flexible, relevant, responsive to organizational needs, well-organized, to-the-point, and not redundant. It should include only enough detail to make clear what needs to be done. With this in mind, you should remember that the job descriptions found in Chapter 12 in many instances will be too detailed, are intended to be modified, and are not intended to be used verbatim. While brevity and focus may not be a good way to demonstrate your command of the language, nor will they be a good way to demonstrate your awareness of the technical issues involved, they will nonetheless ultimately be the descriptors which best characterize job descriptions which have been approved by top management.

Inappropriate Person Prepares Roles And Responsibilities Documents

If someone with a general business background prepared roles and responsibilities documentation for an information security group, and if he or she did not have the benefit of the information in this book or comparable resources, the result will often be dysfunctional. Important topics are often left out and the thrust of the information security effort may be twisted to support another organizational function such as computer operations. The resulting documentation may need to be thrown out and a new version developed, or worse yet, the document may languish in an approving manager's in-basket forever. Accordingly, the person who writes information security roles and responsibilities needs to be a good writer, needs to have inside knowledge about the business in question, needs to know about the technology of information security, and needs to be relatively free of internal politics (an independent consultant is often advisable). This topic is further explored in Chapter 6.

Management Assigns Untrained And Inexperienced People

One of the most common and most serious errors that management makes when setting up an information security organizational structure, is that they assign untrained and inexperienced people to look after information security. This is particularly true at those organizations which insist on promoting from within, which in many cases don't have any employees who are qualified to perform information security duties. Then, to make matters worse, management typically assumes that these untrained and inexperienced people are going to be able to do the job without a significant investment in training. So management doesn't give these people time to become proficient in the very complex and technical information security field, management doesn't give these people the resources to attend college courses or other training events, and then management is disappointed that nothing much happens (or worse, serious break-ins or other problems occur). The information security function is then typically discredited and bad-mouthed. The bad feelings that people inside these organizations have about information security are then carried over to the next group of people, who once again attempt to make things work, and often these new people make the same error. As an aside, the most popular way to measure the knowledge and proficiency of job candidates is see if they have certifications (this topic is taken up in detail in Appendix D).

Management Is Unwilling To Pay Market Rates For Specialists

In many firms, management is dismayed at the high salaries that information security specialists command. Likewise, they are often put-off by the high rates charged by information security consultants. For a variety of reasons, and sometimes a sense of equity with existing employees, management refuses to pay the going rates for information security specialists (be they employees, consultants, contractors, whatever). Typically what happens next is that open positions languish for a long period of time because nobody is willing to take the job when better paying jobs are available elsewhere. Sometimes people who could not get any other job apply for and get these positions. For example, the author knows of one convicted perpetrator of fraud who applied for a position as, and was then appointed as, Information Security Department Manager at a high-tech company. In other situations, inexperienced and untrained people apply for these jobs and get them because nobody else seriously considers the positions. While information security specialists do command very high salaries and consulting rates, to deny the reality of their going rates only causes problems. And the most serious of these problems is that the information security goals and objectives which management established will predicatably not be achieved.

Technical Staff Inappropriately Promoted To Management Positions

It is often bad news to see top management promoting a Systems Admininstrator who did well configuring firewalls to a position of Information Security Department Manager. If this Systems Administrator is a geek, if he or she is focused exclusively on the technology, and if he or she is not a good communicator, there will be trouble. Not everyone can do a good job as an Information Security Department Manager (the essential criteria for this position are defined at length in Appendix B). To lead a person who is tempermentally ill-suited, or otherwise unprepared, to believe that they can do this job when they really can't is not a service to the involved organization or to the individual. To adopt this approach appears to save money in the short run, but in the long run it costs more because important information security projects will be slowed or brought to a standstill, and the Information Security Department Manager recruiting process will need to be once again conducted.

Time Required To Get Top Management Approval Is Underestimated

When it comes to roles and responsibilities documentation, a good number of people underestimate the elapsed time required to get top management approval. While roles and responsibilities documents that are truly tailored to your organization generally sail right through the approval process with few if any objections, others may take up to six months to complete several iterations of a review and revision cycle. To minimize the involvement of top management, you should take a strong stand in favor of adequate up-front research to prepare a document that is truly customized to your organization. Whatever the up-front effort used to prepare the document, be sure to plan for the possibility that several time-consuming review and revision iterations may be required. Additional details about the approval process, as well as a suggested schedule, can be found in Chapter 7 and Chapter 9.

Roles And Responsibilities Are Not Periodically Updated

In many cases, information security roles and responsibilities were defined a long time ago but they have not been updated to reflect changes in information systems technology (such as telecommuting), nor have they been updated to reflect new business structures (such as outsourcing). At the very least, information security roles and responsibilities should be revisited every two years to make sure that they are still relevant. Likewise, when there are significant technological or business changes (such as a merger or acquisition), there should often be changes in the documents reflecting information security roles and responsibilities. A detailed list of the circumstances which imply it's time to update your roles and responsibilities documentation can be found in Chapter 5. The results of outdated roles and responsibilities documentation include (a) diminished respect for the information security function, (b) an increased number of disputes about who is supposed to do what information security functions, and (c) increased management difficulty when it comes to assigning tasks associated with major projects in the information security area.

Staff Performance Reviews Do Not Include Information Security

In far too many situations, staff performance reviews do not consider whether workers carried out their jobs in compliance with information security policies, standards, and other requirements. For example, a Systems Administrator may be judged on technical knowledge, ability to manage multiple projects, problem solving ability, and other factors-but not on compliance with information security requirements. The most important thing that you can do to ensure that information security will be considered in the performance review process is to get it written into job descriptions. In most cases, only the job descriptions of workers directly involved with information security matters will include mention of information security. Over time, it is desirable to include it in the job descriptions of other workers including end-users. The second best thing that you can do to get information included in the performance review process is to get a question included in standard organization-wide performance evaluation questionnaires. These questionnaires typically include questions like, "Does the worker deal courteously with customers?" If your organization does not use a set of questions like this, you may wish to have a conversation with the Director of Human Resources about the merits of adopting such a template. A template can be an effective way to reinforce corporate values and ensure that these values are considered by all workers. Such a template may additionally be a good way to ensure that all workers are being evaluated in a similar manner, that personal bias and inappropriate discrimination is minimized. Performance review considerations are taken up in greater detail in Appendix C.

No Disciplinary Process Exists

Having a well-written set of information security policies is going to do your organization very little good unless a disciplinary process is regularly applied. Without a disciplinary process, information security requirements will be "without teeth" and not worthy of worker attention. For example, if a policy requires users to refrain from taking confidential information out of the office, and if an employee is known by management to have done just that, but the employee does not receive any reprimand or punishment, the absence of discipline indirectly encourages others to do the same. Any attempt to define roles and responsibilities relative to information security will be met with the same attitude. Simply having an impressive looking roles and responsibilities document, a document that workers never follow, a document about which management doesn't seem to care, isn't going to produce the results you want. If you can, you should use the disciplinary process that the Human Resources Department has already prepared rather than come up with a separate disciplinary process. Besides the Director of Human Resources, you may also wish to discuss the disciplinary process and related action-forcing mechanisms with people in both the Legal Department and the Internal Audit Department.

No Compliance Checking Process Exists

It doesn't matter how impressive the information security roles and responsibilities documentation happens to be if no one is checking to make sure that people are working in a manner that is consistent with this documentation. Most often compliance checking is performed by the Internal Audit Department, not the Information Security Department. This is because the Information Security Department is generally responsible for developing the documentation and setting the requirements. To have the same department specify and document control measures, and also review the effectiveness of these same measures, would be a conflict of interest. An Information Security Department with both of these roles would be tempted to tell top management that they were doing a great job, when in fact that may not be the case. Besides the Internal Audit Department, compliance checking could be done by the Legal Department, the Compliance Department, an external consultant, or a government regulator. Increasingly, some software packages can be used to make sure that people are doing their jobs. For example, vulnerability identification software can determine whether Systems Administrators are applying the latest operating system patches. Likewise, license management systems can be used to determine whether users have unlicensed software resident on their hard disk drives.

No Clear Problem Reporting Process Exists

Managers in a position to actually do something about information security often do not hear about the problems that people elsewhere in the organization are having. For example, top management may not hear about a hacker intrusion that a group of Systems Administrators handled on their own. Problem reports may not be communicated for a variety of reasons, including middle management's desire to look good in the eyes of top management. This situation also occurs when roles and responsibilities for the problem reporting and management escalation process are not sufficiently defined. To get a good idea about the problem reporting and escalation process at your organization, you should attempt to identify who would be notified if there were to be a computer-assisted internal fraud at the organization. You should also attempt to determine who is to be notified in the event of a computer related emergency or disaster. You can furthermore attempt to determine who should be notified about information security vulnerabilities as well as violations of information security policies. In a well-structured organization, both the people to be notified and the information that needs to be communicated will be clearly defined in writing. This is not to imply that all these types of information must always be provided directly to top management. Instead, top management should (1) clearly specify what events and conditions they wish to hear about, (2) define what they consider to be important information about information security related events, and (3) specify how, when, and to whom that important information will be communicated.

Appendix A STAFFING LEVELS

The following report, "Information Security Staffing: Calculating the Standard of Due Care", will provide you with a rough indication of the adequacy of an organization's current staffing levels. It is intended for use in so-called "back of the envelope" calculations that provide overall guidance, not precise and definitive results. The survey results should not be taken as a strict standard to which every organization should aspire. Instead, in every organization there will be special circumstances requiring either more or less information security personnel.

While many numbers are included in the following report, you should not be discouraged. The process for using the results is actually quite simple and is based on ratios. For example, the ratios given in the report can be multiplied by the total full-time equivalent workers at your organization to come up with an anticipated average staffing level. This process is described in greater detail in the first few paragraphs of the report. The chapter is thus especially useful when preparing budgets, project plans, or requests for additional information security resources.

Although this survey was performed at the end of 1997, its results are still relevant to organizations in the United States and Canada. If anything, the average staffing levels will have increased in the years that have elapsed since the report was prepared. This is because information security is increasingly being appreciated by top management as an essential business function. Thus the numbers in this report can be used to indicate a conservative minimum staffing level below which organizations should not go.

The author and the Computer Security Institute intend to update this report via a more recent survey. The date when this survey will conducted, and the date when the results will be published, was not known at the time that this book went to press. If you wish to find out whether an updated version of this report has been published, you can view the CSI web site (www.gocsi.com) or the InfoSecurity Infrastructure Inc. web site (www.infosecurityinfrastructure.com).

For a more recent report which addresses some of these same issues, the author recommends that you consult an article entitled "2003: Another Year Of Belt Tightening - InfoSecurity Budgets Are Increasing But At A Far Slower Rate Than Many People Assume," which appeared in the March 2003 issue of InfoSecurity Magazine. Additional up-to-date statistics can be found in the second section of Chapter 18.

INFORMATION SECURITY STAFFING: CALCULATING THE STANDARD OF DUE CARE

Survey Objectives

Overwhelmed with the myriad of things that they are expected to accomplish, many information security practitioners wonder whether their organization has comparable staffing levels to other organizations in the same industry. For many years this question was destined to remain unanswered. But that has now changed with this staffing survey. This survey allows you to provide definitive quantitative reference points that management can use to determine whether an organization is falling behind, or whether it is out in front of the competition.

The idea behind this survey is basically a legal one: to avoid charges of negligence, computer professional malpractice, or breach of fiduciary duty (specifically the duty to protect assets such as information and information systems). To provide a credible defense against such charges, management needs to be able to show that they have exercised due diligence. In the information security arena, this means that management needs to demonstrate that they have deployed controls that are comparable to those found in similar organizations. It also means that management needs to have made a comparable investment in information security. In other words, management needs to be able to show that they have been operating in a manner consistent with the standard of due care.

In response to practitioner claims that staffing levels are insufficient, management often says they don't believe it. Unfortunately, management is often disinclined to take any action until they see detailed quantitative evidence indicating that a change is appropriate. This chapter provides just such evidence compiled by independent parties. Intended primarily to answer budgeting and human resources questions, the numbers found below can also be useful in risk assessments, as well as in both internal and external audits.

Under some circumstances, the numbers appearing in this report can also be used to prevent information security staff from being laid off when management decides that it's time to cutback on expenses. This last suggested use is an especially important one because information security, EDP audit, and quality assurance are all areas that frequently bear disproportionately large reductions in staff when available organizational resources are especially tight.

Survey Structure

The survey used ratios as an expedient way to calculate the level of information security staffing. Ratios are used extensively in financial accounting. One example is the P/E (Price/Earnings) ratio, which indicates the reasonableness of a stock's current price. Rather than focusing on financial ratios, this survey focused on staff head-count. The use of head-count ratios eliminates conversion problems associated with different national currencies, location-related variations in the cost of living, different pay scales for the same job, and different duties for the same job. The use of head-count ratios also allows the results to be readily applied to organizations of any size. The usefulness of the ratios described below is furthermore enhanced because they fall into relatively narrow windows that then reduce decision-making uncertainty.

The questionnaire used to gather data for this survey was distributed in November 1997 to recipients of *Computer Security Alert*, a newsletter published by the *Computer Security Institute* (San Francisco). All responses were anonymous. Incomplete responses were excluded from the applicable ratios, but were otherwise used for calculations. Some 302 usable responses were received.

In general, this survey was not conducted with strict scientific statistical sampling procedures. Accordingly, the results provide only a rough approximation of the real world. The large sample size does, however, allow you to have significant confidence in these numbers.

The average organization responding to the survey had a total of 6,458 staff workers. Like the previous year, most of the respondents hailed from the Financial Services sector, with the Government sector coming in a close second. Unlike the survey conducted in the previous year, there were no respondents in the Retailing/ Wholesaling industry in this survey. To provide a reference point for those working in this industry, we provide the 1996 figures in all the tables shown below. To remind you that the Retailing/Wholesaling industry figures are from a previous year, this topic is mentioned repeatedly in the first several tables. Separately, the "Other" category for industry was primarily pharmaceuticals, oil and gas, law enforcement, consulting, agriculture, and publishing.

Although a formal count was not made, approximately 90% of the responses were sent from American or Canadian locations. The numbers provided should be relevant to other industrialized countries as well.

Figure A-1: Distribution of Respondents by Industry

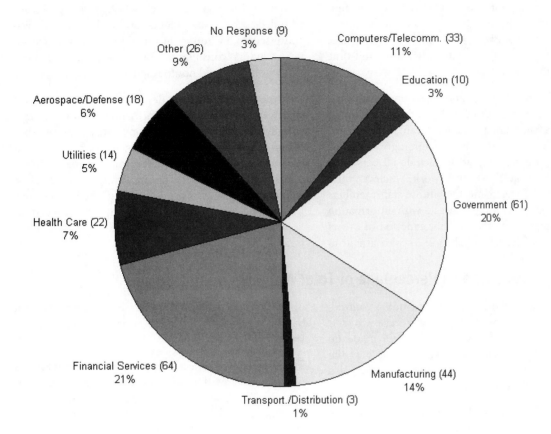

Definition of Information Security

To simplify computations, the study used the term full-time equivalent (FTE) to indicate the sum of both full-time and part-time workers. For example, one full-time and four half-time people would equal three full-time equivalent staff.

The study deliberately ignored organizational structures. Instead, it attempted to include all information security staff, whether they are permanent staff, temporaries, consultants, contractors, or outsourcing personnel. Likewise, the study attempted to include all personnel performing information security work, whatever their title or affiliated department. Only those staff members who have been specifically charged with information security responsibilities that are not expected of others were included in the tallies. Thus users who attend to

their own information security tasks were specifically excluded from the tabulations. The survey was addressed to in-house information security practitioners; vendors, consultants, contractors, and other non-employees were told not to respond.

Information security was described broadly to include all activities that protect information and/or information systems. Thus information systems contingency planning, archival records management, and information systems access control are all considered to be information security activities. Staff in Information Systems, Electronic Data Processing (EDP) Auditing, Risk Management, Legal, and Physical (Industrial) Security departments are considered to be conducting other activities.

Information Security as a Percentage of Total Workers

For the survey as a whole, the staff (including contractors, consultants, temporaries, and outsourced workers) who work in the information security area made up 0.100% of total staff. This is a 64% increase over the prior year's survey (1996). This year's number also represented a 300% increase over the 1989 survey.

This ratio varied considerably by organizational size. Those organizations with fewer than 2500 full-time equivalent staff had 0.638% of staff devoted to information security. Organizations that had between 2501 and 5000 workers had 0.140% of staff devoted to information security. While organizations that had 5001 and more workers had 0.047% of staff devoted to information security. Clearly there are some economies of scale whereby larger organizations can leverage their information security staff better than small organizations can. This significant disparity between large and small organizations also implies that there are some basic things that must be in place no matter what the size of the organization; these include written policies, a user awareness program, and a secure systems development process. In larger organizations, these basic information security efforts can be spread out over more people and thus consume a smaller portion of the total cost for staff.

Looking still at the percentage of total workers devoted to information security, it is interesting to see that small organizations are changing much faster than larger organizations. Smaller organizations are increasing head-count at a 68% annual rate, while medium sized organizations are increasing at a 27% rate, and large organizations are increasing at only a 24% rate. This appears to be a reflection of catch-up efforts on the part

of smaller organizations, which historically have not been as sophisticated in the information security area as large organizations.

The differences between large and small organizations when looking at this ratio are also illuminating. This year the difference between large and small organizations was a factor of 13, but a year ago it was a factor of 10, and back in 1989 it was a factor of five. This increasing disparity between large and small organizations may be a reflection of better risk assessments, which more finely tune the information security expenditures to the unique risks facing each organization. The more a risk assessment accurately reflects prevailing circumstances, the more management is likely to tailor the staffing levels to meet these unique circumstances. The increasing disparity may also be a reflection of more sophisticated information security tools, which often can be afforded only by larger organizations. These sophisticated tools, such as expert systems that help detect credit card frauds, will generally reduce the need for staff.

Continuing with an examination of the percentage of total workers devoted to information security, we found that the ratio was quite different when one looks at the number of years that an organization has had an information security function in place. If a function has existed for five or fewer years, then the ratio is 0.069%. The same ratio applies if the function has existed for six to ten years. But if the function has existed for eleven or more years, then the ratio jumps to 0.181%. The very much larger staffs found in those organizations with a long-standing information security function implies that management understands and supports information security in these organizations. This should be encouraging to all of us who have labored with awareness campaigns year after year, hoping that management will finally understand how important information security is. If you keep at it, management eventually does appreciate information security.

Taking another vantage point on this same ratio, we can examine the effect of military, defense, and diplomatic activities. Organizations that were involved with these national defense activities had 0.188% of their total staff devoted to information security, while those organizations that did not engage in national defense activities had only 0.089% of their staff working in the information security area. It is intriguing to note that the ratio for the national defense organizations increased 55% over the prior year's survey, but the ratio for those organizations not involved in national defense increased 71%. As these year-to-year changes indicate, information security is becoming a business issue to a much greater extent than it had in previous years. The expansion of Internet commerce is partially driving this trend to increased investment in the private sector information security area.

Table A-1 shows an industry-by-industry breakdown for this ratio. Health Care saw the largest year-to-year change, a whopping 564% increase. This makes sense given the US government's efforts to pass legislation to reform the industry, as well as the rapidly rising level of consumer concern about the privacy of health care information. Computers/Telecommunications saw the next largest annual increase at 66%. Education, Utilities, and Aerospace/Defense saw declines over the last year. Because this year had no respondents from the Retailing/Wholesaling industry, the specific numbers for that industry are from the prior year's survey. The specific numbers from other industries, from the prior year's survey, are not provided here in an effort to reduce the possibility of confusion.

Table A-1: Information Security as a Percentage of Total Workers

Business Activity	$\dfrac{\text{InfoSecurity Workers}}{\text{Total Workers}}$
Computers/Telecommunications	0.208%
Education	0.063%
Government	0.161%
Manufacturing	0.035%
Retailing/Wholesaling	0.020%
Transportation/Distribution	0.037%
Financial Services	0.138%
Health Care	0.093%
Utilities	0.092%
Aerospace/Defense	0.047%
Other	0.229%

EDP Audit as a Percentage of Total Workers

Similar calculations can be performed for the EDP Audit (Information Systems Audit) function. In overall terms, organizations in the sample had 0.058% of their total staff devoted to EDP audit. This represents a 49% increase over the prior year. As with information security, the relative number of people devoted to EDP audit was correlated with the information intensity of business activities. In other words, the greater the reliance on information and information systems, the greater the number of both information security staff and EDP audit staff. Table A-2 shows the ratio of EDP audit to total workers. Again, the figure for the Retailing/Wholesaling industry is from the prior year's survey. Similar to information security, the greatest increase in this ratio was in the Health Care sector, which saw a 285% increase. Relatively minor year-to-year declines were noted in the Education, Manufacturing/Production, and Aerospace/Defense sectors.

Table A-2: EDP Audit as a Percentage of Total Workers

Business Activity	EDP Audit Workers / Total Workers
Computers/Telecommunications	0.054%
Education	0.057%
Government	0.114%
Manufacturing	0.017%
Retailing/Wholesaling	0.014%
Transportation/Distribution	0.017%
Financial Services	0.102%
Health Care	0.050%
Utilities	0.060%
Aerospace/Defense	0.043%
Other	0.090%

Information Security Staff Relative to EDP Audit Staff

This year's ratio of information security head-count to EDP audit head-count was 1.75. This means that there are 1.75 information security staff members for every single EDP audit staff member. This ratio has advanced 10% over the last year. The prior year's ratio was a dramatic departure from the 1989 survey, when there were 1.55 EDP auditors for every information security person. In other words, information security continues to grow faster than EDP audit.

Table A-3 provides a set of ratios for information security relative to EDP audit. Major increases were noted in the Health Care area, with an 89% uptick, and in the Transportation/Distribution area, with an 82% upwards move. Decreases were notable in the Government sector as well as in the Aerospace/Defense area. The realignments of priorities in the two sectors experiencing a decline in this ratio are probably a function of the massive cut-backs that they both have suffered over the last few years.

.

Table A-3: Information Security Staff Divided by EDP Audit Staff

Business Activity	InfoSecurity Workers / EDP Auditors
Computers/Telecommunications	3.82
Education	1.09
Government	1.41
Manufacturing	2.11
Retailing/Wholesaling	1.42
Transportation/Distribution	2.11
Financial Services	1.36
Health Care	1.87
Utilities	1.54
Aerospace/Defense	1.09
Other	2.55

Physical Security as a Percentage of Total Workers

Measuring physical (institutional) security as a percentage of total workers, there has been a marked decrease of 52% since the last year. This year's ratio is 0.334%. The decrease in physical security may be in part due to increased automation of burglar alarms, CCTV, and other physical security systems. The decrease may also be affected by the declining crime rates experienced in many parts of North America. A dramatic decrease in the Government sector, and to a lesser extent in the Aerospace/Defense sector seems to have had a major effect in this overall ratio. Health Care saw a very substantial increase of 306% over the prior year.

Because physical security staff typically don't do much work in the information security area, no correlation with information intensity was found in the following industry ratios. As one might expect, the extent to which military, diplomatic, and other governmental activities were performed was a much more reliable predictor of physical security staffing levels.

In previous years, the ratio of information security to total workers was much more tightly constrained in a window than the ratio of physical security to total workers. This variability by industry seems to be decreasing in the physical security area; last year the ratios differed by a factor of 65 for physical security to total workers, but this year they differed only by a factor of 41. The industry ratios of information security to total workers differed last year by a factor of 10, but this year they differed by a factor of 11.

Table A-4: Physical Security as a Percentage of Total Workers

Business Activity	Physical Security Workers / Total Workers
Computers/Telecommunications	0.128%
Education	0.243%
Government	0.509%
Manufacturing	0.452%
Retailing/Wholesaling	0.933%
Transportation/Distribution	0.023%
Financial Services	0.207%
Health Care	0.414%
Utilities	0.148%
Aerospace/Defense	0.195%
Other	0.250%

Information Security Relative to Physical Security

In overall terms, the ratio of information security workers to physical security workers this year was 0.311. This means that for every single information security worker, there are about three physical security workers. This ratio has changed dramatically over the years. Last year the ratio indicated that there was one information security person for every eleven physical security persons, while in 1989 there was one information security person for every twenty physical security people. The increasing influence of information security relative to physical security is clearly showing up in these numbers.

As Table A-5 indicates, the ratio of information security staff to physical security staff is highest in the Computers/Telecommunications sector. Increasing concerns about industrial espionage in high-tech companies may be a significant cause of this high ratio. A relatively high ratio was also found in the Transportation/Distribution area. The latter may be caused by the increased reliance of these industries on high-technology such as satellite-based systems to track the location of vehicles. The lowest ratio of information security staff to physical security staff occurs in Retailing/Wholesaling (again, we used last year's number for this industry), which has significant concerns about shoplifting and cargo theft, both of which necessitate heavy investments in physical security.

Table A-5: Information Security Staff Divided by Physical Security Staff

Business Activity	InfoSecurity Workers / Physical Security Workers
Computers/Telecommunications	1.62
Education	0.27
Government	0.24
Manufacturing	0.08
Retailing/Wholesaling	0.02
Transportation/Distribution	1.58
Financial Services	0.70
Health Care	0.23
Utilities	0.59
Aerospace/Defense	0.24
Other	0.92

Information Services as a Percentage of Total Workers

Similar calculations can be performed for information services (alias data processing, information technology, or management information systems). In overall terms, this year information services made up 3.78% of total workers. In last year's survey, information services made up 3.51% of total workers. Thus information services gained only eight percent over the prior year, while information security gained 64% over the prior year.

This ratio indicates information intensity. In other words, it indicates the extent to which an organization is dependent on information systems. As we might expect, and consistent with the prior year's statistics, Financial Services is the most information intensive. The least information intensive sector was Retailing/Wholesaling (again, we used last year's data for this industry only because we had no respondents in this category this year). Industries that seem to be becoming relatively less information intensive include Aerospace/Defense and Manufacturing. Industries that seem to be becoming more information intensive include Financial Services and Health Care. These changes in information intensity may foreshadow changes in the information security effort for each industry.

Table A-6: Information Intensity by Industry

Business Activity	Information Services Staff / Total Workers
Computers/Telecommunications	0.040
Education	0.024
Government	0.040
Manufacturing	0.016
Retailing/Wholesaling	0.013
Transportation/Distribution	0.059
Financial Services	0.078
Health Care	0.039
Utilities	0.039
Aerospace/Defense	0.017
Other	0.049

Information Security Relative to Information Services

In terms of information security staff relative to information services staff, the ratio this year was 0.027, whereas last year it was 0.017. This 58% increase means that now there are, on average, about 37 information services staff for each information security staff member. Last year there were about 81 information services staff members for each information security staff member. Nobody questions that information services is fast becoming an essential part of modern organizations; what they often fail to appreciate is that information security is moving ahead even faster.

The ratio of information security to information services staff can be broken down by the number of full-time equivalent staff found in the organization. For organizations having less than 2,500 staff members, the ratio is 0.054. For organizations with between 2,501 and 5,000 staff members, the ratio is 0.026. For organizations with over 5,001 staff members, the ratio is 0.019. Thus, as other ratios mentioned above have shown, smaller organizations have a considerably larger proportion of their staff devoted to information security than larger organizations do. This same pattern was evident in previous surveys, although the ratio for smaller organizations is zooming ahead faster than the rest.

The ratio of information security staff to information services staff can also be broken out by the number of years that a formal information security group has been in place. This ratio was surprisingly narrowly constrained no matter how many years an information security function has existed. For organizations with an information security function for five or fewer years the ratio was 0.019, for organizations with an information security function for six to ten years the ratio was 0.023, and for organizations with an information security function for eleven or more years the ratio was 0.019. There has been no appreciable change in this ratio since the prior year's survey.

Those organizations with national defense activities registered a significantly higher number of information security staff to information systems staff than those organizations without such activities. Those with national defense activities had a ratio of information security staff to information services staff of 0.069, while those without such activities had a ratio of 0.023. The ratio for those organizations involved in national defense activities has increased markedly over the prior year. This increase in the information security staff relative to information systems staff may in part be a reflection of recent highly publicized break-ins at these organizations.

As Table A-7 indicates, the ratio of information security staff to information services staff is highest in Computers/Telecommunications. In the prior year, the highest ratio was found in the Government category. This expanded emphasis on information security within Computer/Telecommunication organizations may reflect an increasing appreciation that good information security can be used to sell both information systems as well as communications systems.

Table A-7: Information Security Staff Divided by Information Services Staff

Business Activity	InfoSecurity Workers / Information Services Workers
Computers/Telecommunications	0.051
Education	0.027
Government	0.031
Manufacturing	0.021
Retailing/Wholesaling	0.015
Transportation/Distribution	0.006
Financial Services	0.018
Health Care	0.025
Utilities	0.019
Aerospace/Defense	0.028
Other	0.047

Part-Time Workers

In overall terms, some 14.60% of the information security workforce was part-time. This represents a slight decrease over the prior year's survey, which indicated that 17.27% of the workers were part-time. By far the most part-time workers are found in the Manufacturing/Production sector, while the least can be found in the Financial Services area. Because we received no usable responses to this question from the Transportation/Distribution sector, like the Retailing/Wholesaling sector, Table A-8 reflects the prior year's data.

Table A-8: Percentage of Part-Time Information Security Workers

Business Activity	Percentage of InfoSecurity Work Done by Part-Time Staff
Computers/Telecommunications	15.34%
Education	17.27%
Government	14.16%
Manufacturing	24.43%
Retailing/Wholesaling	12.31%
Transportation/Distribution	6.60%
Financial Services	7.87%
Health Care	15.91%
Utilities	16.06%
Other	11.42%

Use of Outsourcing

When asked what percentage of the information security workforce is outsourced, respondents indicated that, on the average, some 7.44% was outsourced. This is a moderate increase over the prior year, when the average was 5.83%. Like the prior year, the amount of outsourcing again varied considerably by industry, as Table A-9 indicates. A marked decrease in outsourcing took place in the Computers/Telecommunications sector since the last year, perhaps due to concerns about contractors and consultants being eligible for fringe benefits (as the court said they were in a notable Microsoft case). A significant decrease was also noted in the Health Care sector. A notable increase in outsourcing over the prior year took place in the Transportation/Distribution area, as well as in both the Government and Manufacturing/Production sectors. The increase in outsourcing, at least in the Government sector, can be partially explained by the increase in Y2K conversion work which some people consider to be an information security problem (rather than an information services problem).

Table A-9: Percentage of Information Security Work Outsourced

Business Activity	Percentage of InfoSecurity Work Outsourced
Computers/Telecommunications	5.24%
Education	1.50%
Government	11.21%
Manufacturing	10.61%
Retailing/Wholesaling	1.54%
Transportation/Distribution	18.33%
Financial Services	5.89%
Health Care	0.95%
Utilities	6.57%
Aerospace/Defense	4.83
Other	8.07%

In-House Information Security Staff and Total Budgets

When asked what percentage of the total information security budget is devoted to in-house staff, respondents indicated, in overall terms, that some 36.92% was for such staff. This was a slight decrease over the prior year, when they indicated that some 38.92% was devoted to in-house staff. Given the slight increases in the use of outsourcing, the total percentage of the budget devoted to staff of all types seems to be holding stable. There are, however, considerable differences from industry to industry. As Table A-10 shows, the Transportation/Distribution sector, as well as the Utilities sector, seem to be the most dependent on people to get the information security job done. One reason why Utilities may have the highest percentage of the information security budget devoted to in-house staff may be the fact that this industrial segment uses part-time workers more than most others (there may be more overhead associated with part-time rather than full-time workers).

Table A-10: Percentage of Budget Devoted to In-House Staff

Business Activity	Percentage of InfoSecurity Budget Devoted to In-House Staff
Computers/Telecommunications	32.56%
Education	27.50%
Government	39.67%
Manufacturing	20.58%
Retailing/Wholesaling	37.59%
Transportation/Distribution	52.66%
Financial Services	44.81%
Health Care	38.42%
Utilities	55.00%
Aerospace/Defense	30.56
Other	31.00%

Staffing Increases for Next Year

Respondents were also asked about the expected percentage increase or decrease in total information security workers anticipated for the next year. On the average, they anticipated a 14.86% increase over the prior year. This was slightly down from the 17.78% increase anticipated in the prior year. The increase or decrease expected varied considerably by industry as Table A-11 indicates. Major increases are expected next year in the Computer/Telecommunication sector, as well as in both the Health Care and Financial Services areas. The smallest increase is expected in the Transportation/Distribution area, where staffing levels are already high relative to other industries (see Table A-10). Government also has a relatively small-expected increase for next year (7.86%), but then again they had a very large expected increase in the prior year (42.62%)..

Table A-11: Anticipated Increases in Next Year's Staffing Budget

Business Activity	Percentage Increase Expected in Staffing Budget
Computers/Telecommunications	21.27%
Education	11.00%
Government	7.86%
Manufacturing	8.90%
Retailing/Wholesaling	37.59%
Transportation/Distribution	3.33%
Financial Services	20.39%
Health Care	21.09%
Utilities	15.31%
Aerospace/Defense	14.00
Other	17.92%

Annual Budget for Information Security

This year's survey included a few new questions about budgets for information security. If a respondent organization did not use budgets, they were asked to indicate the total dollar amount spent on information security for a single year. Although there may be a difference in practice between budgeted spending and actual spending, for purposes of this study, no such distinction was made. The average annual figure provided was $976,697.

Respondents indicated that they expect the total budget for information security to increase, on the average, 20.42% over the next year. The largest expected increase was in the Education sector, which makes sense given the relatively low levels of staffing that Educational institutions currently have. The smallest expected increase in overall budgets was in the Utilities industry, which by the way now has the largest percentage of its budget devoted to staff of any industry. No numbers were available in the Retailing/Wholesaling area because these questions were not asked in the surveys for prior years, and because there were no respondents in this year's survey which hailed from that industrial segment.

Contrary to what one might expect, the number of years that an information security function was in place did not substantially increase the expected increases in next year's budget. Those organizations with a formal organizational unit in place for five or fewer years expected an increase of 17.67%, while those with a unit for six to ten years had an expected increase of 13.63%, and those with a unit for eleven or more years had an expected increase of 18.61%.

It is intriguing to note that organizations working in the national defense area had a substantially higher expected increase in next year's budget than those organizations not working in this area. Although military, diplomatic, and defense related organizations have been thinking about information security for decades, they have suffered major budget cutbacks in the last few years. Perhaps it is now time for them to catch up? The expected budget increase for those working in the defense area was 24.86%, while the expected budget increase for those organizations not working in this area was 17.90%.

Table A-12: Anticipated Increases in Next Year's Total Annual Budget

Business Activity	Percentage Increase Expected in Budget
Computers/Telecommunications	18.76%
Education	41.38%
Government	13.28%
Manufacturing	18.20%
Retailing/Wholesaling	not available
Transportation/Distribution	25.00%
Financial Services	17.45%
Health Care	14.24%
Utilities	10.71%
Aerospace/Defense	14.22
Other	54.91%

Average Budget Dollars per Information Security Staff Member

We also calculated the average dollars spent on information security for each information security staff person. This was calculated by multiplying the budget for information security at each organization by the percentage of the budget devoted to information security staff. This intermediate result was then divided by the number of information security staff members. This statistic allows an organization to go from the number of information security staff members to the expected budget, or vice-versa. Across all industries, the average was $88,424.

It's interesting that this statistic varies so much from industry to industry. A high average dollars spent per information security staff person could indicate that staff is very efficient, or that sophisticated tools are used to extend the influence of each staff member. On the other hand, a low average dollars spent per information security staff person could indicate that management is unwilling to empower information security staff members by giving them the tools that they really need. We recalculated the average for the Other category because it seemed so different from the other industry sectors, but it is correct. The Other category included a single respondent who claimed an $80,000,000 budget, and thus skewed the results.

The influence of experience in the information security field was profoundly seen in this calculation. Those organizations with information security functions in place for five or fewer years had an average dollars per information security staff member of $35,664. Organizations with information security functions in place for six to ten years had an average of $51,306. And notably, those with an information security function in place for eleven or more years had an average of $101,612. Evidently, as organizations gain more experience with information security, they are able to leverage their staff members much more efficiently. This might be due to the implementation of sophisticated security tools like network management systems, or it might be due to the cumulative positive effects of building information security infrastructure (such as an information security architecture document).

Looking at the same calculation in terms of involvement in national defense activities, we see that there again was a substantial difference. Organizations involved with national defense had an average budget for information security per information security staff member of $34,672. Meanwhile, those without this type of involvement, had an average of $99,398.

Table A-13: Average Budget per Information Security Staff Member

Business Activity	Average Dollars per Worker
Computers/Telecommunications	$20,820
Education	$12,622
Government	$17,893
Manufacturing	$38,896
Retailing/Wholesaling	not available
Transportation/Distribution	$24,552
Financial Services	$41,535
Health Care	$353,461
Utilities	$58,900
Aerospace/Defense	$44,305
Other	$1,166,843

Average Budget Dollars per Total Workers

The last calculation that we will discuss involves average budget dollars spent on information security per worker (for all types of workers). This was calculated by dividing the budget for information security at each organization by the number of full-time equivalent staff at that same organization. The ratios were then averaged by industry.

This ratio provides a way for an organization to quickly back-into an appropriate budget for information security. Simply start with the number of workers and then multiply by the average dollars per worker provided in Table A-14 to get the appropriate budget estimate. The average amount spent for each worker, for all industries, was $7,082.

It's particularly intriguing to see that this calculation provided numbers that varied by industry by a factor of 738. Like several ratios mentioned above, these dramatic differences from industry to industry also appear to be correlated with both information intensity and involvement in national defense activities. For example, as an indication of information intensity, the Computers/Telecommunications industry and the Financial Services industries both have high average dollars per worker. Similarly, as an indication of involvement in national defense, the Government and the Aerospace/Defense sectors additionally showed relatively high average dollars per worker. The average for all respondents with an involvement in national defense activities was $32,409, while the average for all respondents without such an involvement was $1,717.

Table A-14: Average Budget per Worker (All Types)

Business Activity	Average Dollars per Worker
Computers/Telecommunications	$14,766
Education	$671
Government	$12,992
Manufacturing	$660
Retailing/Wholesaling	not available
Transportation/Distribution	$20
Financial Services	$1,079
Health Care	$2,917
Utilities	$142
Aerospace/Defense	$3,100
Other	$1,072

Conclusion

Appropriate information security staffing levels have long been insufficiently-defined, even for many people working in the field. This survey provides specific numbers to characterize the prevailing *standard of due care*. Without question the information security field is expanding at a robust rate. As modern business increasingly relies more on information as an essential factor of production, information security is coming to be appreciated as an essential business function akin to marketing and accounting.

In spite of the trend towards the use of sophisticated technical tools rather than people to perform certain security functions, and in spite of the trend towards the empowerment of users and others to attend to their own information security needs, the relative number of staff with assigned information security duties is growing at a significant rate. Perhaps the most salient example of this is the statistic indicating that the number of information security staff as a percentage of total workers has grown approximately 64% in the course of a single year.

Special thanks are extended to the statistical analyst who helped with this survey, Richard Rohde. This report was originally published in the Computer Security Journal, published by the Computer Security Institute, San Francisco, California. It is reprinted here with appropriate permission.

Appendix B   PERSONAL QUALIFICATIONS

When interviewing candidates for an Information Security Manager (or information security executive) position, it is important to consider the personality characteristics most relevant to the job. This appendix provides both a ranked list of these characteristics as well as the reasons why these characteristics are important. The most important factors appear at the top of the list. The author suggests that you photocopy this appendix and distribute it to all those who will interview candidates (including a third-party recruiter working on the assignment). These people can then rank the candidates according to these criteria to quickly determine which candidates should proceed to the next step in the recruitment process.

Alternatively you may wish to use the following list as a starting point for an in-house brainstorming session amongst those managers who will need to work with the new Information Security Manager. The session can then be used to develop your organization's own unique list of personal qualifications.

The following list assumes that the job candidate has the necessary technical skills to do the job, as demonstrated through both certifications (see Appendix D) and prior experience.

Excellent Communication Skills

More than anything else, an Information Security Manager must act as a liaison between many different groups with different world views, different objectives, and different needs. The Manager must be able to attentively listen, just as he or she must be able to clearly state what needs to be done. This Manager must also be able to persuade management to adopt new and possibly unpopular courses of action. The Manager will be required to write top management status report memos, risk analysis reports, security incident post-mortem analyses, vendor request for proposal documents, employee job performance evaluations, and many other documents. This Manager may also be called upon to act as an organizational spokesperson with the news media and professional society standards setting committees. The Manager may additionally be called upon to give presentations at industry and technical conferences. This Manager must therefore have excellent interpersonal skills, including writing and public speaking skills. While an increasing number of organizations are using a bachelor's degree as a quick-and-dirty indicator of

communications skills, organizations recruiting a Manager should go one step further, and look for specific evidence of excellent communication skills such as papers written, conference speeches delivered, industry standards committees served, etc.

Good Relationship Management Skills

In order to get anything done, an Information Security Manager is going to need to work with and through a lot of people. If the Manager is strictly a work-alone technical type, he or she is going to have a lot of trouble in a position as Information Security Manager. The Information Security Manager in most organizations does not have the power that goes along with a top management spot, where he or she could simply order others to follow policies, standards, and other information security requirements. Instead, acting in a staff advisory role, the Information Security Manager must convince and persuade others to follow these same requirements. In this same regard, many people talk about the Manager's role as a salesperson, selling information security. Some people think it's even more difficult, something akin to converting other people to a new religion. Whatever metaphor you prefer, it's clear that an Information Security Manager must have superior people skills, must know how to maintain good working relationships with a wide variety of people, and must be able to maintain the trust and support of these same people.

Ability To Manage Many Important Projects Simultaneously

The Information Security Manager must be an excellent project manager and must be familiar with modern project management tools and techniques. Many information security projects are complex, have a long time horizon, and depend on the participation of a wide variety of people. The successful Manager must be able to delegate work to, and later manage people outside an information security group (these people will typically include consultants and contractors). In an increasing majority of cases, the pressing information security projects that most organizations need to complete simply cannot be accomplished with the limited information security staff on hand. At the same time, the Manager must stay on top of these projects, paying attention to details, and making sure that progress proceeds as top management intended. The successful

Manager must also be able to put together organization-wide status reports that clearly show trends, problems, and areas in need of top management intervention. Separately, the Information Security Manager often has a dotted-line reporting relationship with a variety of staff that have information security related jobs (Systems Developers, Systems Administrators, etc.). The Manager is thus indirectly responsible for obtaining results, but often not in a position where he or she can force compliance with information security requirements. To get results in this environment, the Manager must be a both a diplomat and a politician. An Information Security Manager must thus be a team player, a team builder, and a team leader.

Ability To Resolve Conflicts Between Security And Business Objectives

The Information Security Manager must be able to clearly see the pros and cons of certain courses of action, and be able to choose and negotiate a compromise which best serves the organization in the long run. Information security is always a compromise because the only absolutely secure information system is an unusable one. The successful Manager must have a flexible personality, and be comfortable making compromises. He or she must also know about the management tools that can be used to arrive at decisions of this nature (net present value, internal rate of return, payback, Monte Carlo simulation, automated testing tools, etc.). In addition to being familiar with information security technology, the successful Manager must also have business skills, business knowledge, and a business aptitude. The Manager must be able to withstand pressure from various groups with competing objectives, and be willing to take a stand for a course of action that is in the long-run best interests of the organization. The Manager should not be overly concerned about being popular and well-liked; a Manager concerned about popularity will soon be fired for getting nothing done. The Manager must appreciate that, in an organization of significant size, information security takes years of dedicated work before it really starts to become part of the corporate culture.

Ability To See The Big Picture

The Information Security Manager must not be easily distracted by the fire-fighting that inevitably comes with the job. Taking care of virus problems is certainly important, but this day-to-day work must not crowd out important but not urgent long-run projects such as compiling a network security architecture. The Manager must be able to prioritize resources in a way that satisfies the organization's urgently pressing needs, but at the same time move the organization in the direction of implementing generally accepted information security solutions. The Manager must also be able to synthesize information from many different sources to come up with a plan for improving information security that is truly responsive to the organization's business needs. A Manager with a narrow technical focus will impede information security progress, because it is only through a broad view of information security that innovative solutions can be conceived. Furthermore, the Manager must be able to read between the lines, identifying the true underlying causes of problems that the organization faces. The Manager must additionally have the guts to tell the truth about these underlying causes.

Basic Familiarity With Information Security Technology

The Information Security Manager must be knowledgeable in information security technical areas such as encryption, smart cards, and system access control. Not only must the Manager not be duped by technical specialists, he or she must know the best technology to apply in response to an organization's information security needs. Without this knowledge the Manager will lose credibility, and thereby jeopardize current and future information security initiatives. Generally a Manager will not have the luxury of learning a great deal about information security technology on the job, so organizations should not hire an inexperienced person and expect that they will be able to pick-up the technology as they go along. Familiarity with the technology does not mean that an Information Security Manager is expected to personally get involved in highly-technical work, for example program a digital certificate user authentication system, but it does mean that the Manager would know when such a technology should be used. In general, a successful Information Security Manager must be familiar with the methods used, the processes employed, and the business reasons cited to justify information security measures. The successful Manager should also be familiar with the successful ways to enforce information security requirements with what is often an uncooperative end-user population.

Real World Hands-On Experience

A successful Information Security Manager is not going to use your organization as the proving ground for untested theories or ideas. This Manager needs to be immediately credible -- your organization can't afford to take the risks that are involved in developing credibility over time. He or she must have relevant prior experience in the real world of information security, and ideally this would be both as an external consultant and also as an internal Information Security Manager. This will give the Manager a taste for what it's like to work in the information security field, and will allow the Manager to bring that prior experience to bear on the problems your organization is facing. Hands-on experience not only helps prevent the Manager from making stupid mistakes or taking positions which are clearly inconsistent with standard industry practices, it also most importantly buys the Information Security Manager a lot of additional credibility. This credibility will be very important when selling information security to various constituencies such as top management and internal technical staff. One additional benefit to having an Information Security Manager with prior hands-on experience is that he or she knows what they are getting into when they take a job, and will therefore be less likely to quit after several months because the job didn't turn out to be what the Manager hoped it would be.

Commitment To Staying On Top Of The Technology

The Information Security Manager must furthermore keep abreast of recent developments in the information security field. Attending a conference or two each year will generally not constitute sufficient effort. The Manager must read technical magazines, subscribe to online news services, and if he or she is located near a major city, attend an occasional professional society meeting as well. A familiarity with the latest developments is essential if the Manager is going to be able to recommend appropriate responses to recently discovered vulnerabilities. A familiarity with the latest developments is also essential if the Manager is going to be grounded in the information security related standard of due care (this will be an essential reference point for discussions about adjustments to information security controls). If the Manager doesn't possess this current knowledge, and if the Manager hasn't applied this knowledge, the organization runs a high risk that it will learn about its vulnerabilities only when it's victimized. If the Manager doesn't possess and apply this knowledge, it's likely the organization will be using information security solutions that are unnecessarily costly, burdensome, and/or antiquated. If the Manager doesn't possess this knowledge, he or she is not going to effectively present proposals for change to top management. The risk of having a Manager who is not in touch

with the latest developments is greater in large organizations where such an individual may be able to hide because others do the technical work; in a small organization it is unthinkable that the Information Security Manager would not also be able to do extensive hands-on work such as install and fine-tune a firewall.

Honesty And High-Integrity Character

The Information Security Manager needs to have a squeaky-clean criminal record as well as an open-minded and questioning personality which inspires trust. Some scrupulous organizations go further with additional background checking, for example requiring the Information Security Manager to have a clean credit report. All this makes sense because the Information Security Manager must be a paragon of virtue and honesty, in addition to being an exemplary employee. Above all, this individual must not be a former hacker because this will often cause others within the organization to be untrusting and uncooperative. In the eyes of many, being a hacker is equivalent to being a malicious and irresponsible person who is out to get them. While hackers are often on top of the latest information security vulnerabilities, they frequently lack extensive experience in the business world, and they frequently lack the diplomacy and people skills necessary to do a good job as an Information Security Manager. There are available people with exemplary characters, who are also on top of the latest developments in the information security field, but you may need to pay them well. Just as a well-managed organization would generally not hire an office employee who had previous convictions for violent behavior, so an organization should not hire a "former" hacker who has run afoul of the law. Even if the candidate for an Information Security Manager position has no criminal convictions, any candidate who boasts about being a former hacker should be avoided like the plague. If a newly-hired Information Security Manager were to send confidential internal information to his or her friends in the hacker community, the hiring organization could soon find itself overrun by unwelcome visitors who are using its networks and systems for illegal activities. If you are still intent on hiring a former hacker, think long and hard about the reputation risk that goes along with such a move. Is your firm really prepared for the negative publicity and the loss of customer confidence that goes along with hiring someone who has demonstrated that they have a different set of ethics than most of the others who work at the organization?

Familiarity With Information Security Management

The Information Security Manager must know about the elements of an information security organizational infrastructure. These elements includes responsibilities, policies, standards, procedures, and the like (a list of these is provided in "Current Documents"). The Manager must also be familiar with, and know how to use generally accepted information security management tools such as risk analysis software and contingency planning software. This Manager must additionally be aware of other information systems management tools that can be used to enhance information security; one commonly deployed example is a network management system. If the Manager is not familiar with information security management tools and approaches, he or she will not be able to marshal the limited information security resources to the organization's best advantage. This in turn will lead to problems like unnecessary costs and delays in developing new systems. For example, the Manager may then suggest a manual solution when an automated solution is current available and more cost-effective.

Tolerance For Ambiguity And Uncertainty

Information security is very complex and full of interdependencies. In many instances, a viable solution to various information security problems has not yet been released as a commercial product. This means that the Information Security Manager must be able to make do with the tools and techniques currently at his or her disposal. The Manager must also be able to make defensible decisions when important or even critical pieces of information are unavailable or too costly to obtain. The Manager must have a strong will and a tenacious personality which does not let these problems cause him or her to become overly cynical. At the same time, the Manager must not live in a fantasy land where he or she does not see the realistic and serious nature of the information security issues facing the organization. A patient, relatively-optimistic, well-reasoned, and level-headed Manager who can adjust to a wide variety of situations will do best in this position.

Demonstrated Good Judgment

An Information Security Manager will be called upon to make many judgments which conceivably could have a profound impact on the future of your organization. For example, if the Manager makes a bad call on an architecture decision, your organization could be widely discussed on the front page of the newspapers. This could cause the organization's reputation to suffer in a very big way. On another note, if the Manager is a former hacker, this background is not convincing evidence of good judgment. It is one thing to know about system penetration tools and techniques, and it is a very different thing to actually use this information to break into a system without the involved organization's formal written consent. A successful Information Security Manager should have a good track record of decision-making in a variety of situations, including those where both management pressure and a quick response were important factors.

Ability To Work Independently

The Information Security Manager must be able to work independently without direct supervision or encouragement. In many cases, top management will not know exactly what he or she is doing. At the same time the Manager must be accountable to top management and the Audit Committee on the Board of Directors. The Manager must be able to stay focused and get things done, even though the resources at his or her disposal are quite limited. The Manager must also be accustomed to taking the lead and not waiting for users or other groups to tell him or her what to do. A deep and abiding commitment to improve the information security status of the organization must carry the Information Security Manager through the inevitable contentious and difficult situations that he or she will encounter. To work independently, the Manager must be creative, proactive, and inspired by a vision of how things could be.

A Certain Amount Of Polish

Although this may at first sound like an unnecessary characteristic of an Information Security Manager, it can be very important when it comes to dealings with both top management and representatives from external organizations. Just as we judge a book by its cover, the Information Security Manager will be judged adversely if he or she does not pay attention to personal grooming, does not take care to dress professionally, and/or does not conduct him- or herself in a professional manner. The Information Security Manager is an important spokesperson who will be a role model and focal point for many people. This person needs to inspire respect and admiration. If the Information Security Manager is disorganized, unfocused, slovenly, and poorly spoken, then people will discount what he or she says, and the projects that he or she promotes will fall on deaf ears. To even mention this point may seem to be an unwarranted emphasis on external appearance and behavior, but this is the way that the world works, and organizations that ignore it do so at their own peril.

Appendix C PERFORMANCE CRITERIA

This appendix discusses both performance measurement metrics and incentive systems relevant to information security. The discussion of necessity involves both individual performance and the performance of groups such as the Information Security Department. A list of possible metrics for measuring both individual performance and Information Security Department performance are provided. You will need to tailor these metrics to your organization because every organization has a unique collection of workers, a unique organizational culture, different societal norms, different human resources laws and regulations, and other situation-specific factors that should be taken into consideration.

This material is an appendix rather than a chapter in the book because the establishment of an information security related performance measurement system should generally be performed after information security roles and responsibilities have been clarified, documented, and approved by top management. You may find it possible to have an information security performance measurement project integrated with the roles and responsibilities clarification project. In most cases, however, it will be preferable to have two separate projects. Two separate projects are desirable because the Information Security Department can recognize two separate successes. Using the two separate project approach is also desirable because these two projects are each quite large, and problems with a proposed performance measurement system will not delay the adoption and usage of documented roles and responsibilities. In some situations, it may be politically astute to postpone the discussion about a performance measurement system until the point where clarified information security roles and responsibilities have already been well established, and are clearly working well. At this point, a significant amount of hands-on experience will be available, and that experience will be important input to the establishment of customized performance measurement metrics.

It is through a formal performance measurement system that information security specialists will get letters of commendation, promotions, raises, bonuses, extra time off, and other acknowledgements that they deserve. In the absence of specific performance evaluation criteria, information security staff members are likely to suffer because management may employ traditional performance evaluation criteria. For example, management

may look to see whether the individual gets along with his or her coworkers, considering confrontations to be evidence of poor performance. While diplomacy goes a long way in the information security field, there are many situations where confrontations are a necessary part of the job. For example, if a major new application has inadequate controls, but is about to be placed on a production Internet web server, the Information Security Department Manager should object, and if necessary, take the matter to top management. If the Information Security Department Manager did not object and make a fuss, he or she would not be doing his or her job.

Having a discussion with top management about incentives to support information security is an essential part of any project to establish an information security performance measurement system. Such a discussion is an excellent opportunity to clarify what management really wants from an information security function. In this discussion, you should point out the many ways in which the current incentive systems encourage people to act in ways that compromise information security. You should then identify the absence of ways in which the current incentive systems encourage people to act in compliance with information security requirements. This should in turn assist management in understanding why workers have consistently been compromising information security in favor of other business objectives. This then allows management to alter the incentive systems to be in support of information security (this should include but hopefully significantly go beyond job performance measurement).

An example should help to make this distinction about incentives clear. In a software firm that is now out of business, a salesman was coming to the end of the fiscal quarter. He had not yet made his sales quota, and he was concerned about keeping his job. He had one prospect who was likely to place a big order, and if this prospect came through, the salesman would make his quota and get a significant commission. The prospect was indecisive and seemed unwilling to place his order at that time. The salesman was anxious to close the deal in the next few days, but he couldn't think of a way to get the prospect to buy. It then occurred to the salesman that if he gave the prospect a copy of the specifications for the next version of the software, which was slated to be released six months later, the prospect would be so impressed with the new features, that he would place his order right away (a free upgrade to the next version was part of the deal). The salesman did this, and the prospect did place his order right away. The incentive systems that influenced the salesman's behavior were the quota and the commission. These systems worked as they should. There was, however, no penalty for the salesman when he revealed confidential internal information without first getting a non-disclosure agreement. In other words, there was no information security incentive system causing the salesman to restrict dissemination of the specifications. Similar combinations of incentive systems can be found in many organizations today, and as long as management allows them to continue, it is not reasonable to expect that workers will comply with information security requirements.

- While there are many other possible combinations of incentive systems, the following list defines some typical ways that organizations are structured to get people to ignore and downgrade the importance of information security:

- Piecework pay systems, such as those for data entry operators, typically pay a fixed amount per piece, and if workers subject to these systems are asked to take on information security tasks, such as checking for fraud, there will be strenuous objections.

- Sales commission systems encourage salespeople to reveal more information than necessary to get additional sales, and this behavior may lead to the unauthorized disclosure of sensitive material.

- Short term financial results are stressed by management bonus systems and this in turn may discourage management from investing in information security because the payoff is long-term in nature.

- Standard industry practice may conflict with organizational policy, for example, stockbrokers may take the contact information about their personal clients with them when they leave their employer, even though this may be a violation of their employer's privacy policy.

- Politeness may conflict with good security practice, as is often seen at the entrance to computer data centers where individuals hold the door open for the person behind them regardless of the authorization of that person to enter the data center.

- Organizational culture may conflict with good security practice, for example, the organizational culture may foster an open and sharing attitude towards information exchange when this is likely to lead to unauthorized disclosure of sensitive information.

- Employees are often pressured to handle the things which management is immediately concerned about, and if they don't receive ongoing information security training then security may be "out of sight and out of mind" and therefore be ignored.

It will not be enough for the people working in the information security area to have clear and rational performance measurement systems. As discussed in Chapter 3, information security can only be successfully addressed if everyone on the organizational team is aligned with the goals of information security. Obtaining this alignment can take many forms such as putting a question in everybody's job performance evaluation form. Such a question could simply ask whether the individual has been doing their job in accordance with information security policies and procedures (yes or no). Other techniques to establish the appropriate new balance between conflicting objectives, like cost minimization and information security, include handing out $100 bills on the spot to people who detect and report information security violations. When designing or redesigning the performance evaluation system for those working in the information security area, you should not miss the opportunity to engage management in a question about incentive systems throughout the organization.

So much of the work in the information security field is negative in its orientation. For example, Internal Information Security Consultants look for and try to prevent problems. Likewise, staff in the Physical Security Department investigate computer crimes. This focus on bad things has an unfortunate side effect which could impact the extent to which management believes that these people are doing their jobs. If there are problems, then management is typically upset and wondering whether the people in the information security area are competent, as well as wondering whether they have been doing their jobs. But if there are no problems, then management is wondering whether the people working in this area are really needed, whether they could be dismissed the next time the organization needs to reduce expenses. So information security is typically either out of the limelight (and therefore in danger of being marginalized) or else in trouble. The former alternative is certainly preferable, but even this needs to be accompanied by ways to communicate to management that the information security function is doing the job it is supposed to do.

An excellent way to show management the contribution that people in the information security area are making is to adopt bonuses. It is also a great way to shift the attitude of the people working in this area from negative to positive. At this point in time, bonuses are already being used in many private sector Internal Audit Departments, but it is rare to find them in Information Security Departments. Credit card fraud investigations and penetration attack projects provide two good examples where bonuses are currently used in the information security area. In the next few years, bonuses will be increasingly used as a way to shift worker pay away from straight salaries and into incentive-based pay systems. Worker motivation is expected to increase with the increased reliance on these incentive-based pay systems. Of course, incentive-based pay systems shouldn't rely on bonuses alone; they should include salary increases, promotions, time off with pay, and other benefits.

To support incentive-based pay systems, organizations will need to create metrics that truly motivate the actions management intends. This can be done by adopting a holistic perspective and focusing on the critical drivers and dependencies needed to get the intended results. For example, suppose an organization has problems with the prompt set-up of new user-IDs and passwords. Suppose user department management has been complaining that newly-hired or newly-transferred workers are wasting time because they don't have system access. An investigation could reveal that the local managers hiring new workers don't notify the Information Security Department until the new worker is actually sitting at their desk. Accordingly, the issue is not so much a matter of Information Security Department response time as it is getting advance notification. Although a metric can be established to measure the response time to new user-ID and password issuance requests, redesigning the new worker arrival notification process would solve the problem better than a metric looking at response time. It would thus be inappropriate to establish a metric which measures the user-ID and password issuance response time of the Information Security Department, because this approach holds the Information Security Department fully responsible for a problem which is not entirely something that they can control.

To the extent possible, each of the metrics that management adopts for the information security function should also be tied-in with specific results for the next year, or perhaps for longer time frames. For example, if the organization has, as one of its goals for the next year, the process of converting all user-IDs and fixed passwords to user-IDs and smart cards, then the percentage of users who are converted successfully might be an appropriate quantitative yardstick. If this type of performance indicator is employed, it will also be easier to predict how many information security people are needed to achieve specific results. (For a discussion about sufficient headcount for the information security function, see Appendix A.)

The following metrics provide a sample of the many potential ways to structure an incentive-based pay system for those workers with assigned duties in the information security area. Because it would be too complicated to administer and track, no real-world organization would have anywhere near all of these metrics. Instead you should choose a few that seem to be most aligned with current business objectives. The chosen metrics should also be periodically reevaluated to determine whether they are creating undesirable side-effects. For example, with a bonus for completing projects on time, employees can get the impression that an individual's ability to meet deadlines is more important than doing quality work.

Information Security Department Metrics

- Accomplished specific project goals as defined in an action plan

- Reduced actual information security losses (based on a reliable loss reporting system, usually managed by the Physical Security Department, to prevent a conflict of interest that might cause fudging of the statistics)

- Received positive comments from internal auditors or external auditors

- Increased the number of internal organizational units which happen to be in compliance with information security policies and standards

- Expanded the percentage of total workers who happen to be in compliance with policies and standards

- Trained a certain number of people (Systems Administrators, end-users, etc.) about information security with a predetermined curriculum

- Actual system logs indicate that user experience was under a threshold of security violations (number of wrong passwords entered, number of lock-outs due to a succession of wrong passwords, etc.) as a percentage of attempted log-ins [*Indicates user training was successful*]

- Was under a threshold ratio calculated by the number of users with privileges revoked for security violations as a percentage of total users [*Users are apparently better behaved, or at least more compliant with information security policies and standards*]

- Met a specific quantitative goal for the number of computer systems in compliance with information security requirements [*This can be monitored in real time with new auditing tools including vulnerability identification systems - it is best if the input to calculations for incentive systems is gathered automatically*]

- Cast the organization in a positive light through information security related publicity a certain number of times over the last year [*As perhaps measured by published articles, TV appearances, etc.*]

- Kept the organization's name out of news stories that discussed information security [*In this case the lower the number of news appearances, the better*]

- Improved the organization's image a certain number of times by publicly showing that it has superior and reliable information security [*A contest to show the resilience of an information security product might be used to do this*]

- Shifted organizational culture related to information security so that information security is now perceived as a necessary business function as evidenced by a certain number of departments using line item budgets for information security [*Results from a staff survey may also be used to measure a shift in culture*]

- Got involved in a certain number of systems development projects to ensure that adequate controls were included in the final production systems [*As perhaps evidenced by sign-offs from the Information Security Department*]

- Created a certain number of new approaches (such as already tested and approved standardized encryption systems) that expedited the systems development process [*These can be combined in an Information Security Department repository or pre-approved solutions to various problems*]

- Enabled a certain number of business activities such as Internet commerce credit card sales that would not have been possible without new security technologies [*This metric has particular merit because it shows that the information security function can help to meet other business objectives, something that many managers don't really appreciate*]

- Developed and documented a certain number of new procedures that help ensure the security of Company X information [*This metric could instead simply involve documentation of new or existing procedures*]

- Reestablished full information systems services within a certain pre-determined time frame after an emergency or disaster took place [*This information should be captured for other purposes, such as determining how complete and up-to-date contingency plans are*]

- Converted a certain number of users from old and insufficiently secured systems (such as those which use shared fixed passwords) to systems that are sufficiently secured (such as those which employ personal smart cards with one-time passwords)

- Eliminated a certain number of insufficiently secure information systems (such as modems inside desktop computers) and replaced these with new and more secure technology (such as an inbound call modem pool which uses extended user authentication technology)

- Brought the organization into compliance with a certain number of new and externally-dictated information security requirements [*The requirements can each individually be identified, rather than combined in a certain law or regulation*]

- Reduced Internet commerce related credit card fraud to a certain dollar level (or percentage of sales) over a defined time span

- Expanded the total number of users supported by a new access control system (such as a smart card with one-time passwords)

- Established a certain number of users as authorized to conduct business on an extranet or trading network [*This could involve setting-up digital certificates*]

- Blocked a certain number of external attacks from the Internet with the help of an extensive logging system and a intrusion prevention system (IPS)

- Reduced the percentage of portable computers (laptops, handhelds, personal digital assistants, etc.) now being used by workers that were lost, stolen, or unaccounted for [*This indicates that end users are increasingly taking responsibility for the security of the machines under their direct control*]

Individual Worker Metrics

Note that a number of the following metrics apply to workers in other groups, such as a Help Desk Department, in addition to the workers found in the Information Security Department. All of these metrics apply to workers in the Information Security Department.

- Achieved a specific desirable result in the information security area related to legal proceedings, whether civil or criminal

- Successfully concluded an investigation of information security violations and incidents

- Posted a certain number of changes to the access control privilege database

- Achieved a certain threshold average time to process new user-ID requests

- Created a certain number of new user-IDs with new passwords and privileges

- Successfully turned-off all privileges of a certain number of workers dismissed in a so-called duress termination situation

- Modified the privileges on a certain number of user-IDs to reflect new duties for the involved users

- Reset a certain number of lost or forgotten fixed passwords

- Restored a certain number of files from backup tapes per user requests

- Reissued a certain number of smart cards, badges, or other access devices

- Answered a certain number of questions from users and others who are confused about information security

- Delivered a certain number of information security awareness training classes

- Reached a predetermined goal involving a certain number of users who viewed the computer-based training (CBT) program developed by the Information Security Department

- Reviewed a certain number of new or enhanced business applications to ensure that adequate controls were incorporated into these systems

- Evaluated a certain number of new information security technologies to determine whether they are suitable for your organization

- Assisted with the classification of a certain number of sensitive documents which had not been previously ranked with a data classification system

- Assisted with the ranking of a certain number of applications according to a previously established system criticality scale

- Eradicated a certain number of computer viruses, Trojan horses, or other malicious software infestations

- Updated all virus screening program definitions within a certain average period of time after these were made publicly-available by the anti-virus system vendor

- Installed and monitored systems which in turn screened at least a predetermined number of viruses and Trojan horses at firewalls, departmental servers, or mail servers, and thereby prevented infestations and other problems

- Updated/patched firewall and router configurations based on publicized vulnerabilities within a certain average period of time from the point when these vulnerabilities were announced by a reliable third party

- Restored a certain number of systems to a trusted state following intrusion by hackers or other unauthorized outsiders

- Installed a certain number of security-related patches or fixes on existing machines for which this individual was responsible

- Configured and placed into service a certain number of new servers/systems

- Responded to a certain number of Computer Emergency Response Team incident alerts

- Fielded a certain number of requests from top management to investigate certain incidents, to clarify certain issues, or to report on the status of certain projects

While there are many other possible metrics, these should get you thinking about the metrics that might be used at your organization. Before any of these metrics can be adopted, you will need to clearly see how the metric can be captured by someone or something other than the person or department whose performance is being measured. For example, the Systems Development Department could indicate the number of new applications that were reviewed by the Information Security Department within a calendar year. Likewise, an Information Systems Auditor could determine the percentage of staff that are in compliance with information security policies now and one year ago, to see whether there has been a noticeable improvement. Alternatively, a help desk trouble ticket system can indicate how many virus infestations took place in a certain year, and how many were taken care of with less than $10,000 of damage (or whatever other criteria the organization wishes to employ). Generally the person or department being measured should not keep track of the metrics themselves because they may be tempted to overstate their accomplishments or exaggerate the contribution that they have made.

As is the case with a trouble ticket system, whenever possible it is desirable to capture the metrics in an automated system as a by-product of doing other tasks. For example, the loss history recording system, typically maintained by the Physical Security Department, will track the number of security-related events and the estimated dollar value of losses. This information can, in turn, be used to help determine how well the information security function is doing. A little innovative thinking will often reveal how metrics can be automatically recorded in the process of conducting normal information technology related activities. For example, auto-discovery software used to assist with automatic software updates could also be used to determine the incidence of unlicensed software on end-user workstation hard disk drives. This could then be used to determine how well the training and awareness effort about software copyrights has been.

Perhaps the most basic of individual worker metrics is to simply add a yes/no question to a standardized form used for performance evaluations. Such a question might go something like this: "Does the worker consistently support and abide by information security policies and standards?" The fact that such a question appears on every worker's evaluation form will underscore the fact that information security is everyone's responsibility. If workers know that they will be evaluated, in part based on their information security related behavior, they will be more motivated to become a supportive member of an information security team. As a variation of this approach, some firms may wish to have one type of evaluation form for management, and another for all other workers. Managers may have a second question, above and beyond the question mentioned at the beginning of this paragraph. This supplementary question could be worded something like this: "Does this manager foster compliance with and support of information security among his or her direct reports?" This supplementary question will underscore the fact that management's duty is not just to mind their own personal business, but that they are obliged to inspire and motivate their direct reports to be supportive members of the information security team.

Perhaps the best metric reflecting an information security function's success is that it saved the organization money. While at first you may scoff, thinking that information security is always an overhead item that only costs money, there are some exceptions. It behooves you to loudly trumpet these exceptions to help change management's viewpoint of information security. One example of such an exception involves software licensing; through the adoption of a new license management system, software costs can actually be reduced. Another example involves an uninterruptible power system (UPS); a power outage of a certain duration can be expected to cost an organization a certain amount due to lost business, and this may be considerably more than the cost of buying and maintaining the UPS. Yet another example involves file backup systems; the cost of recreating files lost in a virus infestation can be compared favorably to the cost of purchasing and operating the backup system. While showing how good information security saved the organization money will definitely help with efforts to get a larger information security budget, it can also show that a specific individual is doing a good job, and therefore deserves a promotion, a raise, a bonus, etc.

Appendix D PROFESSIONAL CERTIFICATIONS

With résumé fraud on the rise, one of the sure-fire methods for employers to be sure that the people they hire are indeed familiar with the essentials of the field is to insist that they have certain certifications. The certifications claimed by applicants can then be checked with the issuing organizations to make sure that they have indeed been conferred on the applicant for employment. Other background checking (vetting) steps are highly recommended, especially because information security personnel often hold significant positions of trust, and because they have access to both the information and tools that could be used to cause your organization significant harm. Reflecting these concerns, it is now common to subject applicants for jobs as Systems Administrators, Information Security Managers, and other computer-related positions of trust to additional background checks which go above and beyond those applied to other types of employees.

The additional background checking that you may want to consider includes a review of applicant credit history, driver's license violation history, references with former employers, and confirmation that academic degrees were in fact obtained. Some organizations also perform psychological honesty tests which subject applicants to a series of questions that have been statistically proven to identify people likely to steal or commit fraud. You may also wish to perform drug testing, verify selected information provided by applicants such as social security numbers, and investigate whether the applicants have a history of civil litigation. While this may sound like a lot of work, and certainly only the military would perform all of these checks, remember that resume fraud has become an epidemic (a recent study performed by Michael G. Kessler & Associates, a New York City background investigation firm, indicated that 25% of resumes contain some form of false claim).

Getting back to certifications, this chapter lists the major certifications relevant to the information security field. There are others, but these are the ones that the practitioner will encounter most frequently, and these are the ones that have the greatest credibility. The following professional certifications are relevant primarily to centralized information security positions. They are not generally relevant to staff working in decentralized information security positions, unless these individuals intend to become information security specialists. You may also look for these certifications on the résumés of consultants and contractors working in the information security field.

You may wish to list these designations in help wanted advertisements, look for them on résumés, and ask about them during interviews. Automatic résumé scanning software can also be set up to search for these strings of characters. The certifications are listed below in rough order of relevance to information security activities (most to least relevant).

Note that vendor-specific security certifications, are deliberately not described below. These include designations such as the Cisco Certified Security Professional (CCSP), the Symantec Certified Security Engineer (SCSE), the Sun Certified Backup And Recovery Engineer, and the Checkpoint Certified Security Expert (CCSE) from Checkpoint Systems. The omission is deliberate, in order to maintain an independent stance, and it also as a reflection of the fact that most employers ask for vendor-neutral certifications. Vendor-specific certifications may, however, be of interest in certain computing environments. For example, if you work for an organization that specializes in a certain type of technology, such as a systems integrator which extensively employs Cisco products, then this type of certification may be what you are after. Vendor-specific certifications can also limit your ability to move from one employer to another. These certifications may additionally suggest a bias towards the use of a particular vendor's security solutions.

While the possession of professional certifications should certainly cause you to more seriously consider certain candidates for an information security position, they are no replacement for breadth of experience. Far too many organizations believe that if a certain individual has a certification, he or she should be able to do most anything in the information security field. This is decidedly not the case. The field has become very complex, and now has many sub specialties. In addition, the field can be accurately described as an amalgam of many different fields such as auditing, mathematics, computer science, human resources, and physical security. Given the field's complexity and multi-disciplinary nature, there really is no substitute for broad and varied background with a wide variety of information security situations and problems.

The large number of certifications listed below is a reflection of the embryonic state of the information security field. Because the field is only a few decades old, it has many contenders for the position of most respected professional certification. This is very different from fields which have been around for a long time. The accounting field provides an example of a field which has been around for hundreds of years. In the United States, a single certification called a Certified Public Accountant (CPA), has become standard and is now recognized in all of the states of the union. The CPA designation is also recognized by government agencies and courts of law as the number one professional designation in the accounting field, and is used as a qualification to get a license to practice certain specialties, such as auditing the books of publicly-listed corporations. No such consensus on a single designation is evident in the information security field, no government entities officially recognize any of the following designations, and no professional licensing is currently available for information security practitioners.

CISSP

Certified Information Systems Security Professional - intended for information systems security specialists, especially those who develop policies, procedures, standards, and architectures, this credential covers topics such as system access control, cryptography, telecommunications security, computer risk management, data classification, computer operation security, and information ethics. This is the premier certification in the information security field and is the one most often requested by employers.

(ISC)2, Inc.

P.O. Box 1117
Dunedin, FL 34697 USA
voice: 703-891-0782 or 888-333-4458 (toll free in North America)
fax: 727-738-8522
web: www.isc2.org

SSCP

Systems Security Certified Practitioner - intended for systems administrators and network administrators, this credential provides a test which recognizes an international body of knowledge related to information security; the topics covered include access controls, systems security administration, auditing and monitoring, response and recovery from incidents, cryptography, data communications, and malicious code/malware.

(ISC)2, Inc.

P.O. Box 1117
Dunedin, FL 34697 USA

voice: 703-891-0782 or 888-333-4458 (toll free in North America)
fax: 727-738-8522
web: www.isc2.org

ISSEP

Information Systems Security Engineering Professional - intended for those who wish to show additional proficiency above and beyond the CISSP. The exam covers the 10 domains found within the CISSP, but also covers certification and accreditation, government policy and regulation, the systems security engineering process, and government protection needs determination. The US National Security Agency (NSA) provides guidelines and content for the exam's certification and testing, but the exam development and administration is handled by (ISC)2. This certification will be required for all people working on information security, including contractors, at the NSA. People who take this examination must first have four years of experience in the field as well as previously passed the CISSP exam.

(ISC)2, Inc.

P.O. Box 1117
Dunedin, FL 34697 USA
voice: 703-891-0782 or 888-333-4458 (toll free in North America)
fax: 727-738-8522
web: www.isc2.org

CISA

Certified Information Systems Auditor - intended for Information Systems Auditors (alias EDP Auditors), this credential covers topics such as the information systems auditing process, business process evaluation and risk management, disaster recovery and business continuity, systems development and maintenance, management and organization of the information systems function, and the protection of information assets. This credential has been in existence longer than any other one relevant to the information security field.

Information Systems Audit & Control Association (ISACA)

3701 Algonquin Road, Suite 1010
Rolling Meadows, IL 60008 USA
voice: 847-590-7474
fax: 847-253-1443
web: www.isaca.org

CISM

Certified Information Systems Manager - This certification from ISACA is specifically geared toward experienced information security managers and those who have information security management responsibilities. This certification is for the individual who must maintain a view of the "big picture" by managing, designing, overseeing and assessing an enterprise's information security. It is business-oriented and focuses on information risk management while addressing management, design and technical security issues at a conceptual level. This credential is relatively new but one of the most popular certifications for information security professionals.

Information Systems Audit & Control Association (ISACA)

3701 Algonquin Road, Suite 1010
Rolling Meadows, IL 60008 USA
voice: 847-590-7474
fax: 847-253-1443
web: www.isaca.org

GSE

GIAC (Global Incident Analysis Center) Security Engineer - intended for systems administrators and others who must respond to hacker attacks and understand operating system logs and intrusion detection software reports; this in-depth certification is unique in that it not only tests an individual's knowledge, it also tests the individual's ability to put that knowledge to use in a real-world environment; separate certifications are available in specific areas: GSEC (GIAC Security Essentials Certification), GCFW (GIAC Certified Firewall Analyst), GCIA (GIAC Certified Intrusion Analyst), GCIH (GCIA Certified Incident Handler), GCWN (GIAC Certified Windows Security Administrator), GCUX (GIAC Certified UNIX Security Administrator), GISO (GIAC Information Security Officer), GSNA (GIAC Systems and Network Auditor), GCFA (GIAC Certified Forensic Analyst), GSLC (GIAC Security Leadership Certificate), and GIAK (GIAC Information Security for Auditors Kickstart).

SANS Institute

5401 Westbard Avenue, Suite 1501
Bethesda, MD 20816 USA
voice: 301-951-0102 or 866-570-9927
fax: 301-855-1633
web: www.giac.org

PMP

Project Management Professional - Granted by the Project Management Institute (PMI), this certification is considered by many managers as essential for implementing complex enterprise-level information security projects. The certification is now the highest-paying certification that an information security professional can obtain. Covering project management principles, project quality metrics, leadership and communication skills, software risk management, and project risk management, this certification involves over a month of in-class courses offered by Management Concepts before candidates are eligible to sit for the exam.

Management Concepts

8320 Leesburg Pike, Suite 800
Vienna, VA 22182
voice: 703-790-9595
fax: 703-790-1371
web: www.managementconcepts.com

TICSA

TrueSecure ICSA Certified Security Associate - Endorsed by (ISC)2, this vendor-neutral practical designation is intended for systems administrators and others who are responsible for security but who may not have the word security in their job title, or for practitioners who wish to show their mastery of security system implementation details; the test covers topics such as widely adopted security standards, standard commercial security practices, commercially available products, TCP/IP networking basics, security law and ethics, PKI and digital certificates, encryption system implementation, malicious code, security system configuration, and Internet security product implementations. A more advanced version of this same certification is called TICSE, or TrueSecure ICSA Certified Security Expert. The latter requires test takers to demonstrate in-depth hands-on knowledge and self-sufficiency in the design, implementation, and deployment of security solutions. The latter is intended for senior network engineers.

TrueSecure Corporation

85 Astor Avenue, Suite 2
Norwood, MA 02062 USA
voice: 888-396-8348 or 703-480-8200
fax: 781-255-0215
web: www.truesecure.com

CCISM

Certified Counterespionage & Information Security Manager - this program seeks to support a variety of career tracks such as application programmers, help desk clerks, database admininstrators, access control system administrators, and information security managers. This is a management level certification which focuses on studying the threats and defeating attacks. Emphasis is placed on both technical as well as human factors related to information security. Topics covered include development of policies and procedures, encryption system usage, network administration, crime scene investigation, surveillance countermeasures, and competitive intelligence gathering.

Espionage Research Institute

P.O. Box 44260
Fort Washington, MD 20749 USA
voice: 305-254-7006
fax: 301 292-4635
web: www.espionbusiness.com/faq.ivnu

SCP

Security Certified Professional - this designation involves a vendor-neutral network security training program intended for systems administrators and other information technology professionals, which is delivered in two discrete levels, and which covers information security fundamentals, network security implementation issues, network defense strategies and countermeasures, encryption including public key infrastructure system construction, and biometrics system implementation.

New Horizons Computer Learning Centers

1900 S. State College Boulevard
(this is headquarters, many local centers exist)
Anaheim, CA 92802-6135 USA
voice: 714-940-8000
fax: 714-940-8418
web: www.newhorizons.com

CBCP

Certified Business Continuity Professional, formerly Certified Disaster Recovery Professional or CDRP (also related designations known as ABCP or Associate Business Continuity Planner, and MBCP or Master Business Continuity Planner) - intended for business contingency planners and information systems contingency planners, this credential covers topics such as business impact analysis, emergency response, developing recovery strategies, testing recovery plans, and awareness training.

DRI International (also known as Disaster Recovery Institute)

111 Park Place
Falls Church, VA 22046-4513 USA
voice: 703-538-1792
fax: 703-241-5603
web: www.drii.org

CCP

Certified Computing Professional (with demonstrated specialty in systems security) - intended for technical specialists like programmers and systems analysts, this credential covers topics such as data resource management, office information systems, systems programming, systems development, software engineering, structured programming, information systems management, and systems security.

Institute for Certification of Computing Professionals (ICCP)

2350 E. Devon Avenue, Suite 115
Des Plaines, IL 60018-4610 USA
voice: 847-299-4227 or 800-843-8227
fax: 847-299-4280
web: www.iccp.org

CIWSP

CIW Security Professional (may also be abbreviated CIW-SP) - intended for network administrators, firewall administrators, application developers, and information security officers, this designation focuses on Internet commerce and the related security matters including information security policy development, risk assessment, development of countermeasures, intrustion detection, and attack response strategies. As a step in the direction of getting the CIWSP certification, some people may wish to be certified as a CIW Security Analyst (CIWSA or CIW-SA). The latter certification is intended for network administrators who wish to move into information security.

Prosoft Training

3001 Bee Caves Road, Suite 300
Austin, TX 79746 USA
voice: 512-328-6140 or 888-303-8749 (in USA and Canada only)
fax: 512-328-5237
web: www.prosofttraining.com

Security+

The Security+ examination is a benchmark foundation level certification for people who have been working in the field at least two years. It covers a wide range of information security areas including general security concepts, communications security, infrastructure security, operational/organizational security, and cryptography. This multiple choice test is based on an industry-wide survey of the topics most relevant to the jobs of people working in the information security field.

CompTIA

c/o CareerAcademy.com
6 Highview St.
Needham, MA 02494 USA
voice: 800-807-8839 in the USA, or 1-781-702-6111 x 201 Internationally
fax: 877-876-3949
web: www.comptia.org

NSCP

Network Security Certified Professional - this is an intermediate level certification intended for information technology specialists, especially network administrators and systems administrators. A similar but less senior designation offered by the same organization is called Enterprise and Web Security Certified Professional (EWSCP). Both include implementation specifics such as how to build virtual private networks, how to deploy intrusion detection systems, how to configure firewalls, and how to build public key infrastructure (PKI) encryption systems.

Learning Tree International

1805 Library Street
Reston, VA 20190-5630 USA
voice: 800-843-8733 or 703-709-9019
fax: 800-698-1015
web: www.learningtree.com

CSM

Certified Software Manager - intended for systems administrators, help-desk personnel, technical support specialists, purchasing agents, value added resellers, and information security specialists, this credential covers topics such as copyright law, software licenses, software inventory tools, software audit process, security awareness training, and virus infestation responses.

The Software & Information Industry Association (SIIA)

1090 Vermont Avenue, NW, Sixth Floor
Washington, DC 20005 USA
voice: 202-289-7442
fax: 202-289-7097
web: www.siia.net

SCNP

Security Certified Network Professional - intended as the designation for information security professionals who wish to demonstrate that they have a hands-on knowledge of defensive network security protection measures. This certification focuses on firewalls and network intrusion systems, but also covers biometrics, public key infrastructure (PKI), network security fundamentals, and network defensive and countermeasures. The SCNP is an intermediate level certification on the way to becoming a SCNA (Security Certified Network Architect). The SCNA designation, which is conferred by the same organization, shows mastery of advanced information security topics such as digital signatures and digital certificates, as well as PKI system implementation.

Security Certified Program

611 East State Street, Suite 626
Geneva, IL 60134 USA
voice: 800-869-0025 or 630-472-5790
fax: 630-472-0190
web: www.securitycertified.net

CFE

Certified Fraud Examiner - intended for internal auditors, forensic accountants, private investigators, academic researchers, and law enforcement personnel, this credential covers topics such as financial transactions, statistical analysis, fraud investigation, fraud deterrence, loss prevention, criminology and sociology, ethics, and the legal process.

Association of Certified Fraud Examiners

The Gregor Building

716 West Avenue
Austin, TX 78701 USA
voice: 512-478-9070 or 800-254-3321 (USA and Canada)
fax: 512-478-9297
web: www.acfe.org

CPP

Certified Protection Professional - intended for directors of Physical Security Departments, this credential covers topics such as emergency planning, sensitive information protection, personnel security, investigations, loss prevention, physical security, and substance abuse.

American Society for Industrial Security

1625 Prince Street
Alexandria, VA 22314-2818 USA
voice: 703-519-6200
fax: 703-519-6299
web: www.asisonline.org

CIA

Certified Internal Auditor - intended for internal auditors, this credential covers topics such as the fraud detection, interviewing for investigations, reporting problems to management, control of information technology, mathematics of statistical sampling, managerial accounting, and financial accounting (also available from IIA: CCSA - Certification in Control Self-Assessment and CGAP - Certified Government Auditing Professional).

The Institute of Internal Auditors

247 Maitland Avenue
Altamonte Springs, FL 32701-4201 USA
voice: 407-830-7600, Ext. 1
fax: 407-831-5171
web: www.theiia.org

Appendix E RESPONSIBILITY AND LIABILITY

This appendix explores a number of issues related to top management's ultimate responsibility for information security. Liability is a vast topic and this chapter is intended to provide only a few starting points for further investigation. The material is intended to be helpful to you in your efforts to gain management support for an information security roles and responsibilities definition/revision project. Consultation with legal counsel is strongly advised prior to having discussions with top management on any issue related to legal liability. The author is not an attorney.

Modern organizations operate in an increasingly regulated environment. Within the last few years alone, a number of state, federal and international laws have been passed that not only impact security and privacy programs of many businesses, but create a number of additional risks for organizations who are not serious about protecting information, especially the privacy of customer data. In fact, most of these regulations specifically require the proper definition and documentation of information security roles and responsibilities. (See Table E-1).

While the regulatory landscape has become more complicated, so too have information systems. Modern information systems technology enables a variety of acts that were not possible in the past. For example, through e-mail, employees can unintentionally bind the organization to a contract, unintentionally libel another entity, or unintentionally trigger charges of a hostile working environment (via dirty jokes for example). E-mail provides a new and easy-to-use channel for the transmission of a wide variety of different types of information including strategic plans, employee performance reviews, as well as merger and acquisition plans. One of the areas where management (which includes the Board of Directors) can be held individually and personally responsible for the acts of employees involves e-mail communications.

Management may also be held liable for the actions of employees if these same employees do not properly handle intellectual property belonging to others. The Software Publishers Association and the Business Publishers Association (both now merged with the Information Industry Association) have conducted many high-visibility audits where they have proven the use of illegal software at major organizations. The resulting fines have been significant and the adverse publicity has been embarrassing. While these organizational risks are serious, management at your organization may not pay much attention unless the risks are to their own personal wealth and well-being. Many managers do not realize that they have a vicarious liability for acts of software piracy by their employees. Managers in the United States can be held liable under the Copyright Act for up to $250,000 in fines and up to two years in prison.

At the heart of the issue related to management's responsibility for information security problems lies the question "Is management legally responsible for the actions of the people who report to them?" In some countries the answer is a definitive "yes," in others the answer is "yes sometimes," and in yet others it is "not so much." In the United States, the answer is "yes sometimes." For example, the False Claims Act, a federal statute that is normally used to prosecute fraud in military contracting, was used against both the University of Utah and the University of California at San Diego. The federal government filed suit to hold management at these two universities responsible for research conducted on their campuses. It was alleged that two professors fraudulently obtained research grants by misrepresenting the results of their research. The suit also alleged that the management at these two universities recklessly certified the grant applications. Beyond the False Claims Act, other statutes such as the Major Fraud Act and the Truth in Negotiation Act can be used by the United States government to bring information security related lawsuits.

When a manager asks you why they should spend money on information security, perhaps the most engaging response is, "Because it will keep you out of jail." Depending on the jurisdiction where your organization operates, there are a number of statutes that attempt to assign greater accountability to management for the maintenance of internal control. And internal control is, of course, critically dependent on information security. Management's ultimate responsibility for all forms of governance, including information security controls, is perhaps best represented by the Sarbanes-Oxley Act in the United States. Enacted in the wake of Enron, Worldcom and other disasters related to financial reporting, Sarbanes-Oxley is the most sweeping legislation that attempts to enforce corporate accountability at the most senior management levels. Under Sarbanes-Oxley, publicly-traded companies are required to file reports, signed by senior management, that attest to the adequacy of their control environment. Companies are also required to disclose "material weaknesses" of their internal controls in their public financial statements.

Another example of such a statute in the United States is the Foreign Corrupt Practices Act (FCPA), which incidentally applies only to companies listed on a stock exchange. Originally written as an anti-bribery statute, the FCPA requires the establishment and maintenance of an adequate system of accounting and management controls. Under the FCPA, top managers can lose their house, their boat, their car, and their savings because they are civilly liable for lapses in internal control. You are urged to investigate the specific statutes that are relevant to your organization and that make management personally liable for information security problems.

Although many people in the information security field don't appreciate their jobs in this light, they have a key role to play when it comes to protecting management against personal liability. The human resources area, at least in the United States, has become a hotbed of litigation with allegations like racial discrimination, age discrimination, wrongful termination, breach of implied promise, and the like. Top management has come to appreciate that the human resources function, if done well, will help to avoid litigation and disputes. The information security function at many organizations has not made this same point clearly to top management, and that is one of the great challenges in the information security awareness field. To be successful with a shift in management attitudes, top management must come to appreciate that information security is not just a technical issue, that it is a management and people issue as well.

Perhaps the most likely type of lawsuit that management will encounter is a stockholder lawsuit. Stockholders may allege that management did not adequately protect their investment, that they breached their fiduciary duty to conserve and protect corporate assets. In the wake of Enron and the stock market decline of recent years, there are literally hundreds of these suits in progress. Even if there are no stockholder suits, the stock price declines related to information security problems can be severe. When one considers the stock options that top managers have at many organizations, talking about these price declines can often help obtain management support for an information security roles and responsibilities effort. For example, eBay, an Internet auction company, saw the market value of its stock decline $4 billion dollars in 1999 because it had a twenty-two hour outage on its auction site. Executives at eBay estimate that the impact included a loss of $3 to $5 million in sales. Likewise, in 1999, AOL saw its stock plunge $4.50/share because it was off-line for nineteen hours. In a similar vein, in the same year, E*Trade saw its stock decline $6.50/share because it had two software related outages that lasted a combined seventy-five minutes. All of these outages directly relate to systems availability, an important information security consideration.

There is a new type of exposure that management may not know about, and it's called computer professional malpractice. This exposure involves those events where computer professionals don't act with the due care that one would expect of a computer professional. In a landmark case involving Ernst & Young when they were still called Ernst & Whinney (in 1990), consultants failed to provide a T-shirt manufacturing company with the professional services needed to integrate a new computer system. The court relied on commonly practiced professional standards, just as is done in medicine, when establishing this notion as legal precedent. It is only a matter of time before this same notion is extended to the information security area, an area fraught with complexity where it's easy to make mistakes. While you may choose not to use this notion in discussions with top management, you should use it in discussions with the Chief Information Officer and others who are computer professionals located within the USA (or other jurisdictions which might have similar case law or legislation).

The notion of exercising due care is also important to discuss with top management. If a person's conduct caused an unreasonable risk of harm to others, then that person can be held liable under common law. In many cases, the standard of due care is readily evident in the information security field. It can be determined, for example, in the area of Internet commerce credit card fraud prevention-credit card numbers should not be transmitted over the Internet in unencrypted form. To do so would subject management to liability for a tort or civil wrong. However, management must be shown to have acted negligently or with wrongful intent. The real issue as it relates to information security is determining what exactly is prudent and what is negligent. The courts will determine this on a case-by-case basis, but it's advisable to stay out of court altogether. Primary to the court's determination of negligence is the notion of a "prudent man," in other words, someone else who was acting diligently and who was facing the same circumstances. You can thus compare your organization to others in the same industry to get a sense for what constitutes the standard of due care. For example, if other firms in the same industry have clear roles and responsibilities documentation, then your firm should also have this same type of documentation. You may also wish to investigate relevant United States cases dealing with the standard of due care such as: Palmer v. Columbia Gas Co., Ford Motor Credit Corp. v. Hitchcock, Delbueck v. Manufacturer's Hanover Bank, US v. Simon, Adams v. Standard Knitting, FJS Electronics v. Fidelity Bank, Diversified Graphics v. Ernst & Whinney, and Price v. Ford.

Going beyond the standard of due care, if your organization does business in the US, you should be aware of what is called the Hooper Doctrine. This doctrine originated in 1928 (Hooper v. Northern Barge Corporation) in a case involving tug boats. An operator of tug boats in the open sea off the New Jersey coast was held liable because he did not have radios on board to receive weather reports, in spite of the fact that other tug boats at that time did not generally use radios. The operator was required to use the latest technology (radios) as a way to lessen the loss associated with a storm in which he was operating. Using this doctrine, courts examine the probability of loss and the dollar value of the potential loss, then compare the product of those two quantities with the cost of a control. In this case, the cost of radios was very small when compared with the dollar value of a loss of several barges loaded with coal. In your own organization, the control could be security measures other than radios, perhaps a disaster recovery plan, or perhaps information security job descriptions. Using this precedent, management can be held liable for the absence of an important control, even if comparable organizations don't generally use this same control. Likewise, with this doctrine management cannot use the absence of a specific legal or regulatory requirement as a way to avoid liability.

Recently discussed in the US Congress, and undoubtedly an indication of more legislation to come, is the notion of holding an organization liable for having Internet-connected systems which don't meet a certain security-related standard of due care. The objective is to get organizations to see good security as clearly in their best interests, in this case as a way to avoid liability. Right now, far too many organizations simply see security as an added cost that they can do without, something which is therefore not in their best interests. The notion of holding organizations liable for having a network-connected system that is vulnerable is particularly important when one considers distributed denial of service (DDOS) attacks. These attacks take place when several different computers are used to synchronously attack a particular computer or a web business. Using

scripted attack sequences, so-called zombie computers, which have been breached and then enlisted to attack another computer, can then be the source of problems for other network-connected users. By having security meet certain minimum requirements, organizations would markedly lessen the probability that their computers would be used as zombie computers. The notion that a vulnerable computer doesn't just hurt the involved organization -- that it hurts other network-connected people and organizations -- is something that will be increasingly discussed in the years ahead, and is something that you may wish to discuss with management at your organization.

Another legal notion that may be helpful in discussions with top management is the concept of legal notice. When management has been placed on notice that there is an information security problem, they have a duty to correct the problem. If management fails to take adequate precautions, they can be held liable. This notion was used against the now-bankrupt Pan American World Airways. Pan Am had received a number of threats about a terrorist act before one of its jets exploded due to a bomb over Scotland in 1988. Because it knew of the threat and failed to take certain precautions, it could be and was held liable for damages to the passengers who died in the crash. In a like manner, if management has been put on notice by a hacker's intrusion, then it needs to upgrade its network security in response to that notice. Worse yet, if management knew a hacker was on its network, and then this hacker went on to use the organization's network to attack another organization, then management might be liable for damages done to that other organization.

Many industries have regulations specific to the industry. For example, in the United States, all federally chartered banks are required to have a contingency plan which meets federal government guidelines. Several legal scholars have implied that management would be personally liable if disaster strikes and a bank did not have adequate contingency plans in place. Unfortunately these directives do not include objective standards, so in the absence of dishonesty or gross negligence, managers would be likely to be saved by the common law business judgement rule (which avoids liability on the basis that managers acted legally, honestly, and in good faith). You should check the laws applicable to your industry to determine the extent to which management is personally liable for failing to be in compliance with information security related laws and regulations.

There are also laws that cut across industries, laws that pertain to certain activities, such as the handling of credit history information. In the United States, the Fair

Credit Reporting Act mandates that organizations handling credit history data maintain the data so that it is complete and up to date. Willful failure to comply can result in actual and punitive damages, court costs, and attorney's fees. The key idea behind this law is willfulness, and personal liability for failing to live up to the standard of due care is not directly addressed.

Beyond multi-industry laws within a certain country, there are certain laws that have been adopted by multiple countries. For example, countries in the European Union (EU) have adopted harmonized privacy laws. Although the privacy laws are more relaxed in the United States, there is still reason for management to be concerned. One such area involves e-mail monitoring. For example, at Epson America an e-mail administrator was dismissed for refusing to monitor the e-mail of other employees. This administrator believed that unannounced monitoring was unethical and that it violated the privacy of the other employees. She went on to file a wrongful termination lawsuit, and 170 employees then joined her in filing a California wiretapping statute violation suit against the company. Although not a part of that case, the California constitution guarantees the right to privacy and gives any citizen standing to bring a lawsuit when they believe that their right to privacy has been violated. You should pay particular attention to the privacy laws of the states and/or countries where your organization operates, and you should be sure to communicate the extent of management's liability for failure to observe these same laws. You should also note that there are United States federal laws that govern privacy such as the Electronic Communications Privacy Act.

The prospect of management liability within a single jurisdiction should be disconcerting enough, but the widespread usage of the Internet compounds this problem many times over. While the legal requirements of doing Internet business in a certain jurisdiction is still evolving, there have been cases where the more stringent standards of one state or country are applied to systems that were physically located in another state or country. The area of pornography is particularly good example here, but there are many other laws related to information security that should be of concern to you. In the United States, at the federal level, these include: the Computer Fraud and Abuse Act, the Copyright Act, the Crime Control Act, the Privacy Act, the Right to Financial Privacy Act, the Privacy Protection Act, the Electronic Funds Transfer Act, and the ERISA Retirement Record Keeping Act.

In whatever country your organization happens to operate, it is customary to have management be personally responsible for problems which are so severe that they jeopardize the very existence of the organization. There are a number of cases on record where the organization went out of business as a result of information security problems. For example, in London, England, a printer who thought that his employer was trying to avoid paying him 2,000 pounds that he believed was owed, used a special password to lock up the computers of Ampersand Typesetting Ltd. The firm was accordingly unable to conduct business, and lost more than 36,000 pounds in sales. Subsequent prosecution under the Computer Misuse Act claimed that the printer's actions contributed to the firm's bankruptcy which followed immediately after this incident. In this case, apparently no contingency plan was in place. Beyond the failure to develop and enhance an adequate contingency plan, management may also be held liable for failure to use virus detection software, or failure to perform proper background checks (the latter is known as negligent hiring).

Management at many organizations is not yet sufficiently aware of its liability for undue reliance on computerized records. In a landmark case in the United States called Ford Motor Credit Co. v. Swarens, the defendant firm was told by the plaintiff that computerized data was incorrect. The data in question involved a loan for a car. The plaintiff provided cancelled checks indicating that the computer records, which said that the plaintiff was seriously in arrears on his loan, were incorrect. Management chose to disregard this evidence, and proceeded to repossess the car. The Kentucky Court of Appeals indicated that management had unreasonably relied on the computerized records and was therefore liable. The management at Ford said that they were not at fault because they relied on erroneous data, and that they had no bad intent. This was not sufficient in the eyes of the court to avoid liability. On this same note, it is useful to ask top management just how much they rely on computerized information when making key decisions related to the organization. Management should be asked whether they really know how often data is updated, who provided it, how it is processed, etc.

In the United States, managers should also be aware of the Federal Sentencing Organizational Guidelines. These 1991 regulations are aimed at white collar crime but they have sobering implications for Chief Executive Officers as well as other top managers such as Chief Information Officers. The regulations hold senior management responsible for crime involving their organization. Management is responsible even if the organization and its members are honest and the crime was perpetrated by outsiders. Organizations are exposed to liability of up to $290 million and the possible loss of a corporate charter. High level managers are exposed to fines and possible imprisonment. To prevent this liability, management must prove its good faith by establishing an effective security program that prevents and deters criminal conduct. While broader in scope than just information security, these regulations nonetheless point to need for the establishment of clear information security roles and responsibilities.

To quantify the exposure that management faces, and to determine how much it is prudent to spend to reduce this exposure, you should perform a brief legal risk assessment. By identifying the serious risks, the likelihood of loss, and the financial implications of each loss, you will be able to go to management with a proposal containing ways to address these exposures. Of course, one very important step that should be included in this proposal is clarification of information security roles and responsibilities. After management receives the legal risk analysis and a proposal about appropriate next steps, it can determine which exposures it wishes to transfer (with insurance), which exposures it wishes to

mitigate (with additional controls), and which exposures it wishes to accept (that is, do nothing about at this time).

After the major legal exposures have been identified, your organization should establish a solid compliance program to ensure that the organization is following the dictates of both laws and regulations. A documented compliance program has been shown to impress the court, and show a bona fide intention on management's part to operate in a manner that is consistent with all aspects of laws and regulations. This can help avert prosecution, not just fines. This opinion is supported by a 1995 report prepared by the U.S. Sentencing Commission, an independent agency of the judicial branch of the federal government. In addition, the United States government has also gone on record stating that the existence of a compliance program would result in reduced fines for firms that have been convicted of statutory violations. A compliance program should be included as one of the responsibilities of the Legal Department, and this topic is further discussed in Chapter 11 and Chapter 12.

Table E-1: Security and Privacy regulations and related frameworks that require proper definition of information security roles and responsibilities.

REGULATION	SPECIFIC REQUIREMENTS
Sarbanes-Oxley Act (Based on the COBIT Framework) International / Applies to all corporations traded on a United States Stock Exchange.	COBIT control objectives Section 4.0 "Define the IT organization and relationships" requires the proper definition and documentation of various organizational roles including: 4.1 IT Planning or Steering Committee, 4.2 Organizational Placement of the IT Function, 4.4 Roles and Responsibilities, 4.5 Responsibility for Quality Assurance, 4.6 Responsibility for Logical and Physical Security, 4.7 Data and System Ownership
Health Insurance Portability and Accountability Act (HIPAA) Privacy and Security United States / Healthcare	HIPAA Final Security Rule Section 164.308(a)(2)- Assigned Security Responsibility. HIPAA Privacy Rule Administrative requirements (section §164.530) requires personnel designations for such roles as Chief Privacy Officer, and for the proper assignment of persons responsible for documenting and implementing the safeguards to protect Private Health Information.

Table E-1: Security and Privacy regulations and related frameworks that require proper definition of information security roles and responsibilities.

REGULATION	SPECIFIC REQUIREMENTS
Gramm-Leach-Bliley Act (GLBA) United States / Banking and Finance	In the auditors checklist within the Interagency Guidelines for Establishing Standards for Safeguarding Customer Information (Guidelines) for GLBA compliance asks: "Is the written information security program appropriate given the size and complexity of the organization and its operations? Does [the information security program] contain the objectives of the program, assign responsibility for implementation, and provide methods for compliance and enforcement?"
Federal Information Security Management Act (FISMA) The National Institute of Standards (NIST) United States / Federal Government	NIST SP 800-26: Self-assessment Guide for Federal Systems that evaluates systems in17 key control areas. Section 6 deals with Personnel Security. Section 6.1.2 asks "Are there documented job descriptions that accurately reflect assigned duties and responsibilities and that segregate duties?" [Reference FISCAM SD-1.2]
FERC Proposed Cyber Security Standard United States / Energy and Infrastructure	Section CIP-003-1: Security Management Controls, Requirement R.3 states "The Responsible Entity shall also define the roles and responsibilities of Critical Cyber Asset owners, custodians, and users. Roles and responsibilities shall also be defined for the access, use, and handling of critical information as identified and categorized in Requirement R2 of this standard."
SECURITY AND PRIVACY FRAMEWORKS	SPECIFIC REQUIREMENTS
ISO/IEC 17799 (Code of Practice for Information Security Management) Security Framework	Section 2.0 Security Organization requires formal definition of: 2.1 Information security infrastructure, 2.2 Security of third party access, and 2.3 Outsourcing. Section 6.0 Personnel Security, section 6.1 requires "security in job definition and resourcing."
The Generally Accepted Information Security Principles (GAISP) V 3.0 Security Framework	Section 2.1 - The Accountability Principle states that "Information security accountability and responsibility must be clearly defined and acknowledged."
Organization for Economic Cooperation and Development (OECD) Privacy Principles Privacy Framework	Principle 8: Accountability Requires the identification of specific individuals or groups who are responsible for privacy within the organization.

Appendix F   SAMPLE USER RESPONSIBILITY AGREEMENT

This form must be completely filled out and signed by the user before it will be processed. Modifications to the terms and conditions provided in this form are not acceptable to management, although additional remarks will be noted. Prior to being processed, all forms must be approved in writing by your supervisor and then forwarded to the Information Security Department.

Please check the relevant categories from the three options shown immediately below and provide the additional information requested.

__User seeks a new user-ID

Provide reason: _____

__ User seeks reauthorization of an existing user-ID

Existing user-ID: _____

__ User seeks additional privileges on an existing user-ID

Existing user-ID: _____

Specify privileges needed: _____

_____

_____

User's name printed: _____

User's department: _____

User's telephone number: _____

User's internal mail location: _____

I am the user whose name appears above. I understand that my continued employment by or contractual work with Company X is contingent on my diligent and consistent compliance with information security policies and procedures. I have read a copy of the Company X information security policies manual, and I understand my responsibilities as defined in that manual. I have been warned and I understand that violation of the rules contained in that manual, or failure to perform my responsibilities as defined in that manual, will be sufficient cause for disciplinary action up to and including termination.

I understand that information owned by or entrusted to Company X is valuable and proprietary, and that it needs to be protected. I understand that my access to this information makes me an important part of the team charged with protecting this information. Accordingly, I agree to take all security and privacy precautions, as I have been instructed by Company X, to protect the information to which I have been given access in the course of my work for Company X.

When I cease to work for Company X, no matter what the circumstances, I agree to turn over to Company X all Company X information which is then in my possession or otherwise under my control. I agree that I will not retain copies of, extracts of, or summaries of, this information, in any form, for any purpose whatsoever.

I acknowledge that the information I obtain access to in the course of my work for Company X is the property of Company X or another organization that does business with Company X. I promise that I will not use this information for my own personal purposes, including operating my own business, selling the information to other parties, or performing analyses of this information on behalf of other parties. I agree not to disclose this information to third parties without first obtaining the approval of the Company X owner of the information.

To support Company X business activities, I agree to do my best to maintain the currency, accuracy, and relevance of information which I have access to in the course of my work. This includes reporting to the involved managers all known errors or inconsistencies in the information.

To maintain the security of the information that I have been granted access to, I promise to choose only those fixed passwords which are difficult for other parties to guess (several words strung together, a combination of characters and numbers, a combination of characters and punctuation, etc.). I understand that my fixed password must be known only by myself, and must not be provided to any other person. I additionally agree not to write my password down on anything, or store it in any computer, unless it has been transformed by a special process which makes it unrecognizable and unusable by unauthorized parties.

I understand that Company X authorizes me only to access that information which I need to perform my job. I agree that I will not seek to obtain access to Company X information beyond that which has been expressly granted to me through a formal request process. I additionally agree not to use Company X information systems to launch an attack on any other computers, whether they are inside Company X's network or outside this network. In this same vein, I agree not to use software which discovers passwords, uses brute force routines to decrypt encrypted files, or in any other way seek access to information which has not been expressly granted to me. I additionally agree not to download any software over the Internet, or with the aid of any other technology, if this software has not been properly licensed and paid for, unless it is an authorized demonstration copy. I furthermore agree that I will not perform any activity which might be expected to lead to damage to Company X information or information systems (writing computer viruses, overloading systems via network games, etc.). I furthermore agree not to use electronic mail or any other system resources to intimidate or harass other people.

I promise to immediately report all violations or suspected violations of information security policies to the Information Security Department Manager.

User's Signature and Date: _____

User's Supervisor's Signature and Date: _____

Appendix G   DISCLOSING ROLES AND RESPONSIBILITIES

A recently-completed survey documented in the research journal known as Computers & Security indicates that there are major inconsistencies in job titles for information security professionals. The author of that report called for standardization of the titles for information security practitioners. The author of this book is however skeptical of the merits of such an effort to standardize, in large part because there currently is no such thing as a standard information security job.

Inconsistencies in job titles are in part a reflection of the fact that information security is still an embryonic field. If that were all that was going on, then standardization of job titles (and by implication of job descriptions) would make sense. But the nature of the job held by an information security professional is dramatically different from organization to organization. For example, if you consider a retail bank, the job of an Information Security Manager it will probably involve looking after the security of automated teller machines (ATMs). But at a wholesale bank, which caters solely to the needs of corporations and government agencies, there will usually be no ATMs, and therefore the job of the Information Security Manager will not involve ATMs. To assume that all information security jobs at banks involve ATMs is thus to make a serious mistake.

Information security is a multi-disciplinary, multi-departmental, and increasingly multi-organizational effort. A standardized set of duties which rigidly applies across all industries, or even a standardized set of duties which applies to all firms within a certain industry, at this stage of maturity of the field, is not desirable. This is not to say that there aren't similarities and common elements in information security jobs, and it is in fact that observation which allowed this book to be developed. Similarly, this is not to say that organizations should not spend time documenting and internally publishing the duties of those who work in the information security area.

This brings us back to the central question about sharing of job descriptions, departmental mission statements, committee charters, and other roles and responsibilities documentation. Certainly within an organization, all this documentation can and should be published (usually on an intranet site). Information security practitioners should actively distribute this documentation to all insiders (including consultants, contractors, temporaries and the like) in an effort to establish the information security function as an accepted and important business function, as is the case for both accounting and marketing. The decision to distribute this material to outsiders is however a bit more challenging, particularly when you consider that many organizations have a policy that says they will not externally distribute details about their internal information security efforts lest these details be used to compromise the security of their systems.

For example, some firms may fear that if they advertise for a SAP security specialist, then hackers will be notified that the organization is using SAP software. The more detail an organization provides in an advertisement, such as the version of SAP now in use, the more easily unauthorized third parties could exploit this disclosure in order to compromise the organization's systems and networks. This concern is especially relevant to on-line job postings, which are by their very nature accessible to anyone. Industrial spies have been known to use on-line job postings to discover inside information about competitors, and there is no reason to believe that determined intruders might not do the same.

With this reasonable and widely-accepted policy in mind, it should not be surprising that astute organizations advertising for security specialists will do some initial screening, and after they have satisfied themselves that the person they are speaking with is a genuine job seeker, and that there is a possibility that they might be qualified for the open position, then and only then will they disclose more details about the technical environment in question. Going back to the same example, the published want ad could simply ask for a SAP programmer. When the candidate shows up for an in-person interview, the ways in which the organization uses SAP, the software version employed, and other implementation details can be revealed.

So you should ask yourself - how could this same concern apply to the information security roles and responsibilities documentation that you have developed? In other words, what might an adversary or an intruder glean from this documentation? Might an intruder thereby determine who to target for social engineering (spoofing)? Might an intruder thereby gain insight into the ways your organization responds to attacks? There are many other questions of this nature that you can ask.

With the exposures that your organization faces in mind, it is wise to use some ambiguity in external communications as a buffer which helps to ensure that sensitive information is disclosed only to those who have a legitimate need for such information. Thus a full job description would not ordinarily be posted on the Internet, lest it be used by attackers to find out who to harass with a mail bomb attack (this involves overloading a person's email box). Abbreviated job descriptions, perhaps only one paragraph long, are much more suitably posted on a public network, distributed to head hunters, and otherwise made generally available to the public.

But where the recipient is known by you to have a bona fide need to know, then disclosure of all the detailed documentation is warranted. For example, when an external auditor is looking at internal controls, it would be fully appropriate to reveal all the roles and responsibilities documentation that your organization has developed. Likewise, if your organization is going through negotiations for a merger, and the other firm is doing its so-called "due diligence process," then all the detailed roles and responsibilities documentation

should be revealed. Nonetheless, for these and other known recipients with a genuine need to know, it is still advisable to get a signed confidentiality agreement.

So what about the establishment of a standard job title and a standard set of duties? Don't hold your breath... it may be a long ways off. In the meanwhile expect considerable divergence in both job titles and job duties from one information security job to another. While you might want to disclose your job description to somebody you met at a professional association meeting or a conference, in order to get feedback and ideas, in general don't expect to get much help by looking at other practitioners' job descriptions. While it can provide a few new ideas, there will be many things in another organization's documentation which do not apply to your organization, and many other important things that are relevant to your organization that will not be mentioned. It is in fact this inconsistency between organizations that the author kept in mind when he wrote this book. To allow you to quickly prepare just the documentation you need, this book provides several exhaustive lists of potential roles and responsibilities, allowing you to simply pick and choose those ideas applicable to your organization.

Appendix H ROLE BASED ACCESS CONTROL

Costs And Benefits

With so many users of information systems these days, the access control privilege assignment and update tasks performed by Systems Administrators and Security Administrators are becoming quite complex, time consuming, and error-prone. In many cases, these tasks are performed on an individual-by-individual basis, where the Administrator defines and updates privileges using access control lists (ACLs). These lists define what system resources a particular user will be permitted to use, and in what way the user will be able to use these resources. For example, a specific ACL may state that user Charles Wood is granted the right to access the customer database, including viewing, updating, and deleting customer records.

To reduce costs, reduce error rates, and increase responsiveness, many organizations are moving instead to what is called role based access control (RBAC). With the RBAC features found in access control software now offered by a large number of vendors, users can be linked to role profiles (sometimes called templates), and role profiles can be linked to privileges to access certain system resources. So, in general terms, a user may be allowed to access certain system resources only if his or her role profile allows this. As an example of this, consider a commercial bank with many tellers. The system privileges of Tellers could be defined once and these privileges could then be set-up as a role profile. Specific users could then readily be linked with that profile, and thus receive the appropriate Teller system rights. This would eliminate the need for an Administrator to specifically grant a variety of rights to each and every teller. An Administrator would typically set-up other role profiles for a variety of different groups of workers such as Accounts Payable Clerks and Physical Security Guards.

One of the most compelling reasons to adopt RBAC involves standardization across an organization. With this approach, a standard set of privileges or rights is granted to all workers who fit into a specific job category. The establishment of a standardized approach for groups of people helps management to understand what they do when it comes to using computers and networks. This in turn is likely to get management thinking about security issues such as separation of duties and dual control (these issues are discussed in Chapter 20). This standardization also enables some important activities, which will be discussed further in the following section entitled Synergy With Clarified Roles & Responsibilities.

With RBAC, the privileges that were previously vested in a single person such as a Systems Administrator, can now be chopped into various sub-sets of privileges, and then assigned to a number of different people. For example, in the UNIX operating system, the systems privileges of a Systems Administrator with "super user" privileges are many and powerful. They typically include turn on/off logging, establish a new user-ID, and shut-down the system. To give all of these privileges to a single person increases the chances of significant errors, invites fraud and other abuses, and furthermore places the organization at grave risk of sabotage from that same person. With RBAC, super user privileges can be sliced into different role profiles, and then these can be given to a bunch of privileged users, thus implementing the notion of least privilege. This approach also overcomes the "all or nothing" inflexibility that operating-system-vendor-provided access control mechanisms previously required.

One of the areas where RBAC really shines is the hiring of a new employee. Because management has already approved a relevant role profile, an Administrator does not need to check with management before granting privileges to a new hire. Thus the traditional approval form with a manager's signature is not required for each user's change of status. The Administrator needs only to determine that the new user now falls into a certain group of people with a previously-approved role profile. This means that the time to establish new user-IDs can be significantly reduced. Likewise, an Administrator's handling of the changes in privileges, which are needed to reflect changes in the duties of existing workers, is expedited and simplified. For example, if a worker leaves on maternity leave, her privileges can be revoked, and immediately reassigned to another person, with only two commands. Likewise, if another individual is promoted from one department to another, two commands can be used, one to revoke the old privileges and one to enable the new privileges. As both these examples show, with the RBAC approach it is less likely that individual workers will continue to have enabled privileges left over from a previous job, and this in turn will reduce abuses and mistakes. Thus, with RBAC, Administrators will be less likely to create dangerous or incompatible combinations of access control privileges.

Because role based access controls are defined in terms of the jobs of specific workers, these access control privileges are readily mapped to job descriptions, committee charters, project team action plans, and other human resources management documents. The mapping of RBAC profiles to human resources documents allows managers and Administrators to think of system privileges in a manner which is more consistent with natural language. The closer the logical structure of access control rules mirrors the way that we think, the more likely it will be that access control privileges will be defined in a way that is consistent with management's intentions, and the more likely it will be that these access control privileges will be defined in a manner that is free from error.

The RBAC approach provides a simplified way to approach access control administration which overcomes some of the problems associated with historical approaches to access control. For example, RBAC is preferable to discretionary access control (DAC). DAC allows end users to determine what access control mechanisms will be applied to objects, such as files, which are under their control. Under a DAC system, a user may delegate privileges to another user without the involvement of an Administrator or a manager. Unfortunately, users most often do not own the information that they access, and the DAC approach thus runs the risk that end users will make access control privilege assignments which are not consistent with management's intentions. With DAC, the risk of user error is also particularly high if the users are not well trained in the access control area. (The concept of information ownership is taken up at length in Chapter 15).

RBAC is also preferable to another historical approach called mandatory access control (MAC). With this approach policies about access rights define whether a user will be allowed to access a certain object, such as a database. These policies assign a data sensitivity classification label to the object, and take into consideration the clearance level of the user. Thus a user would be able to access a database which is labeled confidential if he or she had been previously cleared to access information which was classified at the confidential level. The MAC approach may be appropriate in those environments where users are given clearance levels, and where all system-resident objects likewise have machine-address-able labels. Practically speaking, this means that this approach is most often used in military environments,

and it also means that special operating systems or additional security software is necessary because most popular commercial operating systems do not incorporate a system-wide security classification label mechanism. In contrast, RBAC is more responsive to the common organizational structures found today, as well as now supported by common systems software including operating systems and database management systems.

Since the use of RBAC simplifies access control administration, the job of the Administrator, after role profiles are established, is primarily enabling and disabling certain roles for certain individuals. This activity requires significantly less technical understanding and knowledge, and thus could be performed by a less experienced person within an information security group. Likewise, it could be readily delegated to other individuals outside an information security group, such as Local Information Security Coordinators. The duties of Local Information Security Coordinators are discussed in Chapter 12.

While the initial effort to define role profiles can be significant, in the long run RBAC promises to significantly reduce both Security Administrator and Systems Administrator staff size because it simplifies their activities. To the extent that Help Desk staff are also involved in access control administration, their numbers may also be reduced in those organizations who have adopted RBAC. What's more, the people performing these duties don't need to be as technical as Systems Administrators and Security Administrators, and can thus be lower paid workers.

Many people don't appreciate that as the number of users, and the number of information systems resources that need access controls, are both increasing linearly, the combination of the two causes the number of ACLs to increase exponentially. The incredible number of needed ACLs in many cases means that unused user-IDs proliferate and are not turned off when they should be, and that the review of the logical consistency of ACLs is in most cases an impractical endeavor. Because it can significantly rationalize and simplify access control administration activities, RBAC also brings with it the feasibility of performing audits and management reviews to make sure that privileges have been established correctly. For firms listed on public stock exchanges in the United States, this positive affirmation that internal controls have indeed been set-up properly, and continue to operate propertly, is now required by a law called the Sarbanes Oxley Act. In the future, the law in many other countries is expected to likewise require management to produce some sort of a official statement affirming that internal controls are reliable, that the continue to be in effect, and have been established according to management's intentions.

Synergy With Clarified Roles And Responsibilities

The more clearly an organization has specified roles and responsibilities in the form of job descriptions, the more clearly it understands what particular jobs involve. This understanding in turn allows workers at that organization to more clearly define a set of system privileges, using the notion of RBAC, which accurately reflects the tasks performed by workers. If the organization doesn't understand what people in a particular job actually do, then it will be difficult if not impossible to create a profile to use in RBAC access control administration.

The opposite is also true. The more clearly an organization has defined role based access controls, the more clearly management has thought about which jobs should get which system privileges. This information in turn can be used to document clear job descriptions, if clear job descriptions have not already been prepared. Previous work on RBAC will also assist you in your efforts to clarify the specific information security privileges that should be granted to specific people. This effort needs to be approached in a coordinated manner so that you can see how people work together, how they check each other's work, how they prevent others from abusing their privileges, etc. To assist with this task, you may wish to read about the need to define a coordinated team of people who work on information security. This matter is discussed at length in Chapter 3.

Before an organization can implement a RBAC approach, it will need to thoroughly research the activities of the involved workers. Only when management understands what these workers do with respect to information systems, can it be in a position to rationally make allocations of appropriate access control rights. It is this investigation process which provides a great opportunity for you to initiate an information security roles and responsibilities clarification project. If management at your organization is currently tending in the direction of adopting a RBAC approach, you should be sure to talk about an information security roles and responsibilities clarification project to be performed at the same time. Not only will both projects synergistically support each other, as mentioned in the previous two paragraphs, but both projects will act as double checks on each other, helping to ensure that the work is done consistently, correctly, and completely.

Because the development of job descriptions and the establishment of RBAC access control profiles are often done by different people, it is easy for these lists of tasks and privileges to be unsynchronized, incomplete, and contradictory. To the extent that you can coordinate the update and clarification of these two lists, you will be able to identify excessive privileges that have been granted in the past, or that may still be enabled. To the extent that you can coordinate these two lists, you will be able to identify additional privileges that need to be granted to present and future users. Coordination will additionally pay-off with a deeper understanding of separation of duties, dual control, management review and approval mechanisms, time/date windows in which certain activities can be performed, technical staff member cross-training, and critical staff backup and relief (these matters are further discussed in Chapter 20). This deeper understanding will in turn allow you to see inconsistencies, redundancies, incompletions, and other problems with the information systems security control structure.

Expected Future Developments

With RBAC, users may have more than one role, and thus more than one profile defining the access controls to be employed. For example, a Systems Developer could have rights to create and run application programs on a development system, and that would be part of one profile. He may also sit on an internal committee investigating the ways that the organization could normalize and standardize data definitions. For that role, he may have a profile which gives him rights to access a corporate data dictionary. In the future, commercial products will provide expert systems which will examine the compatibility of different profiles granted to a certain user. Using this same example, such an expert system could inform a Security Administrator or a Systems Administrator if these two roles are incompatible, if they present a conflict of interest, if they might allow a fraud to take place, if they allow a user to approve his or her own work, etc. This logical check on the consistency of roles granted to users can only come about when roles and associated profiles are defined with a level of specificity and consistency that allows this type of analysis.

The use of RBAC also opens up some very interesting new concepts which could not have been implemented in the age of manual systems. One of these involves the traditional notion of static separation of duties (SDOD). With this control measure, an individual is prohibited from having two incompatible roles. Thus, using RBAC, a user would not be able to initiate a purchase order and also approve purchase orders, since these tasks would be in separate role profiles. With RBAC, a filter can be used to prevent an Administrator from assigning to a certain user both of these incompatible role profiles. Unlike the expert systems mentioned in the prior paragraph, this preventive filter is easy to build, and it would avoid problems instead of later detecting the conditions which might lead to problems. In comparison, with the traditional ACL approach, there is typically no such filter, and even if it could be built on a custom basis, it is likely to be way too complex and convoluted to be practical. A more complete discussion of SDOD can be found in Chapter 20.

Another of these new concepts is called dynamic separation of duties (DSOD). DSOD involves those cases where users have two potentially conflicting roles. For example, in a bank, an individual could be both a teller and a branch vice president. Before you object, consider how many small organizations, as well as organizations strapped for budget, are forced to have a single person play several roles, and how sometimes these roles are incompatible. With RBAC a specific user, although they may have been assigned the role profiles for both roles, cannot be both of these roles at the same time. Thus at the bank, this individual cannot simultaneously be using a computer system as both a branch vice president and a teller. The individual can log-in as either one of them, but not both at the same time. This allows the bank to adopt certain control measures such as a mechanism which requires that a teller transaction be completed and submitted before it will be accepted for processing, thus closing a window of opportunity for fraud that otherwise could have allowed a vice president to alter a pending transaction to correct an error. Although this concept is still new, you will probably be hearing a lot about it in the years ahead.

The prospect of tightly-integrating what used to be human resources database information (roles and responsibilities information) with what used to be information security database information (access control privileges information) provides a variety of important potential future benefits. Because RBAC brings these two types of information together, new types of databases, linked databases, or directories can be created. Thus an entry regarding the status of a worker (hired, fired, promoted, leave of absence, etc.)

can be made in a human resources database, and a related message can then be automatically sent to an access control database, which in turn can automatically send a message to multiple operating systems, database management systems, firewalls, communications gateways, etc. The total automated integration of these two different types of information is already starting to allow, and will soon allow to a much greater degree, the following benefits: (a) immediate turn-on of all privileges necessary for a certain type of worker to do his or her job, across multiple operating systems, databases, applications, etc., (b) immediate and synchronized termination of all system privileges across the organization, as soon as a worker no longer needs these privileges, (c) consistent shut-off of worker privileges at a predetermined future time to synchronize a duress termination, a layoff, or some other tense or forced change in employment status, and (d) consistent integration of these two types of data so that they do not go out of synch with each other.

The next step beyond the integration of the two different types of information discussed in the previous paragraph is the integration of these types of information with other information security information. Most often this takes place in an Enterprise Security Management (ESM) system, such as those commercial products now offered by various vendors. Many ESMs bring all this information together via the Lightweight Directory Access Protocol (LDAP). This centralized collection of information security information allows organizations to support single sign-on (SSO) systems through a centralized gateway. Besides allowing an organization to centrally administer all user authentication and user privilege assignment activities, an ESM can be used to consistently enforce security policies such as time of day access restrictions. This type of centralized access control system can also be called by applications, database management systems, systems software, and the like via standardized interfaces. These interfaces eliminate the need for comparable access control mechanisms to be built into all these different types of software. The centralized collection of information also enables a single console which can support 24 X 7 X 365 human monitoring of security events in real-time (these events may be application system events, operating system events, firewall events, network events, etc.).

Such a centralized ESM system can also support the integration of various information security products such as special logging systems (such as those which detect file modifications), intrusion detection systems (IDSs), content management systems, web surfing filtering systems, and vulnerability identification systems. This information integration and information security product centralization in turn will be the source of many new capabilities in the years ahead, such as expert systems which intelligently advise organizations on what to do next in the midst of an attack.

Appendix I   ABOUT THE AUTHOR

Based in the San Francisco Bay Area, Charles Cresson Wood is an independent information security consultant, researcher, and author. As part of his consulting work, he prepares and reviews standards, architectures, policies, codes of conduct, procedures, budgets, action plans, mission statements, job descriptions, and other parts of an organizational infrastructure to support information security. He also performs risk assessments and designs custom information security solutions.

Working in the field full-time since 1979, he has been a computer security management consultant at SRI International (formerly Stanford Research Institute) and lead data communications security consultant at the Bank of America. He has done information security consulting work with over 120 organizations, mainly in banking, telecommunications, and high technology. Many of his clients are Fortune 500 companies. His consulting projects have taken him to Australia, Austria, Belgium, Brazil, Canada, England, Finland, France, Holland, Ireland, Italy, Japan, Norway, Portugal, Saudi Arabia, South Africa, and Sweden.

Mr. Wood has delivered over 125 information security presentations at various conferences; he has also been a keynote speaker at several of these same conferences. He has been quoted as an expert in publications such as Business Week, Computerworld, Information Week, LA Times, PC Week, The Wall Street Journal, and Time. In 1996 he received the Lifetime Achievement Award from the Computer Security Institute (San Francisco) for "sincere dedication to the computer security profession."

Mr. Wood is the Senior North American Editor for the technical journals Computers & Security and Computer Fraud and Security Bulletin. For the last eleven years he has written a monthly information security policies column for Computer Security Alert. He has published over 300 technical articles and five other books dealing with information security. His best selling book is entitled *Information Security Policies Made Easy.* Mr. Wood's work has been or is now being translated into a number of foreign languages including Brazilian Portuguese, Finnish, French, Japanese, Hebrew, Portuguese, Spanish, and Swedish.

Mr. Wood holds an MBA in financial information systems and a BSE in accounting, both from the Wharton School at the University of Pennsylvania. He also holds an MSE degree in computer science from the Moore School of Engineering at the same University (birthplace of the ENIAC, the world's first general purpose electronic computer). In addition to passing the Certified Public Accountant (CPA) exam, he is a Certified Information Systems Auditor (CISA), a Certified Information Security Manager (CISM) and a Certified Information Systems Security Professional (CISSP).

Mr. Wood can be reached directly at ccwood@ix.netcom.com.

Appendix J SOURCES AND REFERENCES

Abrams, M., and Podell, H., *Managing Information Security, Computer Education*, 1991 [out of print]

Anderson, Larry, "*CSO To The Rescue?*," Access Control & Security Systems, 1 June 2002

Alkemi, A., *Computer Security Manager*, Elsevier Science, 1989

Allen, Julia H, *What's My Role In Information Survivability? Why Should I Care?*, slides from a presentation published by the CERT Coordination Center, Carnegie-Mellon University, Pittsburgh, Pennsylvania, 2002

Anonymous, *A Guide To Understanding Information System Security Officer Responsibilities For Automated Information Systems*, Diane Publishing, 1995 [out of print, prepared by the US National Computer Security Center (NCSC), document NCSC-TG-027]

Anonymous, *Board Briefing On IT Governance And Information Security Governance: Guidance For Boards Of Directors And Executive Management, IT Governance Institute, Information Systems Audit & Control Association (ISACA)*, 2001 [free download at www.itgovernance.org/resources.htm]

Anonymous, *COBIT: Governance, Control, And Audit For Information And Related Technology, Information Systems Audit & Control Association (ISACA)*, third edition, 2000

Anonymous, *Code Of Practice For Information Security Management, British Standard 7799*, British Standards Institute, 1997 [now incorporated into ISO 17799 standard]

Anonymous, *Computers - Crimes, Clues & Controls: A Management Guide*, Diane Publishing, 1993

Anonymous, *Information Security Governance: Governance For Boards Of Directors And Executive Management*, IT Governance Institute, Information Systems Audit And Control Foundation, 2003

Anonymous, "More Firms Add Security Managers," *Communications Week*, 14 April 1997

Anonymous, "Preparation And Collaboration Keys To Improving Security, According To CSC; Company Identifies Best Ways To Protect People, Information, And Infrastructure," *PR Newswire*, 10 June 2002

Anonymous, *Principles Of Corporate Governance, Organization for Economic Co-operation & Development (OECD)*, 1999 [includes discussion of Board responsibilities]

Anonymous, "Privacy: HR's New Minefield," *HR Focus*, pp. 1-5, April 2001 [discusses Chief Privacy Officers]

Anonymous, "Proposed: A Protection Committee At Management Level," *Security Management Bulletin*, no. 2215, 10 August 1993

Anonymous, "The Hot Seat - These Days, All Eyes Are On The Chairman Of The Audit Committee," *The Wall Street Journal*, p. R4, 24 February 2003

Anonymous, "Who Is The Chief Security Officer?," *CSO Magazine*, 20 June 2002

Armstrong, Illena, "Evolving A Role In Infosecurity," *SC Magazine*, pp. 30-31, March 2003

Attaway, Morris C., Sr., "What Every Auditor Needs To Know About E-Commerce Outsourcing," *Internal Auditor*, pp. 48- 55, June 2000

Auer, Joe, "Don't Allow Vendor Disappearing Acts," *Computerworld*, 29 January 2001 [deals with outsourcing vendor agreements]

Badenhorst, Karin P., Eloff, Jan H. P., "Framework of a Methodology for the Life Cycle of Computer Security in an Organization," *Computers & Security*, vol. 8, no. 5, pp. 433-442, August 1989

Barnes, Brooks, "Job Hunt - Corporate Cybercop," *Newsday*, 18 August 1996

Barbier, Etienne, "Audit Committes A La Francaise," *Internal Auditor*, June 1998

Beane, William F., "Computer Security: Who's In Charge?," *Security World*, October 1984

Bernard, Ray, "Computer Security: Nerd, Technie, Specialist, Guru or Expert Which Do You Need?," *Security Technology & Design*, pp. 76, 78-79, April 1997

Bernstein, David S., "Certification: For Professionals Only," *InfoSecurity News*, pp. 21-22, March/April 1997

Borck, James R., "Security On A Shoestring Budget," *InfoWorld*, pp. 52-53, 19 November 2001

Botha, R.A., and J.H.P. Eloff, "Separation Of Duties For Access Control Enforcement In Workflow Environments," I*BM Systems Journal*, vol. 40, no. 3, pp. 666-682, 2001

Bound, William A. J., "Discussing Security with Top Management," *Computers & Security*, vol. 7, no. 2, pp. 129-130, April 1988

Briney, Andrew, "2003: Another Year Of Belt Tightening - InfoSecurity Budgets Are Increasing But At A Far Slower Rate Than Many People Assume," *InfoSecurity Magazine*, March 2003

Briney, Andrew, and Frank Prince, "Survey Overview: Does Size Matter?," *InfoSecurity Magazine*, pp. 36-39, September 2002 [covers organizational size and information security budget]

Briney, Andrew, and Frank Prince, "Training Remains The Weakest Link - Large Organizations Have People Problems At All Levels," *InfoSecurity Magazine*, September 2002

Brocaglia, J., D. Foote, T. Lenzner, L. Kushner, L. Regener, and A. Briney, "Infosec Job Market Files," *Information Security Magazine*, January 2001

Brocaglia, Joyce, "Career Corner - The CISO," *ISSA Password*, p. 12, August 2002

Buss, Martin D. J., and Lynn M. Salerno, "Common Sense And Computer Security," *Harvard Business Review*, March/April 1984

Caelli, William J., Longley, Dennis, and Shain, M., *Information Security For Managers*, Groves Dictionaries, 1989 [out of print]

Cale, Doug, "Partners Share Responsibility For Marketplace Security: B-to-B Exchanges Must Establish Security Policies And Protocols That Everyone Agrees On," *Information Week*, 20 November 2000

Campbell, Robert P., "Structuring The Information Security Program," *Data Security Management*, Auerbach Publications, 1992

Carr, Kathleen, and Daintry Duffy, "CSOs For Hire," *CSO Magazine*, January 2003

Carroll, Glen, and Michael Hannon, *Organizations In Industry: Strategy, Structure & Selection*, Oxford University Press, 1995

Ceron, Gaston F., "Staying Focused: Corporate Governance May Be Everybody's Responsibility, But At Some Companies, One Person Has More Responsibility," *The Wall Street Journal*, pp. R7 & R11, 24 February 2003

Chapman, Thomas F., "Privacy & Security In Tomorrow's Global Marketplace," *Vital Speeches Of The Day*, 1 February 1999 (delivered to the Privacy & American Business 5th Annual National Conference held on 2 December 1999) [deals with words in user job descriptions dealing with privacy protection]

Christmas, P., *Network Security Manager*, Elsevier Science Publishers, 1996

Computer Security Institute Advisory Council, "Where Should Information Security Report?," *Computer Security Journal*, vol. XIII, no. 1, Spring 1997

Connally, P.J., "IT Security: Keep It At Home Or Take It Outside?," *Computerworld*, p. 48, 12 February 2001

Copeland, Lee, "Users Look For Protection Against Technology Vendor Flameouts," *Computerworld*, p. 19, 19 November 2001

Dale, Ernest, *Management: Theory And Practice* (4th Edition), McGraw-Hill, 1978

Deloitte & Touche, *Internal Audit: The Nature Of The Transition*, 1998 [defines changing role of internal auditors]

Dean, Joshua, "Report Stresses Management's Role In Boosting Cybersecurity," *Govexec.com*, 14 February 2002

Degner, Jim, "Writing Job Descriptions That Work," *Credit Union Executive*, vol. 35, p. 13, 21 November 1995

DeMaio, Harry B., *Information Protection And Other Unnatural Acts: Every Manager's Guide To Keeping Vital Computer Data Safe And Sound*, Amacom Press, 1992

Dhillon, Gurpeet, and James Backhouse, *Information Security: A Management Challenge*, Inter Thompson Press, 1997

Drucker, Peter F., "Management's New Paradigms," *Forbes*, 5 October 1998 [addresses number of levels in management hierarchy]

Drucker, Peter F., *Management: Tasks, Responsibilities, & Practices*, Harper & Row, 1973 [classic guide to organizational design]

Drucker, Peter F., *The Practice Of Management*, Harper & Row, 1954 [classic guide to organizational design]

Dush, Julekha, "Schools Push Soft Skills For InfoSecurity Majors," *Computerworld*, p. 24, 5 February 2001

Ecklund, Eileen, "Protecting Data Is A Demanding But Secure Career," *Infoworld*, 7 September 1998

Evans, Donald F., "Cooperation In Information Management," *Records Management Quarterly*, p. 32, October 1998 [discusses role of records management function]

Farrow, Rik, "Do Managed Security Services Work?," *Computer Security Alert*, pp. 1, 11-12, June 2002 [discusses people side of intrusion detection system management]

Ferraiolo, David, and Rick Kuhn, "An Introduction To Role-Based Access Control," *NIST/ISL Bulletin* (US National Institute for Standards and Technology/ Information Security Lab), December 1995

Fine, Leonard H., *Computer Security: Handbook For Management*, Trafalgar, 1984 [out of print]

Fitzgerald, Michael, "All Over The Map - Where Does Security Fit Into The Organization Chart?," *CIO Magazine*, June 2003

Flash, Cynthia, "Rise Of The Chief Security Officer," *Enterprise*, 25 March 2002

Freeman, Edward H., "Director Liability In Computer Negligence Cases," *Information Systems Security*, Auerbach Publications, Spring 2000

Frenton, Stacey, and Wei Kuan Lum, *Access Granted: Decrypting Opportunities In Information Security*, NOVA Workforce Publications, 2003

Fried, Louis, "Assigning Responsibility For Security In Distributed And Outsourced Environments," *Data Security Management*, Auerbach Publications, 1993

Fried, Louis, "Distributed Information Security - Responsibility Assignments And Costs," *Information Systems Management*, vol. 10, no. 3, Summer 1993

Fonseca, Brian, "Securing ASP Customers," *InfoWorld*, p. 2, 25 February 2002

Foote, David, "Companies Need Security Pros With More Varied Skills," *Computerworld*, 9 July 2001

Foote, David, "Director, Information Security," *PC Week*, p. 68, 24 January 2000

Foote, David, "Info Security Job Book Inevitable," *Computerworld*, 2 September 2002

Foote, David, "Security Still Pays," *Information Security*, pp. 42-46, August 2002 [discusses professional certifications most recognized by the marketplace]

Forcht, Karen A., *Computer Security Management*, Boyd & Fraser, 1994

Galbraith, Jay, *Designing Complex Organizations*, Addison-Wesley, 1973

Galbraith, Jay, *Organizational Design*, Addison-Wesley, 1977

Galvin, Peter Baer, "The Solaris Companion: Role-Based Access Control," *Unix Review*, September 2001

Gaskin, James, *Corporate Politics & The Internet*, Prentice-Hall, 1996

Gilbert, Dennis, and Nickilyn Lynch, *Sample Statements Of Work For Federal Computer Security Services: For Us In-House Or Contracting Out*, US Department Of Commerce, National Institute Of Standards And Technology, 1991

Gillin, Donna L., "Do You Need A Privacy Officer?," *Marketing Research*, p. 6, Spring 2002

Greenia, Mark W., *Security In Computing: A Sourcebook For Security Officers & Managers*, Lexikon Services, 1990 [out of print]

Greenfield, David, "On The Money? Managed Security Services Mean Cost Savings, But Do They Also Come With Security Headaches On The Side?," *Network Magazine*, pp. 62-64, 66, May 2001

Hagland, Mark, "The Elusive CPO [Chief Privacy Officer]," *Healthcare Informatics*, July 2001

Hayes, Frank, "A Light On ASPs," *Computerworld*, p. 62, 20 August 2001 [discusses risks of outsourcing]

Hayes, Mary, "Impact Player," *Information Week*, 25 February 2002 [discusses role of Chief Information Security Officer]

Hayes, Mary, "Where The Chief Security Officer Belongs," *Information Week*, 25 February 2002 [discusses reporting relationships]

Herberger, Carl, "Integrating Business Continuity And Information Security," *Contingency Planning & Management*, pp. 28-32, July/August 2002

Hill, Lisa B., and J. Michael Pemberton, "Information Security: An Overview And Resource Guide For Information Managers," *Records Management Quarterly*, pp. 14-25, January 1995

Homer, Judy B., "The CSO: A Must Hire," *CIO Magazine*, 1 June 2002

Hopkins, Jim, "Demand Leaps For Chief Security Officers," *USA Today*, 29 Oct 2001

Information Security Forum, *The Forum's Standard Of Good Practice: The Standard For Information Security*, November 2001 [available at www.isfsecuritystandard.com/index_ns.htm]

Isaacson, Gerald I., *MIS Information Security Resource Manual*, MIS Training Institute, 1986

International Information Security Foundation (I2SF), *Generally Accepted Information Security Principles*, exposure draft 2, 1997 [available for free at http://web.mit.edu/security/www/gassp1.html]

International Standards Organization (ISO), ISO/IEC 17799: *Information Technology Code Of Practices For Information Security Management*, First Edition, December 2001 [see www.iso.ch]

Internet Security Alliance, *Commonsense Guide For Senior Managers: Top Ten Recommended Information Security Practices*, Internet Security Alliance, 1st Edition, July 2002

Isaacs, Nora, "Career Planning Guide: Part One," *Infoworld*, p.89, 8 March 1999 [discusses technical/management career options for IT professionals]

Jacques, Elliott, and Stephen D. Clement, *Executive Leadership: A Practical Guide To Managing Complexity*, Cason Hall & Co., 1994

James, Geoffrey, "How Companies Court Disaster In Outsourcing Deals," *Computerworld*, p. 41, 30 October 2002

James, Natalie, "(Still) At Your Service: Managed Security," *Information Security*, pp. 48-57, August 2002 [deals with MSSPs]

Jarvis, Steve, "C-Level Rises: New Exec Job Surfaces," *Marketing News*, vol. 35, issue 5, 26 February 2001 [discusses Chief Privacy Officer]

Joss, Molly, "Do You Need A CPO? Internet Privacy Issues Can Make Or Break Your Company," *Computer User*, June 2001

Kabay, M.E., and Philip S. Holt, "Breaking Into Infosec," *Information Security,* May 2001

Kabay, M.E., "Personnel And Security: Separation Of Duties," *Network World Fusion,* 2000, archived at http://www.nwfusion.com/newsletters/sec/2000/0612sec2.html

Kelly, Beckie, "New Officers Prepare To Protect Privacy: Privacy Officers Describe How They're Taking On The Role And Learning To Prioritize Tasks," *Health & Data Management,* August 2001

Kiefer, Kimberly B., and Randy V. Sabett, "Am I Liable?," *CISO Magazine,* vol. 1, no. 1, 2002

Kovacich, Gerald, "Establishing A Network Security Programme," *Computers & Security,* vol. 15 (1996), no. 6, pp. 486-498

Kovacich, Gerald, "Establishing An Information Systems Security Organization (ISSO)," *Computers & Security,* vol. 17, no. 7, pp. 600-612, 1998

Kovacich, Gerald L., *Information Systems Security Officer's Guide,* Butterworth Heinemann Publishers, 1998

Krause, Micki, "Chief Security Officer (CSO) Training Requires Range Of Skills," *Information Security,* March 2001

Krogstad, Jack L., Anthony J. Ridley, and Larry E. Rittenberg, "Where We're Going," *Internal Auditor,* October 1999 [about the future of the Internal Auditing profession including responsibilities]

Kuykendall, Lavonne, "Privacy Officers Say Role Keeps On Growing," *American Banker,* pp. 1-2, 28 August 2001

Lanz, Joel, and Eric B. Barr, "Managing The Risks In Information Technology Outsourcing," *Bank Accounting & Finance,* Summer 2000

Laurence, P.A., and R.A. Lee, *Insight Into Management,* 2nd Edition, Oxford Science, 1989 [deals with organizational design]

Leary, Mark, "The InfoSec Structure Within An Organization," *Password (ISSA),* pp. 1, 4-5, September/October 1999

Lee, Chi-Lin, "A Study Of Financial Institution's Information Security: Factors That Influence Employee's Willingness To Adhere To Information Security Procedures," *a DBA doctoral dissertation,* Golden Gate University, San Francisco, California, granted 1995

Levinson, Meridith, "Do Diligence," *CIO Magazine,* 1 July 2001 [about outsourcing deals, see http://www.cio.com/archive/070101/vet.html]

Lowenthal, Jeffrey N., *Reengineering The Organization: A Step-By-Step Approach To Corporate Revitalization,* ASQC Quality Press, 1994

Madron, Thomas W., *Network Security In The Nineties: Issues & Solutions For Managers,* Wiley, 1992

Maglitta, Joseph, and Mehler, Mark, "Executive Report-Power Shifts-The New Centralization," *Computerworld,* pp. 85-87, 27 April 1992

Mearian, Lucas, "Banks Pick Up Pace Of IT Outsourcing," *Computerworld,* p. 6, 6 January 2003

Melymuka, Kathleen, "Bench Strength: How And Why To Develop An IT Succession Plan," *Computerworld,* p. 44, 28 October 2002

Melymuka, Kathleen, "The Evolution Of The IT Leader," *Computerworld,* p. 28, 30 September 2002

Melymuka, Kathleen, "Who's In The House? How to Conduct An IT Skills Assessment," *Computerworld,* p. 46, 7 October 2002

Mansfield, Roger, *Company Strategy And Organizational Design,* St. Martin's Press, 1986

Messmer, Ellen, "Role-Based Access Control On A Roll," *Network World,* 30 July 2001

McClelland, Samuel B., *Organizational Needs Assessments: Design, Facilitation, and Analysis,* Quorum Books, 1995

McNeil, Michael, "Integrating Privacy And Data Security: Creating A Culture Of Solutions," *Password (ISSA),* pp. 3-5, May 2002 [covers role of Chief Privacy Officer]

Moulton, Rolf T., *Strategies And Techniques For Preventing Data Loss Or Theft*, Prentice Hall, 1986

Murphy, Bruce, "Beyond The Figurehead Façade," *Security Management*, July 2001 [deals with reporting relationships for information security]

Nadler, David, Gerstein, Marc, and Shaw, Robert, *Organizational Architecture: Designs For Changing Organizations*, Bass Publishers, 1992

Nakatani, Iwao, "How Competitive Are We?," *World Press Review*, August 1988, p. 64 [addresses organizational unit coordination]

O'Farrell, Neal, "Employees: Your Best Defense, Or Your Greatest Vulnerability?," *SearchSecurity*, 21 September 2001, archived at http://searchsecurity.techtarget.com/originalContent/0,289142,sid14_gci771517,00.html

Office of Management and Budget (OMB), *Circular A-130: Management Of Federal Information Resources (US Government)*, 23 October 2000 [covers the ways to drive security responsibilities down to users and managers], archived at http://csrc.nist.gov/secplcy/a130.txt

Oppenheimer, David, Wagner, Avid, and Crabb, Michele D., *System Security: A Management Perspective*, USENIX Association, 1997

Orwall, Bruce, "Hiring A Hacker Brings Headache To A Security-Card Maker," p. B1, *The Wall Street Journal*, 9 October 2002

Osmanoglu, T. Ertem, and John R. Schramm, "ASP Security," *Information Security Magazine*, October 2001 [about Application Service Provider outsourcing]

Paller, Alan, "How Information Security Officers Can Be Successful," *Computerworld*, p. 32, 15 May 2000

Palmer, Ian, *Computer Security Risk Management*, Van Nostrand Reinhold, 1990

Parker, Donn B., *A Manager's Guide To Computer Security*, Prentice-Hall, 1983

Parker, Donn B., "Security Motivation, The Mother Of All Controls, Must Precede Awareness," *Computer Security Journal*, vol. XV, no. 4, pp. 15-23, 1999

Peltier, Tom, "Information Security Fundamentals," *CSI [Computer Security Institute] Conference Proceedings*, February 1998

Peltier, Tom, "Who Should The Information Protection Staff Report To?," *Computer Security Alert*, no. 131, February 1994

Peltier, Tom, "Where Should Information Protection Report?," *Computer Security Alert*, November 1997, archived on http://www.gocsi.com/infopro.htm

Perry, William E., *Management Strategies For Computer Security*, Butterworth-Heinemann, 1985 [out of print]

Peters, Anthony J., "Responsibility For Security Rests With Head Of Agency," *Government Computer News*, 18 December 1987

Pfeffer, Jeffrey, *Organizations And Organizational Theory*, Putnam Publishing, 1982

Phelps, Norman, "Top Management's Role In Disaster Recovery Planning," *Data Processing & Communications Security*, vol. 10, no. 3, 1986

Pine, Evelyn, and Jeff Johnson, "Cyber-Responsibilities," *Computer Professionals For Social Responsibility Newsletter*, vol. 16, no. 3, Summer 1998

Pinkerton Service Corporation, *Top Organizational & Professional Issues For Today's Security Director*, 1997 (survey results)

Plachy, Roger J., and Sandra J. Plachy, *Results-Oriented Job Descriptions: More Than 225 Models To Use Or Adapt With Guidelines For Creating Your Own*, AMACOM Press, 1993

Plachy, Sandra J., and Roger J. Plachy, *More Results-Oriented Job Descriptions To Use Or Adapt With Guidelines For Creating Your Own*, AMACOM Press, 1998

Porter, Doug, "Nothing Is Unsinkable," *Enterprise Systems Journal*, June 1998 [deals with integrated risk management approach to information security]

Power, Kevin, "OMB Will Put Responsibility For Systems Security Into Users' Hands," *Government Computer News*, 13 November 1995

Power, Richard, "How Should You Structure Your Information Protection Unit?," *Computer Security Alert*, April 1998

Power, Richard, "How To Structure Infosec," *Computer Security Alert*, pp. 1, 6 & 8, June 2000

Power, Richard, "Is Your Job Description Out-Of-Date?," *Computer Security Alert*, March 1997

Power, Richard, "Job Descriptions: Excuse Me, Could Anyone Tell Me What I Do?," *Computer Security Alert*, September 1998

Power, Richard, "Where Should Information Security Report?," *Computer Security Journal*, vol. XIII, no. 1., 1997

Prencipe, Loretta W., "C-Level Security," *InfoWorld*, pp. 48-49, 22 October 2001

Purdy, Stephen R., "Information Security: The Tools And Techniques Designed Specifically For The FM," *Today's Facility Manager*, March 2002 [deals with administration of security across departments]

Radcliff, Deborah, "Chief [In]Security Officer: The Exodus Of Some Renowned Security Executives Marks The Beginning Of Turbulent Times for CSOs," *Computerworld*, pp. 28-29, 10 June 2002

Radcliff, Deborah, "Choosing The Best Security Guards - IT Tackles Management Issues Via Service Providers," *Computerworld*, 12 August 2002 [discusses reliability of managed security service providers]

Radcliff, Deborah, "Secure With Your Security Pros," *Computerworld*, 21 August 2000 [discusses the importance of specialty information security certifications]

Radcliff, Deborah, "Security Under The Gun," *Computerworld*, p. 36, 3 June 2002 [discusses IT security job prospects]

Radcliff, Deborah, "Thinking ASP? Don't Forget Security!," p. 58, *Computerworld*, 30 October 2000

Radcliff, Deborah, "Wanted: Security Superman," *Computerworld*, pp. 62-65, 25 September 2000

Radcliff, Deborah, "Security Ambassadors: As Companies Increasingly Put Security In The Hands Of Systems Specialists, They Need IT Liaisons Who Can Translate The Needs Of Business," *Computerworld*, p. 36, 1 October 2001

Rhodes, Harry, "Establishing The Information Security Manager's Job," an article found within *Evolving HIM Careers: Seven Roles For The Future*, published by AHIMA, 1999

Ritson, Philip, "Accounting For Organizational Design," *Australian CPA*, vol. 70, no. 3, April 2000

Ryan, Chuck, "The New Security Pro," *Computerworld*, 7 May 2001

Robbins, Stephen P., *Organizational Theory - Structure, Design, And Applications*, Third Edition, Prentice-Hall, 1990

Ruthberg, Zella, and Tipton, Harold F., *Handbook Of Information Security Management*, Warren Gorham & Lamont, 1993

Saita, Anne, "CISO Strategies: Turnover At The Top," pp. 63-68, *Information Security Magazine*, June 2003

Scalet, Sarah D., "Another Chair At The Table," *CIO*, 9 August 2001 [about Chief Security Officers]

Schneier, Bruce, "Outsourcing Security," *Password (ISSA)*, pp. 4-6, February 2002

Schreider, Tari, "White Paper: The Legal Issues Of Disaster Recovery Planning," *Disaster Recovery Journal*, April-May-June 1996 [includes citations and a discusssion of precedents that could help sell a roles and responsibilities project to management]

Schweitzer, James A., *Protecting Business Information: A Manager's Guide*, Butterworth-Heinemann, 1995

Serpico, Philip A., "What Is Security's Duty To Report?," *Security Management*, pp. 121-122, March 1997

Shachtman, Noah, "Hackers Being Jobbed Out Of Work," *Wired News*, 30 August 2002

Shapiro, Andrew, *The Control Revolution: How The Internet Is Putting Individuals In Charge And Changing The World We Know*, Security Foundation, 1999

Sherwood, John, "Managing Security For Outsourcing Contracts," *Proceedings Of The COMPSEC97 Conference* (London, England), Elsevier Advanced Technology, 1997

Smith, Martin R., *Commonsense Computer Security: Your Practical Guide To Information Protection*, McGraw-Hill, 1993

Spangler, Todd, "Home Is Where The Hack Is," *Inter@active Week*, 10 April 2000 [discusses vendor security responsibility for DSL and cable modem connections]

Spencer, Edward, "Anatomy Of A Security Professional," *Information Security*, August 2001

Straub, Detmar W., Jr., "Organizational Structuring Of The Computer Security Function," *Computers & Security*, vol. 7, no. 2, April 1988

Talbot, J. R., *Management Guide To Computer Security*, Halstead Publishers, 1985 [out of print]

Thibodeau, Patrick, "Feds Considering Terrorism Liability Protection For Vendors," *Computerworld*, p. 10, 16 September 2002 [covers information security vendor responsibility]

Thibodeau, Patrick, "Hearing Stresses Need For Federal CIO Post," *Computerworld*, p. 20, 18 September 2000 [discusses centralized organizational structure]

Thompson, David, "The Social Engineering Of Security," *eWeek*, 11 June 2001

Thompson, Victor, *Modern Organizations*, 2nd Edition, Random House, 1977 [mangement theory about organizational design]]

Thurman, Mathias, "I Hired A Hacker - A Security Manager's Confession," *Computerworld*, p. 50, 26 February 2001

Thurman, Mathias, "New Security Manager Starting At Ground Zero," *Computerworld*, p. 54, 19 February 2001

Thurman, Mathias, "Staff Resignations Put Security Ops In Triage," *Computerworld*, 4 July 2002

Thurman, Mathias, "Security Certification: It's Worth The Effort," *Computerworld*, p. 56, 5 November 2001

Tipton, Harold, and Elliott, Robert, *Data Security Management*, Warren Gorham & Lamont, 1992

Tipton, Harold, and Micki Krause, *Information Security Management*, 4th Edition, Auerbach, 2000

Tipton, Harold F., "Liability Of Corporate Officers For Security Problems," *Computer Security Journal*, vol. X., no. 1, pp. 59-69 (1991)

Tobias, Zachary, "The New Security Pro," *Computerworld*, 7 May 2001

Trombly, Maria, "New York Life Names Chief Privacy Officer," *Computerworld*, p. 10, 23 April 2001

Turnbull, Nigel, *Internal Control: Guidance For Directors On The Combined Code*, report prepared for Institute of Chartered Accountants in England and Wales (ICAEW), also known as the Turnbull Report, 1999 [includes discussion of responsibilities]

Ulfelder, Steve, "Oh No, Not Another O!," *CIO Magazine*, 15 January 2001 [about Chief Privacy Officers]

United States Census Bureau, "North American Industry Classification System (NCICS), Sector 54: Professional, Scientific, And Technical Services," *2002 Economic Census* [includes roles for information security, breaking them down into advisor/strategist, designer, operator/attendant, and examiner]

Vaas, Lisa, "Finding Pros For IT Security: E-Biz Demand For Experts Far Exceeds Supply," *E-Week*, p. 54, 11 Jund 2001

Van Tassel, D., *Computer Security Management*, Prentice-Hall, 1981 [out of print]

Varon, Elana, "Responsibilities," *Chief Information Officer*, vol. 15, no. 10, 1 March 2002

Verton, Dan, "Corporate Security Still Lacks Focus Two Years After 9/11: Survey Finds That Most Companies Have Avoided Centralized Security Oversight," *Computerworld*, p. 13, 21 July 2003

Verton, Dan, "Insider Monitoring Seen As Next Wave In IT Security," *Computerworld*, p. 33, 19 March 2001 [deals with reliance on insiders and appropriate job duties]

Vijayan, Jaikumar, "Build A Response Team," *Computerworld*, p. 32, 15 July 2002

Vijayan, Jaikumar, "Downsizings Leave Firms Vulnerable To Digital Attacks," *Computerworld*, 25 June 2001

Vijayan, Jaikumar, "IT Security Destined For The Courtroom," *Computerworld*, 21 May 2001 [explores management liability for insufficient infrastructure]

Vijayan, Jaikumar, "Outsource Security With Care, Conference Attendees Warn," *Computerworld*, p. 8, 10 December 2001

Vlk, Liliana, "Shadow Management: United Stationers Supply Company Has Been Outsourcing Its Security Management Since 1991," *Security Magazine*, October 2000

von Simson, Ernest M., "The Centrally Decentralized IS Organization," *Harvard Business Review*, pp. 158-162, July-August 1990

Von Solms, Basie, "Corporate Governance And Information Security," *Computers & Security*, vol. 20, issue 3, April 2001

Ware, Lorraine Cosgrove, "The Evolution Of The Chief Security Officer," *CSO Magazine* [Chief Security Officer], 29 August 2002

Watt, Steve, *Computer Security Manager*, Elsevier Advanced Technology, 1989

Weisul, Kimberly, "CSOs Become Indispensable," *Inter@active Week*, p. 94, 17 April 2000 [a CSO is a chief security officer]

Westrum, Ron, and Khalil Samaha, *Complex Organizations: Growth, Struggle And Change*, Prentice-Hall, 1984

Williamson, Oliver E., *Organizational Theory: From Chester Barnard To The Present And Beyond*, Oxford University Press, 1995

Wood, Charles Cresson, "A Policy For An Information Security Management Committee," *Computer Security Alert*, no. 115, October 1992

Wood, Charles Cresson, and Saari, Juhani, "A Strategy For Developing Information Security Documents," *Journal of Information Systems Security*, pp. 71-78, Auerbach Publishers, vol. 1, Issue 2, Summer 1992

Wood, Charles Cresson, "Clarifying Responsibility For Network Security," *Computer Security Alert*, no. 152, November 1995

Wood, Charles Cresson, *Effective Information Security Management*, Elsevier Science Publishers, 1991

Wood, Charles Cresson, "How Many Information Security Staff People Should You Have?" *Computers & Security*, pp. 395-402, vol. 9, 1990

Wood, Charles Cresson, "How To Achieve A Clear Definition Of Responsibilities For Information Security," *Datapro Information Security Service*, IS115-200-101, April 1993

Wood, Charles Cresson, "Information Security Staffing Levels: Calculating The Standard Of Due Care," *Computer Security Journal*, Summer 1998 [provided as Appendix A in this book]

Wood, Charles Cresson, *Information Security Policies Made Easy*, Information Shield, Inc. (Houston, Texas), 10th edition, 2005

Wood, Charles Cresson, "Mandating The Information Security Management Function," *Computer Security Alert*, no. 126, October 1993

Wood, Charles Cresson, "Shifting Information Systems Security Responsibility From User Organizations To Vendor/Publisher Organizations," *Computers & Security*, vol. 14, no. 4, October 1995 [a significantly expanded version provided as Chapter 16 in this book]

Wood, Charles Cresson, "The Information Security Profession: Evolutionary Career Paths," *Information Security*, November 1999

Wood, Charles Cresson, "Why Have Decentralized Information Security Coordinators?," *Computer Fraud & Security Bulletin*, August 1992

Wylder, John O. D., "The Life Cycle Of Security Managers: New Responsibilities For A Distributed Environment," *Information Systems Management*, vol. 9, no. 1, Winter, 1992

Yoder, Stephen Kreider, "When Things Go Wrong-The Main Strength of Networks, Giving Control to Individual Users, Is Also Its Greatest Weakness," *The Wall Street Journal*, p. R16, 14 November 1994

Appendix K   CD-ROM Files

All of the material found in this book is available on the accompanying CD-ROM in PDF, HTML, and MS Word format. To view the PDF version, open the R&RV2.pdf file using Adobe Acrobat Reader (Version 5 or later). If you need Adobe Acrobat Reader, you can download a free copy from the Adobe web site at www.adobe.com. You can also use your web browser to access this book in HTML format by accessing the CD-ROM and opening the index.htm file. For best results, you should use Microsoft® Internet Explorer 5.5 or higher, or else Netscape 6 or higher. To get the materials in the book into your word processor, you will want to open the files which have the extention .DOC, or you can copy text directly from the interactive CD-ROM.

While in Acrobat or your browser, to search the entire book for a certain word or phrase, click the Search tab and enter the applicable word or phrase. For example, suppose you wanted to get some insight into the ways "separation of duties" is implemented in the information security environment. In that case, you would type "separation duties" (do not type common words like of, the, and, are, is) and then click Search. The Search tab will then display all of the topics in the book that contain these words. You may want to print out this response to your query, and then open up your word processor in order to open these same files in a form that can easily be modified.

Whichever type of file you open, you will still need to change the font type, font size, margins, and graphics so that the material matches other documents at the organization in question. It is important to note that each organization is still going to need to customize this material to suit its unique business and technological environment. See Chapter 1 for an overview of this process.

If you are ready to write a mission statement, you will want to open Chapter 11. You can copy the desired text and paste it into a document to tailor the material to the needs of your organization. Or you can simply save the file again using a different name. Likewise, if you are ready to write job descriptions, you should open Chapter 12. If you are interested in reporting relationships, you should open Chapter 13. All other material can be easily located via the Table Of Contents and/or the Index.

If you have trouble opening any of these files, if you have questions, or if you have suggestions for enhancing the next version of this product, please e-mail them directly to support@informationshield.com. There is also a Feedback form provided at the back of this book. If you thought that this product was useful, please tell your business associates about it.

Information Security Roles & Responsibilities Made Easy

Appendix L   FEEDBACK

This book is intended to be a work-in-progress that will be updated as additional information security research is published and as generally accepted practices in this same field are clarified. Input from readers is greatly appreciated and is wholeheartedly solicited. The author pays a great deal of attention to reader feedback, and comments will be used when the next edition is prepared.

Using this page found on the accompanying CD-ROM, please copy and paste this text into an e-mail message and send your response to support@informationshield.com. Alternatively, you can fill out the user feedback form under the "Contact Us" menu at http://www.informationshield.com.

1   On a scale from 1 to 10 (1 is worst and 10 is best), how would you rate the usefulness of the information contained in this book?

2   Using the same scale, how would you rate the extent to which the information in this book is accessible, readily understood, and clear?

3   Using the same scale, how would you rate the way the information in this book is presented?

4   What could the author do to improve this book in future editions?

5   Were there any important roles and responsibilities related to information security that the author forgot to mention?

6   Using the material found in this book, how many hours did it take you to prepare information security related mission statements and job descriptions?

7   What is your job title?

8   To what industry does your employer belong?

9   Roughly how many full-time equivalent employees work at your employer (includes consultants, contractors, temporaries, and outsourcing staff)?

10   How did you first find out about this book?

Information Security Roles & Responsibilities Made Easy

Appendix M OVERVIEW OF BASIC ROLES & RESPONSIBILITIES STEPS

The following checklists are intended to be guidelines to help you see the big picture in terms of integration of roles and responsibilities into your organization's existing information security infrastucture. Read each checklist from top to bottom, staying in the appropriate column all the way.

If Your Organization Is Just Getting Started In The Information Security Area..	If Your Organization Has Already Done Considerable Information Security Work...
Perform Information Security Risk Assessment	Perform Information Security Risk Assessment
Write Information Security Roles and Responsibilities	More Clearly Roles and Responsibilities, as Needed
Establish Information Security Budget	Review Adequacy of Information Security Budget and Staffing Allocations
Write Information Security Policies	Revise Information Security Policies, as Needed
Hire Staff and/or Outsource Information Security Work	Hire More Staff and/or Outsource Other Information Security Work, as Needed
Write Information Security Architecture and Standards	Identify Information Security Organizational Functions that are Not Being Adequately Performed
Purchase, Install, and Run Appropriate Information Security Tools	Identify Information Security Organizational Functions that are Not Being Adequately Performed
Write Information Security Procedures	Purchase, Install, and Run Appropriate Information Security Tools
Develop Information Security	Revise Information Security Procedures, as Needed
Training and Awareness Program	Revise Information Security Training and Awareness Program, as Needed
Develop Incentive Systems and Compliance Checking Process	Revise Incentive Systems and Compliance Checking Process, as Needed
Develop Performance Measurement Systems	Revise Performance Measurement Systems, as Needed

INDEX